Outside Society

Outside Society

People Without a Country

Ayuo Takahashi

JENNY STANFORD
PUBLISHING

Published by

Jenny Stanford Publishing Pte. Ltd.
101 Thomson Road
#06-01, United Square
Singapore 307591

Email: editorial@jennystanford.com
Web: www.jennystanford.com

British Library Cataloguing-in-Publication Data
A catalogue record for this book is available from the British Library.

Outside Society: People Without a Country

ISBN 978-981-5129-54-0 (Hardcover)
ISBN 978-1-003-61921-5 (eBook)

This book is dedicated to all Asian-Americans, Asian-Canadians, Asian-Australians, and British-Asians—the descendants of Chinese, Japanese, Korean, Vietnamese, Cambodian, Laotian, Thai, Malay, Filipino, Iranian, Indian, Bangladeshi, Pakistani, Turkic, and other nationalities from Asia, who grew up in an English-speaking country.

I grew up in New York City in the 1960s with a Japanese mother and an Iranian stepfather. These are my experiences, and I hope that you may find in this book experiences and thoughts that are relevant to your lives.

Names of some classmates have been changed to protect the innocent, especially in the essay *Winter 1983*. Names of musicians and well-known people have not been changed anywhere in the book.

Contents

Part V

Part VI

Acknowledgments

I can't thank Hsu Jui-Ting enough for reading and checking my autobiography and essays. His kind advice has made things so much better.

I want to thank Katsuyuki Aoyagi, Yutaka Kamibayashi, and Miho Watanabe for working on the original Japanese edition of this book.

I also thank Kazuki Takami, Toko Sasaki, Mutsumi Okazaki of Tower Records' magazine, *Intoxicate*, and Kunihiko Yamashita of KB Special for commissioning the original essays.

I would also like to thank a few others who have read the original Japanese essays—Banana Yoshimoto, Yuki Yanagihara, Lisa Yanagihara, Yosuke Jikuhara, Ken Awazu, Iwao Yamazaki, Yoshie, and Eriko Arai.

Thank you to Jenny Rompas for suggesting to publish this book in English.

Part I

One

My first memory/Age 3, plane trip to Berlin/ Kennedy Assassination/New York

Memory is a strange thing.

Whenever I was asked as a child, "What is your earliest memory?" I always answered that it was the first time I flew with my mother on a plane to Berlin, immediately after my third birthday.

"I was on an airplane," I'd say. "The airplane was full of different types of people and faces that I'd never seen before. We flew south and westward from Tokyo, stopping at Asian and Middle Eastern countries along the way."

Before that, all was just a white blank space.

When I had to write a short tale in junior high school, based on my earliest memories, I turned my first flying trip to Berlin into a Cold War spy story straight out of a James Bond movie. I incorporated President John F. Kennedy's assassination into the storyline: the day we arrived in Berlin, President Kennedy was shot and killed. Based on my childhood impressions of spies from watching too many James Bond movies, I, therefore, turned a suspicious-looking white European man in a suit and dark sunglasses into a traveling spy in my short story.

Many people wore dark sunglasses in those days, thinking that it made them look cool, so it wasn't unusual to see people look like that.

I was flying above the clouds with all kinds of people. This was a very exciting experience for me as a child.

I became a foreigner, an outsider, but so was everyone else on the plane.

Years later, when I tried to recollect my early memories, I was unable to distinguish between what had actually occurred, and what I had made up to fit into a later fictional plot. The first memory was superimposed with images from a James Bond film.

I find that when I try to reminisce with someone I haven't seen in a long, their memories don't always match mine.

Many people I've met have informed me that I must have forgotten about them. The truth is, memories are used by each of us to form mental associations, so only the things that are significant to us are left. It's not that any of us have forgotten. People, however, remember things differently because what matters to them varies.

When we create a visual image in our minds, it frequently stays there together with the actual memories. Because of this, when we discuss past events with those who were with us at that time, we frequently wind up discussing different recollections and asserting that things truly happened this way or that way.

A film by Akira Kurosawa called *Rashomon* is an example of a mystery story like this. The term "Rashomon Phenomenon" was used to describe these kinds of events following the global success of this movie.

All people have their own stories. And we are all living our own stories at the same time.

The only instant in time that we could all reasonably agree upon is the "now" that we are in.

My father, Yuji Takahashi, was already in Berlin when we landed; he had received a grant from the Ford Foundation to study composition with Iannis Xenakis, a Greek composer with French citizenship. My father had originally wanted to be a composer and had often insisted that he didn't want to be a pianist, but to earn money for himself and his family, he had to play the piano.

We never heard any classical music at home. My father never taught me music at all; my mother played records of songs from musicals like *My Fair Lady*, and standard jazz. My mother worked as an arranger and accompanist for a Japanese chanson singer named Yoko Kishi after graduating from the music composition department of the Tokyo University of the Arts. After we left for Europe, she had to leave her music friends and became a stay-at-home housewife. She often took me to see musical movies.

I went to kindergarten in Berlin. Because East Germany surrounded West Berlin, there was a plan to transform it into an international city to demonstrate the benefits of a free capitalist society. The Ford Foundation and the Rockefeller Foundation were working with the CIA to promote this plan, which involved bringing artists from all over the world to Berlin to create a city where avant-garde music and art could be performed; something that was not possible in socialist countries. The goal was also to use Berlin as a propaganda tool against the Eastern Bloc.

When I was a child, we used to see a man named Porter A. McCray quite often. After serving as a CIA agent and participating in operations in South America, he took over as director of the arts and introduced Jackson Pollock—a painter renowned for his action paintings—to the European art scene. These details were disclosed in Frances Stoner Saunders' book *Who Paid the Piper*. These people took care of us very well.

I met many such people, and they all seemed to be very nice. Each of them had their own views and thought they were doing the right thing for art, culture, and the world. Without these people, there would not have been the avant-garde art, contemporary music, and other scenes that flourished after WWII. In the 1960s, my father was able to work on his music and support his family by receiving grants from these foundations.

Later, we stayed in Paris, to the south of France and Sweden. We lived in Sweden for over six months. Originally, it was supposed to be a shorter visit, but my father got into a dispute with someone in a high position there; after this argument, other people in the arts stopped talking to him. He had to contact other people in Europe to get our family out.

In 1966, after spending six months in Japan with my mother and her family, I left with her to New York. My father had gone there a few months ahead of us. In both Berlin and New York, there were musicians, painters, photographers, dancers, actors, writers, and directors from all over the world.

Something new was about to happen in these cities. From the '60s up to the early '70s, I thought there was something new happening virtually every day in New York City. The streets were brimming with life. Not only was the music and art exciting, but the age itself was generating a new vibe.

How did this come to be?

After World War II, life settled in the 1950s in the United States and the countries it controlled, including Japan. In the 1960s, as the population grew, so did the number of universities and schools. People were given the opportunity to go around the world to see and discover, as transportation grew more convenient than ever before. People from America's and Europe's suburbs as well as Asia and Africa traveled to New York City, London, Paris, and Berlin in search of the world they had only seen and read about in books and on the radio. People in New York, London, and Paris found a passion for traditional Asian and African arts that even those who had moved there had never considered before.

New encounters are often the starting point for new art. This was an exciting time to be alive. The war had finished, and it was time for people to reassess how they should live. It was a moment when numerous experiments were possible, like never before in living memory.

Two

The Beatles/Rhythm and sound

I first heard The Beatles when I was four years old.

One day, the word "Beatles" came up in my parents' conversation, and I asked, "What are The Beatles?"

"You don't know? Well, how about we go buy some of their records when we go to town today," my mother said.

We lived in a town near Stockholm, Sweden, where my mother, my father, and I went to a record shop in a department store.

"This is The Beatles," my father said and bought me a four-song EP with a picture of the four Beatles jumping up on a rooftop. It was a record centered around the song "Twist and Shout."

On another day, also in Sweden, we bought their album *Help!* That night, we went to a contemporary music concert of avant-garde music, where my father was performing piano. Apparently, the music performed that day was particularly difficult. During the concert, I wrote the word "HELP" in English on a piece of paper and handed it to someone. The person thought I had written "HELP" because I couldn't stand the music.

People would laugh whenever they heard this story.

I was four years old, and I don't think that I heard contemporary music as music. It seemed more like a ritual, where people obeyed certain rules. Sounds were being made on stage, but they were not particularly meaningful to me at the time. For instance, someone who finds the sound of "bang, bang, bang, bang, bang" to be intriguing may find meaning in it.

However, a four-year-old child wouldn't comprehend it, or be able to derive any significance from it.

The Beatles sounded different than this. Their songs were based on beats that beat just a little bit faster than your own heartbeat; they had chordal harmonies; and they had human voices singing the words in easily recognizable repetitive patterns. The melodies didn't have to fit into a strict form like they might in classical music. Even the Bob Dylan-inspired songs on *Help!*, for example, were not about the melody; it was the guitar chords, the rhythm, and the human voices singing over it that made it appealing.

A mass of energy that even a four-year-old could understand as music.

As a child, I was always moving to the beat while playing Beatles' records like Twist and Shout. I heard the English lyrics as rhythmic sounds. Even if I didn't understand the meaning of the words yet, I could enjoy the sound and rhythm in the way the words were pronounced.

Figure 1   Me at age 2 in 1963. The record player was my favorite toy.

When I was in elementary and junior high school, I began to write poems that combined the sounds and rhythms of words with the images of those words. I think the music I write is an extension of this way of writing poetry.

I had the opportunity to see the Beatles perform live at the Nippon Budokan in Tokyo while living with my grandparents in Japan for six months. This was following my time in Europe, and before I left to live in New York. It wasn't as good as many other Beatles gigs in other cities. Many girls were screaming and yelling for no apparent reason. Perhaps they got the impression that was what they were supposed to do after watching film snippets of their concerts in other countries. The PA sound system for rock concerts at the time was also subpar, making it difficult to hear the sound from their little VOX guitar amps.

"Paperback Writer," which had just been released as a single at the time, made the biggest impression on me.

Three

New York in the late 1960s/My mother's artist friends (Yokoo Tadanori, Shuji Terayama, Hiroshi Teshigahara, Kishin Shinoyama, Mutsuo Takahashi, etc.)/The Filmore East/Electric Circus/Terry Riley/ John Cage and Marcel Duchamp/Living Theater/Horace Silver/Joan Gilberto/ Thelonius Monk/Muddy Waters

The late 1960s was a time when rock, jazz, experimental music, theater, film, and many other genres were all energized, and interacting with each other. Such an age has not been witnessed since and may not be seen again for some time. Trying anything for the first time requires a sense of adventure, which is what keeps it interesting. However, once it becomes a set category or a genre, the novelty fades. People start to do what they are already familiar with.

Nobody had ever incorporated free improvisation and modal jazz techniques into popular music before they were brought into rock in the mid-1960s. This was the first time this combination occurred, and it transformed the course of popular music. Because the artists were experimenting with sounds for the first time, experimental music was truly *experimental* at the time. Later, and particularly in the twenty-first century, while "experimental music" concerts and events continue to occur, they frequently execute imitations of previously performed experimental sounds and approaches. As a result, I no longer feel that they can be classified as 'real' experimental music. It evolved into its own genre. The musicians perform what is already known as 'experimental' sounds.

Avant-garde was so named because it was new and innovative. The same may be said about Progressive Rock. It began by attempting to be truly progressive, experimenting with sounds and influences that had never been done before. Since the 1980s, the trend has been for everything to be categorized, which has taken the thrill out of inventing something genuinely new.

When Pauline Oliveros, an experimental music composer and accordionist, came to Japan in the 1990s, she was accompanied by a trombonist whom I had seen as a child. I was surprised to hear him walking around while he was playing improvisation, playing something so similar to what I remembered seeing in the 1960's. What he was doing might have been strange and new in the '60s, but in the 1990s, I felt that it had already become a cliché. He may have been a pioneer of the avant-garde 30 years ago, but it was no longer 'new' in the 1990s. When a particular style or form becomes established, it is no longer experimental or avant-garde. So, for me, a lot of the avant-garde after the 1990s became a formality, or an exercise—not something that came from the bottom of their hearts.

In the '60s, my mother had many friends who were both visual artists as well as musicians when we lived in New York. When she was a child, she lived near Makoto Wada and Toru Takemitsu, and she was in the environment of many pioneers in the arts of the time: Tadanori Yokoo, Shuji Terayama, Hiroshi Teshigahara, Kishin Shinoyama, and Mutsuo Takahashi were among them. When they came to New York, she would cook and prepare parties for them; we often went to rock concerts together.

One of the venues where these concerts took place was The Filmore East. It was at St. Marks Place on the east side of Eighth Street in Greenwich Village. Around the corner from there was a discothèque called Electric Circus whose atmosphere would predate that of the club scene in the late 1990s. Most of the time, they had DJs playing popular psychedelic music records of the time, and people would dance to it.

There were Liquid Light Shows with colored liquid displays, squiggling and moving to the music. Live music was often performed there; every day at a set time, the experimental music composer, Morton Subotnick, played a short piece on his synthesizer. Terry Riley also improvised on organ, saxophone, and tape loops. Other acts would involve a fire-swallowing magic show and a live band.

I first saw Taj Mahal, the African-American blues singer, at the

Electric Circus. There was also a Psychedelic Shop within Electric Circus. There was an event where John Cage played chess against Marcel Duchamp, but I must say that it was not interesting for a child to observe someone else play chess for hours on end. What was more interesting to me, as a child, was when Cream's "Sunshine of Your Love" blared within the light show, or when I looked up from just below the stage to see a guitarist playing with a live band.

Around this time, I saw an experimental theater group called "Living Theater." I was still in elementary school.

Figure 2 A photograph commemorating a party at my home in 1970. In the back row, from left to right: Porter McRae, one unknown, Armond, my mother Utako, Betsy, Betsy's boyfriend, Hiroshi Teshigahara, one unknown, and me. Middle row, from right: Isamu Noguchi, one unknown, Ken O'Hara, and his wife. Front row, from left: Yusuke Suga, my stepfather Mansour, one unknown, Eiichiro Sakata.

In an attempt to express on stage that the first step in becoming free from capitalist society, performers on stage would take off their clothes in public. They would do this, while saying, "I'm going to be free, and I'm going to take off my clothes too." There is a well-known story that Jim Morrison of The Doors saw this performance and was arrested for perversion when he tried to copy this act and do the same thing at a concert in Florida.

This has now become a legendary story in the history of classic rock.

The last heyday of Jazz was in the 1960s, in places like the Village Vanguard and the Village Gate. When I was in the first and second grades, I lived alone with my mother—as my father lived separately in Buffalo—and she used to take me to these clubs. One time, we went to hear a pianist named Horace Silver, and Horace noticed that there was a child in the audience, so he came over to talk to us. He was a jazz pianist, as well as a vegetarian, and he lived a very rigorous, righteous life. My mother became a fan of his, and we went to hear him often. We would go to his house, and he would make us salads. He gave me some pocket money. I had school in the early morning, so I sometimes fell asleep during his live performances at the Village Vanguard.

Joao Gilberto played a solo concert at the Village Vanguard accompanied only by a drummer. It was around the time his album *Waters of March* was set for release. Max Gordon, the owner of Vanguard bought a special microphone for that day, so the audience could hear the delicate sounds of his guitar and vocals as faithfully as possible.

The most memorable act at the Village Vanguard for me was Thelonious Monk. I doubt the music itself was intelligible to me as a child, but Monk wandered around the stage like a completely drunken man in the middle of his band's performance, and I found this very entertaining.

The blues guitarist/singer Muddy Waters, whom I saw a few years later at the Village Vanguard, was just amazing. He got the audience clapping their hands while singing songs like "I'm a Man," which had already become a standard blues number among rock bands. This kind of performance could only be done by a man with a strong charisma. He was no longer young, but his life experiences made his performances incredibly moving and deep. The warmth and depth of his soul conveyed through his voice could even move children, who couldn't understand the meaning of the words. The harmonica player who was playing with him was also incredible. I have never to this day seen any harmonica player as powerful as he was.

At this time, there were still only a few Japanese people in New York City. So many seemed envious when I spoke of all these legendary performances I saw as a child.

Four

Started learning guitar/1968: The year of changes/My parents' divorce/Psychedelic rock/Started writing poetry/Open-tuning guitar

In 1968, when I was in the second grade, I started studying the guitar. My parents had never tried to get me to learn an instrument, or perform music until then.

My parents were the kind of people who thought that children would naturally find their own way. They didn't want to force them to do anything, including learning new skills. When I became an adult myself, I couldn't agree with this kind of thinking of raising a child. The more a child gets to learn when he is young, the more choices he will have when he is older. The child will be able to choose what he wants for himself when he grows up if he studies well in his childhood.

Besides, my parents were too occupied with their desires and problems in life to care about what their children should do. Later on in life, I also found out that my father did not like being forced to study classical music and piano. To play classical music properly, one needs a lot of difficult training from a very young age, and he felt that this stifled a child's natural means of expression. However, I would argue that because his mother forced him to play the piano, he was able to make a living from it in his adult life.

If you deprive a child of learning, he will not even have the chance to choose when he is older. It will be simply too late.

The year 1968 was a year of great change in American society, and that was also reflected in my personal life. My parents divorced between 1968 and the winter of 1969. I was attending public school in New York City at the time. My mother and I had not lived with my father since about 1965, but their official divorce was a new beginning for me, too.

The Doors and Jefferson Airplane were some of the most popular rock bands at the time, and I listened to them a lot. In later years, psychedelic rock came to be seen as a kind of avant-garde rock that was different from the more mainstream pop music playing then, but at the time the primary audience was mostly kids. If you look at old footage of The Doors playing live in the late 1960s, you'll see a lot of 12-year-olds in the audience. Around that time, some 13-year-olds ran away from home to join communes where drugs and sex were everywhere. It wasn't so much that they learned 'early,' but that they didn't understand much about life yet. Freedom is always accompanied by danger.

Figure 3 Photo of eleven-year-old Ayuo playing electric guitar with his mother on piano.

What made me want to pick up the guitar was seeing the film *Monterey Pop Festival*; in the film, both Jimi Hendrix and Pete Townsend (of The Who) were playing guitars while swinging them around, before destroying them—one moment saw Jimi Hendrix setting his on fire with a lighter. It looked exciting to children who would not be allowed to do such things. Psychedelic distorted-sounding guitar improvisation was performed, which sounded cool and got you mentally high, for both adults and kids. The tempi were a little faster than a human heartbeat, with intense repeated beats and plenty of spacey effects. Rhythmic chants were also repeated.

At that time, the anti-war movement against the Vietnam War spread to cities all over the United States. Most of the teachers at my school were of the generation that rebelled against the war and my public school was closed for a strike to protest the war. Even when school was in session, they focused on political discussions and how to write letters of protest to politicians. Teachers taught us to always ask "Why?" and "What for?" toward everything. They also taught us that American history textbooks are full of lies. We were encouraged to participate in demonstrations from the time we were in elementary school. The teachers were not interested in teaching math and science as schools were supposed to do. So, we learned very little about such topics in our early years. It was more important to develop the methods and tools to win arguments, debates, and discussions.

My homeroom teacher was involved in the strike and her picture was in the newspapers at the time. However, she did not want to stop educating their children despite the strike, so the parents of one of my classmates decided to allow the teacher to use their living room in the mornings to continue teaching the children. It was in the building across the street from my apartment. Outside of class, I spent more time listening to psychedelic rock and playing guitar rather than playing or studying with my classmates. We had Jefferson Airplane's album *After Bathing at the Baxter's* in our house shortly after it was released. My parents bought it, not because they were interested in the album, but because they wanted to know what was popular in culture at the time.

There was a woman living on a large ship docked on Manhattan Island in New York City. She was the former girlfriend of my father's first manager in the United States. She traveled around in her boat alongside her pet snake. Her brother had the first two albums of Jefferson Airplane and played them throughout the night. It was a beautiful, clear, starlit night, and the music sounded lovely in the night air on the rocking ship. After this experience, I started listening to Jefferson Airplane all the time.

At this time, my mother and I lived on 72nd Street from 1966 to the beginning of 1968, before moving to 96th Street. We often went to the Greenwich Village a lot, going to live shows and the electric circus, and I would always watch from below how the guitar player was making that sound on stage. I would stare at them when they were tuning up between the songs.

My first guitar teacher was the guitarist/composer named Stanley Silverman. At the time, he had composed an opera called *Elephant Steps*, which was a mixture of classical opera, rock, and electronic music. This opera was later recorded by CBS and released by CBS-Sony in Japan in the mid-1970s.

My first guitar lesson was a simple G chord: press the third finger of your left hand on the third fret of the first string. Then, the G7 chord: press the first finger of your left hand on the first fret of the first string. And a simple C chord: press the first finger of the left hand on the first fret of the second string. Then strum the top three strings of each chord. Next, we practiced playing the top first string on the guitar with alternating fingers using the first and middle fingers. This was my first lesson.

Figure 4   Group photo of my elementary school class in 1968. I am the third from the left in the back row.

It was around this time that I started to write poetry. At first, it was for school homework. My classmates consisted of a few Hispanics, a couple of blacks, a half-Hispanic/half-Chinese girl, a few Caucasians, and a few Jews.

My teacher and classmates told me that my poems were unique. She told me that I was expressing things in ways that were different from others.

In a city like New York City, everyone is an immigrant. Black people in New York have their own way of pronouncing and using words. Jewish people often have their own way of expressing things using the English language. The English language does not have to be spoken and written in the same way everywhere. Different locations and nationalities will develop their linguistic preferences, and they have the right to do so—because if you grew up speaking the language your way, then that is your language, *whether your ancestors spoke it or not.*

Writing poetry is also an act of arranging sounds, and in this process, the use of rhythm comes into play. I later came to understand that music for me was an extension of my use of the English language.

When I was in the third grade, besides the exercises I learned from my guitar lessons, I was also playing the songs by The Who and others by looking at the chord diagrams or guitar in the songbooks.

Then, in the fourth grade, I began studying with the experimental avant-garde music composer and guitarist William Hellerman. He taught me mainly using Matteo Carcassi's classical guitar method book.

I remember being surprised when, in the sixth grade, my classmates chose me for one of the lead roles in the Christmas school play. I even asked my friends why they liked my reading. But this was something that gave me confidence as a human being. I was usually quiet in class and didn't stand out much, but when I read poetry or made up short stories, a different person emerged, and my classmates accepted the world I was presenting.

When I was 13, I bought a book by Stefan Grossman called *Open Tunings for Guitar.* This book changed the way I played. It was an introduction to open-tuning guitar playing—a style of guitar playing where the guitar strings are tuned to sound a G chord, a D chord, or a more complex chord when played without holding down any of the strings.

It is often stated in encyclopedias covering an instrument's historical development, that guitars were played in a variety of tunings until the 20th century. For example, in a 19th-century book of Irish folk tunes, the guitar was tuned to the E chord.

Nowadays, the guitar is usually tuned from the low 6th string to the 1st string as follows: *EADGBE*. However, open-D would mean it's tuned as follows: *DADF#AD*.

If you raise this pitch by two chromatic half-tones, you get the Open-E chord (*EBEG#BE*). In this case, Open-G would be tuned as *DGDGBD*.

Keith Richards of the Rolling Stones took out the 6th string and tuned his 5-string guitar to *GDGBD*. Blues guitarists who played traditional music often used these tunings because they fit the music better than standard tuning, which was after all created to play Western chordal music easily.

Stefan Grossman also introduced some of the tunings that British guitarist Martin Carthy often used when playing British and Celtic folk songs. Carthy was awarded an OBE (Order of the British Empire, 4th class) in recognition of his important cultural role in the British nation. One of Carthy's modal tunings was *DADGAD*: this tuning is suited to modal music such as English folk songs. This tuning was popular among many British traditional players in the early 1960s because it gave a different sound to the music than the chord progression in standard tuning.

Carthy would later develop more complex tunings such as *CGCDGA*, making the guitar sound like a medieval European instrument. His playing became very percussive.

The above is the most popular way of tuning a guitar, but there are many other ways of tuning a guitar, including the tunings for Joni Mitchell's *For the Roses*, a songbook I bought in 1975.

This was an important innovation because the tunings made by Joni Mitchell created sounds that no one else had played before. Her music influenced British groups such as Fairport Convention, Anthony Philips, and Mike Rutherford, who founded Genesis and experimented with completely different and original tunings. "The

Cinema Show" was tuned E, A, D/a, G/e, B, and E on a 12-string guitar. There is a fifth and a sixth in the fourth and third course of the guitar. These unusual tunings were what created the unique sound in early Genesis releases.

Joni Mitchell's songbook had a big impact on me. It introduced me to a lot of different open tunings, and the music and lyrics were more in line with what I wanted to talk about.

After reading these books, I started experimenting with different tunings and writing songs using them.

For me, knowing all these different ways of tuning strings has opened up a whole new world of musical expressions.

Toward the end of junior high school, I started to arrange my version of a melody from the medieval European tune "Kalenda Maya," and played it in the *DADGAD* tuning. Medieval European tunes are composed with what music theory terms as modes. Jazz improvisers such as Miles Davis, Bill Evans, and John Coltrane started to use old European modes to distinguish their new compositions. Miles Davies was trying to find a way of playing music that wasn't Western, but more African, and therefore closer to his roots.

There is also a lot of evidence that music from North Africa influenced Medieval European music. Many musicians came from the Middle East and North Africa, introducing new instruments to Europe such as the guitar.

Some of the more commonly used modes are Dorian mode (with notes *D, E, F, G, A, B, C, and octave D*); Lydian mode (*F, G, A, B, C, D, E, F*); Mixolydian mode (*G, A, B, C, D, E, F, G*); and Phrygian mode (*E, F, G, A, B, C, D, E*), among others. These modes are classified as such, if we use the key signature of C major (with no flats or sharps). Even today, many British and Irish folk songs and dances are made of these modes. American Country music and Bluegrass also retain some of this tradition.

Much later—in the 2000s—a modal improvisation I played on the Greek Bouzouki was played a few times on an American Bluegrass radio program.

If you've ever listened to Scottish bagpipes, you'll notice that much of the music has sustained drone notes on the 5th and an octave. For example, in the Mixolydian mode, the 5th degree of *G* and *D* and the octave above *G* are sounded, and the following real notes are played on them: *G, A, B, C, D, E, F, G*. The notes used are the same as the white keyboard solfège (*do-re-mi-fa-so-la-si-do*), but the sequence is different. The sequence of the notes has a set of rules that create a particular mode.

I hadn't even composed music using Western harmony or chord progressions before I began making music using these old European modes. It wasn't because I was interested in music theory, but the music I listened to was based on these modes, so it became more natural for me.

I had never made music using solfège theory before. I knew nothing about chord progressions or harmonic music. But by discovering books like this, I was learning about pre-classical medieval European music even before classical music or the chords used in jazz and pop music.

Apart from this, I was to become influenced by the way Thomas Binkley played the Lute, and other Medieval and Renaissance plucked string instruments that were the ancestors of the guitar. Binkley was the leader of Studio Der Frühen Musik, an ensemble that played Medieval and Renaissance European music. They were one of the first to popularize Medieval music.

The sound of medieval European music is similar to that of East Asian music. That was one of the first things that I noticed before I learned anything about history and culture. My interest in Medieval European music and culture grew substantially when I was in the 6th grade. Our teacher Brenda tried to teach by simulating life in the Middle Ages in our modern classroom, but I will write about this in more detail later on.

When I first heard Steeleye Span's rendition of "Blacksmith" and the Scottish folk song "Cam Ye O'er Frae France," my mind was filled with images of a world I had seen in Kenji Mizoguchi's film *Ugetsu Monogatari*. The music was also a bit similar to the music in this Japanese film. Perhaps life in Medieval feudal societies produced music that was somewhat similar. Similar lifestyles producing similar music? I was to try to find out more about this, later in life.

These were also the roots of our modern-day storytellers and minstrel music—the lyrics and songs of singer-songwriters, such as Joni Mitchell, Sandy Denny, Richard Thompson, Peter Gabriel,

Anthony Philips, and many others. They sounded different from much of the Western music that we were exposed to every day. Was there something common in the lifestyles during the medieval age?

This would lead me to a study of world traditional music.

And this was the beginning of the music I would come to make.

Five

My mother's marriage to Mansour Malekpour/Jethro Tull/Ten Years After/ Alice Cooper/Emerson, Lake & Palmer/Pink Floyd/Fairport Convention/Earth, Wind, and Fire/Steely Dan/The Who and more

My mother, after divorcing my father, married an Iranian named Mansour Malekpour, who became an American citizen. Both my mother and I got green cards for permanent immigration status. We moved to Greenwich Village to an apartment on 14 Horatio Street named Van Gogh.

My stepfather came from a family of court musicians in Iran on his mother's side, but he did not choose that path. He would sing traditional songs in the shower every day, and occasionally at parties. He worked for an American bank called Banker's Trust, Monday to Friday from 9 am to 5 pm. Every morning, we would go out together; I went to school, and he went to work. My mother read books and listened to music late into the night, and often slept until I got home from school.

On weekends, my stepfather and mother woke up late, but my stepfather usually prepared breakfast. Weekend breakfasts were usually muffins with eggs and bacon. When the weather was nice, we would go to Central Park, rent bicycles, and ride around the park. We also went swimming in the pool.

My stepbrother, David (from my stepfather's first wife), would often come to stay with us then. We would listen to records and try to play songs like "Your Move" by Yes.

My stepfather and I often went to rock concerts together on weekends. He especially liked Led Zepplin because Robert Plant had a great singing voice. Robert Plant and Jimmy Page also studied a lot of Middle Eastern and North African music, as would I in the future. When I heard more Persian classical music, I could hear some similarities in musical expression.

If you think about it, people who can sing like Robert Plant are preferred in both Iranian traditional music and Pakistani Sufi music. If you know the work of Nusrat Fateh Ali Khan, who was popular in Europe and Japan in the 1990s, you can probably understand what I mean.

This was a great life. I still think of my early years in NYC with Mansour and Utako (my mother) as the happiest time in my life. This is despite the fact that in the 1980s, I was able to get record companies to fund me to record in England with some of my favorite musicians.

(a)

(b)

Figure 5 (a) 1970. In Central Park. From left to right: my stepfather, my mother, and myself. (b) The apartment where our family lived at that time. (Photographed by Ayuo in 1986.)

Here, I will write about some rock concerts I saw around this time as I remember them:

The first time I saw Jethro Tull at the Fillmore East, I went with Yokoo Tadanori. It was right after their third album, *Benefit*, came out. Glenn McCormick was on bass and Clive Bunker was on drums. There was also John Evans, a pianist who played a mixture of classical music and jazz. They started the evening with just the leader and main songwriter, Ian Anderson, playing guitar and singing alone. Then the band started playing together from the middle of the song. It was very effective, but this showed that this band was virtually

Ian Anderson's one-man band. Other members probably had limited freedom to express their ideas, even though the musicianship was great. Later in the concert, they did a song that incorporated a piano solo by John Evans and a long drum solo by Clive Bunker. The band mixed English and Scottish traditional elements with progressive rock.

I saw *Ten Years After* in 1970 at the Filmore East. They were very popular at the time because the movie *Woodstock* had their performance of the song "Going Home."

The concert started that night with only a light show and a DJ playing records over the speakers. Unlike the electric circus, all the seats were reserved so that the audience did not dance during the light show.

The performance of *Ten Years After* was quite good, playing hard blues rock with the same energy as I saw in *Woodstock*. In the last song, during the free ad-lib sections, the guitarist Alvin Lee tuned down the lowest string on his guitar until it just sounded like a croaking sound. Eventually, he tuned up and started to play bass lines at the same range as the bass guitar. I tried to imitate this at home.

I saw Alice Cooper at the Fillmore East with the poet Mutsuro Takahashi, who performed wonderfully. It was right after their third album *Love It to Death* was released. The music was masterfully produced by Bob Ezrin, who would later produce Lou Reed's *Berlin* and Pink Floyd's *The Wall*. *Berlin* represented for me the depth of what my once happy family life in NYC would sink into.

At this time, Alice Cooper was a full-fledged group. They mixed avant-garde sound with hard rock in a very interesting way, which had something in common with Captain Beefheart's avant-garde rock. After this period, the band started to concentrate on becoming more popular and commercial by becoming more entertaining to normal American audiences.

In the days when Alice Cooper was a band, all the members wrote songs. When they started to make it big, however, conflicts began to arise among them. The singer of the group, Vince Furnier, would eventually take the name for his solo career, starting a one-man musical show—like a Broadway show with rock instruments. Mutsuo Takahashi told me at that time that he already felt there was something fake about Alice Cooper's performance, even back then.

Emerson Lake and Palmer also played their first New York show at the Fillmore East, but I went to see their second New York show at Carnegie Hall. I went to see this one with Yokoo Tadanori. Carnegie Hall is a classical concert hall. While I lived in New York City, I saw only three rock concerts at Carnegie Hall. The other two were Pink Floyd and Fairport Convention. Emerson Lake and Palmer were especially conscious of playing in a famous classical hall. The program was in two parts: the first part was a rock arrangement of Mussorgsky's *Pictures at an Exhibition*, and the second part was a program of mostly songs from their first album.

They started with "The Barbarian," an arrangement of Bartok's *Allegro barballero*. Then they played "Take a Pebble,"

"Lucky Man," a song with a long drum solo; and finally, "Knife Edge." The encore was "Nut Rocker," based on Tchaikovsky's *The Nutcracker*. Keith Emerson rode on top of the organ like he was riding a horse in the rodeo, and played the organ while it was rolling all over the stage, much to the delight of the audience. The Moog synthesizer was also used for the first time on stage by a rock band. Emerson didn't try to break it, but he did improvise by swinging a big stick-like thing connected to the synthesizer and showing how the sound changed as he did so. All this was done for entertainment. The other two members tried their best to stand out as well. Greg Lake sang "Lucky Man" alone with his acoustic guitar. Carl Palmer played a long drum solo.

Pink Floyd played a concert at Carnegie Hall. It was right after they released their album *Meddle*. Many of the songs that they played that night can be seen in the film *Live at Pompeii*.

Pink Floyd's show was the first time I saw and heard a surround sound system used effectively. On the blues song "Mademoiselle Knobs," which is still not on any of their officially released albums, the sound of a person walking down the hallway was heard from the back of the hall up to the stage. Pink Floyd at the time still had a loose, improvisational feel to their music, which was nice. It was still psychedelic and experimental. I preferred this period more than when they became commercially successful with *Dark Side of the Moon*. They played improvisation within a set song structure, with such songs as "Embryo," "Atom Heart Mother," "One of These Days," "A Saucerful of Secrets," "Be Careful with that Axe, Eugene," and "Echoes."

After this period, they started to hire people to create an elaborate stage, and their music became more commercial and accepted as entertainment. For me, it was their first period with Syd Barrett and the period that followed up to their album *Meddle* (1971), which was interesting. Syd Barrett wrote great lyrics, where he used words for their sound and rhythm. Barrett was influenced by James Joyce; studied as a painter; and was well-read. I also liked psychedelic music more than progressive rock because it was more experimental and avant-garde. For me, *The Wall* (produced by Bob Ezrin), and *The Final Cut* which followed it were their next great period.

My stepfather and I also went to see the Fairport Convention concert at Carnegie Hall. It was around the same time as the release of the album of the same name. Sandy Denny sang "A Sailor's Life" that day. Sandy Denny became known in the United States after her song "Who Knows Where the Time Goes" was covered by Judy Collins, but she didn't perform that song for the concert.

A concert that was nearly halted by the police was the Flash concert at Philharmonic Hall. This is the hall where the New York Philharmonic Orchestra usually plays. The concert also featured Dr. Hook and the Medicine Show, and Earth, Wind, and Fire on the bill. Earth Wind and Fire were not yet well known at that time. They had just released their first album, and the first song started with a hugely amplified sound of an electric kalimba. Then, they started playing a song with funky rhythms and lots of improvised ad-libs. The groove was great. The music was closer to Miles Davis's *Pangea* and *Dark Magus* from the 70's than later Earth Wind and Fire. The band members invited the audience to come up on stage and dance, which startled the hall manager, who called the police. He turned on all the lights in the hall and came out on the stage with the police. He made Earth Wind and Fire stop playing and forced the audience members back to their seats. He announced that if they left their seats, he would stop the concert. I was horrified.

Figure 6 A photo of my room in 1973. Tadanori Yokoo, who went to see ELP with me, later made a poster at the request of their record company in Japan. (The poster behind me was made in 1973.)

I knew the stage manager from the concerts that I saw there, as conducted by Seiji Ozawa. I talked to him many times during breaks and after the concert. When I told him that I started learning how to play the guitar, he asked me what I wanted to be when I grew up. I remember telling him that I wanted to start a band like Jefferson Airplane or The Doors.

When I saw him forcibly pulling everyone down to their seats, I thought he was acting horribly. But he had probably never seen such an audience reaction at the Philharmonic Hall, and I guess he was shocked and scared. After that, the concert went on more quietly than usual.

Dr. Hook and the Medicine Show was a band of about eight people that mixed stand-up comedy with folk rock. Most of the songs were written by Shel Silverstein, who was known as a cartoonist and picture book writer. Their shows were fun. There weren't many other bands like them who mixed rock with comedy performances. Their first three albums were particularly interesting, but I still haven't seen any live recordings of them.

Flash was the band created by Yes' first guitarist, Pete Banks. They sounded similar to the early days of Yes, with a bit of American pop that reminded me a bit of Steely Dan. The band was rumored to be intense on stage, but they played the songs stoically, probably because Earth, Wind, and Fire were interrupted that day.

I had also seen Steely Dan at the Philharmonic Hall. It was right after their first album came out. They were opening for Electric Light Orchestra, led by guitarist/singer Jeff Lynne, Steely Dan later stopped playing live because the audience reaction to their work was not good.

I was sitting in the front row and an audience member next to me was screaming, "You suck! Try playing 'Topographic Ocean' [by Yes]! How about it—you can't do it, can you? You can't play!" The band must have had a hard time trying to play in front of such an audience. From what I remember hearing, I don't think their performance was that bad, but the atmosphere was so horrible that it must have influenced their playing. Maybe that's why they stopped playing live and remained a studio band. They would spend weeks and months polishing their songs in the studio with some of the best studio musicians of the time.

I saw The Who, Jethro Tull, and It's a Beautiful Day play in Tanglewood, Massachusetts in the summer of 1970. Tanglewood is a rural town where the Boston Philharmonic plays in the summer. It was truly a beautiful day. There was a big screen set up on the lawn to show the performance on the stage. The lawn was covered in soft grass. It was clean and free of trash, as this is where the classical audience usually comes from. You could lie down and listen to the music. It's a Beautiful Day was a psychedelic band from San Francisco, formed by a violin player, which was rare among bands at that time. They started playing in the evening. It was quiet electric folk. This band was also in the films *The Last Days of the Fillmore* and *Stamping Ground*, but they didn't play as wildly as they did in the latter festival and film. They were probably able to play that wildly at the Stamping Ground festival because a large part of the audience was high on drugs and started going crazy, grooving to their intense performance.

Their first album had just come out. One of the songs from that album, "White Bird," was sung in male–female harmony and sounded beautiful on the lawn. I listened to it while watching the clouds at dusk. It felt good. Their entire performance, as well as the performances of Jethro Tull and The Who, were filmed that day and are available on YouTube for anyone in the world to see.

Jethro Tull was next on the bill. They had the same members as the time I saw them at the Fillmore East, playing mostly songs from their third album *Benefit*. However, they didn't stand out very well at this festival. Many people in the crowd were just walking around, waiting for The Who to appear. The long piano solos and drum solos were good, but the audience was not receptive to their efforts. It must have been experiences like these that led Jethro Tull to record and release very well-organized concept albums such as *Aqualung, Thick as a Brick*, and *Passion Play,* one after the other. I like those three albums the best. The jazzy improvisational parts took a backseat to more organized performances.

The Who's performance that day was exceptionally good. Some of it is included in their video *30 Years of Maximum R&B.* Following Bill Graham's announcement, they started with "Heaven and Hell" sung by bassist John Entwistle. John Entwistle was my favorite bass player along with Jack Casady (of Jefferson Airplane). They are the musicians who really created the style of electric bass playing in rock music.

If anyone asked me what the best examples of great bass playing in rock music are, I would point toward the albums that they play on. For Jefferson Airplane, that would be *Bless Its Pointed Head* or *Volunteers.* John Entwistle sounds the best on The Who's *Quadrophenia* or on most live recordings from around this time in the 1970s.

One thing that John Entwistle and Jack Casady had in common was that they both started out playing lead instruments, while the lead guitarist in their bands originally played rhythm guitar to support them. When they were both eleven years old, John Entwistle began performing melodies on the trumpet and flugelhorn with Pete Townshend providing chordal accompaniment.

When they were in their teens, Jack Casady began playing lead guitar with Jorma Kaukonen of the Jefferson Airplane on rhythm guitar. When Entwistle joined The Who and Casady joined Jefferson Airplane, they became the bassists, while Townshend and Kaukonen became the lead guitarists. They would inspire many bassists. Yes' Chris Squire was influenced by John Entwistle. Jack Casady influenced Anthony Jackson.

Keith Moon was throwing his drumsticks around, drumming in his unique style. The first thing you need for a rock band to sound great is to have a good bassist and drummer playing energetically and tightly together. The first half of the show focused on the songs from *Live at the Leeds*, including the new songs they had started recording for *Who's Next*, which had not been released yet. Roger Daltrey, the singer, then announced "We were told not to play this tonight, but we're going to play *Tommy* in its entirety from now on." Wow! Just what I wanted to hear.

The song "Overture" started amidst intense joyous shouts and claps from the audience. The band played all the long instrumental parts including "Underture." The band was well organized, so these instrumental parts were especially good, even better than the studio recording. After the last song "See Me, Feel Me," they started playing "My Generation," similar to the version they released on *Live at Leeds*.

Seiji Ozawa, the conductor of the Boston Philharmonic, got us box seats for this show and we went to see the concert together. The box seats are in the center of the audience, and for classical music, they are the best seats to hear an orchestra, but for rock music, it was a little different. When The Who started, some of the audience wearing sneakers with suction pumps started to climb up on the wall. People in front of me also started to stand up. Seiji Ozawa stood up to scream out loud "Sit down!"

Lots of musicians came to Tanglewood for the summer music festivals. Stanley Silverman had rented a house there, and that's where I played my first electric guitar. I especially liked the noise that you could get from the distortion in high volume. Even if I messed up some of the notes, I could get intoxicated by the noise itself. It made me feel like Jimi Hendrix.

The next year, I got my first electric guitar for my 11th birthday.

I loved writing short stories and couldn't wait to read them to my class when I was in middle school. The fact that people heard, liked, and commented on my words every time was encouraging. If this hadn't happened, I would probably never have chosen to continue to write lyrics, stories, and non-fiction essays.

In an article, American novelist Kurt Vonnegut stated that picturing the person he wished to tell a story to serve as his initial inspiration. It's fun to write while imagining someone's reaction. In my case, my first imaginary audience was my middle school classmates. This is how I was inspired to tell stories in front of an audience.

There's one thing that was most influential in my life at that time: the lyrics and storytelling, by Peter Gabriel of Genesis.

Six

Influences from Peter Gabriel's performances

From 1973 onward, I was most inspired by Peter Gabriel's work with Genesis. He would tell stories using very simple mime techniques that he picked up from watching performers, such as Marcel Marceau and Lindsay Kemp. Unlike David Bowie or Kate Bush, Gabriel never took lessons from Lindsay Kemp. However, Peter Gabriel said in many of his early interviews that he was influenced by Lindsay Kemp in mime. He simply took from what he saw and liked.

He wrote stories and lyrics inspired by a wide range of literature and arthouse movies. He knew classical literature, and world mythology; and read Kurt Vonnegut, Carl Jung, and many other books that I loved in the early 1970s. "Stagnation" reminded me of Edgar Allen Poe; "The Fountain of Salmacis" was based on Greek mythology; and "The Battle of Epping Forest" was based on news clippings he kept of a gang war in Epping Forest. "Dancing with the Moonlit Knight" described many of the problems in Britain of the early 1970s through images and clever use of wordplay. "Supper's Ready" was inspired by a spiritual encounter Gabriel had one night at producer, John Anthony's home in London (according to Spencer Bright's biography on Peter Gabriel). Many other early songs were like English folk tales and nursery rhymes, but distinct and often macabre.

When I saw Peter Gabriel's mime in "The Musical Box" and "Supper's Ready," I thought it was one of the greatest things I'd ever seen. I would adapt some of Peter Gabriel's hand movements to recite a macabre story in front of the class. My friends at school often told me they loved my recitation and loved the hand movements that I adapted.

I felt that Peter Gabriel used mime movements better than David Bowie. It was original and unique. He wasn't trying to do mime properly like David Bowie would during his Ziggy Stardust tour.

Genesis was touring the United States a lot at this time, and I went to see many of their concerts. The ones I attended in 1973 and 74 included the following: Felt Forum NYC on November 22, 1973; Capital Theatre Passaic NJ on March 1, 1974; Academy of Music NYC on May 4, 1974; and Academy of Music NYC on December 6, 1974. I took my camera to the March 1 concert in New Jersey and the December 6 concert at the Academy of Music. No one stopped me from taking photos in those days. I took a photography class at school and had great shots of their concerts. Peter Gabriel flew up in the air like Peter Pan during the end of "Supper's Ready."

During *The Lamb Lies Down on Broadway* show, I sat in the front row; Peter Gabriel came down to the front of the stage during "Anyway" and stared straight into my camera. Unfortunately, when my mother ran off to London and separated from my stepfather in a divorce, all my belongings including notebooks and all those photographs were thrown out. No one knew where they were. It was heartbreaking! I was depressed for years.

How I wish I could get on a time machine and save those photos because they were like nothing else, and I haven't seen any photographs that were like those I had taken. They also represent what rock music was like during the early 1970s. I had taken many photographs of Lindsay Kemp which were professionally published in magazines.

Peter Gabriel used to tell the stories of the songs briefly before the band played them using simple mime hand movements. I always enjoyed the way he did it. Before the song "The Cinema Show," he told the story of Romeo and Juliet with a touch of black humor. Before "The Musical Box," he told the story of a girl in kindergarten who kills a boy in a game called Crochet with a big stick that hits the ball, and the boy comes back as a ghost in the form of an old man.

When he told the story and sang, he used his hands and arms skillfully to express the words with his movements. For example, when he sang that there was a clock on the shelf, he first stretched his left and right arms out to the side with five fingers straight to represent the straight line on the shelf and then swung his hand from right to left like the pendulum of an old clock.

In the song, "Watcher of the Skies," he would either stand very still or make sudden agitated movements. He knew how to use rhythm very well. This wasn't dance, but something entirely different. It reminded me of movements in silent film classics such as *The Cabinet of Dr. Caligari* or *Nosferatu*. He made these movements with great concentration. I often watched him from the center of the front row in the theater. I was deeply affected by his lyrics and his movements like nothing else. This influence remained strong deep inside me for years.

Their unique guitar sound was originally created by Anthony Philips and Mike Rutherford on 12-string guitars for Genesis, while they were still in their late teens. Anthony Philips was influenced by the open-tuning guitar methods played by Joni Mitchell, Fairport Convention, and other guitarists who adapted traditional British music for the guitar. I found it amazing that Anthony Philips created so many great songs with open tuning 12-string guitar when he was still in his teens. He formed this group when he was only fifteen years old, and he quit when he was eighteen for health reasons.

But it was the way Peter Gabriel used simple mime techniques to tell the story that most influenced me. This continued to be my role model. The performance I liked the most was *The Lamb Lies Down on Broadway*, which I saw live in its entirety. This performance was on December 6, 1974, at the Academy of Music in NYC. It is one of the two greatest rock concert shows I have ever attended. (The other is the *Preservation* musical show by The Kinks which I will write about later.)

Peter Gabriel is very well-read and was inspired by *The Tibetan Book of the Dead* and Carl Jung's journals, as well as by the film *El Topo* by Alejandro Jodorowsky.

I loved *The Lamb Lies Down on Broadway* (henceforth shortened as *The Lamb*) from the moment I heard it. I particularly liked the story and the lyrics. I thought that it was and still is one of the greatest works of art from the 20th century.

I completely identified with the character of Rael. I lived in NYC at the time I heard it in 1974. There were a few Puerto Rican kids in my school, and I had a close friend who would carry a spray gun and paint graffiti on the subway. There were Italian gangs in my neighborhood. Some of them would threaten to beat us up just because Puerto Ricans were in our school. The Elgin cinema, where Peter Gabriel may have seen *El Topo* (which influenced this story), was three blocks from my apartment house. I also saw it there at the time. Friends of my mother who came from Japan, such as Tadanori Yokoo, also saw it there and were impressed by this film.

When my stepfather and mother suddenly separated, while I was visiting relatives in Japan, I couldn't go back to NYC—even though I was already enrolled in high school. I would listen to *The Lamb* for hours feeling that the lyrics represented my life, and I was trapped underground in a country whose culture I couldn't understand. I felt that "The Lamb" is my life in art. I am sure people with similar experiences will understand this. And the title track has the most poetic lyrics about NYC that I have ever read.

I developed an interest in philosophy, mythology, and world culture. *The Lamb* is very much influenced by Carl Jung and *The Tibetan Book of the Dead*. Once you read these works, the meaning behind the words becomes clear. "It" is about 'individuation' in Carl Jung's analytical philosophy—the lifelong psychological process of differentiation of the self out of each individual's conscious and unconscious elements. Jung considered it to be the main task of human development.

There are also many books published by his disciple, Marie-Louise von Franz, analyzing the meaning behind mythology and fairy tales, and Jung's influence is definitely felt in *The Lamb*. "It is here. It is now," Gabriel sings in "It"—this is from Buddhism. It is true that many hippies adapted words like this, but there was something deeper in Gabriel's lyrics. Jung noticed similarities between Buddhism and Eastern traditions such as Taoism and the I-Ching to modern physics. Buddhist philosophy, of course, is the basis for *The Tibetan Book of the Dead*.

The lyrics for "The Lamia" reminded me of a story in *One Thousand and One Nights* from the Middle East.

A lot of progressive rock fans have said that they found the story of *The Lamb* to be difficult to understand, but I have never found it to be so. I have always felt that it represented a part of my life and culture in the arts.

I would also come to love some 20th-century opera classics such as *Lulu* by Alban Berg and *Pelléas et Mélisande* by Debussy, but I've always felt that *The Lamb* is as artistically as refined and creative as these works. I still feel that this was the greatest work by a rock group in the 20th century!

Throughout my musical career, the influence of the way Peter Gabriel presented the stories and lyrics he wrote remains the strongest.

Later during the 1980s, when I became a professional musician, music producer, and music journalist, I was introduced to David Lord, who co-produced Peter Gabriel's fourth album *Security*. I worked on five albums with David Lord; three of my solo albums; one that I produced for the Koto player, Kazue Sawai; and one of Celtic mythology in which I was a guest player.

During a recording session in 2000, I visited Real World Studios and asked to interview Peter Gabriel, but he never got back to me. I didn't realize then that David Lord had had an affair with Peter Gabriel's first wife, and that they weren't exactly the best of friends.

Seven

David, the actor/Experimental films/The Strawbs

Toward the end of '74, I got to know a bisexual actor named David Haughton. At that time, he was the lover of a dancer and mime actor named Lindsay Kemp. He was from the south of Ireland and had the type of Gaelic (Celtic Irish or Scottish) face you often see with dark hair. He had a unique way of reading; his reading of Oscar Wilde showed me a world that I had never known before. I was not gay, and had no interest in gay culture, so my friendship with David was purely platonic.

Looking back, I think it was an old-fashioned way of reading English, like the way that Shakespeare was often read, but it wasn't a common reading I would expect in my time in New York City. I began to experiment with that kind of voice when I read stories. At school, I developed a reputation for speaking like an Englishman even though I was from East Asia. America had been a part of Great Britain for about two hundred years before that, so speaking in an English way reminded Americans of their roots. In fact, he may have been creating a kind of pose on purpose to have that effect on people.

He was an Irishman, but he talked very much like what people imagine English people talked like centuries ago. David and I went to a few concerts and movies together; I was fascinated by experimental films and experimental music. We went together to an experimental film festival at the Museum of Modern Art in New York. There was a film playing then, with Marcel Duchamp and music by John Cage. I had met John Cage with my mother and father, but this was the first time that I consciously listened to his music. This was also the first time I saw Luis Buñuel and Salvador Dali's *An Andalusian Dog*.

On March 1, 1975, I went to New Jersey with David Haughton to see the band The Strawbs play at the Capital Theatre. This band had just released an album called *Ghosts*, and they played mainly songs from this and their other recent album, *Hero and Heroine*. This was their most progressive rock period. The Strawbs started as a folk group, and Sandy Denny was a singer in the band for a while. But they first gained attention when Rick Wakeman, a keyboard player who could play fast phrases in classical piano style, joined the band. Then, they received more attention after Wakeman quit the Strawbs and joined a more famous progressive rock band called Yes. This meant that Yes fans became interested in bands that Wakeman was previously involved in. The Strawbs responded by changing their sound to a more progressive one.

When we saw them at the Capital Theatre, John Hawkins, formerly of Renaissance, was the keyboard player. John Hawkins looked like a mad scientist as he played the intro theme to *Hero and Heroine*, with the strong white lights shining down on him. The song was centered around a funky bass line played on a synthesizer, and it was getting a lot of radio play on black radio shows at the time.

Listening to it now, it has the same feel as the black funk music that was popular at the time, such as Isaac Hayes' *Shaft* and Curtis Mayfield's *Superfly*. But what was distinctive about The Strawbs' music was that they retained more folkish characteristics in their music than many of the other groups. The medley of "Out in the Cold" and "Round and Round" was particularly good.

David started appearing in Italian B movies in the late 1970s. He played the leading role in Joe D'Amato's *Caligula 2*. Joe D'Amato is the director of films such as *Madame Emmanuelle Meets the Cannibals*. The title *Madame Emmanuelle Meets the Cannibals* came from the fact that the Indonesian actress Laura Gemser was in one of the sequels of the erotic film *Madame Emmanuelle*, which was a big seller at the time. It was a project to bring together fans of *Madame Emmanuelle* and fans of horror films at the same time. The idea was that when Laura Gemser starts a sex scene, a cannibal comes out from behind her and turns it into a horror movie. As it turned out, neither type of moviegoer showed up. But Joe D'Amato didn't give up and continued to make film after film like that. When *The Night of the Living Dead* became popular, he made a movie called *Sexy Nights of the Living Dead (Zombie '99)*. Joe D'Amato's films always went into debt.

In the early 1980s, David told someone that I used to be his lover, but this wasn't true. In 1986, I got to work with his brother, Richard Haughton, who became a well-known photographer—taking many photos of rock musicians as well.[1]

---

[1]He took the photographs used on my *Nova Carmina*. Mr. He also did some other jobs for MIDI records and a few Japanese magazines in the 80s.

Eight

The junior high school I attended/Studying medieval European history/Teaching methods that make the students think for themselves/The Italian school in my neighborhood

Most of the students at the school I went to had parents of different nationalities and ethnicities. Some spoke a different language at home. The type of people whom I didn't meet at school were the WASPs (White Anglo-Saxon Protestants) who are usually supposed to represent America. There were people of Chinese descent, Puerto Rican descent, German-Jewish, Russian-Jewish, Ukrainian, African-American, Japanese, and a mixture of these combinations. But we were all raised in New York City. The American culture, we understood, was different from our parents. We were raised in the English language, and we deserve to be recognized that the English language is *our* language. It is not a second language, or an adapted tongue.

We were all educated as members of one multi-ethnic nation-state, the United States of America. No one was a foreigner; otherwise, we would *all* be foreigners. One day in the seventh grade, the history teacher said that this class was 'cosmopolitan.' But I don't think this was 'cosmopolitan' at all. It was very much what New York City is all about—people from different backgrounds, congregating together to study one culture in the English language.

Our school was famous for its progressive education based on liberal ideas, as evidenced by the fact that the children of Bob Dylan, those of the group Peter Paul and Mary, and (in the 1990s) Patti

Smith's children attended our school. It was believed that to create a new society, a new way of education was needed.

The first year of junior high school focused on the history of medieval Europe. The Metropolitan Museum in New York exhibited many items brought from Europe, and there is a medieval European monastery called Cloisters in Fort Tryon Park near 190th Street in Upper Manhattan. The building's stones were carefully disassembled, one by one, and reassembled with items brought from Europe. There were tapestries and beautifully decorated medieval manuscripts. The tapestry of a woman with a unicorn was so beautiful that its image lingered long in my memory.

Brenda, our history teacher, wanted the students to feel the Middle Ages as realistically as was possible in our school curriculum. She had the class create a virtual medieval European space within the classroom, to make us feel as though we were living in the Middle Ages. We read medieval English literature, listened to medieval European music, cooked medieval European food, and performed a medieval European historical drama.

The play we performed was about King Arthur, the legendary king of England, who is said to be buried in a tomb in Glastonbury (a town in the southwest of England) according to one legend. The play involved a group of people on a quest to find the legendary Holy Grail buried there with him. First, we all read the novel, and then we all wrote the script for the play in class together.

That same year, I wrote a play alone myself, based on the biography of Jane Seymour, the third wife of King Henry VIII of England. I remember watching a TV historical education program, buying various books, borrowing books from the library, and writing a play of about 60 pages. I don't have any of this with me anymore, as I lost everything in 1975 when my mother walked out on the family.

In our school, teachers tried to strive to provide pupils with real-world experiences that made the students feel and think for themselves rather than only reading history texts.

This was also true of American history. When we studied the War of Independence from Britain, we were given the task of figuring out who fired the first gunshot. Usually, the American side would say the British side. The British side would say the American side. You had to read various documents of that time in class and had to analyze it yourself, think about it, and submit a report. Of course, there is no right answer. The important thing was how well you could research and write your own opinion. William, our American history teacher, always told us not to trust American textbooks. He also told us to be careful with newspapers as well as any media reports, saying: Why does it say this? Why are they saying this? What is the position of the people who are saying this? Who benefits from this news? He told me that we would never know the truth unless I looked at it from various angles.

Figure 7   The secondary school Little Red School House, as photographed by Ayuo in 1986.

Figure 8   A photo of me dressed as a medieval European knight, with my Little Red School House classmates at the Metropolitan Museum of Art, 1972.

My eighth-grade history teacher, William, was a black man.

He always said that the current US history textbooks are written from the white man's point of view. For example, Thomas Jefferson, who wrote the *Declaration of Independence*, is usually taught to be the father of American freedom and democracy, but he was also a slave owner. On top of that, he impregnated several black women and refused to recognize them as his children.

From a black man's point of view, Jefferson was a racist. When he wrote, "All men are created equal, and that they are endowed by their creator with certain unalienable Rights, that among those are life, liberty, and the pursuit of happiness," he did not include black people in the "All men" category. He did not see them as human beings.

It was the same for Native Americans, Asians, and Orientals. White people did not see us as human beings at that time. I remember his next words well.

"America was not at first, a free country or a true democracy. If you go to the South today, the majority of students here will be discriminated against and treated very badly. We are only beginning the struggle to end racism and discrimination in the world."

What I learned in this class continued to influence me for the rest of my life.

At the time, I thought that this was the normal education that one gets in school. It wasn't until much later that I learned that in most parts of the world, they use textbooks approved by the government and do not teach students to think for themselves. They are taught to become proper 'nationals'—to uphold their country as patriots and become a cog in a wheel to support it. In East Asian countries such as Japan, individualism does not even exist in traditional culture, so the kind of education I received was not understood at all.

The school adjacent to Bleecker Street in the Village was a catholic school for people of Italian descent only. When I walked past the school, I could hear the students talk in Italian. It was co-ed, but the students all wore uniforms. Outside the school, there were stained glass window panels with a picture of Mary holding Christ. Unlike our school, it was a school where they read Biblical class and prayed. The way they taught history was probably completely different from our school.

Many of the students at that school came from Little Italy, a part of downtown New York City, which was just around the corner. Little Italy was protected by the mafia. The students from this school started bullying the students from our school.

Toward the end of my first year of junior high school, there was a day when each student in my class had an interview with our homeroom teacher. As I was walking to school alone, I saw an Italian boy standing in the street with a baseball bat.

'Hey, if you don't give me all the money you have, I'm going to smash your head in with this bat!" he said.

I only had a quarter in my pocket, but I gave it to him. By the time I reached the school grounds, I couldn't bother to tell the teachers what had just happened. Things like this started to become commonplace. It didn't seem important, and he didn't hurt me in the end.

New York City culture in the 1970s was often stimulating, but it could also be dangerous. One night, I heard pistol shots and looked out the window to see a dead Italian boy covered in blood. Another day, a pair of robbers entered our apartment with knives, threatening to kill us all. They just took whatever money there was in the house. They were never caught.

I had heard rumors that a boy in the grade below me had been beaten and kicked by some Italian students in Washington Square Park. Things got a little more violent in the eighth grade when some Italian middle schoolers with big knives stormed into a night party at our school and scared everyone. At the time, the schoolteachers were there, but they never called the police because they all knew those Italians were from the school next door. I wasn't there at that party.

The Italians were often referred to by the racist term 'guineas.' In New York City, there were several racist terms for different races and ethnicities. All Orientals (East Asians) were chinks. Blacks are niggers. Hispanics are spics. The term Mongoloid, which comes from 'Mongolian,' had also been used to describe a certain type of mentally handicapped person, as well as referencing East Asians.

The Italian students would attack the kids in our school because there were a few Puerto Ricans in our school. One might think of the musical *West Side Story*, by composer Leonard Bernstein, about a gang war between an Italian gang and a Puerto Rican gang. Truthfully though, I don't think the Italian students cared about the "ethnicity" of others. I think those boys just wanted an excuse to become violent when they became middle schoolers and high school students—the age when boys go through puberty.

Both Puerto Ricans and Italians are Catholic and of Latin blood. Many Puerto Ricans are mixed with African blood, and Spanish blood and have some native 'Indian' ancestors. People from southern Italy and Sicily are also said to have Mediterranean North African blood. These kinds of bullying are more likely to happen between people who are 'similar, but slightly different.' I think it is the same when we grow up. The various sects of Christianity in Europe don't seem very different from each other when observed by outsiders, but very small differences can lead people to wars.

Of course, we can't deny that there is often a power struggle in the shadows among the rulers and elites that everyone cannot see, but this is usually not enough to overturn an entire country unless masses of people are involved.

Colin Wilson wrote in *A Criminal History of Mankind* about the time of Emperor Justinian in Byzantine, Greece, when the citizens of Constantinople were divided on the question of whether the divine and human natures in Christ were joined together or separated. One side called themselves the Greens, and the other side the Blues. They began to act like modern-day hooligans, reinforcing their argument by murdering one another. In the riots in 532 A.D., half of Constantinople was set on fire. Justinian's general, Belisarius, took his army into the streets and killed thirty thousand people, which convinced both the Blues and Greens factions to end their argument.

Often, people who have similar but not exact political opinions with one another, wind up killing each other. Many communists and Marxists with slightly different political opinions killed more of their same faction, compared to the capitalists that they attacked, for example in Japan during the 1960s.

I believe in the following:

Patriotism and nationalism were both created during the creation of Western nation-states from the 18th to the 19th centuries.

Although tribal nationalism exists among many tribes, state nationalism did not exist until it was invented in the West. Countries around the world were forced to adopt this system of nation-states and to think of themselves as members of this new order.

Originally, the native Americans were recognized as Hopi; Sioux; Cheyenne; Cherokee; Iroquois; and others but were renamed 'Indians' by European settlers mistaking the land for Europe. When the Americans and the Europeans called people living on the island of Japan 'Japanese,' they became Japanese from then on. Until then, most people were not allowed to leave the village in which they were born. People who are not aware of the existence of different people in the world cannot identify themselves as belonging to a particular nation-state. The people in neighboring provinces, which were called countries before the age of the nation-state (*kuni* in Japanese; *guo* in Chinese; *gok* in Korean) were like foreign countries. They are now provinces in the modern age. There were no such people as the Japanese before the modern age, except in theory among the elite who wished to unify all the people or rule over all of them.

This is how I interpret history.

Recent scientific studies show the following results: all human beings (*Homo sapiens*) spread from around Tanzania in Africa to all over the world 50,000 to 60,000 years ago. I believe that all people are connected, but that tribal warfare and discrimination divide people.

For example, there is the following theory:

In *The Autobiography of Malcolm X,* Malcolm X posits that among black people, some are born as albinos. Albinos are white, but slightly weaker than others. They were discriminated against and thrown out of African society. Thus, the albinos who were thrown out of Africa later became the ancestors of the white people.

From the way I saw how people discriminated against each other in all of the countries I have lived in, I can easily see that this kind of bullying led to the division between tribes and later nationalities.

Every human being carries the same RNA signature from the very first life on Earth. This is the same as what the Old Testament says: "In the beginning was the Word."

This human being has the memory of all living things, from the first life on earth to the birth of oneself as that human being.

I have it. You have it. It is within the genetic codes that make us.

The genetic changes that occurred before we came into existence are all recorded in our bodies like a book of genome. Science now allows us to read it like a book.

Another new revelation, thanks to the progress of scientific discovery, is that race and ethnicity are not as important as was previously thought. An individual is markedly more different from one another than nationalists and conservatives would like to think. The culture that one is raised in; the food that you ate when you were a child—all these parasocial influences inform you in a way that your nationality and race cannot by themselves. There are also small things, like blood types, which also delineate further differences between people.

This is, of course, true not only for personality differences, but is also important knowledge when it comes to treating diseases, especially cancer. According to science journalist Matt Ridley, in one experiment, the genetic difference between two Swiss people was greater than the overall genetic difference between one Swiss person and a Peruvian person.[1] The difference is greater for each individual than for ethnicity or race, proving that ethnicity and racism are not as meaningful as it was once assumed to be. Individual differences are far greater.

---

[1]See Ridley's foreword to *The Red Queen*.

Nine

The disintegration of my family life/ Suddenly leaving New York City in 1975

In 1975, when I was fifteen years old, I had to abruptly leave New York City, where I had grown up from kindergarten until junior high school.

In the hours between December 31st, 1974, to January 1, 1975, a tiny tarot card dropped out of a book I was taking from the shelf. It was a stray card from a tiny deck of tarot cards I had given away, featuring a scythe-wielding Grim Reaper. I had long believed that the tarot card that had fallen that evening represented change. For me, it marked the end of one era and the start of another.

This was a warning that something was about to change.

A few years later, when I informed my mother about this, she remarked, "You gave the playwright Shuji Terayama a set of tarot cards the last time he visited our apartment in New York.

Yes, Mr. Terayama had the remaining cards.

I spent much of my life after I had to leave New York City to reflect on all the influences I was exposed to while growing up there and find ways to express them in my work.

The reason I had to leave this city had nothing to do with my own decision. I wanted to stay and continue this life. After all, this was my home! The place where I grew up. My culture was here.

In 1974, my stepfather's father died in Iran, and he had to go back several times that year and the next. This seemed to be the catalyst that brought to the surface the gap between my mother and stepfather that had been simmering below the surface. My mother was just about forty years old. The age when one has a mid-life crisis.

Up until about 1969, my mother was listening to mostly Frank Sinatra, jazz standards, and occasionally The Beatles. Things began to change in New York City, because her friends from Japan would come to taste the new rock culture that was emerging in New York. I was the one listening to Jefferson Airplane, The Doors and Grateful Dead.

As the 1970s progressed, she began to come into my room and take the rock records that Mansour and others had bought for me. The orchestra conductor, Seiji Ozawa, once bought me records by The Kinks, Moody Blues, and Deep Purple in England, and brought them back to me as a present. At first, my mother didn't like them. My mother began to take the magazines and books I had and read them herself. She used to stay up all night and sleep at dawn, reading books and listening to music on the headphones. She would often still be asleep when I came back from school around 4 pm.

I hated the way she would take my things and make them her own. A child of thirteen or fourteen wants his own private space and music that he listens to on his own. When your mother starts to take your records of David Bowie, The Kinks, Roxy Music, and Genesis and starts to play them endlessly, you lose a part of your own space. A thirteen- or fourteen-year-old wants to go out with his friends and develop what would later become his art, on his own. He doesn't need a mother or want a mother hanging around him taking away his things.

I used to have a subscription to a magazine called *Circus*, from which one issue had an interview with Peter Gabriel. In that interview, he mentioned that he was influenced in his theatrics on stage by the mime and dance artist, Lindsay Kemp. David Bowie and later Kate Bush would study dance and mime with Kemp. My mother kept this in mind. One night she went to see a performance of the English dance and mime company, the Lindsay Kemp Company, performing "Turquoise Pantomime" by herself. I don't remember why I didn't go. Perhaps I had schoolwork and was visiting friends to do them together. She noticed that the members of the Lindsay Kemp Company were all poor and often didn't have the money to buy dinner. She began to invite them back to our apartment to feed them.

From then on, my house had become a very uncomfortable place. My mother started seeing and later sleeping with some of the members of The Lindsay Kemp Company. Every night, a lot of people would come over to my house and party all night. Many of them were on LSD or magic mushrooms. My mother would take the rock records Mansour had bought me and play them loudly all night long. I couldn't even sleep; the walls were always shaking.

At one point, one of the dancers brought in a white woman besides my mother, and the three of them had sex for hours on end. My mother stopped taking care of things around the house and started telling me things like "go crazy" and "drop out." I would go to the kitchen to get food and a naked man with his penis out would be there. Not a sober person in sight. My mother came to say, "It's more fun to be able to choose who you want to sleep with than to be chained to one man." I couldn't even leave my room.

LSD can make you see the world differently and understand things you wouldn't normally notice, but it can also make you so wrapped up in your world that you can't see what's going on around you. I was only 14 years old at the time. Mentally and physically, I was still a child. In today's American law, if something like this happened, my mother would be accused of child abuse. It was as if a dam had suddenly burst. Our family home life evaporated.

Looking back, I tried and tried to analyze the reason for my mother's breakdown; it was probably because she had been living the life of a housewife with me and my stepfather for so many years that her stress suddenly overflowed like a dam bursting. Another thing may have been that she wanted to go out and have a relationship with young men again.

Whatever the reason, she lost complete control. Children should not have to face such situations.

At school, they were worried about me. A psychiatrist was brought in. They noticed something deeply wrong was happening in my life, but they didn't know what it was. I hadn't thought of my mother as the type of person who would suddenly explode like this. Maybe I didn't know, because I was still a child and didn't understand the complexity of adult human beings. My stepfather, who had returned from Iran for a time, went to the school and tried to reassure the teachers. Looking back, I really feel sorry for him. His whole family life collapsed while he was away for a short while.

My mother used to often ask me around this time, "Why don't you go out and date girls?" But in junior high school, you don't have that kind of relationship yet. I think the situation changed in high school. In my class, there were only two groups of kids who had girlfriends or boyfriends at that age. One of the girls was nicknamed "whore" by her peers. She didn't have a father, she lived with a single mother, and she would walk up to the boys in her class and say, "Give me some money."

Around this time, the British filmmaker Ken Russell made and released the film *Tommy* based on The Who's rock opera.

I had been listening to *Tommy* since I was in the second grade of elementary school. I went to see this movie with my mother and her dancer boyfriend, Robin. He didn't have any money, so my mother always paid for it. The movie is about a boy named Tommy. His father was missing in action during World War II.

Tommy's mother becomes close to a man named Bernie, who runs a summer camp for boys. One night, when she and Bernie start to have sex in bed, Tommy's father comes home. Bernie is so surprised that he kills his father. Tommy sees the scene and is shocked. His mother and Bernie implored Tommy: "You didn't see it. You didn't hear it. You won't say nothing to no one ever in your life. (You can't tell anyone about this, you didn't see anything, you didn't hear anything, you can't talk.)" And Tommy remains in a state of shock and does exactly as they say. He can't hear anything, he can't speak, and he can't see. After seeing this movie, my mother and her boyfriend looked at me and said, "You act just like Tommy." My life was getting messed up and I knew it.

Junior high school students have to do a lot of homework and reports. I was studying to get into high school. But my home became a difficult place to study. I started inviting my school friends to go and study at the library. It made me closer to them. It became normal for me to go to my classmates' houses at night after school to smoke weed and listen to music. This was the time when I had the most friends.

Later on, in the 2000's, with the internet and social networking, I looked up what happened to my friends from that time and found that some were in the music industry as singers, rappers, producers, road managers of nationally touring rock bands, etc. We would exchange music that we were making.

What would have happened if I had stayed in New York? I could have been writing poetry and making music with my friends. I missed the opportunity to continue with my education. I missed the opportunity to be with my friends. My future had to be sacrificed because my parents wanted to do things in life, and didn't think about me.

In the summer of 1975, I had to leave for a summer vacation in Japan. My mother's boyfriend, Robin, the dancer, had already gone back to England that spring. I asked my mother what she was going to do after that. She only told me what she was going to do that day. Then I left for Tokyo from Kennedy Airport.

Ten

Arrival in Tokyo/Father, Yuji Takahashi/ Stepmother, Karen/Enrollment in Yokohama International School

When I arrived in Tokyo, my father—Yuji Takahashi—was there to pick me up at Haneda Airport.

He had married Karen, an Irish-Polish-American, in 1970. Karen was born in Texas and raised in Oklahoma. She worked as a radio personality in San Francisco. At the time she met my father, she was the girlfriend of Lukas Foss, a prominent contemporary music composer and conductor in the United States.

Karen and I talked a lot, and she recommended various literary works to me. Her recommendations introduced me to Kurt Vonnegut and Aldous Huxley, who had a profound influence on the stories and poems I wrote from then, all the way to this day. I composed a song, "Ophelia," based on Vonnegut's novel *Jailbird* in the 1990s, and recorded it in the 2000s with Jadranka Stojakovic, a Bosnian singer from the former Yugoslavia.

As soon as I arrived, my father told me that he would be gone for a while because he had to go to Australia for almost two months. Thus, from the middle of June to August, I spent time with my stepmother Karen and my half-brother Haya—the son of my father and stepmother. Karen was studying Asian history and culture at the graduate school of Sophia University and had rented an apartment in Takanawa, Tokyo. A day or three after I arrived, I bought a Yamaha acoustic guitar.

Once my father left for Australia, Karen told me that she and my father had already divorced that winter. After a short time in Japan, she began to realize that Japanese culture was very different from what she had imagined in America. She was pregnant at the time. Once the baby was born, there was a period when she could not get back on track—but my father, who was supposed to be her husband, didn't help her at all. Even when Karen got sick and collapsed in her room for a few hours, he never asked her if she was okay. He just ignored her and left her alone for the rest of the night. My father just kept on working on his writing for hours in front of her collapsed body. How could he do that?

Karen told me that she felt at that moment that my father was a man who did not care about other people at all. "I think it must have been the same with your mother," she said.

She had written to my father a few months before that: 'I am afraid of you. I try to talk to you, but when I get close to you, I get too scared to talk to you.'

For my father, being "different" was how he attracted attention. He could appear to be a 'genius' or a crazy person. Years later, Aki, his younger sister, told me that she believed he had Asperger Syndrome, a type of autism spectrum disorder (ASD). She said that when one reads about Asperger Syndrome, it seems to point out my father's problems. His sisters have known him since he was born, and his 'weird' attitude and inability to understand others may be attributed to this. Yet at the same time, people in Japan knew that he was still very much a Japanese of the old traditional kind. This is what made him popular in Japan, rather than in any other country.

The two months I spent with my stepmother and half-brother were peaceful. We even went to a pottery factory in Fukui-ken run by Hiroshi Teshigahara, where we made our pottery.

I was supposed to go to Elizabeth Irwin High School in Soho in September. I had written to my friends in August that I would be seeing them there. However, I suddenly got a letter from my mother that she left New York to follow the dancers in the Lindsay Kemp Company to London. She was enjoying herself there and didn't want to go back to New York City.

So, what would happen to my school? What about my education? What happened to what I thought was my family? Did she care?

My mother later said that she shaved her head and danced naked for three days, and she no longer felt guilty and felt refreshed. She told me that this was a 'Japanese' traditional custom of saying sorry. I had never heard of such a tradition.

Is shaving your head and dancing in London, at a time and place where I'm not there, a way of 'Japanese' apology? It sounds ridiculous to me. But she said that by shaving her head and dancing, she was forgiven and did not need to apologize any further. Was she forgiven by the gods?

In Japan, I noticed that people do not apologize when they bump into you in the street unless you know them—or if you are recognized as a foreigner (meaning if you're recognized as 'white'). I could never figure out this strange attitude in Japanese culture.

I told Karen about the situation in New York. In September, my stepfather wrote to me asking about how this situation could be resolved. I was still 14 years old; I had no experience in how to solve this problem. He suggested in the letter that if I went back to New York, my mother would probably come back from England. Karen told me that it would be better for me to stay in Japan because the situation was complicated and messed up. She said that if she were in my situation, she would stay in Japan because I would be used as a pawn between them.

Two years later, my mother came to Japan with a 19-year-old boy, who had been a part of the Lindsay Kemp Company at that time. We got along very well because he was around my age and we both had the same interests in music and culture.

After my father returned, my stepmother and father decided to let me attend Yokohama International School. This was a school in Yokohama for English speakers. It was the only school in Japan at the time to offer both the British GCE and the US SAT exams. There were teachers from both the United States and Britain.

I was at first very disappointed that I could not attend Elizabeth Irwin High School. I missed my old friends. Most of the children at

Yokohama International were children of businessmen. They came from more conservative backgrounds than my classmates in New York City, who came from more progressive and artistic backgrounds. I did have much in common with them. However the kids with whom I had the most difficulty communicating were the Japanese kids. I knew nothing about how to communicate with ordinary Japanese male teens.

One day, a Japanese guy beat me up in the locker room before the gym, screaming at me that I'm *not* 'Japanese.' "I'll show you what a real Japanese is," he said, and he used his fists to give me a beating. Throughout my lifetime, I never forgot this. I realized that being raised abroad meant that the Japanese would never accept me as one of them. I was much happier in New York City, where I was one of the many children of immigrants. I had my own identity as an individual. I didn't know what he meant by 'Japanese.'

Much in Japanese culture is unspoken. No one, not even your parents or your relatives, will explain to you these unspoken rules in culture and society.

"You're *not* one of *us*" is what many will tell you.

In the 1990s, many Japanese-Brazilians and Japanese-Peruvians came to Japan to look for work, but they could not integrate into Japanese culture—even though many were 100% Japanese by DNA and blood. They were raised in Hispanic culture, and once their cultural ties are formed, people cannot change them later to become part of Japanese culture—even if their ancestors came from Japan. The Japanese government saw them as trouble and paid them with tax money to leave Japan and return to Brazil or Peru. President Lee Kuan Yew of Singapore pointed this out in his writings and speeches about how Japan was not able to accept foreign-raised Japanese, even though their parents may have been 100% Japanese in blood. Lee said that Chinese immigrants could be accepted better than these Japanese-Brazilians. Perhaps it is the similarity in having a Confucian background, but Western or Hispanic-raised individuals with Japanese faces are the last to be accepted in Japanese society.

As part of her graduate studies, Karen wrote a long essay about the atomic bombings of Hiroshima and Nagasaki.

Yuji Takahashi read this text and taped a song that electrically modulated his voice. At a festival called Media 3, organized by composer Shigeaki Saegusa, he played this piece on tape and showed a slide show of photographs to accompany it. Yuji Takahashi and my half-brother Haya walking in Hiroshima were shown on the screen.

At the end of the year, Karen went to the Philippines to study musical anthropology. My father, Haya, and I lived together in an apartment in Takanawa for two years. This was the only time I lived with them.

Eleven

My father's recordings/Left-wing political activists began to visit our residence. Takehisa Kosugi/Steve Lacy/Aquirax Aida/ Meeting Ryuichi Sakamoto

My father was still very active as a pianist back then, recording and releasing album after album of Bach, Satie, Messiaen, Xenakis, and other composers for Columbia Records. At that time, Mr. Kawaguchi, the classical music director of Nippon Columbia, was a fan of my father. However, my father was growing weary of these activities. There was about to be another major change in my life.

Many left-wing political activists began to visit our residence. They were people who talked about Asian solidarity and anti-Americanism. The underlying reason for this, I believe, is that my father lived for around ten years in both Europe and America, during which time there were several cultural conflicts and failed relationships in his personal and professional life. In addition, he harbored nostalgia for the previous Japan, where he had spent his postwar and elementary school years. I think the stress from all that led him to become politically and socially active at this time. Why he did so in the late 1970s, when the left-wing activities were coming to an end in the world, must have been for personal reasons.

Throughout my life, many radical ex-left-wing activists would contact me, trying to get me involved in some radical political activity. There were people who would drop copies of selected works by Stalin and Kim Il-Sung on my doorstep. Some were hoping that I would get my father to become involved in their political activities.

Although I'm getting a bit ahead here, one time around the year 2000, the promoter of my album *Songs from a Eurasian Journey* tried to get me involved with Takuya Shiomi, the ex-intellectual leader of the Japanese Red Army Faction who had just gotten out of prison. He had been in prison for organizing the hijacking of an airplane, known as the Yodo-go Hijacking Incident—when, on March 31, 1970, nine members of the Red Army Faction (armed with katana swords and a homemade bomb) hijacked Japan Airlines Flight 351 out of Tokyo International Airport carrying 129 people aboard. He was not on the airplane because he was already arrested, being mistaken for a common thief, but the hijacking went on as planned.

The hijacked plane went to North Korea, and they asked the North Korean government to help them train the Japanese Red Army to overthrow the Japanese government and take over. They would then make Japan the headquarters of a worldwide revolution against the United States of America and its allies. The hijackers were granted political asylum by the North Korean government and remained there for years.

Between February and July 1971, Red Army Faction members who remained in Japan carried out a series of relatively successful armed robberies of banks and post offices to secure funds for their armed uprising.

However, after the loss of Shiomi's ideological leadership, the Red Army Faction split into two. One faction formed the United Red Army, which became notable during the Asama-Sanso incident—when it murdered 14 of its members on Mount Haruna in July 1970, before a week-long siege involving hundreds of police, leaving a bystander and a police officer dead. Another faction called itself the Japanese Red Army, which attacked Lod Airport (now Ben Gurion International Airport) on May 30, 1972, near Tel Aviv. This incident caused the death of 26 people and injured 80 others.

Their ideology was that of extreme anti-Americanism. After Shiomi got out of prison, he became an ultranationalist while still maintaining contact with the North Korean government. He and my ex-promoter started to organize music concerts. Some were charity concerts to send money to North Korea because there was a famine there at the time. Some well-known names such as Shoukichi Kina also appeared in these concerts.

I was asked to go to a meeting, where Mr. Shiomi talked about how the United States needs to be destroyed. I said that I have no hatred against the United States because I was raised there. Mr. Shiomi then pointed out another person at that meeting saying this man also studied in the United States, but now hates it "as we all do." I immediately noticed that one major difference between this man and myself was that I was raised in NYC with an Iranian-American stepfather, while he went to study in the United States as a grown Japanese adult.

Most people in Japan don't understand that the country where you grow up is your home. I heard of many Japanese men who went to the United States when they were already in their late teens and came back a Japanese nationalist or a racist because they could not understand the cultural difference. I was the opposite of this. I always see my apartment home in Greenwich Village as my home and my culture. That never changes, no matter what happens.

Coming back to 1975: *Distant Voices*, an improvisation record of Steve Lacy (an American jazz saxophonist living in France), Takehisa Kosugi, and Yuji Takahashi, was to be recorded at Columbia Studios. I went to see this recording. It was the first time that I saw a recording in a big studio. The three musicians recorded three pieces of complete improvisations in a single night.

In the studio, each of the three occupied his own space to play. Yuji was at the grand piano. Takehisa Kosugi had a tablecloth on which he had placed cups, glasses, and various things used in the kitchen. On it were his violin and a microphone for recording his voice. Mr. Kosugi's violin and voice were particularly interesting. He had tuned his violin to his own unique tuning. I remember it was tuned *GDGD*; this made it easier to play in modes using a glissando style learned from Indian violin playing. Normally, classical violins are tuned to *GDAE*.

To me, it sounded like the way early blues was played on an open-tuning guitar. I thought what he played was very similar to the musical expressions in rock and blues. I was surprised that this was coming from someone who wasn't involved in rock music. Other avant-garde composers and musicians were mostly writing and performing atonal music, which was a little difficult for me to understand at that time. I became greatly interested in the music by Takehisa Kosugi from then onward.

Columbia Records had signed a licensing contract with Virgin Records in the United Kingdom at this time and were trying to sell artists such as Gong, Can, Steve Hillage, Tangerine Dream, and Faust. But they didn't sell at all in Japan at the time—Faust sold 100 copies; Henry Cow sold 56 copies. In other words, the company went into debt because of these records. Rock was not yet a major thing in Japan. A style of J-pop, known as Kayokyoku for the youth and Enka for the mature audience, were the two major styles of pop music in Japan.

Akira Aida (as Aquirax Aida), the author who wrote the Japanese liner notes for these albums at the time, was also Takehisa Kosugi's manager. When we met and talked, he realized that I knew a lot about these genres of music. He suggested that I write liner notes for Columbia Records. So, two projects came up. One was for the liner notes of Tangerine Dream's first four recordings, which featured a discussion with Yuji Takahashi about Tangerine Dream and the music that inspired them. The other was liner notes for Can's *Unlimited Edition*, in which I was asked to do an interview with Akira Aida, as well as write commentaries on the individual songs. I had already finished writing the commentary in English, but before it was translated into Japanese, the record company stopped releasing Can because their albums didn't sell too well.

Ryuichi Sakamoto, who was still a student at the Tokyo University of the Arts, used to come to our apartment often. He was already working as a studio musician in pop music. Columbia Records planned a joint album with the jazz drummer Masahiko Togashi, and Yuji Takahashi. The music that Yuji Takahashi wrote for this album was inspired by the poem "Twilight" from a collection of poems by Ho Chi Minh of Vietnam. I had already written a school report about these poems when I was in junior high school. So, when Yuji Takahashi asked me to buy this book for him, I told him that I already had it, so I simply gave him my copy.

I went to see the recording of this album. The recording started late at night and finished at midnight. Yuji invited Ryuichi Sakamoto to join him on this song. He had long hair and a beard at this time and still looked like a hippie.

He came to the studio and said, "I haven't eaten anything yet today." He was assured by Columbia Records' music director that he could eat at a nearby restaurant on the company's tab. "Twilight" was an improvisational work about twenty minutes in length with meandering, wandering melodies performed on synthesizers by Yuji Takahashi and Ryuichi Sakamoto. Yuji intended to use one hand to play a phrase and the other to play the drone portions, which are sustained bass notes, but he was unable to do it at the same time—therefore the first take ended in the middle of the composition.

It was past midnight by then, so Yuji invited me to play the sustained drone parts in the recording.

Aside from the rock records that Virgin was releasing around 1975, by the artists I have mentioned above, I was mostly listening to European medieval music and Steeleye Span, a group that performed traditional British music.

Troubadour, Trouveres, Minstrels by Thomas Binkley, as well as a series of CDs by Peter Abelard and others on the German label Reflexe, are all masterpieces. Thomas Binkley played the chitarra and the lute in the same manner as traditional plucked string instruments from Central Asia and the Middle East. Bowed string instruments performed in modes, frequently with portamentos between notes, similar to that of Asian music. I also discovered music performed by the Kazakh people of Central Asia on the Tambour. These kinds of music appealed to me more than most rock and pop music at the time.

The fact that many of Thomas Binkley's and Studio Der Frühen Musik's recordings were created in the 1960s and early 1970s may have influenced their perception of medieval music. Jazz players recorded modal jazz, and psychedelic rock musicians recorded lengthy improvisations in medieval modes.

The records of Thomas Binkley from the 1970s have the same feel as the psychedelic rock and modal jazz of that era. Ten minutes of drone and mode playing, in which ornamental notes were added to the melody and repeated riffs were played over the drum rhythms, were similar to rock and jazz music of the period. Andrea von Lamm's beautiful voice brought medieval tunes to life for the present era. Thomas Binkley's distinctive improvisational adlibs on lute, chitarra, and all the guitar-like instruments he played had a big influence on me.

Another ensemble that made fascinating adaptations of medieval music around this time was the Vienna-based Clemencic Consort. Their album *Carmina Burana* was given to me by the music director of Columbia Records. It featured a male chorus singing while slamming chains against the wall.

On one of the songs, René Zosso of the Clemencic Consort sang powerfully over the beat of slamming chains against the wall with the drone of the Hurdy Gurdy. The lute, percussion, winds, and strings ensemble had a sound straight out of *A Thousand and One Nights*. The way each piece was arranged was very exciting for me. Their CDs *Cantigas De Santa Maria* and *Troubadours*, released on Harmonia Mundi, are also 1970s gems. They featured an Iranian percussionist who performed several pieces in traditional Persian rhythms. It was a creative development based on the drawings and written records of Persian, Arab, Greek, and North African musicians from their time as court musicians in Spain.

Steeleye Span is a British band that began with two couples: an East England folk duo, and an Irish folk duo; all joined by the bassist from Fairport Convention, Ashley Hutchings. They created electric folk versions of folk music from England, Ireland, Scotland, and Wales. Some of their songs were sung in medieval music modes or in Renaissance music harmony. Their melodies were inspired by centuries of folklore, fairy tales, mythology, and traditional legends passed down from generation to generation. The stories in the lyrics captivated my interest.

"King Henry" is a Scottish song that tells the story of Beauty and the Beast with the genders reversed, becoming a medieval-style song about the story of a prince and a hideous lady beast. "Two Magicians" was a traditional song sung in Europe during pre-Christian ceremonies. People who practiced old European religions were frequently punished as witches throughout the Middle Ages; therefore, the song is claimed to have been sung in secret at times. When I read the lyrics, I noticed parallels to both Hindu mythology and Greek mythology. I was intrigued by the unique story given by the song, which prompted me to learn more about the traditions behind the songs and the similarities between other world mythologies and traditions.

The interesting thing about the Yokohama International School at this time was that the music teacher was Frank Becker, and the art teacher was Stelarc. Frank Becker was an avant-garde composer who won prizes for his classical works. He later became a synthesizer player and released many albums on Toshiba EMI Japan, arranging Beatles songs and classical compositions, such as *The Four Seasons* by Vivaldi. Stelarc was interested in how technology could make human beings evolve. He developed a third hand that he could attach and control with his stomach muscles. He felt that future artists could use technology to re-design human beings. His ideas were to influence David Bowie, who quoted him during the promotion of his album *Outside*. In Stelarc's class, I worked on photography and presented a slide show at the end of the year.

It was during my second year at Yokohama International School that I got the chance to write an entirely new work specifically for the Tokyo Symphony Orchestra. I was able to get this opportunity thanks to Frank Becker. This was scheduled to be played at "The Young People's Concert."

Over the following few months, I worked on it bit by bit. I decided to write variations based on three medieval German minstrel songs. Before this, I had no experience composing music for an ensemble or piano, and certainly not for an orchestra. I commenced my study of orchestration utilizing a book authored by Walter Piston.

If I had the chance to do this over again, I could have produced something better. Even though the work had ideas I would eventually develop as I matured, I was unprepared for it because I lacked experience. I cringe when I look at this work now. It was a chance that was lost. I wish I had some guidance from someone, but even if I had been advised at that age, I might not have listened to it well. Maybe I had to fail once to understand what I needed to learn.

In the summer of 1976, I was supposed to go to Australia with my father. He had a few concerts already booked in a couple of cities. First, we were going to take Haya to his mother, Karen, in the Philippines. But a few days after we arrived in the Philippines, Yuji told me he did not want to go to Australia. "All Australians are crazy.

All Swedes are crazy, too. I don't want to be with crazy people," and he said he was going back to Japan. When a white person hears this, it sounds like he is saying that all white people are crazy. To this day, I don't know what he meant by this.

Karen and my father got into a fight. Karen said, "Please take Haya with you to Japan. I am too busy with my studies and don't have the time to take care of him."

There was a part of me that felt that Karen was right about the leftist ideology. In the US, we were all concerned about 'Real Democracy.' We felt that the government wasn't truly democratic. The movie *Easy Rider* was about looking for the real America. America began as a social experiment for a utopian society. Freedom of Speech, Freedom of Thought, and Freedom of Religion was guaranteed. These were the important ideas that made many Europeans come to the US to look for a new life in pursuit of happiness. In the 19th century, there were many religious communes in the US. Fredrich Engels, who would later write *The Communist Manifesto* with Karl Marx, was very influenced and inspired by the utopian ideas behind a particular protestant commune in the state of Indiana in the US. The communist ideal of "For each according to their needs" comes from this. Western communism grew out of Christianity, and the word communism comes from the word *commons*, a land the church held where things were shared. Jefferson Airplane, a rock band popular with the hippies and youth in the 1960s, was so named because Thomas Jefferson had written the *Declaration of Independence*, which stated that all men are created equal.

The hippies and leftist youth in the United States were certainly not anti-American. They simply disagreed with many of the government policies.

This was very different from the leftist activities in Japan, which were essentially anti-American and pro-socialist or pro-Maoist. In the post-war era, many who were once nationalists and rightists became leftists because they remained anti-American. Meanwhile, many politicians of the pre-war rightist regime were protected by the US after World War II. The United States wrote and gave a new constitution for Japan, and after the United States occupation ended in 1953, the new rightist party in Japan was a combination of members from the family of the old regime and pro-US followers.

Therefore, the leftists in Japan were very different from the leftists in the United States.

In Japan, women are also lower in social status than in the United States. Even in the 1970s, the wife would eat alone in the kitchen when friends of her husband came to the house for dinner, after serving her husband, the Master, and his friends. In Japan, the husband is even called *Goshujin-sama*, which means Master. Most women were expected to become housewives, and working careers were very limited. Serving tea was what most office jobs for women were about. Other than that, most other jobs were called *Mizu-shoubai*, serving alcohol as hostesses. Sometimes this would include a sexual act. So, any woman who is raised in a Western country would feel the oppression living in Japan.

Sometimes, when Karen got drunk, she would suddenly yell to my father, "You don't like me because I'm American," and point a knife at my father. It was as if Karen had become a different person from the Karen I knew, and all her pent-up emotions would explode at once. I had never seen Karen like this before we came to Japan. She had never shown this side of herself when it was just the three of us: me, Haya, and her. She became like this only when she was with her husband.

I interpreted the problem between my father and stepmother as an inability to understand each other's culture. I began to see yelling, screaming, the sound of breaking glass, and frequent fights with a knife. My father began to reject American culture at this time. I felt it was based on personal experience.

The writer, Yukio Mishima, wrote that what the Japanese leftists were saying looked superficially similar to what the American leftists were saying, but in fact they were quite different. The American left and liberals were talking about the true nature of democracy. The Japanese left was anti-Americanism. So, from an American point of view, the Japanese left-wing sounds like it is advocating a nationalism similar to that of the American right wing.

In our everyday life, my father often made fun of Americans and the American way of thinking. It was a habit of his.

Those who know my father often witnessed him criticizing others without consideration for their feelings. This was not only to those he lived with, but also to other composers and colleagues in his work. He was not afraid to publish his criticisms of other people. It may have been a bit of a joke to him, since he would do this very lightly without thinking, but the other person was often hurt as a result. When something like this accumulates too much, it is very human to suddenly explode emotionally.

Karen used to say to me, "You grew up in America, so you'll understand what I mean." It stuck with me in the same way that I was often told later by various Japanese people: "You don't understand anything about Japan because you didn't grow up in Japan."

Japanese culture, and the normal Japanese way of thinking, is very different from that of Americans. In the '60s, the hippie generation thought that all people on earth were the same. This was viewed as the liberal and politically correct way to view things. All humans are equal in value; I can understand this. You can't say one is better than the other.

However, it is the culture that is not visible on the surface that makes the greatest difference between human beings. You are often not aware of this until you crash into that invisible wall. Many of the generation in the 1960s didn't understand this. They viewed human beings in a better light than they actually were. I would say that they were seeing an illusion, like a utopia that cannot come into existence except in your mind. And I think this generation faced this cultural clash the most.

For some people, understanding this through experience changed their life for the better.

Angela Carter, one of the most important women writers of the 20th century, spent several years in Japan in the 1970s. Based on the experience of having a Japanese lover, and facing tremendous psychological difficulties and difficulties in cultural communication, she was able to create wonderful literature that truly explores the depth of the human psyche. She wrote that working at a hostess bar while living in Japan made her understand what being a woman was like; she meant that she learned from negative experiences.

It was the fruit of the lessons she learned from her bitter experience.

Twelve

Going to Yokohama International High School/ Friends/Cannabis/LSD/"The Lamb Lies Down on Broadway" by Genesis

For a time in my late teens, I used to smoke strong hashish or marijuana around noon every day, but I never bought or had any on my own since. Other people always had it, and I was just there. In the '70s, that wasn't that difficult. Now, I do not need these drugs. The last few times I had them, I got a headache.

At that time, I had a purpose to try these drugs.

These kinds of substances change the way you perceive sound and space, and I wanted to express this in my music and poetry. Once you understand how to view things in a new way, you no longer need these substances. It becomes just one of your experiences.

Drugs were common among the contemporary music and art people in downtown New York. In Japan, these people may seem quite elite, but for those avant-garde art people in New York, life was difficult unless some of them became drug dealers. Psychedelic experiences can also lead to creative imagination. It often leads to the creation of unique works of art. It can also give you a surreal experience.

William was one of my high school friends at Yokohama International School. He was an honor student, at the top of his class, especially in physics and mathematics. His teachers used to say that they never thought there were students like him in this day and age. Once, I said to him, "I don't know how you can understand such difficult things so easily." He responded that as you reach higher degrees in mathematics and physics, imagination becomes the most important thing.

He and I first started talking because we took the same train to school every morning. He was from Texas. He was tall, with long blond hair down to his shoulders. He had a very intelligent face, but he also looked like many hippies from the '70s. I told him about the many rock concerts that I went to see in NYC and the bands I listen to. As I was speaking to him, I mentioned that there wasn't much marijuana in Japan. He asked a few confirming questions and then said, "I know how to get marijuana here," to which he added: "But you have to be really careful."

We had a teacher who taught science and physics, but he was also doing and selling marijuana and hashish on the side.

He was English, and he had originally wanted to be a folk singer, singing songs like Bob Dylan. He had traveled to India many times. He came to Japan and lived there, working as a science teacher and singing folk songs on his guitar at night. By the time I met him, he already had a thinning head of hair and wore big glasses. He was often late to class in the morning, and he was always teaching in class with a bored look on his face. His concentration would return when his favorite topics came up. As a student activist and a hippie, he probably had big dreams about Asia, but when he arrived there, he was disappointed to find that it was nothing like what he had dreamed of. I had his class as the first thing in the morning, and he often didn't get too mad at me when I was late for class. He couldn't be bothered to get angry.

Rumor had it that the other science teacher, the one who taught biology, was also doing drugs. He was a red-headed Irishman who loved sports. He was fired a year after I entered the school for sexually harassing a Korean female student. But there were also rumors that the truth was completely different. It was said that the English teacher in charge of English language and literature wanted to fire him, so he told the female student—who was about to fail the course—that if she wrote such a testimony, she could pass the course. I heard this story from another teacher. In this school, the teachers were not on good terms with each other because they were competing with each other for positions.

This student was rich, but she didn't study well in any of the subjects she took. I thought this rumor might have been true.

The art teacher was dressed like a hippie, but he was into meditation. Meditation was rumored to get you high.

We met at lunchtime in the park by the school: William; his girlfriend Dorothy; his brother Henry; my classmate Tina; Ross, who was a year older; and me. Henry wore silver thin-rimmed glasses and had short, light blonde hair. Ross was a dark-haired young man from Long Island in New York. This was unusual.

Figure 9 1977. Photo of me at Yokohama International School.

Most of the Americans at the school were from rural areas, instead of from the city. They were country people at heart.

Ross was a fan of the British rock band Yes. He also liked to listen to fusion music. He especially admired fast guitar playing. He talked fast.

Tina had long, thin, dark hair that reached down to her waist, and she didn't talk much to other people; when she did talk, she was very slow. She always sat in the back of the class with her girlfriends. She was from rural America.

Dorothy was an American country girl who liked to talk loudly in a rough voice.

We all went to a cliff in a park where there were not many people. There, we would smoke a couple of joints or hashish pipes each and pass them on to the next person. It was like one of those Indian ceremonies you see in the movies. We didn't have much in common except that we smoked in secret together. The afternoon was either art or music class. Listening to Bartok after we smoked, the music gave me cinematic images. In addition, I could feel each sound deeper than normal. It was easier to feel the direction that one sound was heading and the emotion in that sound than in a normal state. There could be something I could learn from this if I pursued this further.

There were no Japanese students who smoked with me. In Japan, people thought about marijuana and hashish in a completely different way than in the US. It was simply a crime to most, even teenagers. In East Asia, drinking alcohol is often a part of traditional customs. In Japan, it is often required to go drinking with your boss and your fellow workers in companies.

In the United States, alcohol and cigarettes were often considered more harmful than marijuana. Students who drank alcohol were more likely to be caught by the police.

One day, when I got to class, a Japanese boy, who was a student at Yokohama International School only because he was expelled from a Japanese school, and his Hawaiian friend were causing a commotion with a loud voice. I asked the teacher, "What's going on?" He replied, "Oh, it's very unpleasant."

The Japanese boy says, "Tina is smoking marijuana, her eyes are all red—I'm going to tell the police." Tina looked like she was about to cry. The teachers are trying to calm the situation down. These two students were the students with the worst grades in the class. They didn't study at all. They were always being yelled at by the teachers in class. If there was trouble, one of them was usually the root cause. The teachers and other students always looked at them with disapproving eyes. Probably one of them must have tried to get his hands on Tina. She must have rejected him, so he threatened to report her to the school and the police. One of them had been interested in Tina for a while.

The school solved this case in private. The teachers and the headmaster knew what these two were likely to do, and everyone in the class saw that they were unreasonably threatening Tina.

Perhaps the headmaster and some of the teachers told them off. The next day, when I went to school, class resumed as if nothing had happened. Tina was there too. The two of them were sitting quietly at the front of the class. No one wanted to talk about the incident.

We continued to get together to smoke around lunchtime as usual. The music and composition teacher at school told me that Ross was coming to school looking too much like he was on strong drugs, so I told him to be careful. The teacher asked me if I was sure he wasn't on methamphetamines, to which I replied that he was only on marijuana. Most people who did marijuana, hashish, and other psychedelics looked at methamphetamine and heroin as an abomination.

One day William got some LSD and gave it to me and Ross. I took it and then got on the train home.

At first, everything seemed normal. Nothing changed.

Then suddenly it began to work.

I noticed that the people on the train were under a lot of stress, and LSD makes you notice things that we humans usually filter out and don't notice. We don't usually pay attention to the stress of others on the train. There's no point in noticing it, so our brains filter it out. However, when I took LSD, I started to notice small details.

The old man in front of me began to look like a big hard stone. He must be living with such a heavy load. He looked like he was under so much stress that he might get sick.

The high school girl next to me looked like a chicken. Her face seemed twisted with troubling thoughts.

All the people on the train were tired. Perhaps because it was time to go home from school or work. But to me, it seemed as if they were tired of being alive itself.

People who can see human auras may have the ability to see people in this way. If you were sober, you wouldn't have noticed that much.

When I arrived at Shinagawa station and got off the train, I was relieved for a moment.

In those days, I had to pick up Haya from preschool every day after school. As I was walking to the nursery, I was again seeing detail after detail that I hadn't noticed before.

I arrived at the daycare center and said hello to the teachers there; then, I walked back to our rented apartment house in Takanawa with Haya. On the way, my eyes fell on a leaf on the road. The leaf had water on it. I was curious about the movement of the water: when the leaf shook, the water moved. I began to think how the water was shaking in the history of 'here' and 'now.' It may not be something you would normally think about, but each detail seemed to be important. Various words came into my mind. Haya was singing and talking by himself. I had lost all sense of time, but since I was walking with Haya, I was probably walking at the same speed as usual.

I looked at Haya's face. Normally, I see it as a child's face, but at that moment, I began to see the faces of the people in my life as they grew older and matured. I thought that I must be seeing what I was imagining.

When we arrived home, I went to my desk and started writing words. Just word after word without thinking. It was as if I was doing automatic writing, like the surrealists used to do. The family was at home, but no one seemed to notice anything particularly unusual about me. I turned on the TV and the faces of the people on it looked different than usual. I noticed the shape of the Asian's teeth. I noticed that they had fang-like teeth like Dracula. I had never noticed that before. I looked at myself in the mirror. I also noticed my face and the shape of my fang-like teeth. I looked different than what I imagined I looked like. Perhaps this was how others saw me.

I decided to listen to a record. I put on a German psychedelic band called Amon Düül to see what would happen. The first record I put on was called *Disaster*, which is a recording of music played while the musicians were completely stoned on drugs. It sounded like a storm of noise. It was more interesting when I was sober, because I could feel the druggy atmosphere of the music, but when I listened to it while my senses were also altered, I couldn't get any enjoyment from it. Next, I listened to the album *Yeti* by Amon Düül II.

Amon Düül II was a German psychedelic band that separated from Amon Düül because the original Amon Düül was more interested in drugs and communal living than in music. Except for the drummer, who played in a jazz style, the other members played psychedelic music that was almost close to hard rock, with some influences from Turkish music. The noise and distortion of the music became more noticeable. The distorted guitar sound sounded as harsh as the sound of breaking glass. It became painful to listen to.

So, I went back to writing words. I began to wonder what I was doing in the current history of time. I kept writing to try to answer that question. After a while, the effects of LSD were over.

Dropping acid (taking LSD), I realized then that the Genesis album *The Lamb Lies Down on Broadway* must have been influenced by the LSD experience. *The Lamb Lies Down on Broadway* was the greatest Genesis show I had ever seen.

It was about a young Puerto Rican teenager in New York City, who, after painting graffiti with a spray gun on the subway, goes out of the subway and ends up in another dimension. A few music journalists have written that the imagery of the other dimension in this work is inspired by the imagery and analytical approach of the psychologist, Carl Jung. But at the same time, it was like the world I saw on LSD. It could easily have been a 'bad trip,' a state of over-imagining after seeing too many details. Peter Gabriel said somewhere in an interview that he was once influenced by taking LSD a few times in his early twenties, and I think this album—and possibly the lyrics to "Supper's Ready" from the album *Foxtrot*—could be a manifestation of that influence.

I had become an enormous fan of Genesis in 1973 and attended as many performances as possible in the NYC and New Jersey area. I saw the live performance of *The Lamb Lies Down on Broadway* on December 6, 1974.

As soon as the intro to the first song started, Peter Gabriel came out on stage and started singing, dressed as a young Puerto Rican teenager with short hair wearing a black jumper.

Three slides were projected on a screen behind the band. The concert began with photographs of New York City at dawn. The teenager is going about the city, as he usually does daily, but suddenly he becomes trapped in an underground world in another dimension. It suddenly overpowers him as he's walking down Broadway. At first, he felt that he was wrapped in a warm cocoon, but the cocoon changed into a cage that he was trapped in.

During the song "In the Cage," a strong straight light from the ceiling played the role of the cage. The various slides on the screen kept showing worlds of another dimension.

The work of Ken O'Hara, a Japanese cameraman I know, was also used in the show. Ken O'Hara had published a book of close-up photos of various faces in New York City, and I remember a particularly striking face was chosen from it. My mother called Ken O'Hara after seeing the show and told him that they were using Ken's photos and that he should go see the show.

I later read that Alejandro Jodorowsky, the film director of *El Topo*, had been interested in making a film of *The Lamb Lies Down on Broadway*. If this had happened, I think it would have been a great film which would now be regarded at least as a cult classic.

From a world in the other dimension, Rael starts to remember his young life in NYC as a gang member. He also remembers his first date, which ended in failure.

In the song, "The Chamber of 32 Doors," the main character sees himself between his parents. Like everyone else, they are pointing around them. But every door that Rael goes through leads him back to the same spot. And he is trying to get out.

A blind woman named Lilith helps him to get out. He meets death as the Supernatural Anesthetist. Walking through a long passageway, he enters a magnificent chamber with a rose-water pool. He is soon surrounded by three Lamias—beautiful half-snake half-woman from Greek mythology. They nibble all over his body, but as they drink his blood, they begin to die, and he eats their remaining carcass as his food.

In "The Colony of Slippermen," Peter Gabriel appeared on stage with squishy balloon-like balls all over his body. The character Rael had been bitten all over his body by the three Lamias. His only cure is to be castrated.

As he is walking down a gorge's edge, he starts hearing the sounds of a NYC subway and smells the scent of his spray gun. He cries "My home!" He sees a window above his head showing his home, but just as he is about to return, he hears the screams of his brother, who is drowning in the river below. He wonders between returning to the freedom he had in the 'rat race' or saving his brother. He chooses to save his brother, and the window disappears into the void.

But as he reaches out to save his brother, Rael realizes that it is he, and not his brother, who is drowning.

For the last song, "It," there was a mannequin the same size and shape as Peter Gabriel standing on the side of the stage. while Peter sang from the center. It had the same costume as Peter, so it looked like there was another Peter on stage.

This work is not only a masterpiece of progressive music and psychedelic influences, but I consider this one of the great artistic achievements of the 20th century. I would compare this with the 20th-century 12-tone opera *Lulu* by Alban Berg. It is especially the lyrics and the story that moves me.

What also moved me the most was that I would come to identify myself with the character of Rael. I was at first living as an immigrant in NYC. My stepfather was from Iran. My mother was from Japan. But when I went to Japan for a vacation in the Summer of 1975, I could not return. My home in NYC was gone. I became trapped in a culture I did not know. All my parents were divorced many times over, so I had no home. I could not read or write Japanese. When I first lived alone, the police would often come asking me what country I came from. Some people imagined I came from Korea. To me, it was like living in the underground world. Everything was upside down.

However, it was not just a story of experience: this story represented many aspects of the 'shadow' in man's life.

Since *The Lamb* was very much influenced by Carl Jung and *The Tibetan Book of the Dead*, once I read these works, the meaning behind the story and lyrics became a little bit clearer.

In his solo career, Peter Gabriel would continue to be inspired by the traditional cultures from around the world. The festival WOMAD helped spread this interest around the world as "World Music." In Japan, they tried to set up the WOMAD festival, but the people presenting it did not fully understand Peter Gabriel's concept, and there was no support to make this festival happen. There were many interesting performers, both from abroad and from Japan. I first saw Jadranka Stojakovic's group at the WOMAD festival.

About 14 years ago in 2010, I discovered that Hula dances tell their narratives with hand movements and that some of the hand movements reminded me of what Peter Gabriel was doing in the early 1970s. From the 1990s, I had been performing "The Lamia" from *The Lamb Lies Down on Broadway* in different arrangements (including one for shakuhachi, koto, accordion, and percussion— and a different one for a string trio), but when I saw videos of these performances of Peter Gabriel in early Genesis again, I realized that it was these kinds of performances that I wanted to do in my life.

In June, at the end of the school year, William and Henry went to the Northeast to pick up marijuana—but they were arrested and sent back to the United States. In September when they went to school, none of the friends they had smoked with in the park, were there. They had all gone back to the United States.

Whatever happened to William? Did he go into physics or science? Or did he become a junkie? Or perhaps he is now teaching science or mathematics in rural America.

Until then, I had only talked to Americans, Westerners, and foreigners when I lived in Japan. It was as if I wasn't actually living in Japan yet. One thing was clear. The students who took marijuana were clustered in the honor roll group. And their imaginations were richer than the other students.

I was also able to expand my imagination while listening to the tape music of Pierre Schaeffer's sound collage. And it had a unique peaceful atmosphere when one listens to it while intoxicated with marijuana.

The group of Japanese delinquents who started drinking alcohol now wanted women when they reached their late teens. It was obscene.

Our marijuana smoking group didn't have that feeling then.

Thirteen

Father forces me to drop out from high school for political reasons/Separated from father/The music activities in Tokyo in the late 1970s/Keiji Haino/Kichijoji Minor/Live performances at Seibu Auditorium, Kyoto University/Aunt Sally

Toward the end of 1977, my father began to focus his activities on left-wing politics and said that he no longer wanted to play the piano. He gave away his piano and began to live by playing a small Japanese instrument, the Taisho Koto, at political meetings—getting 10,000 yen at best or not at all. Naturally, money was running out. He began to write letters asking for donations for his group to carry out social activities. Many people refused. I and many other people couldn't understand why he was doing this when he could earn money by playing the piano. Perhaps both my biological parents wanted to live their lives by doing what they wanted at the time, not considering my future, or taking responsibility for the people around them. It was like I didn't matter except as an afterthought.

My father's mother, however, looked at him quite lovingly, saying that he was trying to do something that was going to benefit people and society as a whole. Maybe there was something deeper psychologically at play.

In 1978, my grandfather (from my father's side) fell down a flight of stairs and died unexpectedly. He used to be a music critic, introducing new European music. He was the chief editor of a magazine called *Ongaku* (Music) and corresponded with European composers such as Bela Bartók. Before the war, when proletarian literature was popular among the intellectual classes, he was also active among the left-wing intellectuals.

There is a certain mystery about the Takahashi family background. My father's grandfather was a protestant missionary in Pyongyang, which is now the capital of North Korea. He published a book written in Korean about the life of Jesus Christ. A biography about him was also published, written by someone who knew him. I saw both these books in the late 1970s, but when I asked about them many years later, my father didn't know who took the books. My grandfather's elder brother took over as a missionary, but he would become influenced by Marxism. He was rumored to mix Marxism with protestant Christianity at his church. He also published his own books, including a book of poems. However, he died in his thirties from either tuberculosis or pneumonia.

I saw a television drama called *Pachinko*, written and directed by Korean Americans; one of the main characters is a Korean protestant priest, who was active in Pyongyang. He later moves to Osaka with his Korean wife, and the two become involved in Marxist left-wing activities. They raise two children together. The elder son realizes that his father is not his biological father and runs away from home, living the rest of his life pretending to be Japanese. Not even his wife and children know that he is Korean. The protestant priest is arrested as a left-wing activist and dies from tuberculosis.

I thought there were some similarities to my family background, although my father's family has always identified themselves as Japanese.

My father asked me to leave home and live by myself; he said his girlfriend was not obligated to take care of me. It was when Haya was just about to enter elementary school. A little later, Yuji and his new partner moved into a new house together. I rarely went to their house. The few times I went, I would hear his girlfriend say: "Your son is downstairs, I can't go down until he leaves." It made me very uncomfortable. Many people who have no experience of this realize what this can do to people. I was not an adult yet, but still in my teens.

My father also asked me to quit high school in 1977, and I had to oblige. The school was expensive, and he couldn't afford it because he no longer wanted to play piano to earn money. He also told me that I was being brainwashed by US imperialism. At the time, I was an honor student whose name was on the school's Honor Roll.

I started living by myself from the beginning of 1978. After that, we saw each other at concerts and outings, but our relationship as a family was over.

I loved to read and recite. I was a great reader. I won prizes in poetry reading contests every year. One of the poems I wrote at that time in ninth grade became one of the themes in my future album. Mr. John Tanner, my history teacher (who later became the headmaster), told many people at school that he thought I was one of the best students he had ever taught, and that it was a shame—that he hoped my father would reconsider. But there were ideological and financial reasons for this.

Since he was now only involved in playing the Taisho Koto and talking at left-wing political rallies, he had no way to earn money to pay for my school. He also told me that he disagreed with the ideology my school was teaching. He was himself raised in a traditional Eastern 'master and disciple' style of education. He did not understand that students did not have to follow their teachers but were allowed to discuss and debate their opinions. He had taught at a few schools in the US, but students wouldn't come to his classes, and he was fired in the end. I think that he tried to teach in the manner in which he was taught, which was too strict for the American students to follow.

Many who are taught in Japan don't seem to understand individualism. I was told that higher education was not necessary. I had no choice. Being forced to leave school had a much greater negative impact on my life than anything I had ever experienced before.

My father said that the piano is not necessary to compose music, so I wouldn't need it either. He would say: "Going to America was the biggest mistake in my life." He had told me that he would only do musical activities at far-left-wing rallies from then onward.

I found myself wandering alone in what was for me a foreign country with a culture I never knew called Japan. I knew no one here; I wasn't allowed to go to school; I had no friends, and no one to learn from.

My parents both seemed to have lost their minds, but the world called them geniuses. People only think of themselves. If people are like this, I feel that there is no way to create an ideal society or future. This showed me that when human beings fall apart, they can become completely messed up. This is one of the central themes I depict in my work.

After spending a few years wandering around Tokyo, not being able to go to school or work, I managed to contact my old school, Yokohama International School in 1982. I was not even a high school graduate, but I was told that there was a way for me to go to college.

At the urging of the school's headmaster and other teachers, I took the SAT for the UCSD (the University of California, San Diego) test and passed. Again, my father was against it. He said that he would neither support me nor help me. He said that I could go with my own money, but I would probably run out of funds before the year was over.

I have never received any education in Japan, nor did I ever learn how to read and write the Japanese language properly, but this was not my choice either. My father never tried to teach me music. The irony is that many people would assume that my biological father taught me music without understanding the complexities of our family connections. Many people would think I was rebelling against my family, when in fact it was my father who was rebelling against tradition.

In the late 1970s, I started recording improvised music at home on a cassette recorder with a few people that I happened to meet. We weren't all aiming for the same musical direction.

I knew nobody in Japan. If you didn't go to school, there are only a few ways that you can meet people, and the kind of people you can meet is very limited. One of us was essentially interested in old Japanese traditional music and played the shakuhachi. One was interested in contemporary piano music. The other was playing the violin. At the time, the various underground theater and music scenes of the 1970s were coming to an end. In the small apartment I was renting, I had electronic effect devices that Takehisa Kosugi had left behind when he moved to New York City. They included echo machines and phasers.

I started recording music with them.

Some of the songs I wrote around this time include "Annabel Lee," which I later recorded for the album *Silent Film*, and "Across the Seasons," which I later recorded for *Nova Carmina*.

I bought many records of traditional music from around the world and tried to learn from them by ear. What else could I do? I was not allowed to go to school by my parents, not because I couldn't study. My parents were very anti-academic. However, I always did well in an academic environment and had been an honor student. Living the life of a hobo was going to ruin my chance of a future and possibly destroy my life.

What I could not do was to communicate with the Japanese people. I was going to be completely isolated in a society that was foreign from the culture and environment that I was raised in.

I listened to the ensemble music of the Kazakh people in Central Asia and wrote a piano piece that incorporated this methodology in my own way. I further developed this style in a set of compositions I named *Eurasian Tango*, which I composed around 1997. This series has been performed by various musicians, including accordionists Mie Miki, as well as pianists Aki Takahashi, Yuji Takahashi, Ellen Uglik of Norway, and Ross Kelly of New Zealand. So far, this piece has been played by more people than any other composition I've written. The entire set of five compositions was choreographed by Martin Lawrance and performed many times on tours by the Richard Alston Dance Company of Britain.

One day, someone I knew as a music journalist invited me to come to an improvisation workshop. I went to a place called Space Jola in Takadanobaba in Tokyo, near Waseda University. Keiji Haino, Chie Mukai, Takashi Kazamaki, and others were there, performing noise-like improvisations. I remember Chie Mukai saying that Keiji Haino had turned up the volume on his amplifier so loud that she couldn't hear the sound of her Kokyu (a bowed string instrument that originated in China).

I took my violin and tried to play a little like Takehisa Kosugi. First, I tuned the violin like an open-tuning guitar: *ADAD*. Then, I played a lot of glissandos, sliding between the notes. I thought I sounded like Takehisa Kosugi's glissando violin and Daevid Allen's glissando guitar in the band Gong.

We got together again the next week with the same members. That day, Keiji Haino came closer and closer to me and we started exchanging ad-libs. He looked very pleased. My playing was in a rock style. It often reminded people of the Velvet Underground and Jefferson Airplane at their most psychedelic. After the performance, he invited me to come talk to him. We talked, and it turned out we liked the same medieval European music ensembles and the same bands that I listened to in elementary and middle school. This was highly unusual. I hadn't met people with similar musical tastes since I came to Japan. He also asked me if I wanted to join him in a new band he was trying to start.

At first, he asked me if I wanted to play the bass, but I was more interested in playing the lead instrument. We started practicing with the guitar and the violin, just the two of us. We started doing sessions with a drummer named Takashima as we went along. He had never played drums before and was a vocalist. He had helped Magical Power Mako, who later became a progressive rock legend, both musically and in promotion. That's how he knew Keiji Haino.

We started practicing at Takashima's house for about eight hours each day. However, the music Keiji Haino wanted to play at that time was hard rock. He was writing 8-beat rock songs, where he would sing on top of simple chord progressions, such as AAAA/FFFF/AAAA/FFFF while strumming these chords on the guitar. That's why he wanted to add a bass player to the band.

Other than that, he also improvised around unusual rhythms used by people like Captain Beefheart and the medieval European composer Francesco Landini. This kind of music sounded unique and interesting.

In the meantime, Keiji Haino invited a bass player to join us. He was about my age. He was a guitarist, but Haino invited him to quit his own band, Gasaneta, for a while and form a band with him. He wasn't too keen on the idea at the start. After a few rehearsals together, he told us that he wanted to quit. Haino told him, "Then you can play an instrument other than bass," He wanted to try the cello. "Okay, let's all try different instruments," said Haino. We practiced with a euphonium and two guitars (he played euphonium and I and Haino played guitars). But Haino wanted to make a three-piece hard rock band as the foundation.

Haino said we should all buy three stacked Marshall amps, which have been popular since the 1960s in hard rock. He said he could buy one for 200,000 yen. Haino had enough money to buy his own amplifier at that time, but the other members did not. The drummer said he knew a way to make money fast. He didn't tell us what it was, but we found out later in a surprising way. I didn't know how to make 200,000 yen, and I didn't need a Marshall amp.

Mr. Haino and I had the same taste in music, but I didn't need nor want a Marshall amp.

I wasn't that interested in playing hard rock.

Mr. Haino said, "If everyone buys Marshall amps and I don't, we can't work together." He wanted to play in a band with a loud, ear-splitting sound. But I found myself getting tired of practicing loud for hours on end. Furthermore, the music in this band was Haino's idea, and I wanted to learn more about composing to create my music.

One day at a meeting, I told him I was quitting. The drummer told me not to quit. He said he could see how it would sound with just the two of them, but that it would be more interesting to see how it would turn out with me in the band. He had made me a special pick-up mic in his workshop so that I could be heard even in the loudest sound. The bass player wasn't particularly interested in me from the start. So, I quit the band. I was only 18 years old at the time. I still had a lot to learn.

At that time, I also improvised with Chie Mukai, Junichi Kawahara, and others. There was a live house called Kichijoji Minor, and a place called Space Jola (pronounced hola) for live concerts and dance performances. Kichijoji Minor was a small dirty live house with a capacity of about 20 people. They had mainly performances of noise rock, free jazz, free music, and improvisation, which other venues didn't have. Keiji Haino, Tori Kudo, and others often played there.

It later became a legendary avant-garde venue, but at the time it was a small, dark space where music made up of screaming and noise was played every night.

The shop's master, Sato, also played drums and keyboards.

One day, he asked me to improvise with him.

They had about four acts lined up that night. The first act had already started. The sound was ear-crushingly loud. It sounded like a space invaders game played unbelievably loud. The sound was completely distorted. There was one man alone, wearing a long, huge cape jumping up and down in front of a synthesizer with no audience.

I got deeply tired the moment I saw that. Why do that sort of thing? Are they doing it because they want to get rid of the stress from their daily lives? If that's the case, I don't want to listen to other people's noise and screaming filled with stress. If they had something to say, I wanted to hear it in a way that made sense to me. When people who lack good musical ideas simply generate noise, it becomes just that—noise. I rested on the stairs outside the live house until it was my turn, trying not to get too tired from the stressful noise. When it was my turn, I felt like all I could do was play quietly.

The first guy playing the synthesizer had been playing classical piano since he was a child. When a university classical composition student handed him a score of Liszt's piano music, he was able to play it properly, even though it was a very difficult piece. Then why didn't he play properly when he played solo? What's wrong with people like him? Do they think it's so cool to pretend not to be able to play? Did they think they were rebelling against the elite and the educational system by pretending not to be able to play?

I could not figure out why.

There were a number of people there who could play well, but only played with noise. Tori Kudo was also a person who could play the piano relatively well. Of course, there were also people who couldn't play at all. Some people could only make noise, so they just made noise. Alternatively, after hearing that someone could play the piano well, some people were later found to just be amateurs who could only make noise.

There were a few musicians whom I first met around this time that I would continue to work with later in my life—such as Takuya Nishimura and Wataru Okuma. However, I found this whole scene to be depressing. This was not what I wanted to do. I was not impressed with what was going on. I simply felt that I had no choice because I was living in a country whose customs I didn't understand. I was longing for the NYC culture that I knew in the early 1970s. By the end of 1979, I wanted to be out of this noisy Japanese scene.

One day, a guitarist named Mr. Ohki invited us to go with him because his band, Factory, had broken up, but they still had a gig scheduled at Kyoto University's Seibu Auditorium. We all got in the car and headed for Kyoto. I never learned to drive, but two of the others took turns driving, and it took us all night to get there.

There were three bands from Kansai: INU with Machida Machiz, Aunt Sally with Phew and Bikke, and Ultra Bide. Aunt Sally was so good that I bought their record right after the show. The guys I went with laughed at me. They were like, "Why are you buying their stuff?"

We were the last to go on stage. Ms. Mukai sat in the middle of the stage and concentrated on her Kokyu. Kawahara played the clarinet whenever he felt like it. I could hear the droning sound of his clarinet.

It was the kind of performance that I wouldn't want to hear if I were in the audience.

Phew later said in a magazine interview, that because one of the people in the group was the journalist, Kenichi Takeda, who was treated like a 'god' by some musicians, she came out to see what it was like. But all she saw was a bunch of dirty hobo-looking creeps. She said: "Gee, I wondered what they were going to do, but then they started banging on the floor and walls, so I thought it was crap."

Later, Mr. Ohki often invited Ms. Mukai to join him, and they formed a reggae band called Stereos with her as the lead vocalist. He developed a love interest for Ms. Mukai, but she did not respond to him. One day, Mr. Ohki became hysterical, took all the strings off his guitar, and said that he would never play guitar again.

He stopped playing music after that.

A few years later, I called a company called Fostex to ask how I could repair my broken cassette player and gave them my name.

"Oh, I've heard about you. Mr. Ohki told me about you a long time ago. Did you know that he killed himself?"

"What?"

They found his body below a tall building.

I was shocked and called Kawahara, who had gone to Kyoto with me in 1979.

"I can't believe it," he said. "If I hadn't met him, I wouldn't be doing music."

Back in 1979: Mr. Haino and his group played their debut live at a small live house in Fusa. A friend of mine went to see them. When I asked him how it was, he said it took about two hours just to tune up their instruments. He didn't say much about the contents of the gig.

Two weeks later, I got a phone call from Keiji Haino. He asked me if I would like to join him for his upcoming live performance at Kichijoji Minor. I didn't feel a need to say no, so I said yes. He also asked me if I could bring my Echo Machine; he wanted to use it for his vocals. The drummer Takashima called me and said that the pick-up mic he was making for me was finished and that he would give it to me for free. I asked him if they had all bought Marshall amps and he replied that they had.

That night, I thought the bass player was acting very strangely. After the show, he was lying on the floor laughing by himself. Seeing him like that reminded me of a Grateful Dead concert that I saw when I was 10 years old, where the audience member sitting next to me was on LSD and he couldn't stop laughing the whole time the band was playing.

The tape of the live performance that an audience member recorded was later copied and passed around in various music circles. Two years later, I found and listened to this tape in Nagoya.

Two weeks after the show, I got a call from a friend of mine. I was still sleeping.

"Hey, did you see the evening edition of yesterday's paper?"

"No. What happened?"

"It says, '*Avant-garde* musician caught as a drug dealer.' The drummer of Fushitsusha, Takashima, got caught. He was making a living as a heroin dealer."

"What?"

I realized then that this was what he meant when he said he had a way to make money fast.

"You know. The bass player was doing it too, and it was bad drugs. He was throwing up blood all over the place."

"What?"

"All the other musicians he was selling to got caught too, quite a lot of them. All the bands in Fusa got caught. All the members in the band 'Z' got caught. It's the biggest drug bust in years. It's on the last page of the paper with a full-page picture."

"What was Haino's reaction?" I asked.

"He had no idea what they were doing behind his back."

I had no idea either.

About a month later, I received a phone call from Mr. Haino.

"What have you been up to lately?"

I told him I was learning many things. I had also started learning the Satsuma Biwa. At that time, I wanted to take a break from the band's music for a while.

Two years later, I met Mr. Haino again.

"What did you do with that Marshall amp you bought back then?" I asked.

"It's at home," he said. "It's too big to carry without a car. I might be able to roll it over to Gatty in Kichijoji."

Another two years passed. I had taken a job of programming and playing Erik Satie's piano compositions, *Gnossiennes 1-3*, for a computer-programmable player piano. This was a job resulting from a misunderstanding: a music producer called me, imagining that I must have studied classical piano because my biological father was Yuji Takahashi and my aunt was Aki Takahashi. I later learned that they went to Aki Takahashi first, and she refused the job. I couldn't play it at all, but they offered money which I didn't have. I couldn't survive without it. I was trying to live by $3 per meal in US money.

So, I took the job. I spent about 10 hours trying virtually typing in the notes, little by little by hand. Of course, it sounded awful. Why did I have to do this? The presentation for this event took place at a place called Inkstick, which is a combination of a live house and a bar in Roppongi. A guy wearing sunglasses was sitting next to me.

After the presentation, the organizer said to me: "The guy sitting next to you, didn't he used to work with you and Haino? He finally got out of jail the other day, so I gave him a job to build the stage set."

I'm sure he knew who I was, but by the time I realized who he was, he was gone.

Fourteen

Performances with Junichi Kawahara, Chie Mukai, Takeo Suzuki, Takuya Nishimura and others in the early 1980s/Kansai tour

Around 1981, I began to hear something like a scream coming from inside me. The screams permeated my body like liquid. It was difficult to keep the screams to myself. All I could do was breathe slowly and tell myself that it was my parents, my parents' parents, my parents' parents' parents. Maybe it was because I couldn't communicate with anyone, including my two parents. If I had been in America, I would have seen a psychiatrist. When I told my father that I wanted to do so, he replied that psychiatrists were only for rich people.

In the spring of '82, my father told me that he would not support me going to college. If I went with my own money, I would barely last one year; I would have to return because he isn't going to help me with the money. All the arrangements had been made for me to go that summer. I spent most of one year, preparing for exams, getting letters of recommendation, and being accepted. Yet, I found out that I could not go to college after all. I was not allowed to. My father told me that he did not have the money and hated the college. He was against it and insisted it was a waste of time.

"People like the composer, [Toru] Takemitsu never went to College, he only has a junior high school education," he would say.

I would say that it was because there was World War II and the destruction afterward, so they couldn't go, but he wouldn't listen to my arguments.

"Don't talk back" was the kind of response I got.

Around this time, I started playing again with Junichi Kawahara, Chie Mukai, and Takeo Suzuki, whom I had worked with in 1979. I didn't like free improvisation and the music they were making, but I really had nothing else to do, and nowhere to go. Japan was, after all, a foreign country and I knew nobody.

I had no choice. My future seemed to have been taken away from me.

Our first live performance was at a place called Shinjuku JAM.

It was at this time that I was first introduced to a bass player named Takuya Nishimura. He and Kawahara used to work part-time as dishwashers at the same hotel where I used to work.

At Shinjuku JAM, I had an idea for a group improvisation that started by playing rhythmic repetitions of music phrases to create ostinato patterns, riffs, and loops, and superimposing new repetitions over them. This idea was put together a few years later in a composition I called "Symbolic Interplay."

After that day, I became friends with Nishimura. He, a singer named Keiko Koyama, and I would play improvisations at Koyama's house all night long until morning. At that time, I played many improvisational gigs in a month with these members.

Suzuki told me that they often went to the Kansai area. Since I came to Japan in 1975, I had never been anywhere other than Tokyo, Yokohama, and Kamakura, except for the trip to Kyoto with Mr. Ohki and his friends in 1978 as mentioned earlier.

When I asked them how they got there, they answered as follows: "About four of us would get together, buy the cheapest tickets in Tokyo, and take a local night train to Osaka." When they arrived at the station, one of them would tell the station staff that he had lost his ticket and went out through the ticket gate. He would then buy the cheapest ticket for all four people and enter the station, cutting the tickets for the remaining three people with scissors, imitating the shape of the cut end of the scissors, and everyone exited through the ticket gate. We decided to go on the Kansai tour in this way.

At 11:30 in the evening, Suzuki, Mukai, the drummer Takahashi, and I went to Tokyo station to get on the all-night train to Osaka.

We bought some drinks and snacks, talked a bit, and then everyone started to sleep. Around 5:00 in the morning, we were woken up, when the conductor asked us to show him our tickets, but of course, we had no money, so we all kept pretending to be asleep.

"Hey. Hey. Sir. Sir!" The conductor kept trying to wake me up. Maybe he knew that we were pretending to be asleep. After a considerable time of effort, he finally gave up.

After the conductor went to the next car, everyone opened their eyes.

"That was a close call," Suzuki said.

We changed trains near Nagoya at about 5 o'clock in the morning, arriving at Osaka between 8:00 and 9:00 am.

Kawahara and Nishimura had more money than us because they were washing dishes at the hotel where I had previously worked.

The first day of this tour was in Osaka. The first section was "Symbolic Interplay." For the second section, I wrote some words in very bad Japanese based on the Greek myth "Orpheus."

We played some improvisation around it. It was in three parts.

In the first part, Orpheus meets Eurydice and recites love poems to her. But she is taken away to the underworld. In the second part, Orpheus goes on a journey to the underworld to look for her to try to bring her back. This was expressed through improvisation. In the third part, Orpheus finds Eurydice. He is promised that he can take Eurydice back to the world above if he does not try to look at her while they are in the other world. But he falls to temptation and looks back at Eurydice who is following him from behind.

Chie Mukai played Eurydice. I played Orpheus. Chie Mukai composed an instrumental theme for the performance. I wrote and recited all the words. The owner of the live house liked our little play and told me that I should continue to write and perform these kinds of theater pieces.

At that time, with this group of people, if you came up with an interesting idea, there was a good chance that they would get on board and do it.

The next day, I invited them to play an English folk song called "Blacksmith" in a version that Steeleye Span was playing. I played the melody on an Indian harmonium and accompanied Chie Mukai with drones and melodies. Mukai sang. Nishimura played the *charmela*, a reed instrument often used by street vendors who sell noodles at night.

In Kyoto, we all stayed together in a spare room in an apartment. The space was shown to us by Mr. Ishibashi, the organizer of the live concert at Kyoto University. When I asked him whose house this was, he told me that the surrounding rooms had tenants, but this was a room that no one rented, so they let people stay there when they came. At first, they separated the men's room from the women's room, but later that distinction disappeared.

During the daytime, he played the Fairport Convention album *Liege and Lief* and Sandy Denny's *Rendezvous*.

I also went to see the Todaiji Temple and other old temples in Nara with Mukai.

I went to Osaka, Kyoto, and the Kansai area about two more times that year.

Kawahara started to get interested in the drawings I would do during our trips. When we were in a coffee shop, he would ask me, "Hey, try to draw a penguin. He was a designer who had studied properly, so he could draw very well. Sometimes a complete amateur will be able to express things in a way that a trained professional could not. This is why I think he became interested in my drawings. He always wondered why my drawings always looked like children's doodles. He made me draw a lot of pictures and later printed them as a picture book.

I often said to Nishimura, "Let's do a power trio of guitar, bass, and drums next time." We once played a fake hard rock trio at the Tsukuba University festival with a drunken drummer. I began by playing a riff from Hawkwind's "Master of the Universe," but the whole music sounded like a cacophony of dissonance over an unsteady 8-beat rhythm. The Tsukuba University people danced to our music, probably because they knew we had come all the way from Tokyo and they wanted to be nice.

One time I stayed at Nishimura's apartment. He played the bass part of the song "Fat Old Sun" by Pink Floyd, which he copied from a bootleg live version. I told him that he was a great player. He seemed to have his own style as well as being able to play the bass part. I asked him why he didn't try to play like this when he was playing with people who were improvising all the time. He replied that it was because he met Takashi Kazamaki, a free improviser, when he got tired of playing only the standard stuff. There are various times in a person's life, and depending on when you meet someone, your impression of that person will probably change.

I asked him to put on something soothing before bed, and he played Deep Purple's "Burn."

Thirteen years later, in 1995, Nishimura and I formed a full-fledged guitar, bass, and drums trio.

Around this time in the early 80s, Suzuki organized a concert series named 10 Minutes Solo. It was a project in which various people would each perform a 10-minute solo.

It was an interesting idea that allowed me to see various aspects of individual improvisation that I normally wouldn't be able to see if we were all improvising together.

I used and expanded this idea, organizing a concert called the 20-Minute Solo Project in 2005.

Fifteen

1983, Record debut is decided/First solo album, *Carmina*/Interviews where communication is not established/Morgan Fisher/Moonriders

One of the few things that saved me from going insane or dying was the fact that I could play the guitar.

I grew up in an English-speaking society from the time I was a child until the age of 17—from living in New York City until I left an international school in Yokohama—and I am still an outsider in Japanese society. But even if I couldn't express myself in Japanese, I could still express myself in music. I would learn that it wasn't possible to have deep communications with people who did not share the same culture that you were raised in.

However, I was able to communicate by going back to the music of my childhood such as Syd Barrett, The Doors, Jefferson Airplane, The Grateful Dead, Fairport Convention, Steeleye Span, Joni Mitchell, and the Velvet Underground.

Another saving grace came in the early 80s when a manager-record producer suddenly offered me the chance to make a solo album for Epic-Sony. This led to *Silent Film*, my first album for MIDI Records, which was recorded and produced in New York with a production budget of 5 million yen. The jacket production also cost about 1 million yen. They also gave me a budget of 5 million yen for publicity, and the album was advertised and reviewed in all kinds of magazines and newspapers in Japan.

The album after that, *Memory Theatre*, was also produced and advertised for 8 million yen. The third album, *Nova Carmina*, was recorded in England with a production budget of 2 million yen. For someone who had been feeling crazy and completely battered up until that point, this was nothing short of a lifesaver. It was a miracle. It's not something that happens very often.

One day, the former manager of Eikichi Yazawa—who made him a star from the time he was in the rock 'n' roll band called Carol—left me a message at a record shop in Ikebukuro called Art Vivant, saying that he was looking for me.

I contacted him. He said, "You know, New Age music is going to sell big." He said that it started with Brian Eno. I knew about Brian Eno, but I had never heard of New Age music. In fact, I don't believe such a genre existed back then.

Brian Eno was at first a visual artist, who became influenced by John Cage, Cornelius Cardew, and minimal music while he was still a university graduate student. His debut as a singer was on one of Cornelius Cardew's albums released by Deutsche Grammophon. He joined a group with Andy McCay, which later became Roxy Music. At first, Roxy Music incorporated many influences from the avant-garde and experimental music. This influence shows especially on their second album, *For Your Pleasure*. After leaving Roxy Music, he made two solo albums of vocal rock music, before setting up Obscure Music—a label of experimental music, releasing music by John Cage, Michael Nyman, Harold Budd, Gavin Bryars, Christopher Hobbs, John Smith, and many other contemporary classical composers. He then came up with the concept of ambient music. He had been thinking about sound and music that was in the background like ambience, but which can influence people by influencing the environment around them. This concept was influenced by Erik Satie's concept of "Furniture Music." Around the 1920s, Erik Satie coined the term "Furniture Music," and Eno was beginning to reference it for his Ambient Music. His *Music for Airports* is literally a piece of music for airports. It was made to be played in the background in airports as a part of the environment.

The manager-producer who called me didn't really know himself what New Age music was, but he had a vague, confused idea that it was something like Brian Eno's ambient music or perhaps the music of Kitaro or Richard Clayderman. And he was going to find someone to do it. His wife, who had seen me playing guitar at a party a few years back suggested me to him. She told him that I may be the musician he was looking for. She also told him that my father was a famous pianist and not too bad-looking. In other words: here was a young man who grew up in New York City, in a good family, and had probably been exposed to classical and contemporary music since childhood. This was a misunderstanding, of course, but at the time, Japan still had a huge admiration for American culture, especially of what was fashionable in New York City.

They also seemed to think that I could naturally play the piano and keyboards just because my father was a well-known pianist. They never checked my real background—the fact that my parents were divorced and that I grew up in a very dysfunctional family listening to rock music and doing drugs.

I was only taught the guitar and had never been taught the piano at all. In fact, my biological father always told me, "You don't have to learn the piano," because he himself didn't enjoy studying the piano when he was a child. I was also very influenced by my life with my stepfather from Iran. The manager-producer simply assumed things without checking them out.

He got Epic-Sony to come up with a recording budget to record and mix a solo album at Take One studio in Shinjuku. I think the budget was around 2 million yen, but I was never shown receipts, so I'm not sure.

He had just started a new company. He had been in a lawsuit with his previous recording artist, Eikichi Yazawa, who thought he was being ripped off and quit. When I first met him, he began by telling me how he decided on the name of his company. He and his wife were flipping through an English dictionary and his wife found a cute picture on one of the pages.

So, he chose the English word explained in the picture as the name of the company. The name was Juggler.

However, when he read the slang meaning of the word many days later, he discovered it meant a deceiver and a cheater. By the time he realized it, it was too late because they had already registered it as the company name.

When I told a friend of mine with whom I had been doing improvised music how I was scouted, he said that I must be getting deceived. Even if I had heard this story objectively as somebody else's story, I might have said to him, "Someone is trying to trick you."

I liked a lot of Brian Eno's music. There are many songs on *Before and After Science* that I like. The drums on this album were played by Dave Mattacks, formerly of Fairport Convention, who I got later to play on my albums. My favorite part of Eno's music was his more rock side. So, if they wanted something ambient in the Eno vein, I was going to give it that vibe plus something a little closer to my own thing. No demo tapes were required. It was before the days of MTR and a proper studio recording was still very expensive.

Eno's *Music for Airports* itself was improvised, layered, and recorded in multiple recordings, so I told the manager-producer that I would use this same approach.

I was very much interested in traditional instruments from all over the world. I told the music director that I would bring various traditional instruments to the recording studio and improvise with them in multi-track recordings to create experimental compositions. The director answered that was fine. Looking back, I don't think he understood that experimental music and New Age music are actually two different things.

So, I borrowed some instruments to bring to the recording studio. I started by summarizing how I perceive ambient and new age. Then, I started reading American New Age books, books on brain research, and books on ancient religious mantras. I thought that, in order to create effective New Age music, I needed a concept—a way of thinking and creating, rather than a musical technique. Eno would also often come up with the concepts before the music, and he would be able to explain them very well and convincingly.

Instead of writing songs normally, I created some motifs and themes that I could improvise in the studio. I tried to repeat some mantras in my head for about two hours before I went to bed. That was one way to get myself into a self-induced trance.

In Brazil, Haiti, and some other countries in the Caribbean and Latin America, there are religious ritualistic traditions from Africa that are still practiced today, such as Candomblé and Santeria. In these traditions, the drummers would repeatedly beat rhythmic patterns, making the people enter a trance-like state. This kind of trance music existed and still exists all over the world. I wanted to try this in my head by myself and see if I could change my consciousness.

In addition to this, I also did some odd experiments on myself. I set the timer on my tape recorder so that I could hear the music when I was half asleep, and I tried to see how my consciousness would change. Listening to Grateful Dead's *Dark Star* again in this way, I realized that the music alone could create an experience akin to a psychedelic drug trip.

I still have some songs I like from this album. My favorite is the song "A Grey Town."[1]

I wrote the lyrics to this song on May 1, 1982—Mayday.

One day before May 1, I came to Tokyo from Kamakura, where I was living at the time; after meeting my designer friend, Kawahara, I went to Yoyogi Park to find a quiet place. But it was extremely noisy that day. Many helicopters were flying in the sky, and the sound of speeches from megaphones and loudspeakers could be heard everywhere.

Figure 10   1983. One of the photographs was taken for the *Carmina* album jacket. Photo by Ben Simmons.

---

[1] I later renamed the song, "A Town Covered in Ashes" and included a version of this on my *Early Spring* album on ayuo.bandcamp.com.

Amidst this noise, I managed to write some lyrics under the shade of a tree. "A Grey Town" is intended to depict a near-future science fiction landscape of the world after an atom bomb missile explosion or a nuclear power plant accident covers entire towns and cities in nuclear waste and ashes.

A Grey Town by Ayuo

A grey town
Shadows of monsters
Living in cold steel
The rain doesn't stop
Drunk with a foggy heart
A town already dead
Mountains made from wrecked toys
I picture you in my mind
With the tears of a child
Wrapped in fantasy
Forests of junk
Sands eat the walls
Wanderers walk slowly
Towards the fields
Toes drawing waves

This song was a conscious effort to incorporate the old Japanese *biwa* song style of music making. The form is based on *biwa* music, but the sound itself became rather similar to the music of medieval Europe—likely because of the drone and mode used. On top of this, I overdubbed a glissando guitar that slid like a cello, a vocoder that sounded like a whispering voice, and a Prophet synth drifting through the overtones of the root drone note in a sustained bass. The combination of these sounds gave it a psychedelic feel. However, I think the people who really liked this song liked the feeling of a wounded boy singing honestly, not the way the song was written, or the method used. That kind of honesty is not something that can be consciously created. It may or may not happen by accident while recording. I still play this song live from time to time.

I also like the composition "Lament." The original song version of this composition was later included in the album *IZUTSU*, released by Tzadik Records in New York City. I wrote this song in 1980. When I composed it, I thought that I finally realized for the first time my own unique voice in the melodies. I felt, though, that other people around me did not recognize this at the time.

The lyrics are based on a poem by the Tang dynasty poet, Li Bai, which I translated into simple but rather poor Japanese. The story in the lyrics was, for me, similar to the Japanese Noh play, "Izutsu," and Poe's "Annabel Lee." It is the story of a boy and a girl who grew up together in a small village. They grow apart because of shyness when they realize that they have become a man and a woman. However, they are able to confess their love for one another, and they marry. Their marriage goes through some difficulties as they grow older, but their love for one another never dies.

This kind of situation was the opposite of the situation that I grew up in. My parents both went through so many marriages and divorces, that I grew to fantasize an eternal love like this in a village that never changes like in the olden days.

On "Vanishing Point," I played a Chinese moon-shaped lute called *gekin* in Japan, which I tuned to *GAE*. *Gekin* (*yuèqín* in Chinese) was once popular around Nagasaki in Japan, where many Chinese traders came to do business during the Edo period (17th to 19th century). I borrowed an electric bass from Takuya Nishimura and played it with distortion effects. The song is written in the form of *ABAB*, but in the *B* part, I also played the high piercing sound made by rubbing wine glasses and made music with the sound of water and ice being transferred from one glass to another.

I used a microphone at a close distance to capture the sound of water and ice being transferred from one glass to another.

The album was originally scheduled to be released around October 1983, but it was pushed back to February 1984 because I was suddenly hit by a car while I was walking near the Hachiman shrine in Kamakura.

I was interviewed for several magazines to promote my album. However, no communication was ever established—just misunderstandings because the journalists arrived with fixed notions of who I was supposed to be. All the writers who came to interview me mistakenly thought that I was someone who grew up listening to classical and contemporary music with my father, or that I learned music from my father to follow in his footsteps.

The record company had asked me for my profile. I wrote in my profile draft only what I had really experienced. This included the fact that I had not lived with my father since I was five years old, but with an Iranian stepfather in NYC. In fact, I didn't even mention my father in my profile. If I had written that I learned music from him, it would have been a total lie. I had read the finished profile printed by the record company, and there was nothing wrong with it.

Then, what happened?

The promoter must have told the journalists, by word of mouth, a complete lie. A record company promoter later told me that it is not the job of a promoter to understand the artist. The promoter's job is to make his music sell by whatever means necessary. It doesn't even matter if the promoter doesn't listen to the artist's music. The promoter doesn't have to tell the truth. This is how many journalists work in Japan.

A keyboard magazine arranged for me to have a dialogue with Toru Okada, the keyboard player of the Japanese band Moonriders, because they were told that I was a classically trained pianist. It was supposed to be a dialogue between a classical-trained pianist and a pop keyboard player. At that time, there were suddenly many keyboard magazines because of the popularity of Ryuichi Sakamoto and YMO. Ryuichi Sakamoto was trained in classical piano and became a famous pop musician. Sakamoto also said that he respected my father, Yuji Takahashi, in many interviews. Toru Okada had never heard of me before, nor had he listened to any of my music before meeting me.

Because this project started with a misunderstanding, the conversation didn't go anywhere, and the magazine canceled publishing the interview. However, at the time of the interview, Okada said to me, "I'm recording a new album with my group now, so come and visit me at the studio in Ginza."

That same week I met a keyboard player named Morgan Fisher who was in Japan for the first time.

Morgan became known in the early 1970s as a member of a band called Mott the Hoople. The band became famous for an album produced by David Bowie, and they often appeared on TV. Around that time, they toured the US with Queen, who had just made their debut album. I was in junior high school at the time and saw both bands in a concert on Broadway in New York City. After Mott the Hoople broke up, Morgan continued with bands like Mott and British Lions, while releasing solo albums in a variety of genres. Some were instrumental ambient albums, and some were song albums.

At that time, he had just come and had not yet met many musicians in Japan. After hearing my album, he asked me if I would like to be a guest on his live show.

We practiced in the studio of a radio program production company called Genonsha. Mr. Yokota, the president of the company at the time, let Morgan use the studio for free. At that time, I told Morgan, "I met a member of a band called the Moonriders, and the keyboard player invited me to visit them while they were recording a new album. Do you want to come with me?"

It was a studio called Onkyo House in Ginza. Producer Shigeki Miyata was directing the recording, and the members were waiting for their turn to record. Keiichi Suzuki, with long black hair, was on acoustic guitar practicing a song to be recorded. I met Mr. Miyata for the first time here. Only a few months later, I signed a three-year record contract with Mr. Miyata for MIDI Records. We were introduced to everyone there. Everyone behaved quietly until the recording was finished. On the way home, Morgan said to me. "Was that a rock band recording? It was like waiting at the dentist's."

Morgan told me about wild parties with the bands he toured with. After Mott, The Hoople broke up, he was also the touring keyboard player for Queen. He told me the story of how "every night we'd go on a bender, and after dark we'd tear up the hotel room, breaking the windows with the table and throwing the TV set out the window."

I told this story to John Zorn and a concert organizer at Hosei University, whom I met soon after that. John said, "Oh, one of those.

How about we get him to come over to Hosei University Hall next time and organize an event called 'Smashing up Hosei University Hall.'"

Figure 11   1984. Attending MIDI's inaugural press conference with Ryuichi Sakamoto, Taeko Onuki, EPO, Moonriders, Saeko Suzuki, and others.

The concert with Morgan was attended by a lot of people from Rajneesh's commune. Rajneesh, also known as Osho, was a guru from India who organized a commune in Oregon, where it became known that free sex was allowed. They must have had a branch in Japan, and Morgan must have contacted them. He had told me that he had been to Rajneesh's commune in Oregon in the United States. They were all wearing pink clothes and trousers; I happened to be wearing pink trousers at that time. It was a coincidence.

Mr. Yokota, who had lent me the practice space, was there with his eldest son, Taro.

After that visit, Taro would ask me many times, "Aren't you a member of the Rajneesh commune, too?"

Sixteen

1984, signing with MIDI records

In 1984, I took the completed album *Carmina* to various people I knew and had them listen to it. When the slide show "Shinorama" (presented by photographer Kishin Shinoyama) aired on NHK TV, they used my music, and my name was clearly credited.

Shinoyama gave a party at his office for a private showing of "Shinorama." He invited me, Ryuichi Sakamoto, his then-wife Akiko Yano, and the people who were to become a part of MIDI Records, including the president, Hiroshi Okura. Shinoyama introduced me to all the people there. I hadn't seen Ryuichi Sakamoto in years since he became famous in Japan. The music worked great with Shinoyama's photographs. I still think that it was this show that convinced the staff of MIDI Records to sign me as a recording artist on their label.

At that time, I had already started to make demo tapes of the songs that would be recorded for the next album, *Silent Film*, on a cassette MTR, and had a lot of people listen to them. Most of the people who listened to *Carmina* and the demo tapes were excited about what I was going to do next.

I had Morgan Fisher listen to the demo tape. He told me that he would like to produce this album. When I told this to the president of the company that produced *Carmina*, Juggler ("The Deceivers") responded negatively: "He's just an ex-rock 'n' roller who came to Japan because he was not selling records anymore. You can do something different. Next time you should record music like Erik Satie."

When I told Morgan what was said, he replied, "He's talking through his ass, don't you think so? You're not a piano player. You don't play the piano. You can do things that are completely different from what he is saying you should do. He doesn't understand you at all."

"Oh, I know. I understand all that, but what could I do?"

I was thinking that maybe that was the way things were. I already given up on trying to tell them what I could and could not do.

I had Ryuichi Sakamoto listen to it. He told me that he was going to start a new label in the near future, and that he would invite me to join it when it was ready. That label was to become MIDI Records.

In 1984, my career took a sudden turn when MIDI Records was formed, and through the introduction of Ryuichi Sakamoto, the company agreed to produce my next album. In fact, I signed a contract with them to produce and release three records, including *Silent Film*. I was allowed to record the first album in New York City.

The company that produced my first album, Juggler ("The Deceivers"), initially offered me a 2% royalty deal. About a month after the album came out, I got a phone call from the president saying that they could only give me 1%. Even when everything was decided at MIDI and we decided to go to New York to record, the contract for the first album was not drawn up.

Of course, I didn't tell him that I was negotiating with MIDI. After a while, he said: "Sorry, I can only sign with you for 0.5%. But we're talking with Epic-Sony about doing a second album." They kept lowering the percentage they had to pay. So, when my contract with the new company started to become public knowledge, I called up Mr. Okura, the president of MIDI, to discuss the matter.

He told me the following:

"That's not what he promised you at the beginning, is it? If he said 2%, tell him to give you 2% as originally promised. Make that clear to him."

So, I called up Juggler ("The Deceivers") and told him exactly what Mr. Okura had advised me. Then, as if he already knew that I had consulted someone, he answered:

"Okay, 2%, right? Okay, we'll give that to you."

Seventeen

Silent Film album/The misunderstood promotion/*Memory Theatre* album

Silent Film was produced in New York City in the summer of 1984. My mother had met Steve Elson, who played saxophone with his group Strange Party and Borneo Horns, and who would go on to join David Bowie to play the sax solos on hit singles like "Modern Love" and "Let's Dance." My mother told me that he was coming to Japan, and we met for the first time in 1983, when he came with David Bowie on his "Serious Moonlight Tour" (The Let's Dance Tour). Before *Carmina* was even released, I asked Steve Elson if he could help me to record an album in NYC. He got together some session musicians and the engineer, and he booked the recording studios.

There are a couple of songs that I like on the album, and I still perform them sometimes. One of the compositions I quite like is the improvised track with the New York actress Cynthia Hunton, reading Sylvia Plath's diary entry about what she felt on New Year's Eve in 1956. Plath took a night train from Paris to Marseilles in the south of France on New Year's Eve. The description is gorgeous and truly poetic. The night sky looked to her like a painting by Van Gogh. I layered all kinds of instruments and sounds over a loop track of drums played in reverse. The drums sound like an old train moving through a rural area. I played violin, glissando guitar, bowed bass, plucked bass, and an instrument I picked up at a shop near the studio called Woodstock Bells. I thought the music I made described the scenery well. Cynthia Hunton, who did the reading, was Steve Elson's ex-wife. When the album was re-mastered in 2000, I made this the opening track of the album, which is what I should have done when it was first released.

"Birds of Paradise" features Takehisa Kosugi on violins. He plays very passionately on this track. This was another track where I used a lot of loops, this time of David Baker (the engineer), Steve Elson (my co-producer), and myself chanting a repetitive music phrase and a drone.

"Be the Night of My Darkness" was recorded with cello sounds from an emulator, making this song sound unusual and unique. However, I have been performing this over the years live on a guitar with dropped D tuning.

Carlos Alomar, who was a member of David Bowie's band since the mid-1970s, plays all the guitars on "Nothing Left to Say." I had heard him on albums like *Young American*, *Station to Station*, and *Scary Monsters*. He overdubbed all the parts, the lead guitar and rhythm guitar parts. It was great to see a master like him playing my music.

However, I now feel that other songs could have been done a little bit better had I had more experience. For example, I've been playing a new version of "Annabel Lee" since 2006, and this sounds better than the one we recorded back then. This was a song I wrote back in 1978 with an open-tuned guitar in the G chord. Later on, I would play this in an open C 9/11 tuning that I picked up from listening to Joni Mitchell. The recording of this song during *Silent Film* didn't really convey the character of an open-tuning guitar. It was drowned out and buried in a 1960s rock sound. The one thing interesting about this arrangement is the electric saw played by Page Wood. If I understood more about recording in those days, I might have been able to come up with better arrangements. I have only myself to blame for not being able to do this back then.

These days, I tend to think that an arrangement that could bring out my recitative vocals over the unique sound of an open-tuning guitar would have worked better. My vocals in many such songs are more like telling a story or a poem over chords and modal movements rather than 'singing.' The arrangement on Lou Reed's Berlin achieves this very well. Even though Lou Reed's singing is accompanied by a full band, the recitation of the poem becomes the main focus. Bob Ezrin produced and arranged these songs marvelously.

Many people saw me as something I wasn't, so I wanted to show this in an ironic way. This is why I wear thick white makeup on the jacket of this album. However, I don't think people understood what I was trying to do. In fact, I wasn't sure if I could communicate at all with the people around me in Japan, and so this is what I wanted to covey on the jacket.

The lyrics are also purposely vague. At this point, living in Japan, I realized that people didn't say things directly, but often in a very roundabout way. I, however, did not understand the way the Japanese do this. I was so used to thinking in metaphors, and that was how I spoke and wrote things. At the time, I felt that perhaps someday, some people would understand what I was trying to do. I wanted to make it so that the audience would see my true, buried feelings only when they started to analyze it. It would be like unraveling a puzzle. But this wasn't really possible: people don't have that much time to spare on you, and since so much false information had been disseminated to the public, besides this cultural difference, that difficulty was compounded further.

I was given a mask by people who were supposed to know me. My true self lived behind that mask. But I also made a mask that I put on myself to hide my feelings, as well, because I thought that was what I was supposed to do in this culture. However, not many people would have the patience and time to listen to it with that level of analysis. Some of the people who told me they liked the album said they couldn't understand how interesting it was until they could feel what was going on behind the scenes.

Another problem was that I didn't practice guitar much before recording this album. I also had some personal problems that got in the way of spending more time on the music before I started recording. Most of the songs were written at home on a guitar, but when I actually went into the recording studio, the fact that I didn't have much studio experience yet was another problem. I didn't really know how to record them effectively yet.

So, although there were a lot of good parts and things I liked about it, something just didn't feel right.

It was an album that had some parts that weren't there.

This album was promoted more heavily than my first album *Carmina*, with more coverage in magazines and newspapers than anything else up to that point in my life. However, I was still often written about as a person different from my true self. The false preconception—that I had received an education in classical music from my father from childhood—dominated the people who interviewed me, and those who promoted the album. A lot of the interviewees had questions about this nonexistent person, and there were a lot of mistakes in the information released by the record company and in the translation of the lyric sheet. I did not know Japanese well enough to be able to stop this.

I didn't realize then how many misunderstandings this was going to cause.

The illustrated advertisement in the magazine also seemed to intentionally further those misunderstandings. It said: "Webern, Mahler and medieval music are all around me." I had never listened to Webern and Mahler until I was twenty years old.

Figure 12   1984. At Gramavision Studios, New York, with engineer David Baker.

No one from the record company came to see me record this album. They were talking about it without knowing exactly what I was doing. I heard from the managing director of the company at the time that one of the reasons for signing me to MIDI Records was that he wanted me to bring an academic image to the label to boost Ryuichi Sakamoto's academic image. He told me that it didn't matter what kind of music I made because they had already decided that I would be promoted with an academic image. Whether I came up with a rock album or a classical-sounding album didn't matter to them. MIDI Records did not want to work with Yuji Takahashi because they felt he would be too difficult to control, but with me, they could control the promotion of my album more easily.

Confusing articles appeared one after another. One newspaper article stated: "An album by the son of Yuji Takahashi, famous for his piano performance of Erik Satie, produced by Ryuichi Sakamoto, is now on sale. It sounds just as expected from someone of this kind of background," said another. The author must have written the article without listening to the album at all.

There were times when I thought the interviewer got it right, but when I read the finished article the person wrote, "an alien named Ayuo."

When it became clear that the 'person' the record company was selling me as and the actual 'me' were two different things, various rumors began to circulate. One of the rumors was that I was a classical musician, but the record company forced me to make a pop album by bringing in a pop producer. My co-producer in NYC, Steve Elson, is a serious jazz musician, even though he toured with David Bowie on the Serious Moonlight Tour. It was also me that contacted Steve Elson to help me record these songs in NYC. Not the record company. I wanted to get back to where my cultural and musical influences came from.

There were also rumors within the record company that I must have been influenced by the musicians I was working with to make it a pop album. There were also rumors that I must have been originally playing classical music but was rebelling by performing pop music; or that I made pop music for the 'people' because I was thought to be a left-wing political activist. There were even rumors that I couldn't communicate properly. The promoters also seemed less and less interested in promoting me because they thought I was being difficult.

Sometimes, potential music jobs were cancelled because of mistaken rumors. Among the jobs I was asked to do at that time, there were a couple that were suggested to me through these kinds of misunderstandings. One of them was to play Erik Satie's piano pieces to record on a player piano. I later heard that they had actually wanted my aunt, Aki Takahashi to do it, but she had turned them down. I couldn't play the piano, but I wanted work. Well, I thought that I could manage somehow.

People often thought that I was being modest when I told them that I really can't play the piano. Maybe it was something to do with cultural differences as well. People in Japanese societies often show themselves to be more modest than Westerners, especially Americans.

I chose a piece called *The Three Gnossiennes*. I somehow managed to play the first one because the left hand is doing only the same thing from the beginning to the end. Being taught as a guitar player, I don't know what to do when my right hand and my left hand have to move independently. In No. 2, the left hand doesn't move so much, so I managed to play it by doing it a few times, but No. 3 was very difficult. The left-hand chords change, and the right-hand plays something different while keeping the same tempo. No matter how many times I played it, I couldn't do it. It took hours and hours. The people around me finally realized that I couldn't really play the piano, so we had to make do by stringing together the different takes.

The fee for this job (including videography of the performance scene) was 600,000 yen. It was a job for Asahi Beer with Dentsu, a Japanese international advertising and public relations joint stock company, doing the co-ordination. The people who hired me probably couldn't report to the company executives that I was not a piano player and that I was given this job by mistake.

However, this gig didn't prove that I was a guitar player and not a piano player. Rather, it just made me seem to be someone who was difficult to work with.

The company told me that *Silent Film* sold about 5,000 copies. Actually, I don't even know if these are the correct figures; later on, the president of the company told me that he would adjust the sales figures on all the records on his label, so that it wouldn't look so bad. He said that he would write down 5,000 copies to anything that sold less than 5,000 copies. I still don't know what the actual sales figures were like. We talked about what to do next. It was only when we were about to start recording the next album that I had a long talk with Mr. Miyata, the managing director of MIDI and the music producer for EPO and Taeko Onuki. He seemed to realize that I wasn't a pianist or a keyboard player. He suggested that I should make an ambient album like *Carmina*.

The next album, *Memory Theatre*, was inspired by concepts about the idea of a *Memory Theatre*, which are said to have influenced the design concept of the Global Theatre where Shakespeare premiered many of his plays in England during the Renaissance. The label thought that the album would work out well in the planning stages.

To create the ambient elements of *Memory Theatre*, I asked the synthesizer manipulator and the engineer who worked on the first album to help me, and mixed in the rock elements from *Silent Film*, with support from Ryuichi Sakamoto, Taeko Onuki, EPO, Saeko Suzuki and EPO; so, the album was produced with the support of all these MIDI artists.

The accompanying booklet and most of the lyrics were written by Kisaragi Koharu, the playwright. I decided to do an album with songs in Japanese, because I thought that one of the problems that made many people say that they didn't understand my album was that it was not in Japanese. Kisaragi Koharu had written plays that I liked, and I liked the sound of the words she used. This was especially important for me. Years later, in 2020, a compilation album entitled *Kankyō Ongaku: Japanese Ambient, Environmental & New Age Music 1980–1990*, was nominated for a Grammy award in the US. It showcased the track "Nagareru" from *Memory Theatre*, sung by Kisaragi Koharu herself.

However, during this recording, Mr. Miyata told me that my intonation in Japanese was wrong. He told me that I sing like a foreigner. No one told me about this problem before, although when I studied Japanese Biwa songs for some time, other students would laugh and say that I sounded like I was intoning the Japanese alphabet, AIUEO. They said that it was because people listening could feel that I obviously did not understand the meaning of the words but was simply trying to phonetically pronounce them. Even when I was past sixty years old, I would try to record recitations in Japanese, and the engineer would inform me that I was pronouncing the words in Japanese all wrong.

The president of MIDI Records came to my concert many years later and told me that I should stop trying to talk to the audience in

Japanese because they didn't understand what I was trying to say. This interrupts the flow of the concert. A film producer told me that I should sing in my language, which is English, and stop trying to act Japanese because it "makes you sound weird." I'm sure that many Asians who grew up in an English-speaking country were told the same thing when they went to visit the land of their parents and ancestors.

I asked the violinist Kishiko Suzumi, who was known as a virtuoso in the world of classical music, to play on one track. She did a great job.

The results of the album were not as good as I had hoped and imagined. Of course, there were some interesting parts and some things that worked, but it wasn't as cohesive as it could have been. If I had more experience, I would have done a better job.

When an artist is still inexperienced in music, a producer is inevitably needed. When we first started recording *Memory Theatre*, Mr. Miyata used to come to the studio, but slowly, he stopped coming to the recording sessions. Maybe it was because EPO, Taeko Onuki, and Ryuichi Sakamoto's albums were being recorded at the same time, or maybe he decided that he didn't need to come because he had already decided on the direction, to a certain extent. But I needed someone to advise me, and I didn't know who to ask.

In this album, the composition that I was able to complete in the most satisfying way was probably "Mizuiro no Kagami,"[1] which was played by Kishiko Suzumi on the violin. This was actually not an original piece; after recording *Carmina*, I had already recorded a song titled "River of Light" on the SWITCH label with a band of guitar, bass, drums, synths, and vocals. I thought it would be interesting to change the guitar part of this song to a violin and make it a classical-style composition for violin and piano, so that's what I did. I added some ambient synth sounds in the background of the violin and piano. The tone was something similar to the one I used in *Carmina*.

I liked the first song, "City in the Sky," as a composition, but later when I performed it live, those performances were better. In the 1990s, I used to play this with my trio (Ayuo Trio), with long extended jamming like the Grateful Dead and Jefferson Airplane used to do in the 1960s. This song was certainly more interesting

---

[1]Later titled "A Turquoise Mirror"

live when I played it with Takuya Nishimura, who also played bass in this studio recording. and we would expand the improvisational parts to make it about 20 minutes long. The performance of this song on this album is very short and doesn't show the possibilities that an extended-form version of this song could.

The same can be said for other songs on this album, such as "Summer's End" and "Fushigina Yoru (A Strange Night)." I liked the melody of "Summer's End," and I later made a version with just the acoustic guitar and the melody. The version on *Memory Theatre* sounds simply 'psychedelic.' Many musicians participated in "Fushigina Yoru (A Strange Night)"—Ryuichi Sakamoto played piano, Saeko Suzuki played drums, Takuya Nishimura played bass, and Jun Tohyama, who was a synthesizer programmer for EPO, created the synth sounds. I play the electric guitar and sing. However, I later felt that there were too many elements in the song. I felt that all the different ideas of the performers were cluttering up the overall sound.

But since we had already asked all these well-known musicians to come, even though they were all busy, we couldn't really afford to cut them out from the recording. In 2009, I recorded an open-tuning guitar version of this song with just the acoustic guitar and vocals for my album *dna*. Although it's fine to have well-known musicians play on your album, sometimes it can take away what you're trying to convey through your music. The 2009 version is more direct and to the point.

The melody of "Into the Light" was used for a television commercial for Renown Incorporated, a clothing company. This was often broadcast every weekend on movie shows shown on television. Listening to the original version now, it sounds very much like the 80s. Some music magazines said it reminded them of music by Virginia Astley. Perhaps this was because some of Astley's music was produced and arranged by David Lord, whom I would come to meet. In 2009, I also recorded an acoustic version of "Into the Light" with open-tuning guitar, violin, and a chorus. Some music critics wrote that my guitar solo in the song "Hymn" reminded them of Steve Hackett (of Genesis).

I also recorded an arrangement of "Marie's Lullaby" from an aria by Marie in the opera *Wozzeck* by Alban Berg, a composer of twelve-tone and atonal music of the early 20th century. I did this by using emulators and synths to create each note. The complex harmony of this piece has a sound that would come to be used in modern jazz and later in Brazilian pop music. In hindsight, I should have interpreted them as bossa nova chords on an acoustic guitar and made the arrangement around a guitar. Perhaps I was too interested in how synthesizers and emulators would develop at the time. If I had been a keyboard player, that might have been an interesting result, but it was hard to see myself as a keyboard player when I was recording one note at a time using sequencers.

I did not like the 1980s pop sound that dominated all the recordings from this period. Many bands went on to re-record their 80s catalog or re-mix them to lessen this 80s sound. Pink Floyd re-recorded all the drum parts for their 80s album and re-mixed it. Marillion, a band that was very much influenced by Peter Hammill as well as Genesis, re-mixed their 80s-sounding album Fugazi. Peter Hammill re-recorded two albums from the 80s to get rid of many of the typical 80s sounds that were on the original album.

Today, I am aware that there are people in this world who feel nostalgic for this kind of sound. However, I was disappointed in the 1980s by the 80-ish sound of *Memory Theatre*. At the time, the albums that had the sound I liked were few. What music did I like in the 1980s? From the mid-80s, I liked Prince; New Order; Siouxsie and the Banshees; The Cure; and in the late 80s, My Bloody Valentine. My Bloody Valentine brought back alternate tunings in guitar in their own unique way. Brian Eno said that they were able to create a unique electronic sound by mixing records in a way that no one had done before, but it was their use of open-tuning guitar that I found most intriguing.

In 1988, after visiting Guy Evans, drummer of Van der Graaf Generator in London, I tried to get in to a live show of My Bloody Valentine, but it was packed full. David Lord's sound on Peter Gabriel's 4th album was one whose sound I loved.

The various problems I felt with *Memory Theatre* were soon to be resolved on my next album.

Eighteen

Departure to record in the UK in the summer of 1986/Stopover in New York City/John Zorn/Arrival in London/ AMM/David Lord/Fairport Convention/ Photographer Richard Haughton/Steeleye Span and Renaissance in concert/ Recordings at Crescent Studios/Dave Mattacks/Maddy Prior/Peter Knight

In July 1986, I received 2 million yen as a recording budget from MIDI Records in the form of a traveler's check. I went to England alone to record the next album with this money. Now, 2 million yen is actually a very small recording budget for a major record company. Only an independent minor label would have made an entire album with that kind of budget.

I will tell you what happened.

I first went to New York City to spend a week there. I had bought a cheap round-trip ticket from Hong Kong to New York. I took the flight from Tokyo but could go on to Hong Kong with a free one-way ticket after I got back to Tokyo. This was what I planned to do.

My mother had been living with an Englishman named Martin since about 1976. They had lived in New York City since 1978. He had suggested that we could get a cheap round-trip ticket from New York to London after I arrived in New York City, so that's what I did.

When Martin was still 17 years old, he started going to Lindsay Kemp's workshop to study performance art. This was how he first met my mother. He and my mother came to Japan briefly in the late 1970s, where Martin started to study Chinese acupuncture. He began giving shiatsu as a business in New York. His clients included people like the actress Isabelle Rossini, who acted in David Lynch's *Blue Velvet*. He would later study psychology and earn a degree, after which he became a professional counselor.

Martin's parents lived in England. His father had met and married his mother in Malta, a former British territory in the Mediterranean Sea, when he was in the British Royal Army. After returning to England, his father worked at a bank. I had never been to England before, so Martin told me that I could stay at his parents' house in Kent, while I was trying to find a recording studio and musicians to record with. I knew very few people in England at the time. But I had a feeling that I was going to make a good album.

First, I flew to New York and spent a week there. Then, Martin and I both bought round-trip tickets to England. It was a Kuwait Airways ticket. Because it was an airline from a Muslim country, they did not serve alcohol on board. I don't drink alcohol, so it didn't really matter. I had never met Martin's family, so I went with him, and he introduced me to his family.

I enjoyed my week in New York City. When I arrived in New York on July 15, I called up John Zorn. He is a New York composer and musician whom I had met in Tokyo a year before. He had been coming to Japan frequently since around 1985, renting an apartment in Koenji and playing gigs with various Japanese musicians. I once interviewed him and wrote an article about him for a magazine called "Keyboard Special." Later in the 21st century, he released three CDs of mine in a row on his label TZADIK. These CDs introduced me to the music-buying public in the US and Europe.

When I rang his house, the first thing I heard was what sounded like music from a scary horror movie. Then I heard the music suddenly stop and a voice spoke in a static, serious tone, "State your name and message."

I waited for the beeping sound so that I could put in a voice message.

After a few moments, the voice repeated, "State your name and message."

"Isn't this a recording?," I asked.

"No. This is not a recording," he said.

"This is Ayuo."

His voice became friendly.

"Ayuo! You're in New York now?"

"I'm on my way to London, so I'll only be here for a few days."

"How are you doing these days?"

'This week, I'm recording a composition called "Spillane" for the Nonesuch label. It's at the Radio City Music Hall studio. The 18th is the next recording date. Do you want to come visit the studio, while we're recording?"

"Oh, yeah, I'd love to see you recording."

"Alright, then, let's get together on another day. How about tomorrow at noon?"

"I'm free."

"Well then, I know a good Thai restaurant. Want to go eat there?"

So, on the next day, the 16th, I had Thai lunch with him, a saxophone player/composer named Ned Rosenberg, and a Japanese composer and performance artist named Ushio Torikai. It was a restaurant near Chinatown. John gave me the phone numbers of some avant-garde musicians living in London. After lunch, we all went shopping in Chinatown.

That night I saw Lou Reed live at a big club called the Ritz. It was right after the release of his album *Mistrial*, which was produced by the bass player Fernando Saunders. At the time, Lou Reed was a rock star. The venom of the Velvet Underground and Berlin was gone, and he was making more of a pop sound in the 80's style. The show started with "We're Gonna Have a Real Good Time Together" from the Velvet era. They played songs from Reed's Velvet days and songs from *Mistrial* as energetic rock and roll songs. Many in the crowd were conservative-looking white boys who came over the bridge or under the tunnel from New Jersey to New York City to enjoy the weekend. They seemed to listen to Lou Reed in the same way as they listened to Bruce Springsteen's *Born in the USA*. These were the kind of kids who would have booed and thrown bottles on the stage in the 1960s and 1970s. Lou Reed's performance itself was really good.

On the afternoon of the 17th, I bought a round-trip ticket to London on Kuwait Airlines because it was cheaper than most others.

In the evening, Tsuguhito Tsukada, the guitarist, and Ken Awazu, my lifelong friend who was living in New York City at the time and I had a round-table discussion to be published for a Japanese language newspaper called OCS NEWS. Tsuguhito Tsukada was a member of the group Mitch Live, and he also played lead guitar prominently in Hajime Tachibana's show. OCS News was edited by Akiko Iimura, and published many interesting articles about Japanese-Americans and Asian-Americans.

On the 18th, I went to see John Zorn's recording at Radio City Music Hall studio.

The title of the composition "Spillane" is named after mystery writer Mickey Spillane, whose novels featuring detective Mike Hammer provided the basis for the album's title track.

Arto Lindsay, Robert Quine (former guitarist for the Lou Reed Band), and Anton Fier were reading from a text written by Arto Lindsay. John had written what he wanted to do with the song on index cards, and as he laid them out, he thought about what he would record in the studio.

On the 20th, I met David Baker, the engineer for *Silent Film*, and Steve Elson, the saxophone player. I also met Arto Lindsay (who was staying at the apartment of a Brazilian percussionist named Nana Vasconcelos), who told me a lot of stories about what he was doing at DNA and his plans for his group, Ambitious Lovers.

That night, I went to see Ryuichi Sakamoto mixing his live album at the Power Station with my friend, Ken Awazu. Power Station was a popular recording studio at the time, and by the mid-1980s it was filled with Japanese artists. The recording room was made entirely of wood, like a country house. There were microphones and speakers in the elevators and toilets so that the whole building could be used as an echo chamber for the mix. I had a chat with percussionist David Van Tieghem who was there that night. He told me that he had just started recording a solo album and invited me to visit him while he was recording.

On the 22nd, I went to see David Van Tieghem's recording. He was recording with Fairlight—an expensive synth sampler that cost 10 million yen at the time—connected to a sequencer. When he was invited to Japan for Ryuichi Sakamoto's tour, he liked the sound of stones clacking into one another that he heard at a Japanese restaurant so much that he recorded the sound and sampled it with the Fairlight to create the "clack, clack, clack" sound. He then made a V-sign with the fingers of his right hand and sampled the sound of his left middle finger hitting the valley of the V-sign to create a percussion-like sound. In the 1980s, many people spent a lot of time on this kind of sound experimentation. In those days, such sounds could only be made with instruments costing over 10 million yen, but in the 21st century, you can now do it with free samplers.

That night, I boarded the plane to London.

England was a place I'd never been to before, so I could start from scratch. Nobody knew me. I had a record company paying for my recording budget, but I didn't have any introductions from them to any studio or any musicians. I was working completely on my own. There were no misconceptions about me unless I made them myself. In the first two weeks after arriving in London, I met one musician after another. John Zorn advised me to call a lot of phone numbers that he, Morgan Fisher, and others had given me: Nina Hagen had just moved to London; Steve Beresford was a musician whom I first heard on Brian Eno's experimental label. He played handmade instruments, produced pop music, and did improvisation with John Zorn and others. Particularly memorable for me was his playing and arranging on albums by the female punk band, The Slits. I met him near Notting Hills in London. I also went to see Michael Nyman. I heard about studios and engineers from these people.

Tower Records in London had just opened, and I was one of the first customers there. Here, I discovered *Silent Film* in the imported rock section of the store. It was imported through Tower Records in the United States. I bought an old duo album of Maddy Prior and Tim Hart of Steeleye Span.

In the magazine *Time Out*, there was a schedule of an improvisation band called AMM playing at an art gallery in Hyde Park. This band was a veteran of the UFO Club and other venues with Pink Floyd and Soft Machine in the late 1960s, when Syd Barrett was with them. I have read somewhere that Syd Barrett learned various techniques from Keith Rowe, the guitarist of AMM. In the early days of the group, the contemporary composer, Cornelius Cardew, was involved. He was originally influenced by the New York experimental music group Fluxus, John Cage, and the experimental music of Karlheinz Stockhausen. Cardew also worked with John Cale of the Velvet Underground, before Cale left London for New York. Brian

Eno also learned a lot from Cardew's experimental music activities. In the 1970s, however, he became more "political" in his musical activities. In the early eighties, he was killed by a car on a London street corner while waiting for a bus.

There was an exhibition of graphic scores at the gallery.

There was also a piece written by William Hellermann, my guitar teacher from NYC, on the wall. I was surprised to know that he wrote such interesting graphic scores.

At this gallery, AMM played a set of improvised pieces. Percussionist Eddie Prevost's performance was particularly impressive. Keith Rowe used a steel ruler and coils of wire between the strings of his guitar to create a metallic bell-like sound.

I spoke to the band members after the concert. I had done a concert in '82 where I played some of Cardew's songs. They seemed to know about it. I told them about my father, that my guitar teacher was William Hellermann, and that I was looking for a studio to record a new album.

Eddie Prevost told me that an old experimental music colleague of theirs, David Lord, has a recording studio in Bath where AMM also recorded one album.

I already had several albums recorded by David Lord. I had heard many of the albums he had produced, such as Peter Gabriel's 4th solo album (titled *Security* in the US), the compilation he made for the first WOMAD festival, Virginia Astley, Peter Hammill, and so on.

I asked him for his contact information. Eddie Prevost called me the next day and gave me the studio phone number.

Then I called up David Lord. David Lord told me that he was going to London that week to record a rhythm track for a band called Latin Quarter, so I arranged to meet him then. The studio in North London where he was going to record it was owned by Jerry Boyce, an engineer who had produced many folk-rock albums for Steeleye Span and others. I took a sample of my sound there and asked him if he wanted to work with me on an album, even though we didn't have much of a recording budget. He seemed interested.

The following week, Fairport Convention played a show at a pub called Half Moon.

I went to see them. I was impressed by drummer Dave Mattack's performance, but the whole atmosphere of the concert was a bit strange for me. I liked the sound of Fairport Convention around the time of "Liege and Lief;" I also liked their concert that I saw when I was in junior high school back in 1974. But the Fairport I saw that night was a drunken band. Of course, they played good songs, and they played well. There was great tension in their rendition of "One More Chance," written by Sandy Denny; Jerry Donahue, the guitarist I saw in '74, was a guest on this song. I was listening to cassette tapes of Sandy Denny's Fairport days and Sandy Denny's solo albums backed by the members of Fairport, a lot during this trip. The title of her song "Who Knows Where the Time Goes" itself carries that sense of suspended time. It's like the feeling of an infinite expanse of sky. A feeling you can get when one gets high with cannabis. It's a sense of freedom that you can hear from the music. This sense of freedom was no longer present in Fairport Convention that night. As is the case with Middle Eastern music, when tastes change from hashish to alcohol, the feeling of the music changes somehow. A band influenced by alcohol and a band influenced by cannabis sound different, because they both influence our sense of time in different ways.

I visited the studio of the photographer, Richard Haughton. He was the brother of the actor David Haughton, whom I met in NYC when I was in junior high school. On the way to Richard's studio, I bought a *psaltery*, a European instrument from the Middle Ages, at a shop selling books and records. This instrument played a big role in the album I recorded this time. Richard used to take pictures of many musicians, so a lot of musicians were always coming in and out of his studio. He had taken photos of Siouxsie and the Banshees, videos of Thomas Dolby at that time, and later, of Phil Collins. I met Thomas Dolby there that day.

That night, after smoking pot in his studio, we went to a Vietnamese restaurant for dinner with the members of the band Rip Rig and Panic, a woman who played the viola, and a Hungarian designer. Richard bought all our drinks. I asked him to do a photo shoot for the album cover. I called up MIDI with him and we agreed that he would take the promotional photos for the album as well. He had met the managing director of MIDI in Japan before.

In the basement of Schott's, a music store in London, there was a shop called Early Music, which sold kits and complete pieces of restored medieval European instruments from the Yorkshire region of England. I bought a kit of a medieval harp, which I had been interested in for a long time. However, it was a kit that could not be made without certain tools, such as a saw. I asked David Lord if he knew anyone who could make one, and he introduced me to the violinist Stuart Gordon. He was a former member of the Incredible String Band, and later became a member of The Korgis; he used to play with Peter Hammill at the time. The following week, I saw Steeleye Span and Renaissance at the Royal Festival Hall. Steeleye Span was great live. They had just released an album called *Back in Line*. They played songs from this album, as well as songs I've wanted to hear live for a long time.

By comparison, Renaissance, who played first, sounded tired. When I saw them at the Academy of Music in New York in the early 70's, they were a tight-playing progressive rock band. The female vocalist, Annie Haslam, had a crystalline high voice with incredible vocal technique and this band mixed classical music with folk-rock in prog-rock suites. They borrowed musical phrases from late 19th-century Russian classics and Debussy's piano pieces and mixed them into songs to create an excitement similar to spectacles and dramatic film music. However, times changed, members changed, and in the early 80s, they were releasing more pop records. In this era of Duran Duran, their music no longer sold well. Their outfits were out of fashion. They wore the same things as in the 1970s, but their '70s style costumes looked tacky in the '80s when more glamorous fashions were in vogue. Renaissance that day consisted of Annie Haslam and Michael Danford, who wrote most of the songs, with guests on bass and piano. The pianist was from Long Island, New York. They played a series of old songs, but Annie Haslam had lost her once clear voice. She sounded out of tune and now had a husky voice. The two guests played like they were copying the music from the old records.

After seeing this show, I told David Lord that I wanted to ask Maddy Prior of Steeleye Span to sing on my album. I knew that Jerry Boyce, the studio owner, knew many of Maddy Prior's acquaintances. I asked David Lord if he could ask around. One of the people he asked was involved in organizing the concert I had seen with Steeleye Span and Renaissance, who suggested that I should invite Annie Haslam as well. He said that she was at a point in her career where she was wondering what to do in the future. Apparently, she knew that Renaissance no longer had much of a future at that time. They had run its course. If I hadn't heard her current voice at the concert, I might have been happy to ask her, since I had been listening to their albums when I was in junior high school. But I turned it down. If it were now, I probably wouldn't have refused. Now I wonder how she would have sung if I had asked her then.

Then, through Stuart Gordon, I asked Dave Mattacks of Fairport Convention to play drums. Stuart had played with Dave Mattacks on the Incredible String Band's *Earthbound* in the seventies.

In this way, I was able to ask many musicians that I have been listening to since I was in junior high school. In my heart, I was really surprised at how it was working out. I didn't expect that I would be able to work with these musicians, some day. Paul Kantner of Jefferson Airplane once said that in 1966, the year before the 'summer of love,' he felt that everything he wanted was coming true. For me, that's what it felt like when we recorded this record in 1986.

Recording and mixing at David Lord's Crescent Studios took ten days—the recording took 7 days, and the last 3 days were for mixing. For a rock album to be released on a major label, this was very quick.

I arrived at his studio in Bath the day before recording. James Warren, formerly of Stackridge, was there recording his solo CD. Andy Davis from Stackridge was there too. I said I was going to watch a video and then go to bed, so I borrowed a videotape of a horror movie called *Texas Chainsaw Massacre* that was in the studio and went to the back of the studio to spend the night. But as I was watching the movie, I started to get very scared. So, I went back to the studio and told them that I was scared. Both James and Andy laughed at me. I asked to stay for a while at the studio while they were recording, as I couldn't sleep.

The first thing that surprised me about working with David Lord was that we were able to communicate with each other as though it were by telepathy. In my previous recordings in Japan, such a thing wasn't possible at all. Rather, I was treated as someone who couldn't communicate. But here in the studio, before I could even say a word, he was precisely initiating the next step. This is one of the reasons this recording went incredibly fast.

In recording in Japan, people tend to wait until they are given specific instructions. They tend not to initiate or suggest anything unless they feel they know you well enough. Since I didn't have much experience when I started out recording in Japan, I didn't know what to tell them. It was also difficult to communicate with them the kind of sounds I was hearing in my head, so I would bring albums by various bands to the studio. I would make them listen to it, and say, "I want to make this kind of echo sound."

The first two days at Crescent were spent programming patterns into a drum machine, and then overdubbing guitar, bass, and keyboard pads (sustained chords, notes, and drones) to the drum machine.

The third day was spent recording all my parts except for drums on "Across the Seasons," "With Eyes Closed," "Sounds of You" and "End of Earth." On the third day, I recorded all the parts of the *psaltery*. From then on, every day, a different musician would come in to overdub parts.

All of Dave Mattacks' drum parts for the four songs were recorded in one day. He came to Bath the night before recording and stayed the night before, just before he left for a tour in Germany. He gave me a lot of advice on everything, from the sound of the drum mix to the overall arrangement. He mixed the sound of his drums himself and saved it on the mixing board computer.

Maddy Prior left the eastern part of England by car at 6 o'clock in the morning, arrived at Bath, and worked hard until about 7 o'clock in the evening without eating at all. She said that eating would change her voice, and she wanted to give her best performance. I was amazed and very much moved. No one else before had given me such an effort to give me their best performance. This is what a real professional should do.

The first piece was an arrangement of a piece from Carl Orff's *Carmina Burana*. The second was a piece from the medieval *Carmina Burana*, a German melody from around 1200, which I had transcribed from several medieval recordings. Maddy Prior sang in Latin on the hit single, "Gaudete" by Steeleye Span, and also a song in Renaissance four-part harmony, so I assumed that she could read music. But, in fact, she couldn't read music and had to learn everything by heart. She had Peter Knight, Steeleye's violin player, come to her house and play the scores I'd sent her over and over again to help her learn them. Maddie sang them beautifully and they still sound wonderful today. I can feel the power and energy she put into it.

I was blown away by the musicians' sincerity toward music and their hard work ethic. In Japan, I had never seen musicians work so hard on my project. Even if you called up studio musicians, many would not have taken their jobs as seriously as these musicians I met in England.

Figure 13 1986. At Crescent Studios. Photo by Richard Haughton.

Figure 14 1986. Photograph taken for the cover of the album *Nova Carmina*. Photographed by Richard Haughton.

David Lord was a man who couldn't stop when he really got into his work. After I finished dubbing my keyboard pads for "Veris Leta Facies," he started programming in all those little volume and dynamics changes by himself into the mixer's computer. These are the small intricate changes that many people would not even notice. At around 2 am I told him I couldn't stay up any longer and he said he wanted to continue to do some more work on his own. And yet on the next day, he would start working early again.

Over the weekend, Richard Haughton came to take some photos for the album. We drove to towns like Glastonbury and Wells to take photos. The one taken in a church in Wells became the cover photo. After the shoot, we went to a rock festival in Somerset together. Latin Quarter (a group that David Lord was in the middle of producing work for) was there, and so was Steeleye Span. It was a beautiful day, and we laid down on the grass and listened to the music being performed. There were a lot of good bands out there, but not many people in the audience. I had invited Peter Knight, Steeleye's violin player, to record on the album and we had come to pick him up after the show. After Steeleye Span finished playing, I said hello to Maddy and took Richard's car back to Bath with Peter and his American girlfriend. The last band to play was It Bites; Richard had filmed them a while back for work, but he didn't see them as he didn't really like the band.

I asked Peter Knight to record violin on two compositions. One was a medieval-style piece I had composed, and the other was an instrumental version of a composition I had originally written for the Japanese koto player Kazue Sawai, entitled *Eye to Eye.* Peter had studied classical violin at the Royal Academy of Music, but he became more interested in Irish fiddle music. While working in a bookshop and playing Irish fiddle tunes in his spare time, he was invited to join Steeleye Span by Martin Carthy, a folk singer and guitarist, who was already well-known in the United Kingdom. This was in 1970. When I met him, he told me that maybe he got too much into Irish music since he was English and not Irish himself.

What he was worried about had to do with his identity. Irish fiddle tunes remained an important part of Steeleye Span's repertoire, and his playing was a perfect fit for my album.

I wanted to include a reading in Latin over a harp solo piece I played. This is how I met Peter Hammill.

Nineteen

Meeting Peter Hammill/Visit to Peter Hammill's house/Interview with Peter Hammill

I wanted a reading of a poem from the *Carmina Burana* written by Peter of Blois, Archdeacon of the town of Bath in the 12th century, over my performance of the medieval harp—backed by my sound recording of the sounds of water in Wells. Peter of Blois was known to have composed several poems preserved in *Carmina Burana*, which he composed in his student days in Paris; this included "Vacillantis trutine libramine," a well-known song that I later often covered in concert. When David heard my suggestion, he said that Peter Hammill would be perfect for this reading and that I should invite him to the recording. At the time, David had been working on Peter Hammill's solo album.

I was surprised because I knew about *Fool's Mate* and *In Camera*, as well as the Van der Graaf Generator albums he was involved with. David called Peter as soon as I said yes.

Peter lived in a small town that had only two streets in the mountains about a twenty-minute drive from Bath. He came over right away and we recorded the reading. That weekend, he invited me to his house. He picked me up at the studio in Bath and we drove to his house together. His children were still young at the time, and he was living with his family and recording his solo album at home. In the car, pointing to the mountain landscape, he said, "My children live where they were born. My children have grown up with almost the same children they've known since they were born, which is quite unusual in this day and age."

I told him that my family was constantly moving when I was a child, so I grew up in Berlin, Sweden, and New York City. Peter

Hammill told me that his family was also constantly moving when he was a child, but it was all in England. He wanted to give his children a place that they could look back on as their home. This conversation was what inspired me to compose the suite of songs, *E no Naka no Sugata* (What We Look Like in The Picture), which I recorded on Kazue Sawai's album in 1987. I would record this again on the Tzadik album *Red Moon* in 2003 (with the English title, "A Picture of You and I"), and then again on *What We Look Like in The Picture* in 2006.

When I entered the house, I found a 24-track tape recorder in the back room on the first floor. At the time, an analog tape recorder with that many tracks was still very expensive, and not many musicians owned one themselves. He told me that he had started buying equipment when he was recording *Fool's Mate* in the seventies because he felt that the time might come when he would have to own his equipment to continue to record the music he wanted to create. At first, he started by experimenting and trying things out as if he were working on a homemade recipe, but by the time I knew him, he was already very proficient. He would buy more and more of his equipment as they came out.

In the 1990s, he started to record his solo albums on ADAT, and in the 21st century, he started to record his solo albums on his laptop. He had many years of recording experience, and so the quality of the finished product was already comparable to that of David Lord's recordings and mixes. He recorded, mixed, and mastered all his recordings by himself; ordered the pressing and jacket printing from the factory by himself; and packed and sent them all over the world by himself. The album he was recording at the time was called *As Close as This*. Paul Ridout, a designer, synthesizer and keyboard programmer, and PA operator for Peter's gigs, was helping him record the album. After he let me listen to the songs he was recording, we went upstairs. Near the stairs of his house was a collage of photos of musicians he had worked with hanging on the wall. Some of the photos were used for the inside cover of Van der Graaf's live album, *Vital*. David Lord's photo was also on the wall.

In this upstairs room, I did an interview with Peter for a magazine called *Keyboard Special*. Here is much of the original interview. I have taken the liberty of re-organizing it, so that people who may not know much of Peter Hammill's works can also enjoy and understand it.

===The Interview with Peter Hammill in 1986===

In 1967, just as Peter Hammill (hereby referred to as PH) was about to graduate from university to study medicine, he dropped out of college because he was more interested in playing music.

The band he formed became Van der Graaf Generator.

Ayuo: When did you start [performing music]?

PH: Professionally, 19 years ago; I began [performing in] 1967–1968. I began writing songs before that, around 1965. But at that time in 1967, I was at university, and I formed Van der Graaf Generator there... and after nine months, you know, before exams, I decided that this was the thing that I wanted to do.

Yeah. In fact, it was very much a thing of the moment, and really, if I'd thought about things today, I imagine I would end up writing prose, writing books, and then maybe I'd be lucky enough to have had two or three years in music.

Of course, I realized when I started doing it that this was more important for me.

Ayuo: With basically the same members?

PH: Yes, basically the same people.

It's the question of communication that you build up with people. A lot of people don't understand why Van der Graaf can break up, and yet it's still possible for the musicians to play together, and what's the difference?

There are differences, of course, but when a band is in existence, it dominates everybody's lives and it's the main thing, and yet the individual musicians still have their own aspect.

But it would seem foolish to me to throw away the knowledge that you've built up with different people. Not having to use words and, say, so that you can say to somebody "I would like you to play this like concrete or like stainless steel." If you've played with somebody for a number of years, they know what you mean and what those images mean to you; if it's somebody else you've never met before then they just go "Well, what do you mean? Does concrete mean slam, slam, or [what] does it mean, huh?"

So, this kind of thing is really important.

Over the last few years, I've often toured with quite a few normal groups. There've been three or four records with a normal group—

two guitars, bass, and drums; or piano, guitar, bass, and drums. There are a couple of records that were made—more or less—with that lineup, and until about two years ago, that was mostly the way that I toured.

But, occasionally with duos and trios, you know, I quite like to have a different lineup for each tour, so that there's an element of surprise. I don't like the idea of going and playing the same thing. I've never particularly seen the point of that.

So, I've had lots and lots of changes over time.

Ayuo: What kind of musicians did you play with?

PH: Mostly, they've been musicians from Van der Graaf.

Guy [Evans], the drummer, has been almost continuous. Obviously, a lot of that is due to the fact that we have played together as a section for (by now) nearly 19 years.

So, the amount of understanding that there is, that one doesn't really even have to look at each other for syncopations because you know [it] without it entering the brain. And also, in a certain sense, rhythmically, because I have his drumming or his percussion in some way imprinted on my psyche, I tend to write in a way that follows his way of thinking.

And in fact, even if I ever play drums myself, I find myself playing what Guy would. So, he's been almost continuous.

Ayuo: The years 67–68s were very psychedelic.

PH: That's right, yes. We were just at the tail end of the psychedelic period, and then there was the progressive period. It was in between the two, which we had kind of fitted uncomfortably really. We were put in those categories, but it was a bit uncomfortable. It was also at this time that people really started doing this thing of playing the same thing every night.

(Peter Hammill later told me that he didn't enjoy how Genesis would play the same solos as on the record every night, when they toured together in the early '70s. He felt it was predictable, but then he realized that times were changing. Van der Graaf Generator would be more adventurous and play differently every night. Some nights were great, but others weren't as good. Hammill told me that he knew Genesis were going to make it more than Van der Graaf. Their way of doing things made it so there weren't many bad nights.)

Trying to play exactly like the records, which is something I've never really liked, and [which] Van der Graaf never did. We had an interesting reputation that one night we'd be brilliant and two nights we'd be average and one night we'd be terrible.

But the brilliant nights were really reaching for something that wasn't completely known. So sometimes you fall. If you try to do that then sometimes you fall down, obviously. Sometimes you manage to catch [yourself], but you have to accept that you will fall down at times.

Which I still think is the proper approach to music.

Ayuo: When was your first record?

PH: It was in 69. Oh, there were two records actually.

The Aerosol Grey Machine, I think was just in 68.

And then *The Least What We Can Do* was in 69, so it's a long way back.

The Aerosol Grey Machine was only released in the States at the time. It was one of those things that was released and then deleted straight away. And now it's been released about two or three times since. The first real one (as Van der Graaf Generator) was *The Least We Can Do is Wave to Each Other*.

My solo things occupy entirely different territory as well. Sometimes it's quite like Van der Graaf, and sometimes it goes in lots of other directions too.

Ayuo: I know of *Fool's Mate* and *Nadir's Big Chance* from the 70s.

PH: They're actually the two 'kind-of' pop albums.

Fool's Mate was done at the same time that Van der Graaf was going in the first [psychedelic] period. And so, you know, it was territory away from Van der Graaf because Van der Graaf could really play in any style, but not normally the little three-minute songs.

Nadir's Big Chance, in fact, was made after we decided to reform. It was the first time we played together, having decided to be Van der Graaf again, but not wanting to do that yet.

That again is one side of the solo stuff.

And the other albums, I mean, there are more extreme albums, in terms of sound and subjects, length of songs, you know—there's one record that has a 20-minute piece, rather like "Lighthouse Keepers" on *Pawnhearts*, so in the sense that there are lots of interlocking tunes and passages that eventually combine. There is a bit of musique concrète in there, and all sorts of things.

Ayuo: Has the approach to your songs changed? They have been quite consistent, haven't they?

PH: Yes, there's been a consistent approach. There're some things that are still the same, I think.

In terms of what I think a song can do, lyrically and musically. I mean, I normally write in a fairly traditional way, with some odd spikes. I use some funny time signatures—not to be difficult—just how I hear it because I was never formally trained at all.

In a way, I'm a blank sheet of paper, so some of those things remain the same. The differences obviously are that I know so much more about [composing] now, about the way to use words, the way to use music.

I've become a musician as well somewhere along the way. When I began in 68–69, I was a singer and songwriter, and not really a musician. If I played anything, I would play (more or less) the chords that I wrote the song with, but I wasn't comfortable [exploring yet].

I learned the psychology of being a musician really from the others in Van der Graaf, who were all very good musicians, and somewhere along the way [I] became more of a musician—which in turn meant that I could write slightly more complicated songs, which meant that I had to become a slightly better musician in order to play them, and so on.

So, there's obviously an accumulation of knowledge. But, still, the fundamentals are the same, I think. And naturally as well, the other main difference is that I'd be foolish if I tried to write songs from the perspective of a 19-year old.

Although, a lot of people in their 40s and so on seem to want to write songs about going out to parties and doing 19-year-old things. I think it devalues the form, because the form can hold much more than that, and I think it can deal with adult songs.

So, I try to write adult songs or universal songs, I should say.

Ayuo: Many of the songs that you do are lyrically very strong.

The other day, before we rang you up, David Lord just showed me a bit of this video that he had.

PH: Oh, the BBC one?

Ayuo: Yes, I think so. You booked into a hotel in London to write a song.

PH: Yes, that's right, I've done that quite often. It's that hotel. It's actually right by the railway station now and obviously, you know, I spent a lot of time over the years in hotel rooms.

When you've spent a lot of time [there], your experience becomes different from most people. Most people don't stay in the hotel for a long time; maybe if they're on holiday or on a trip or something. So there's something exciting and active about the hotel room.

But I've stayed in so many that I look on them as very passive places. It's going to be my room for a little while. And I find it's very good for just cutting yourself off from any outside influences. I mean, [the house] here, obviously, I work downstairs, and the family is upstairs. There's always lots going on, and it's a different mental discipline.

I find, for writing lyrics, that often it's good to just be [on the road] like that, but I haven't done it for some time. I mean, lately, I've found that I can write lyrics anywhere. Or it's that the writing is inside, rather than depending on any outside stimulus. But I don't divide off the words of songs.

I think I see myself really as a songwriter, which is a very different thing from being a poet who writes music. You know, I think that things are very much band up.

(From here, PH talks about the spoken word from Carmina Burana *that I asked him to do.)*

Even if one's taking coming to *Carmina Burana* and recording spoken word, I think that's the fascinating thing.

The rhythm that's imposed, the rhythm section that's imposed is actually just in the meter of the words, which makes a song really, doesn't it? There's a melody line in the harp, but the real melody line is just off somewhere in between things.

It's in the water, I suppose. But even with that, you know, it becomes something different once you put words and music together, and I obviously always try to write with a lot of a mixture of logical sense in the words and intuitive things, spaces in between them.

But also, a large part of it is simply the sound of words, because one of the wonderful things about English is that—for any idea—there are normally at least eight or nine different words, and they have slightly different meanings themselves.

They also have very different meanings in terms of their sound—there's the actual technical meaning and the sound meaning. And sometimes that's more important—in fact, it's more important when [the words] are sung.

So I work hard at that end. This is why, sometimes, I need to go to hotels.

Ayuo: I remember that the more popular image attached to you is that you are singing dark songs. Showing a darker side of life.

PH: Yes, I think that was true to an extent. It's one of these things that hangs around me like a millstone.

Ayuo *(speaking about one of the songs from "As Close As This")*: Well, the song that I just heard, especially the first one today that I heard, is very different from that.

PH: Yes, well, a lot of these songs are very different. On the last record, some would say would be quite dark. There are a couple of dark songs. It's not because I find it hard to write happy songs. Not that there's less of an interest there. I kind of find that the subjects that demand to have songs written about them, are generally other things that you ought to look at, but we don't like to look at too much.

And if you're happy, you know you're just happy; so if you don't normally examine that, you just say I'm happy.

There were a lot of songs that were in that [dark] area, and sometimes, you know, people think that's all I write about, or even that I feel negative or go around in a dark cloud all the time.

My attitude has always been, "This is something one must look at." If you don't look at these topics, they won't go away; sometimes, they get bigger. So, a lot of the songs are in that territory.

And, again, some of the things—that I think pop songs or rock songs, or whatever you want to call them—some of the topics they deal with are things like faith and religion and questions of time. Time is really the big thing that obsesses me, or has over the last several years; say, the last 10 years or so.

The one thing I keep writing about is time, and the way we perceive it, and in terms of our own lives, and future and past lives.

So, I think that songs are an ideal medium for dealing with this sort of stuff. If you simply write prose about it, then you're almost into philosophy, and you have to approach it from a non-emotional angle.

If you paint, then of course there's no direct line. So, it seems to me that songs can deal with this kind of territory because of the spaces that there are inside them.

Ayuo: Were you traveling around a lot in those early days?

PH: Oh yes, nearly all the time.

Ayuo: Were you writing most of your songs when you were traveling?

PH: Some. In the very early days of Van der Graaf, we played only in Britain and that would be, I suppose, three or four times a week. I obviously had a lot of songs already and the rest I would write after we've been going for about a year.

We toured nearly all the time, mostly in Europe. Sometimes I'd write on the road but, I mean, there's always... you have a week at home, and at that time, you know, if I had any time off, then I'd be writing away. And still, it doesn't take so long to write songs, really.

Once you have the idea, then it's all right. I think generally I tend to write quite fast, once I know what to write. Maybe a day or two to write something once the idea is there. In fact, even in solo days I used to tour an awful lot. Van der Graaf used to tour eight months a year. Something like that, and then I still did four or five months a year until now. As you see, I have a family now, and it became more important to be at home. So, now I tour very little. In fact, you know, this time [in Japan] will be the first since I was in the United States six weeks ago. After that, I'm doing maybe five days in England and two weeks in Europe, and that's all for this year.

It's important, not only from the family point of view, but because I want to be fresh each time—not just go around the world, you know, being a hologram of myself. It's still important to me to be excited about playing, and if I don't do it too often, I can be.

Ayuo: Can you tell me more about your approach to songwriting?

PH: Okay, yes.

Well, one of the main things about songs for me is that music is non-specific. I mean, it carries messages, in terms of emotional messages and musical messages, but it's not dogmatic. And that's something I try to preserve in songs, normally.

I don't like the idea of songs that just have one meaning: "That's the meaning. There you go."

That is just one of the problems, having the endlessly repeating choruses—you can only have one meaning there.

So, I usually try to write songs that have two or three lines that you can follow down. If you start thinking along one line, you can follow it all the way down the song, and it means that.

But by the same token, there are two other lines as well.

And the "true meaning" of the song is a combination of those and none of them at the same time.

I sing an "*I*" normally in the song, but that isn't necessarily me. It's a character in the song, and even the character doesn't know, he's not saying exactly if it's like *this* or if it's like *that*.

And I try to put this in, whether it's a love song or a more philosophical song, or something like that. Because I think it's important, really, that the process of writing songs for me is to clarify something for myself. It is to understand for myself, in a slightly obscure way because it's not a specific *me*.

And if I can get it outside in that way, whether it's a story or just playing on words or talking about dreams, time, faith, something like that; I can get it outside and see, *oh yes, sometimes it's like* this, *sometimes it's like* that.

Then, I think, what happens for somebody else hearing it is that they can get the same kind of effect. But not from me, it's not me telling somebody this is how it *is*, it's them relating to the song.

It's important in that case not to, for me, be saying it is like this, it is so, and not to be dogmatic. So, that's one of my main efforts, whatever kind of song it is—so that, in a way, the song exists between me and the audience.

Otherwise, you know, it would have been insufferable for me to go on for 19 years constantly just saying *this is what I think*, on and on.

The important thing is that *it is the junction between me and the audience*. And secondly, that there is doubt or uncertainty somewhere in the song. That it is not dogmatic.

On a technical level, I'd like to have something different between different verses and choruses musically, as well as lyrically.

I don't normally like choruses that repeat the same thing. They're quite rare for me.

There may be only 5, or 10 percent of my songs that have choruses that come out the same. Usually, there's an extra—there's either a change of words or there's the insertion of an extra couple of lines of music.

Um… very many, very many of my songs, in fact, are a little bit like jigsaw puzzles. As I realize when I'm teaching them to other musicians, you know, I usually have about nine parts that fit together in different ways.

So I always have to teach people the nine parts and then—so, right now, let's call Part A a verse. And that's the first kind of verse. And then take *that* verse and add a little bit to it. That's the second verse.

And it usually works out like that. So that there's a kind of continuous, a "continuousness" thing about it, rather than the kind of hiccup of a song, you know, that you reach a certain point and then go back to the start, and so on.

I like it to flow through. Which is most exemplified in the opera. That which is absolutely continuous and no choruses or anything.

Ayuo: I hear that you're writing an opera?

PH: Yes, this is *The Fall of the House of Usher*, which I have been writing for 15 years now, and it's now almost completely written in the song sense, in the melody sense. The next stage, obviously, is to record it and have other people sing it. And that—it bears some relationship to a song. It is really like an enormous song.

I'm simply doing the music as well. For lyrics, I have Chris Smith, who started Van der Graaf with me. He is doing the libretto, which is quite interesting. I don't think I… if I'd been working on it entirely by myself, I couldn't have done it for 15 years.

But you know, he presents me with another piece, and then I present him with another piece, and we egg each other on. It's also quite interesting for me to simply write music rather than words.

Ayuo: And what does he do?

PH: He writes songs, and he writes musicals, generally, and he works for an architect. He does a mixture of things. He writes songs for other people, generally musicals. I still do some of his songs occasionally because I think he's very good. He also writes tunes. So, we've divided up the responsibilities.

Ayuo: When you're writing your songs, do you think of them as short stories?

PH: Yes, very much so. Short stories. Or: they divide in a certain way, there's the ones that are like short stories. There are others that are like little scenes from films. Quite often when I'm writing, especially love songs, I have a picture in my mind of a room as a *frozen frame* from a film.

And then there are others that are maybe more, as I say, more *philosophical*, but usually set in the same way that a short story can contain an idea as well as a story. This is usually what I try to do, especially these days.

And this is maybe the big change in my being a professional songwriter between now and 1968 when I started. I didn't really appreciate how much one could do that.

In exactly this way, in a short story or an extract from a film, you can compress lots of experiences and lots of ideas into one little thing.

So they're very much in that area, yes.

Ayuo: Would you say that your earlier songs were more based on your own experiences?

PH: Yes. This again is something else. There are early songs that are, in which the "I" is indeed a proxy of my experience.

Naturally, there's an inclination to write like that, in any case when you're in your late teens or early 20s. The world at that age is very much in your head. Then, when we get older, there are different ways of living and understanding. I suppose, understanding more about other people's points of view or other aspects of the world.

Ayuo: Most of the songs on *Fools Mate* are quite early songs.

PH: They're early, yes. Most of them are ones that were penned quite early. The "*I*," yes.

I wouldn't have felt happy carrying on just writing about me. I would think, in a way, that would be false trading. I wouldn't want to sell my life to songs or to start regarding the living of my life as being source material.

I think this is something, actually, that anybody who writes or does any creative endeavor, at one point or another—you have to realize that you cannot just live your life and want to just provide source material from yourself because in the end, the source material will become corrupt. You have to live a life outside of that, and then you come across the material that you work on by that. But it has to work that way. So obviously at some time, I had that realization—I think it was when I began to write proper characters in songs. So that there would be an '*I*' in a song and I would sing the '*I*.'

'I think,' 'I do,' but in the same way as an actor.

Ayuo: And when did you realize that on the more conscious level?

PH: I think probably in the period between the two Van der Graafs in the 70s. Because the Van der Graaf songs were always slightly more impersonal because I was writing for a band. Anything that we played had to be for the music to be played honestly.

Even if the others weren't singing it, the concepts and feelings involved in the music had to be ones with which the others agreed. I think it's unreasonable to expect a musician to play [something they don't agree with], if it's a band.

So it's different.

You know, it's one of the differences that people outside wouldn't really understand.

If you're making your own record, you can ask a musician to play anything. You may disagree with the whole idea of the song, but if it's your project you say, "Please, will you just do this?"

Then, there's no problem.

But if it's a band then everyone has to agree about what the whole thing is; even if the drummer is just playing a backbeat, he still has to agree or be prepared to debate at least what the song is about.

Therefore, from necessity, they tended to be more impersonal, broader songs, and in the period between the two Van der Graafs, where I did four solo albums that were more personal. Because I've been doing it for four or five years, at that point, I began to realize this other thing.

I hope the learning never stops—that discoveries about how to do things, why one does them, and what the result is continue. The *what it is* changes because if that isn't the case, then *it* isn't really happening. So nothing is ever definitive.

Ayuo: In your solo albums, when you had other Van der Graaf members, would their attitudes toward it be more kind of like session musicians?

PH: Yes, exactly in this way as I have just said. The responsibility was obviously mine. So there was no reason for them to argue about something that they might have argued about if it was in the Van der Graaf album.

By the same token, I had no reason to argue either, because it was my project. But it's hard for people who aren't musicians to understand this area of things. Obviously, any time a musician plays properly, he's playing with his soul.

But still, there are different ways of doing it. Sometimes, the soul and your beliefs are more important, and other times, your technique is important. So, whose project something is, it's [a] very shifting ground. I don't think people outside [the industry] can conceive of that, really.

It's a very complex cauldron, obviously, in the area of musicians' arrangements and what their commitment should be. Session musicians generally have something of a negative feeling about it, but in fact, it's the most fantastic thing. It can be a great thing to come in and just for somebody to say, *I want this feeling*, and you play it and then go away again. It's been a pure activity, in a way that you've had the idea for the project and you've planned it for a month and you've been recording for two months.

You can never come in just with that pure '*vah*' and then walk away again. One tries to do this naturally, but I think anyone serious about music tries to capture that however long they've been doing it. Every time they record something, it is the all-important *thing*— if you're a musician, a singer, or a writer, the moment that you're performing, *the world* depends upon you or at least your contribution to the world.

But it's hard if it's your project; if you're just coming in for somebody else, then it can be quite exciting.

I sang three songs on one of Robert Fripp's solo album, very much in that sort of way. I went to New York City, heard the backing tracks, saw the lyrics, went in and sang. Two takes of each of the songs. That's it.

Ayuo: Which album was that?

PH: *Exposure*. It was wonderful to sing in that way because that was exactly like being a guitarist, going in. It's quite normal for a guitarist to go in and be told, "Can you give me a solo over this? Here are the chords."

To have that in singing was great. You know, it's not just that important lack of knowledge that means you can cross over some boundaries that maybe you shouldn't cross over, because you don't know they're there… actually, you can find something very positive there.

Ayuo: How do you feel about the music scene now compared to the days when you first started?

PH: Well, it's very complex really. Technologically, it's a completely different universe. I mean, when I started, eight track recording was the norm. Nothing existed. Synthesizers didn't exist. The effects would be a tape machine and a plate echo and that was it. Period.

So, there are obviously many more possibilities now. On the other hand, then it meant that you had to push a lot more.

Now, you know, a million wonders of sound are there, waiting at your finger-tips, you know; just kind of close your eyes in the studio and just go bomb on the button on the rack, and something else will come in, instead of sometimes deciding what we want to get and having to spend a long time doing it. So, there's a balance that works out there.

I think generally the balance works out between different times as much as it does in people's lives.

It's obviously now much more industrial. Music now is much more important as a business than it was then. There was something cowboy about it still in the days of '69 or so. Yeah, I mean, in terms of playing live—maybe more than records, because we used to be sent out to Europe, as I say—and nobody really understood at that point how to do concerts. They wouldn't understand that you had to have electricity.

Now you can go around the world, and there are always two or three promoters and different sizes of halls, and everything will be sorted out. I mean, there, I think my regret there is maybe for younger bands, because there was a real element of adventure when we went. Many experiences that I've had were quite extreme. I wouldn't want to have them again, but I'm glad that I had them.

But I know at the same time that now, because the system is more *organized*, it's possible for somebody to go off for a six-month world tour and just see the 25 people on the crew and never meet, never see the outside world, or have a chance to understand the culture that they're passing through—which has always been, if you like, a selfish attitude that I have.

I like the idea of going to different places and performing because it means that you're *there*, you have a *meaning* in terms of the place, rather than just passing through and observing. And because you're in there, it means you have the possibility to try and get some understanding that would take you a month of just walking around and looking. So that is obviously a change.

As far as the music goes, I think it's an interesting time at the moment.

Ayuo: At the moment?

PH: I think at the moment it's an interesting time, not because of now, but because of *what will be*. I think that now it is a very big business in terms of record companies because they are looking for [products that are] enormous sellers.

Ayuo: It's more oriented toward videos, and it's kind of like visuals and records. I think that album sales have gone down.

PH: Yes, certainly, but my belief is that this is a kind of a peak of that kind of thing because there's an enormous uniformity about music. It's all chasing this one market?

It's all got the same kind of *video*. The same kind of *sound*. The same system. Which obviously in a way the audience wants or quote 'wants.' I believe that, already, that wave has broken. In the next two or three years, one will probably start to see many more minority music. Always staying minor but achieving some kind of substantial steady state.

Ayuo: Do you mean minority music, in terms of those released through more independent units?

PH: Maybe, yes, maybe through independent units. If I were running a large record corporation, instead of trying to get everything to be a great hit, which is what I think they're doing at the moment. They're even taking interesting people, and they then try to put them into this one route of the 'hit.'

I don't knock companies for doing that. I mean, they have to survive. But I think [making music as an independent unit] is the right kind of thinking because if you're just dealing with the hits, you have this very short time span, even for the most successful people, you know—people will succeed on a global level for two or three years and then you have to find another one. Whereas cultivating, quote *minorities* unquote—I don't mean to assign any value necessarily, but into areas of ambient music, jazz; all these kinds of things are going to have a longer time span.

Also, my real feeling is that the audience is going to demand these kinds of things. Never to compete with the enormous platinum records and 12 million sellers and what have you, but there's almost a law that says that something that achieves that state doesn't have so much *soul* inside it, or whatever kind of music it is.

So, I believe that this is the way that companies will go in the future, whether it relates to me or not, because I honestly don't know. I have no idea by now, what areas of music I fit into at all. I don't think it's rock music as such. I don't think it's pop music as such. It's not really jazz. It's simply the stuff that I do. It's simply my observations of other things. Like the different areas of jazz and so on. And I think this will happen over the next two or three years.

The *other things* will continue. Maybe even videos now are starting to roll down, because—for the average member of the audience—how many more times can you be excited by a thunder flash going through the air?

And, still, wonderful videos are being made and that will continue. But I think that the possibility is there. Well, maybe it'll be the point where the coin is flying through the air. Either way, the possibility is there, and we can look forward to generally and globally having a kind of healthy music for the rest of the century.

Or, well, one just kind of goes, *oh, well, yes, that was a good 20 years*; lots of interesting things out of rock music. And now all there is, is buff, baff, *buff, baff,* you know; endless eight-beat guitars and videos.

I believe that it's going to be the other way, and that the possibilities that are still there in this loose form... the possibilities are so enormous because you don't have to go through the conservatory route that you obviously have to do for "modern serious music."

You don't, in fact, have to take this jazz route of having played with the famous musician, then forming your own group, and getting the new hot young guns and *so on,* which is again fine, but just a different way.

If you have the will, you can go in and make whatever you want. So there's always an awful, awful orthodoxy about rock music as well as one sees with punk music. I mean, you know, by now it's not even a joke.

I mean, the original things, of course, were vital. But now, anybody going around going, "I'm a punk in 1985" is literally 10 years away from any kind of idea of what the original point was, and what the original whole basis of that music originally was.

'Enough of that. Let's have something different.'

And now, 10 years later, still people get up, and now the *something* different is just completely embedded in rock, and [that something]'s just ran a lot. But as I say, I'm positive about things and I think that they will go in that route.

You have to have *hits* to pay for everything. But then, even in—not in a kind of philanthropic way or kind of charitable arts way, for the health of the company—you have to have things on different levels.

And I think that's it. If I was running a record company, that's exactly what I would do. Even on this basis, this is why I think so. I'm positive. I think that's based on just sound business sense, rather than any kind of artistic value.

Ayuo: Well, one thing was that the early 80s for me was kind of like a very dull period, musically, because every band sounded the same.

You had the same voicing on every record. You could turn on Duran Duran and some other band and they sounded the same. The voice sounded the same. Everything sounded the same.

PH: It's a negative thing, really.

The problem, really, in the 80s was the technology. The jumps in technology, in recording, and in performing. It's been an absolute revolution, really, and what one heard in the early 80s still happens to a certain extent. Trevor Horn discovers a wonderful new sound, makes an astonishing record, and ten minutes later.... Because in terms of this technology if somebody discovers a sound it takes you a hundredth of the time once you hear a sound, to be able to make a copy of it. That's maybe not a hundred percent, but close enough.

So, Trevor Horn makes a sound and ten minutes later every other record is also going *Pow*! This is because technology now has many possibilities. Too many possibilities. I think it's very, very early in terms of that. That's on the recording side. And on the instrument side, because of the whole Midi area, and the use of the new synth and sampling as well. I think there's a lot of interesting stuff to be done there, as well, in a positive and "musician-ly" and soulful sense, rather than the way that it's been used so far, which is more or less about getting control or replacing musicianship.

I mean, not really being negative, but that's the way it's been used rather than pushing for the things that it can do.

It's really why I'm interested in doing this, sticking the performance into the computer (using Midi), just two hands.

(Hammill is talking about his album *As Close As This*.)

And then, obviously, something is playing an arrangement with two hands, but then to take out other things.

It's a world of possibilities. It means that traditionally you'd record and record your sound and your performance simultaneously, but now to be able to record your performance and then decide what sound will suit what part is a wonderful tool really.

So yes, I think this must come forward now.

Ayuo: There's also a whole lot of nostalgia for the earlier years. The psychedelic period because of what has been going on. A reaction.

PH: Yes, that's right. I think the other thing that characterizes it, that's negative about the '80s, is that there aren't so many *songs* written anymore. I speak as I am coming from that time, I have this idea of a song usually having a beginning, a middle, and an end.

So I don't like things to repeat. I very rarely have choruses that are the same; more or less, you have the verse, chorus, verse, chorus, mid-verse, chorus, chorus structure.

But often these days, again because of technology, people don't find that necessary. You can write a good chorus and half an idea for a verse, and what you're going to do is do your half an idea for a verse, then a chorus, then just a quarter of the verse, and then chorus, chorus, chorus at the end to bash it into people's heads.

And those choruses will all be the same as well. So somewhere in there, it seems to me that the craft of song has *gone*. But I think that the craft of songwriting will come around again as well.

Ayuo: When is this album you're now working on going to be released?

PH: Yes, I'd like it to be in November, because, as I said, 19 years I would have been doing this. The 25th album—and I think, you know, a lifetime's amount of work—I'd be happy with 50 records.

I think... as long as the other 25 [albums] can be all as different and varied as these have been, and that they aren't just *normal*.

I think 50 would be a reasonable target for a lifetime. I'm graced with a long life, and I've been doing it for 19 years—and in November, I'll be 38. So I will have had half of my life. It seems to me that the numbers are lining up.

I ought to have this one out in November. You know, I think one should sometimes pay a bit of attention to these things where they observe the anniversaries.

Ayuo: Do you feel that it's really a record to celebrate?

PH: I think so, yes. Yes, I think so. Well—still, as you were saying in the car—it's always the newest one, the one that you like. I mean, if that's not there and if you're not excited, I mean the excitement is obviously different now for me. I mean, it's not the same thing as first going into a studio and just getting a record for the first time.

I mean, you can never repeat that. But unless you're still excited and positive about music, well, there's no point in doing it, really. And I still, I love doing it and I'm maybe obsessive about it, you know, work with it all the time.

But, you know, it's still there.

Ayuo: Did you say *The Fall of the House of Usher* is finished?

PH: The writing is finished. But now, the arrangement... and we have to persuade somebody that it is a good business venture because to put it on will be a very big, much bigger thing than what I could manage alone.

But it's close.

Having been going for 15 or 16 years, you know, now... it could be a year and it could be out, which would be very exciting.

Ayuo: So you have many exciting plans now?

PH: Yeah, oh yes, always.

Yeah. Lots of things to do.

Figure 15   Photo of Peter Hammill and Ayuo in 2010. Peter and I have remained friends since then. Photograph by Masahiko Miyazaki.

Figure 16   Peter Hammill, Ayuo, and David Lord.

Twenty

Completion of the album, *Nova Carmina*/ Seeing Steve Marriott live

I decided that the title of the album would be *Nova Carmina* before we began the mix. The mix was done very quickly. Dave Mattacks had already mixed his sound on the computer mixing board, and we applied all the effects as we recorded—so all we had to do was to balance them out. Most of the songs were mixed in two hours, and the mixing was finished in two and a half days. I walked around Bath listening to the finished mix on a cassette on my Walkman.

This was much faster than any recording I had done in Japan. In Japan, people at record companies had spread the rumor that I was very slow; they were not talking about the recording process. The problem was in trying to communicate my ideas to the staff.

Because many people in Japan talk in a roundabout way, people said that I could not understand what my fellow musicians, the engineer, and the staff at MIDI Records were trying to communicate to me. People didn't understand the sounds I wanted either. When I spoke directly, other people would make strange interpretations. A musician told me that when I walked out of the room, someone would say that Ayuo says *this*, but I think he meant *that*, doing something which was the opposite of what I requested. I don't speak in the roundabout way that many Japanese do, but this meant that trying to get my thoughts across without being misunderstood was going to take hours. This was very frustrating. The musicians I walked with in England were mostly people that I had always respected from the time when I was in junior high school. I had always wanted their sound; I no longer had to explain what I wanted.

The day after we finished, Andy Partridge from XTC came to mix a 12" single. He told us that the world-famous American musician/producer, Todd Rundgren, had produced the XTC album, but they had disagreements halfway through the recording, so they decided to release a 12" single with a song they had recorded on the A side and a mix of Andy's original demo tape that he had recorded at home on the B side. The original demo tape was a 4-track cassette tape.

I had about a week from the time I got back to London from Bath, until my flight back to New York.

I went to see Steve Marriott—formerly of Humble Pie and the Small Faces—live in a small pub in north London. He was playing pub gigs all year round at this time. The band was Steve Marriott and the Pack of Three. The venue was an ordinary London pub with a stage and PA system. Steve Marriott played songs from Small Faces, Humble Pie hits, and some old favorites. His blues vocals were as powerful as ever. His power had not diminished at all. The crowd was mostly local and was mainly drunk.

A middle-aged fat English lady was laughing and dancing with some Indian or Pakistani guy. The atmosphere was one of drinking and enjoying old songs. I was enjoying myself too, but in my mind, I thought back to the days when he used to play in front of 20,000 people at Madison Square Garden when I was in my mid-teens. That had only been about twelve years ago, and yet he was already considered an oldies entertainer, even though his music was as good as ever. That made me sad.

Then there is the theatre. I've always felt that London is the best place to see a theatre play. I went to see Shakespeare, Renaissance plays, and Chekhov's *Three Sisters*. I hear it's very competitive to start a play production in this city, but that's why it's so hard to find such high quality anywhere else.

When I arrived in New York, Martin picked me up alone at the airport. I spent a few days with him. I also contacted Ken Awazu. While I was having dinner with him, I asked him about his father Kiyoshi Awazu's designs and the opening title sequence he made for many of Hiroshi Teshigahara's films, such as *The Man Without a Map* and *The Face of Another*, one of my all-time favorite films. I asked if there was any chance that his father might do the jacket artwork for me if I asked him.

"I'm sure it wouldn't be a problem," he said.

I went back to Japan at the end of September, and one of the first things I did was to ask Kiyoshi Awazu to do the jacket for *Nova Carmina*, and he agreed.

Twenty-One

Prolific creation in neurotic states

Nova Carmina turned out to be a lot better than I expected. I was able to record it in an environment that I had longed for, with musicians that I had admired. It seemed like a miracle that I could do this. It was also my first trip to England by myself, and I recorded it amid so many good encounters. Rarely does something like that happen. But when I returned to Japan from England, trouble was waiting for me.

First of all, the pressing machine at the JVC factory broke down several times as they were trying to press this album. No one knew what was wrong. Usually, when we release an album, we press the sample disc one month before the release and distribute it to magazines and writers. It was already too late to properly promote this album. The sample disc was not ready until a few days before the release date. Someone at the record company half-jokingly told me that maybe I was cursed. This made me feel worried and depressed. Things went so well during the recording, but now I was facing unexpected difficulties.

In the UK, no one knew anything about me, so I was able to meet people with a completely blank slate. However, when I came back to Japan, I had to face communication problems and misconceptions about myself again. To make matters worse, I had been speaking almost exclusively in English for about three months, so my way of thinking had become English, and it had become awkward to speak Japanese for the things I wanted to say. As a result, I was no longer able to articulate myself clearly enough to be understood.

In addition, the MIDI promoters had begun to lose interest in promoting my music. Mr. Miyata told me, "The promoters don't want to talk to you because they don't know how to communicate with you. I think the only type of people you can talk to in this country are university graduate students in philosophy. I am a graduate student in linguistics, so I personally find your conversation to be interesting, but not many others will feel the same, especially not rock musicians because many tend to hate school and the elite."

At a meeting, I asked Mr. Miyata why he signed a record contract with me.

'We wanted to give the label an academic image, regardless of what *Ayuo* is really about. And I think we succeeded in doing that. And I'm grateful to you for that."

Another MIDI executive had this to say:

"Do you know why we wanted to release an album by Ayuo record instead of by Yuji Takahashi? It's because Ayuo's music is less esoteric and seems to have more general appeal. It's just that we haven't figured out how to sell it yet."

However, I felt that the contract I signed 'to give an academic image' and the misunderstandings that developed from that gave rise to the image of me as a difficult person.

After *Nova Carmina* came out, one critic from the magazine *Rockin' On* said: "The music on this album sounds like it is by a second-generation Japanese-American asserting his identity."

I think it is because my feelings and the way I express things are not Japanese. I understood clearly that the most difficult thing for people to understand is about those who have the same face on the surface as you but were brought up in a completely different culture.

Around this time, a French DJ was living in Japan who came to some of the concerts I played. Her job was to introduce Japanese pop and rock to a European audience. She told my friend: "Ayuo will have a hard time. His music is not Japanese, but it's not German or white American either. So, this makes it hard to be understood by the Japanese, and hard to be understood by the Europeans at the same time. It is of his own culture."

I became neurotic. However, I was able to write songs and poems, one after another, in this state. It may be different for some people, but I can write a piece of work by taking anger and sadness as a source of energy and transforming them. Of course, not everything I write in this state is good, but the message I want to convey is clear, and the emotion comes through.

For instance, when you listen to Joni Mitchell's *Blue* or *For the Roses,* it reveals that she composed these compositions while in such a condition. A sense of calm washes over you whenever you listen to music that expresses emotions similar to your own. It's as if someone told you that you are not alone in your feelings.

For me, Joni Mitchell's *Blue* is healing music. So were *Clouds*, *Hejira*, and *Shadows and Light*.

Lou Reed's *Berlin* was healing music to me as well in the same way.

In a different way, Grateful Dead's live recordings of "Dark Star" also work as healing music. Grateful Dead's performance of "Dark Star" in the late 1960s and early '70s centered around long improvisations, and the performance of each evening was distinct from the one that came before. I feel a sense of security while listening to this because it is possible to perceive that individuals can profoundly communicate with one another through their music, even in a world where few rules exist.

People won't come near you when you look like you're feeling down, however. I just kept writing one song after another. From around October 1986 to the spring of 1987, I wrote the suite of songs *E no Naka no Sugata* (What We Look Like In The Picture); "Kimi ni Narareta," later recorded as "Wrong Footed" for *Songs from a Eurasian Journey*; "Evolving" and "Standing at the Edge," which I later recorded for *Earth Guitar*, and "A Song to a Fallen Blossom" and "They Sat on Two Bamboo Stools Gazing at the Moon and Its Reflection in the Lake," which I recorded for Kazue Sawai's CD *Eye to Eye* in 1987.

For the first song in *E no Naka no Sugata*, "When I was Eight," I wrote the words and melody at the same time in the middle of the night, over a repeating arpeggio pattern of notes. Considerable emotional depth was infused into each note, approaching it as if it were a spiritually moving prayer. Even when I listen to the song today, its potency is still perceptible to me. This piece of music is not influenced by any particular compositional technique. However, such songwriting left me emotionally drained. This is due to its similarity to the method of releasing *chi* (the Chinese term for spiritual power) or a supernatural incantation into an object or a stone.

In addition to these compositions, I also wrote a song called "Dancing at Ease in Spring." There are two versions of this song. The version I did with a rock band is available on an album called *Blue Eyes, Black Hair*, which is now on Bandcamp. The other one is a suite of compositions for the Shinobue flute and percussion which was recorded on the CD *DUEL* by Tosha Suiho and Sumire Yoshihara, released by Sony in 1988.

Not all of the songs I wrote back then are good. Certain tracks contain lyrics that are so neurotic that I am unable to listen to them because the lyrics reveal too much of my neurosis. For instance, I included "We Will Be Together Again" and "A Letter in Song" on the *Private Tapes* compilation of demo tapes, but I wouldn't want to record them today. Initially, I had the intention of releasing all these tracks on a single CD as my next solo album. A major label album production cost between two and three million yen at the time, and I couldn't find any company to finance this album's production.

The order of the songs on the solo album that I couldn't make at the time was as follows:

1. Song of Songs
2. Kimi ni Narareta (Wrong Footed)
3. Evolving
4. Photographs
5. They Sat on Two Bamboo Stools Gazing at the Moon and Its Reflection in the Lake
6. Standing at the Edge
7. Dancing at Ease in Spring
8. Song to a Fallen Blossom

Twenty-Two

1987, Producing Kazue Sawai's album, *Eye to Eye*/David Lord/Hiromi Ota/Peter Hammill/Guy Evans/Sara Jane Morris/James Warren

Around that time in 1986, Yoh Hirai, the then-manager of *koto* player Kazue Sawai, asked me if I would produce her next CD. Mr. Hirai had been listening to my music since the time of *Silent Film* and was thinking of having me work with some of the performers he was managing, which included Kazue Sawai on *koto* and Sumire Yoshihara on percussion.

This recording was released with the title *Eye to Eye*. At first, I was going to record just my song "Eye to Eye," which was originally commissioned and composed for her, and the *koto* and vocal version of the suite *E no Naka no Sugata* (What We Look Like in the Picture), but then I decided to record some of the songs I was preparing for my next solo CD. They were from a series of songs I was preparing, based on the Chinese novel *Dreams of a Red Mansion*. This included "Song to a Fallen Blossom" and "They Sat on Two Bamboo Stools Gazing at the Moon and Its Reflection in the Lake."

Kazue Sawai had heard *Nova Carmina* and liked its sound, so she suggested that we record and produce the album in the same studio, and with the same engineer as this album. That was how I was able to record at David Lord's studio again.

The recording took place in August 1987. Again, the recording went smoothly and took only about five days.

On the first day, we had a meeting and rehearsed the material, confirming the songs to be recorded. At the same time, David was preparing the studio for the recording. That night, the first song, "Across the Bridge," was recorded solo by Kazue Sawai on a 2-track digital recorder, after the effects were decided. At that time, digital recording was still rare and expensive.

On the second day, we recorded the three songs from *E no Naka no Sugata*,[1] recording Hiromi Ota's vocals and Sawai's *koto* at the same time. We recorded them on a two-track digital recorder after deciding on the effects, then determined the best take after several performances. In the evening, we recorded "Eye to Eye" on a 24-track analog recorder, using the new Dolby system for noise reduction. I used David's Prophet 2000 synth to add some octaves and pads. First, Hiromi Ota sang and Sawai played; then, Hiromi Ota and I added background vocals. Finally, David and I added effects to each sound.

On the third day, we recorded the 14-minute song "A Song to a Fallen Blossom" with Peter Hammill, Guy Evans (the Van der Graaf Generator drummer), and Sarah Jane Morris, a female singer who Peter recommended; this was recorded on a 24-track analog recorder. This was completed in one day, which is very fast for a multi-track band recording. I played electric lead guitar, back vocals, and Prophet 2000 on this track.

In the evening, James Warren, who lived nearby, came over and recorded some backing vocals. James Warren was a member of Stackridge in the '70s—a band whose albums I had since I was in junior high school. In the '80s, he had a band called Korgis and they had some hits in the UK. Many years later, in 1999, I went to a Stackridge reunion show and James introduced me to the band's new keyboard player. The keyboard player told me he was a fan of Keiji Haino and Fushitsusha.

'It's a small world,' I thought.

On day four, we started with a solo seventeen-string *koto* piece—"A Letter from A Stranger's Childhood," composed by Robin Williamson, formerly of the Incredible String Band. I had come across the albums of The Incredible String Band at my first guitar

---

[1] I translated the title of *E no Naka no Sugata*, three times because I was never satisfied with the translation since languages have different nuances. It is called "A Painting of You and I" on the Tzadik album *Red Moon*, "A Picture of You and I" on Kazue Sawai's album *Eye to Eye*, and my own album *E no Naka no Sugata*. It is the same composition. The title "What We Look Like in the Picture" refers to this composition.

teacher's house back in 1968. In 1967, their album *The Hangman's Daughter* reached number five on the UK album charts.

It is said that their unique psychedelic sound using traditional Indian, Middle Eastern, and Chinese instruments had a great influence on The Beatles, The Rolling Stones, and Led Zeppelin. In their sound, you can hear a fascinating part of the hippie culture; this sound later came to be known as 'acid folk.' Much of the work I came to do in the 80s and 90s as 'World Music' was more influenced by this kind of approach that I heard when I was a child, rather than what I would hear when the term 'World Music' became fashionable.

Robin Williamson later wrote and published his autobiography. In it, he described how—in the late '50s and early '60s—people who had read Jack Kerouac's *On the Road* had created numerous beatnik communities in areas from Scotland to France, where they had apartments to stay wherever they went. People like him who desired to live a new style of life banded together and formed communities where they could travel and discuss new ideas on their own. He joined them and learned a lot.

Both men and women took on this journey; there, they became lovers, wrote poetry, and continued their journeys. It was a community where people made friends and trusted each other. Some of these people crossed the English Channel and then traveled from Spain to Morocco. There, they found new instruments and were influenced by *Sufi*-inspired dances. So far, this seems quite romantic and idealistic. A part of me wishes I could have participated in it, but I believe that such a life would not be sustainable.

This kind of Beatnik community life was followed by the hippie community in the sixties, and then the commune. Stuart Gordon, who used to work at Crescent Studios in his free time, later told me that he was a member of the Incredible String Band commune in the late 60s and it was a painful experience. The commune became a place where free sex and drugs took center stage, and then it became a place to practice a new religion. They would all get up at 6 am and start the day with some exercises that they learned from who knows where. There was no privacy, and the men and women were all sleeping with each other. In this situation, people started to hurt one another and the people around them. No one knew which person belonged with whom. As a result of this process, they all eventually joined Scientology to try to clean up their lives.

Ever since I was a young child, I wondered what kind of person Robin Williamson was; when he came to the studio, I felt that he was still a very charismatic man. The way he spoke and moved was also full of charm. He brought Kazue Sawai a bell as a gift.

I've seen leaders of political groups, religious groups, cults, and both rock stars and classical star pianists exude a unique charisma. That's why people follow them. People who have this special kind of charisma are often not aware of their distinct allure. For example, I felt that my father began to emanate a certain magnetism when he returned to Japan in the early 70s.

Robin Williamson mainly became a harpist in the '70s and '80s, rediscovering traditional Celtic music. He researched, restored, and performed old Scottish harp tunes, recording, and releasing CDs of them. He also edited several books of Celtic music tunes—I had one of these. Some of his harp pieces had a Japanese or East Asian sound.

Figure 17   Live performance in 1989. Photo by Masashi Kuwamoto.

As a result, I wondered what he would write if he composed a work for the Japanese *koto*. Before the recording, I was surprised to receive a score that was written in 5-line notation. I asked him if he wrote this himself. He replied that he had written down a rough copy himself but asked someone to transcribe it properly for him.

This work, *A Letter from A Stranger's Childhood*, is still being performed by Kazue Sawai, and is part of the repertoire in the *Sawai Sokyoku-in* (Sawai Koto Academy of Music).

The next composition we recorded was a traditional composition for *koto* titled *Midare*. I asked David Lord to do an electronic mix for this song, and we both sat at the mixing desk and experimented with different sounds before mixing it down. It was fun.

At night, we recorded "They Sat on Two Bamboo Stools Gazing at the Moon and Its Reflection in the Lake." Peter Hammill brought two women from his neighborhood to read the two cousins' parts from *A Dream of Red Mansions*. They were sisters who both attended local poetry readings. The text was translated into very beautiful English and sounded like Shakespeare's poems. We first recorded the sisters reading the text; then, we recorded the main melody I composed and asked Kazue Sawai to improvise to the images conveyed in the text. She did this very well, despite not understanding English that well. Then, I played with some samples from the Adagio of Mahler's *Symphony No. 4* on David Lord's Prophet 2000, adding a Pink Floyd-esque keyboard pad thinly behind it. This sound came from David toying around with the keyboard. The bell-like sound at the end of the song was added with the Prophet 2000—this was David's idea, too. Peter Hammill also stayed throughout the recording, giving us some advice and chatting with us, making us all feel comfortable.

This was the end of the recording period. The next day, we started mixing everything, and it only took a day and a half. This was because we had already done most of the mixing and effects while recording and David had a computerized mixing desk. The SSL was one of the first of its kind. It was incredibly fast. Everyone involved in the making of this CD—Hiromi Ota, Peter Hammill, David Lord, Kazue Sawai, and myself—thought it turned out great, but this CD wasn't much talked about.

Critics in magazines once again accused me of looking at traditional Japanese music from the viewpoint of a foreigner, or a Japanese-American.

Figure 18   Hiromi Ota, David Lord, Kazue Sawai, and Ayuo.

Twenty-Three

The Hungerford massacre/
J. G. Ballard

The Hungerford massacre occurred on the road between Bath and Heathrow Airport in London, the day we started mixing Sawai's album. This is the road that most people use to go to Bath—where David Lord's studio was located. A 27-year-old man shot and killed 16 people, including a police officer and his own mother, before killing himself. The perpetrator was a local citizen, born and raised there; he was seen as very quiet, and sometimes the victim of gossip. He had no criminal convictions nor a record of medical problems. No motive for the killings was ever established.

The novelist, J. G. Ballard wrote the short novella *Running Wild* immediately afterward because he felt that the world would start to see more of these types of mass shootings. He was right. Until then, such 'spree killings' had been rare. After this, the world was witness to the Columbine shooting, the Las Vegas mass shooting, and many other tragic incidents.

J. G. Ballard became one of my favorite novelists because I felt he depicted human psychology with incredible accuracy. J. G. Ballard was born in Shanghai in 1930. He was just a child when the Japanese Imperial Army occupied Shanghai and began a war of invasion up the Yangtse River. As a result, he and his family were sent to an internment camp established by the Japanese Army—a prison for European and American citizens who were residents in Shanghai. This was where he grew up until the end of the war in 1945. In 1945, the Japanese Imperial Army ordered that all the Europeans and Americans there were to be killed before the army left China because they did not want to leave evidence of having imprisoned them. The Japanese Imperial Army had killed all inmates at the notorious Unit

731, a covert biological and chemical warfare research facility that conducted human experiments on the scale of Auschwitz, to hide its existence. However, at the camp where Ballard's family was interned, the Japanese commander decided to disobey his order and released all the prisoners before they could be killed. Many people in Japan were not aware of all the brutal crimes committed by the Japanese Imperial Army during the Pacific War until left-wing journalists started to investigate and reveal them after the war ended.

The things that happen to you between the ages of 10 and 15 have a lasting impact on your life. Ballard said in an interview:[1]

> I don't think you can go through the experience of war without one's perceptions of the world being forever changed. The reassuring stage-set that everyday reality in the suburban West presents to us is torn down; you see the ragged scaffolding, and then you see the truth beyond that, and it can be a frightening experience.

Ballard continued to depict this aspect of human psychology throughout his life. J. G. Ballard influenced a whole generation of people including many musicians. Joy Division, Siouxsie and the Banshees, Trevor Horn (Yes), Gary Numan to Madonna have acknowledged his influence.

His novel *Crash* was based on a childhood friend who tried to escape the camp and was caught and beaten. Ballard used to play hide and seek with him when they were children. When his friend grew up and returned to London, he would race down the street in his car, and once hit a car with two Japanese stewardesses. His memories of the beatings he received would suddenly surge up. Then one night, he collided into a car with a cellist returning home after a concert; the cellist was killed by accident. The court found that he was traumatized by his childhood experiences in the internment camp, and he was sent to a mental institution.

My favorite novel by Ballard is *Super-Cannes*, an imaginary ideal utopian community on the surface near Cannes in France, in which the psychiatrist prescribes violence as a cure for stress. Arab immigrant laborers are assigned to the community, not only to do work but also to be subjected to discrimination and torture.

---

[1]The quote from J. G. Ballard is from this interview: Livingstone, D. B. (1996?) "J. G. Ballard: Crash: Prophet with Honour" https://spikemagazine.com/0899ballard/

As part of my work, I also strive to reveal the reality of human behavior. Living in Japan showed me this aspect of human psychology, not just because of Japanese culture, but because it exists below the polite suburban culture around the world.

This is the reason why I chose a part of the semi-autobiographical novel by Jerzy Kosiński, *The Painted Bird*, as an inspiration for my chamber ensemble work in 2023. Even though I was never interned and beaten at a Japanese camp, I can identify and understand what he is depicting.

I have always admired lyrics that depict the human condition and psychology with honesty. This is why I admire Peter Hammill and Ray Davies's lyrics. On the Van der Graaf song "Man-Erg," Peter Hammill sings:

> *And I too, live inside me, and very often don't know who I am,*
> *I know I'm not a hero, but I hope that I'm not damned,*
> *I'm just a man, and killers, angels; all are these,*
> *Dictators, saviours, refugees in war and peace;*
> *As long as Man lives...*

I feel that this is more powerful than just singing about love and peace; this insight would help the people of the world to understand one another.

Christian Bale—the actor who portrayed J. G. Ballard as a child in the semi-autobiographical film, *Empire of the Sun*—later played the role of an American mortician in Nanjing. The narrative focused on the Nanjing massacre in 1937. This film, *The Flowers of War*, was a huge hit in China.

Twenty-Four

From 1990 to now

If the best time of my life so far was the period of my life in New York from 1966 to 1975, the next best time for me was from the 1990s onward, especially after having a child of my own.

The main difference between before and after the 1990s is that I began to meet people with whom I could work together and perform in Japan. Perhaps the fact that 'World Music' was becoming a respected genre had something to do with it as well. People began to ask me to make 'exotic' sounds. I was not interested in exoticism; it is similar to categorizing Japanese culture as 'Fujiyama, Geisha, Harakiri.' It's like identifying a culture based on its most superficial aspects. Many people did not understand why I was studying Iranian or medieval European music, but at least I was getting some jobs.

The following is a brief list of some people that I began working with from this period onward:

Suzuki Cohji (Cohjizukin), Jadranka Stojakovic, Akinobu Imai, Moco Matsumoto, Mai Yamane, Epo, Yoko Ueno, Takuya Nishimura, Shuichi Chino, Natsuaki Fuyuharu, Takako Takase, Emi Shirasaki, Maha, Akiko Takada, Chizuko Miura, Torsten Rush. Danny Thompson, Clive Deemer, Wataru Okuma, Joji Sawada, Keisuke Ota, Hoppy Kamiyama, Yae, Zabadak, Bice, Toshiki Sawada, Yoshie, Junzo Tateiwa, Makiko Sakurai, Sara Yoko Benito, Shintaro Asizawa, Yoichi Okabe.

When I met Clive Deamer, he was the drummer for Portishead and Roni Size. He was a jazz drummer living in Bath, England who was interested in various world percussion styles, including the Middle Eastern style of Turkish *darbuka*. He said that his studies of Chinese

Tai Chi helped him perform in the faster drum and bass (DnB) style, and in the 2000s he joined and co-produced Strange Sensations, the band of former Led Zeppelin singer Robert Plant. Listening to Plant's work from the '00s makes it clear why he needed Deamer. He can play percussion from all parts of the world, as well as play jazz and strong rock drums. On my album *Earth Guitar* released in 2000, Clive plays on "Standing at the Edge," which is one of my favorite rock tracks that I have ever recorded. Later in the '00s, he would become the touring drummer for Radiohead. He plays in many of their videos, such as those in the DVD *The King of Limbs/Live From The Basement.*

Figure 19   1997. Photo with Danny Thompson (left) and Dave Mattacks (center) at Crescent Studios.

The first time I met Danny Thompson was when he came to Japan to play a show with Richard Thompson, and we went out for Thai food together. He was known for his British traditional folk band, The Pentangle, from the '60s and was the one-time lover of Sandy Denny of Fairport Convention. Sandy Denny's classic "Who Knows Where the Time Goes" was a song about him during their romance. This was also one of my favorite songs from grade school. It became a worldwide hit as the title track of the album Judy Collins made with Stephen Stills of Crosby, Stills, Nash and Young (CSNY).

Danny plays a unique bass that no one else can. Musicians like Peter Gabriel, Kate Bush, T Rex, Nick Drake, Rod Stewart, Donovan, Marianne Faithfull, Tim Buckley, Loreena McKennitt, The Incredible String Band, and Savourna Stevenson have all asked him to play—and when you hear him, you can see why people seek him out. It's one of my proudest achievements to be able to do a jam session with him and Dave Mattacks and release it on CD. He included my *Songs from a Eurasian Journey* in his discography as well.

There were no musicians of this level in Japan at the time.

Musicians and people like Carlos Alomar, who performed on my album *Silent Film* in the '80s, taught me what a real musician is. Carlos Alomar was James Brown's guitarist, before working with David Bowie from the mid '70s to the late '80s as his band leader, arranger, and songwriting collaborator. He, too, has tremendous expressiveness and skill. Behind every charismatic musician is an excellent supporter—this is what makes the concepts that the singer is envisioning come to life.

I started doing more live performances in the 1990s. There was a time when I was constantly performing, and the albums I released after the mid-90s were the first time I became satisfied with many of my recordings. I created more works in this period than at any other time in my life, many of which are now available on ayuo.bandcamp. com.

The president and the former managing director of MIDI Records began to come to my concerts. It turned out that I was one of the few early artists of that label who never took out a lawsuit against MIDI Records and its publishing company because of contractual issues. In contrast, artists such as Ryuichi Sakamoto and Epo both had problems with their contracts.

Hiroshi Okura, the founder of MIDI, told me that he always wanted to hear what the next album after *Nova Carmina* would be like. He gave me a recording budget that was twice as high as *Nova Carmina* and asked me to make an album in England. Hiroshi Okura said that when he first started out working for a record company, he was assigned to promote The Pentangle and Fairport Convention; he always liked British traditional folk, he told me, and was listening to my albums recently. I accepted his offer and made *Earth Guitar*, which was released in 2000—14 years after *Nova Carmina*. It is these two albums that I like the most out of all my releases from MIDI.[1]

When I went to England again, I was much inspired by watching Peter Hammill's work in the '90s. He had told me, when I first met him in 1986, that he started to buy recording equipment in the '70s when he began making solo albums so that he could be prepared for the day when record companies could no longer give him a recording budget to rent a studio. By the late '90s, he was recording, mixing, mastering, and sending his recordings out to pressing factories on his own, and they sounded as good as all his previous albums, recorded and mixed by some of the best professional recording engineers of the day.

I was also introduced to John Anthony at this time, who had produced many of the early albums of Van der Graaf, Genesis, Peter Hammill, and Queen.

If I was going to continue to work in music, I had to learn to record and mix on my own.

Technology has gotten so much better since the '80s that today it's become possible to make relatively good recordings at home with computer software and distribute them yourself either in person or online. The process of promoting them has changed.

In the 80s, you still had to rely on newspapers, television, radio, and magazines; today, social media, and having friends and supporters on the social network will help you with your work.

I got married to Yuki Yanagihara in the mid-90s and remained married until 2007. We had a daughter together. Raising a child was a wonderful experience in my life.

When Peter Hammill came to Japan in 2003, I told him: "My child is learning new things every day."

He said, "That means you're learning new things every day."

There is so much we can learn from our children. Watching them teaches you a lot about yourself and what it means to be human. You might also be able to turn your life around by having children.

---

[1]Some songs, however, I prefer the versions I uploaded to ayuo.bandcamp.com. I like "A Language You Can No Longer Speak" on the Bandcamp album *Ambient Guitar* more than "Different Languages" on *Earth Guitar*.

In the 90s, things changed. Even though we are now divorced, I have nothing but admiration for how my ex-wife was able to hold up our family. She became my interpreter and my translator in Japanese. I learned a lot during this time. Living with a Japanese partner meant that—at last—I could learn more about its culture. We often had guests for dinner, and we went to see concerts and movies with friends. We spoke in Japanese all the time, so my language ability improved exponentially like never before.

Word processors and computers enabled me to start to write in Japanese. In the '80s, I only knew a part of the language. I knew *hiragana* and *katakana*, but not much of *kanji* (Chinese characters). I didn't know the grammar of the language either. The editors in the '80s would treat me to a meal, then rewrite my primitive Japanese into something usable for print. In the '90s, computers became cheaper, and it became possible to make home recordings that were often as good as studio recordings—many of them were published on Bandcamp in later years.

I met Yuki Yanagihara while she was working as an assistant producer for a theater production company. When the production company went bankrupt, she started work at another company that promoted events such as the Fuji Rock Festival. My ex-wife knew that I had problems being accepted in Japan, but I don't think she knew to what extent this was. She insisted that I just keep working on my music, and said that if I tried to get a regular job amongst the Japanese, they would probably beat me up.

I once showed her a book of short stories written by a Japanese-American woman. My ex-wife said that most Japanese would laugh at her photo on the cover jacket because she is wearing the Japanese *kimono* all wrong. These are the kind of things that will make the Japanese make fun of the Japanese-Americans and those raised abroad, she said.

I began teaching at a music college. Since East Asians still have the tradition of 'master and disciple,' it is not too difficult to teach once you get the hang of it. I learned not to do the kind of discussions and debates I did when I was at school in the United States—I adapted. More work came for me as a journalist, since my Japanese improved considerably. My ex-wife and editors were willing to rewrite my Japanese or translate my English into Japanese.

There were now fewer misunderstandings. I met music journalists, who helped promote my albums and concerts. One journalist, Tetsuya Uchida, was especially helpful; he had been writing articles about 'world music'—especially European music from Greece, the Balkans, Ireland, Scotland, Steeleye Span, Fairport Convention. One day, I noticed in a magazine that he interviewed Dave Mattacks and included comments about my album *Nova Carmina*. Tetsuya Uchida also wrote about psychedelic and progressive rock music. Other writers, who did not write well about me in the '80s, started to write more understanding articles about my music.

I saw that the 'World Music' movement encouraged individuals to be more open-minded and tolerant of diverse cultures. Until then, both popular and serious classical music were influenced by major trends. In the '60s, there was folk, folk-rock, and psychedelic; in the '70s, progressive rock, fusion, disco, and punk; in the '80s, techno, neo-romantic pop, and new wave. In 'serious' music, there was serial music, cluster music, minimal music, neo-romanticism, and Western music influenced by Asian and African traditional music. Western rock itself was not popular in Japan; instead, popular music in Japan at the time was Western trends superimposed over *enka* and *kayokyoku* customs. People were encouraged to join major trends and movements.

World Music trends also somewhat influenced social behavior. People became willing to explore other rhythms and expressions from other cultures.

In the early 2000s, Maddy Prior and the Carnival Band came to Japan to perform at a classical music festival. The Carnival Band essentially plays arrangements of early music, including John Dowland and Henry Purcell. Their repertoire focuses on popular music from the 16th and 17th centuries, in the spirit of medieval and renaissance Carnival.

I interviewed them for the Classical and Jazz music magazine *Intoxicate*. A few years before this, I was surprised to see my album *Nova Carmina* in Maddy Prior's profile, so I asked her about it, and she said that it was the first time that she had sung early music. I said that I thought she had sung early music before that because she sang "Gaudete" in Latin with Steeleye Span, and it was a hit in 1973. She said that the *Carmina Burana* song, "Axe Phoebus Aureo" was difficult to learn—since she does not read 5-staff notation, she had the violinist, Peter Knight, play the melody until she could memorize it.

During the interview, we talked about how the genre, World Music was being perceived in England and Japan. Shortly before this interview, I had talked to a musician in Fanfare Ciocărlia, a twelve-piece Romani Balkan brass band from a northeastern Romanian village. He told me that what he really wanted to do was to play jazz, but to tour different countries, he had to play Balkan brass music. I also knew an African guitarist, who wanted to play like Santana, but picked up the *Kora* to improvise in his own style and started to dress in traditional African clothes. This way, he would be invited as an African musician.

Then, I talked about a Japanese jazz/rock musician friend, who played in England at a world music festival in front of an audience who was expecting more traditional Japanese music.

(Excerpts from the interview)

Maddy Prior: If you booked a Japanese group, you'd expect them to be playing Japanese music.

Ayuo: Whereas in reality, it's a bit more complex. 150 years ago or so, when Japan opened up to the West, a lot of Irish and Scottish songs were taken in and translated into Japanese of that time. And because they're pentatonic, and in the old Japanese of that time period, people think that they're traditional Japanese songs. But they would be most often famous Irish songs. Like there's a song called "Last Rose of Summer" that's translated as "*Niwa no Chigusa*."[2]

Maddy: That's quite an interesting idea, isn't it, but I suppose it's the same as what we were saying about the carols. A lot of them are French tunes or different tunes, but we think of them as English folk carols, as English, but then we think of Christianity as being English, really, you know what I mean? When something has been there all your life, it is yours, it's your culture. You don't kind of question go around saying, is that really English? You just don't do that, You just say, oh, "Ding Dong Merrily on High" is English.

I think this quote from Maddy, "When something has been there all your life, it is yours, it's your culture," is very important.

---

[2]I recorded this song on *Red Moon* and released it on Tzadik Records, as Ayuo/Ohta Hiromi.

The language you grow up with, the culture you grow up with, is your culture and will remain so for the rest of your life.

After my ex-wife and I divorced, I lived with my daughter only on the weekdays, because my ex-wife felt that changing schools suddenly as well as her living environment would not be good for her. I enjoyed living with her: I would make breakfast, see her off to school, and later we would go out for dinner, or I would make something simple like spaghetti and then check her homework.

Figure 20   Ayuo and his daughter, Lisa.

Living with my daughter reminded me of my childhood. However, I knew that she would need her mother to be raised properly. Both my ex-wife's father and brother died suddenly and unexpectedly, and my ex-wife had to take care of her mother, who was now alone.[3] As a result, my ex-wife had to return to her family's house. Her family had a better house and lived in a better environment. She later remarried and became a stay-at-home housewife, giving her more time to take care of her family and my daughter and enjoy life.

---
[3] Her mother would eventually die of dementia.

My daughter would get to live a better life and receive a better education. She would get the education that I never had.

I believe that having a child at a stable age is vital. As you get older, there are certain things you learn from experience. It's too early to get married in your early 20s.

When I was in my teens, I met a woman who used to be Haruomi Hosono's manager and YMO's coordinator and later became a palm reader. She told me: "You will have a child someday, and unlike your parents, you will take care of your child very much."

I think it is the duty of the previous generation to think about how the next generation can live properly. In traditional society, children were educated by their parents to be able to live in society; or in the case of craftsmen, they would learn the necessary skills, so that the next generation could become their successors.

When I was born, my parents were in their early twenties. They were too young. My father was 21 years old when he realized that I was going to be born. It was an accident, and my parents were not prepared. They still wanted to have a life of their own before settling down.

In fact, I was lucky to be born. My mother had at least 4 or 5 abortions after my birth because my father and mother didn't want a family. My mother finally had a birth control ring inserted to prevent pregnancy. But years later, this ring caused an infection, and she had to have an operation, after which she lost the ability to get pregnant.

I wanted to be different, for my child.

The generation born before and after World War II was a generation of rebels, as exemplified by the 1950s film *Rebel Without a Cause* with James Dean. They wanted to "change society," with slogans like: "I don't believe in the system;" "I want to change the world;" "I want to liberate the people from old conservative ideas."

"Revolution!" These ideas were seen as progressive.

But what will the next generation do, when they look at all the things that have been destroyed? There must be an example for the next generation to follow. You can't tell them to start everything over because what their parents, grandparents, and ancestors learned was all wrong. I used to refer to my works as "Neo Trad" in the early '90s because I was yearning for a new "tradition."

I hated the period from the late '70s to most of the '80s. Disco, fusion, techno, and romantic pop became the main trend. People stopped using music, literature, and the arts to question humanity and seek answers about philosophy and psychology. Hippies turned into yuppies. Psychedelic Rock, Progressive Rock, and experimental avant-garde music went underground, except for the few that had become established. The few who became established became either more conservative or pop in commercial music. Joni Mitchell once said that the '80s were a cold age. It was about making money.

I was also very isolated. I had no family. My father and stepmother asked me to leave home and live alone without going to school.

I often wondered why my father did not play much of a father figure when I was a child. I later learned that my father did not get along with his father. His father—my grandfather—kicked him out of his home when he was in his teens. I do not know the reasons why.

If you did not have a father figure when growing up as a son, you don't have the experience of how a father figure can raise a son.

However, this might not be all. Sometimes when I would ask my aunt about my father, she would tell me that Japanese men don't do things that way. Since I was raised by an Iranian stepfather, and not a Japanese father before I was 15 years old, I wouldn't know what traditional Japanese fathers are like. I simply don't have that experience.

"What We Look Like in the Picture," as well as "Annabel Lee" (based on Poe's poem) were my fantasies about the old life—a fantasy of a traditional old-fashioned town. Yet, I also knew that this kind of dream was just an illusion. There was a reason for me to seek out traditional music and literature in the late 1980s and 1990s. What can we pass on to future generations? What kind of future society do we want for our children and our children's children?

The birth of my child triggered my interest in life science, genetic science, physics, and so on. And I began to think about them together with philosophical thought, which I had been interested in for a long time. I read Jung and Freud again and discovered Slavoj Žižek, Jacques Lacan, and Jared Diamond. I also came into contact with the scientific papers of Michio Kaku, Lynn Margulis, Dorion Sagan, Matt Ridley, and Keiko Nakamura.

I composed the following dialog, "What is life?," for an improvisational work that would be performed alongside the reading.

It is a conversation between a father and his child.

What is life?

A: Please tell me, what is a human being?

B: What do you mean, my sweety?

A: What are we made of? Why are we alive? What is a living thing?

B: I once heard a great scientist say that all living things are created from stardust from a distant universe. The origin of living beings came floating to Earth with the wind from a distant universe. These are too small to see with the eye.

A: Then are we all aliens?

B: *(shakes head)*

No. But, you know, if what that scientist says is true, then we are of the energy from very strong stars.

All living things on earth live on the power of the sun that we can see in the sky.

A: It gets very hot when the sun is out.

B: Yes, it does, doesn't it? It feels hot because it gives us strong light. Plants like flowers, grass, and vegetables grow by the power of the sun. And this is what cows, pigs, and birds eat. When we eat plants and meat, the power of the sun enters the human body from these foods as well.

A: But how do you become human?

B: Once upon a time, a long, long time ago, on this planet that we live on—humans were not created yet.

A: There wasn't anyone?

No people here?

What about cats then?

B: There were no cats either.

A: What about birds?

B: There weren't any birds.

A: Were there any flowers?

B: There weren't even any flowers.

A: Then what *was* here?

B: Very, very tiny little creatures. Big creatures are from little creatures, you know? We're made up of a lot of small creatures.

A: But I look like one living being. Not many beings. Aren't I?

B: It took many, many years to become what we are today.

In the beginning, a long time ago, a little stardust from outer space turned into tiny creatures that live on Earth.

A: How? Did they move here?

B: Yes. Our ancestors, who were not yet human beings came to this new place called Earth. It took years to get used to the way of life here.

First, those little creatures that came from space regrouped here and over the years became little creatures that lived in the water. Then, over time, they became fish. The grass grew in the sea and on top of the earth. Those that moved on land became crocodiles and lizards and birds and big dinosaurs. Then there were rats and cats and dogs and monkeys and finally humans.

It's been a long, long road to get to where we are now. Even today, before we are born, we all have to go through a long journey in our mother's tummy to become a person. It is said that this journey is like the journey of how human beings were created.

A part of our brain is the same as a bird. A part of our brain is the same as a mouse. And we have many parts of our brain that are the same as monkeys.

Many people in the past felt intuitively that people were made up of many different beings and creatures, so they came up with many different gods and goddesses to represent them. This was how they explained how completely different ideas can come into their minds.

A: What is God?

B: People say different things about what God is, but I think that it is the great power that moves the universe. It is all the energy of the universe combined. It can neither be created nor destroyed; it can only be transferred or changed from one form to another.

The various gods and goddesses that appear in stories of mythology are the various manifestations of that power.

People are all made from a combination of different creatures, so we are able to use all kinds of powers.

A: Am I alone in this world?

B: *(shaking his head)*

No. We are not alone.

We came from our mom and dad, and they came from their moms and dads and before them, and their moms and dads before them too. Back in the long, long ago, I was a monkey, and before that, I was a bird, and much before that I was a flower.

And we are all part of the universe.

As my life settled down, I produced more creative works. I began writing numerous poetry and melodies. The pieces I created when I was younger may have had the intensity that I wanted to portray, but I often lacked the technique to present my ideas in the manner that I desired. When I examine my works from before and after I was thirty, I notice a significant difference in my technique. The 1986 album *Nova Carmina* is good, but it still seems naive and not as developed as it could be. But that's part of the charm of this album. I believe my technical abilities have improved since I was in my thirties.

The '90s and the '00s were my most active period. The following is a brief list of the works I made from my thirties in chronological order:

1990

- I performed regularly at Kichijoji Mandara 2 and other venues.
- I performed with Suzuki Koji, Akinobu Imai, Moco Matsumoto, Cement Mixers, and others.

- I composed music for the architect Hiroshi Hara's videos and performed music at his lectures.
- I started to make a lot of music for TV commercials around this time. In 1991, One of the music I made for a commercial for Cupee Mayonaise won an award at JAM for the best-sounding commercial song.
- I started teaching a songwriter's course at Musashino Music Academy.
- I started doing interviews and dialogues for the magazine *Keyboard Special*.
  - ○ I published dialogues with various musicians such as Haruomi Hosono, Minako Yoshida, Yoko Ueno, Zabadak, Morgan Fischer, and others.

1991–1992

- I composed a few songs and performed guitar for actress, Saki Takaoka's album, released by JVC Victor. "Ni-Ya-oo," the single composed by Ayuo for Saki, entered the Oricon chart (the Top 100 hit song chart).
- I provided music for an increasing number of documentary films. Some of them are still frequently screened today, such as Noriaki Tsuchimoto's *Minamata Disease: 30 Years of Minamata Disease*.
- I also composed and performed music for documentary films by Osamu Wakatsuki, Takashi Fukuda, and John Junkerman. I also composed and performed music for the theatrical dramatic film *The Wind in the Valley*, produced by Komatsu Kakumasa. Most of the music in that film was performed on my acoustic guitar. Other actors in the film included Kazuko Shirakawa and Mie Mizumori.
- I composed a tango for a TV commercial for Okasan Securities Co. Ltd. This tango song featuring Asuka Kaneko's solo violin was often broadcast on TV.

1993

- I composed a suite titled *Alien Zero* for the Paul Dresher Ensemble and toured Japan with them. The ensemble featured Philip Aaberg who was the keyboard player for Peter Gabriel's first tour promoting his first solo album produced by Bob Ezrin.

- Started performing with Yoko Ueno. Around this period, I called my music "Neo Trad (New Traditional)" to mean a new form of traditional music.

1994

- I composed music for three plays organized by the Hyogo Performing Arts Center.
  - Anton Chekhov's *The Seagull* featured Kenji Sawada, Leona Hirota, and Manami Fuji. The Women Without Gardens, starring Kirin Kiki, Shiho Fujimura and Mariko Okada.
  - Sophocles' *Oedipus the King* is a musical-style production featuring Isao Natsuyagi, Kyoko Enami, and Yuri Haruna.
- From 1994 onward, I wrote the stories and scripts for contemporary dance performances by the dancer, Takako Takase. I also wrote poems to be recited, composed, and performed music for her dance performances every year.[4]
- I started performing with Yoko Ueno and contributed English lyrics to Zabadak's album *OTO (Sound)*.
- I started writing regular columns for Tower Records' magazine *Musée*, where I would interview Bill Bruford, John Cale, Ani Di Franco, Steve Hillage, Maddy Prior, Donal Lunney, Hossein Alizadeh, film director Alex Cox, Philip Garrel, and many others.
- On Yoji Yamamoto's CD *Your Pain Shall Be Your Music*. I composed most of the music for the words recited by filmmaker Wim Wenders (the film director), John Cale (the musician and composer), Wolfgang Wagner (grandson of German composer Richard Wagner and opera director), Otto Sander (actor), Charles Lloyd (saxophonist) and others.
- I went to Athens, Greece, and bought a 1930s model 3-course bouzouki. I got married this year to Yuki Yanagihara.

---

[4]Her daughter, Fukiko Takase, would later become a well-known dancer in both Europe and Japan performing in contemporary dance as well as in videos of pop music such as for Thom Yorke, Hikaru Utada, and others.

1995

- Three solo CDs are released on independent labels.
  - *Blue Eyes, Black Hair* was released from Belle Antique with an introduction by the writer Tetsuya Uchida.
  - *Heavenly Garden Orchestra*, a collection of music for plays, dances, and films, is released from FOA Records.
  - A collection of demo tapes is released from PSF.
- Ayuo Trio (Ayuo, Takuya Nishimura, Chizuko Miura) begins regular live performances with Takuya Nishimura and Chizuko Miura.
- I started a duo performance with Keiji Haino.

1996

- I went to Scotland to perform music for the Saiga Ballet.
  - Shinichiro Shinozaki, a former student of mine at Musashino Music Academy became a music producer and contacted me to discuss the possibility of recording a new album in England. Motohiko Maeda, also a former student of mine at Musashino Music Academy became the recording engineer for a new recording project. We started making an album at Toy's Office where they both worked.
- I started recording *Songs from a Eurasian Journey* with the members of Ayuo Trio, Yoko Ueno, and Epo and completed it in England with Peter Hammill, Danny Thompson, Dave Mattacks, and Aoife Ní Fhearraigh.
- I commissioned Tadanori Yokoo to make the CD cover jacket.
- I composed "Where I Was the Day the Second World War Ended" and "Ophelia" based on two works by the American writer Kurt Vonnegut, and presented them at Spiral Hall.
- I composed *Izutsu*, based on a Noh drama by Zeami. This was later released by TZADIK Records in the US.
- I composed the piano composition series *Eurasian Tango*, a suite of five piano pieces.

- o In the 2010s, this piece was widely performed in Europe as music for contemporary dance performances.
- I composed music for the theatre play *Futsuu no Kuma* (A Normal Bear) by the theater group EN.
  - o The original story was by Yoko Sano, the script was by Tomomi Tsutsui, and theater production was produced by Kyoko Kishida, who played leading roles in Hiroshi Teshigahara's films, *Woman of the Dunes* and *The Face of Another*.
- Ayuo's single "Song of Songs" is released from FOA Records.
- I composed and performed music for a Shiseido TV commercial.

Figure 21   Photo of a 1996 live performance with Keiji Haino at Mandara 2, Kichijoji.

1997

- *Songs from a Eurasian Journey*, Ayuo's first UK recording in 11 years, is completed and released from JVC Victor. Epo was the guest singer at the live performance to commemorate the release.

- I began writing English lyrics for the singer, Bice (real name: Yuko Nakajima).
- I formed a techno unit "Alien Zero" with synthesizer player, Shintaro Ashizawa and we started recording.
- I performed with the jazz pianist, Kensaku Tanikawa.
- I recorded one song for FOA Records' compilation album *Landscape from Earth*.

1998

- At Shobi Music College, I started teaching world music studies, songwriting in English, music history, cultural and social studies, and music ensembles.
- Started to participate in live shows organized by Suzuki Cohji (Cohjizukin).
- I was introduced to the Bosnian singer Jadranka Stojakovic, and I started writing English lyrics to her songs.
- *Eastern Tradition* is released from Belle Antique with Suzuki Cohji (Cohjizukin)'s jacket.
- I composed *Ulysses and the City of Dreams* as a suite of two piano pieces.
  - This piece was later included in the CD *Aoi* on the Tzadik label.
- One song by Ayuo was included in the compilation disc, *Healing Voices from The Sea*, on FOA Records.
- I sang and played *bouzouki* on the ending theme of the movie, *Beautiful Sunday* starring Masatoshi Nagase.
  - "Never on Sunday" by Greek composer Manos Hadjidakis served as the closing theme song.
- I composed a commercial song for a Toshiba mobile phone.

1999

- The recording of *Earth Guitar* began in Japan and was completed in the UK. The album features 22 musicians including Jadranka Stojakovic, Peter Hammill, Clive Deamer, Yoko Ueno, Wataru Okuma, Keishi Ota, Sara Yoko Benito, Takuya Nishimura, and Chizuko Miura.
- Ayuo Trio performs more often with 7–8 additional members.

- I performed with Brandon Perry of Dead Can Dance on the Irish Mythology CD *Voice of The Celtic Myth* (released under the name Greenwood).

2000

- *Earth Guitar* is released from MIDI records. It's one of my favorite albums. Tadanori Yokoo designed the front jacket. Suzuki Cohji (Cohjizukin) designed the flyer for the live performance in celebration of the release of the album. For this show, Suzuki brought a big cardboard robot and made it dance. Belly dancer Maha danced on stage. Yoko Ueno and Sara Yoko Benito sang, and my stepfather, Mansour Malekpour from NYC, who was in Japan for a vacation, joined in with a traditional Iranian song. I accompanied Mansour's singing with a *bouzouki*, which was tuned similarly to the Persian *setar*, a traditional Iranian instrument. The clarinet was played by Wataru Okuma. The violin was played by Keisuke Ota. Akinobu Imai performed on electric guitar. Takuya Nishimura on bass guitar. Double drums were performed by Chizuko Miura and Tsuno Ken. We continued to play live with different combinations of these members in this period.
- Alien Zero's song "If Tomorrow Never Comes" was released on a FOA Records compilation CD.
- The CD of Ayuo's mono opera, *Izutsu*, is released from John Zorn's label Tzadik in New York.
- A one-hour program about Ayuo, including an interview by David Garland, is broadcast on the WNYC FM program "Spinning on the Air" in New York City.
- My daughter, Lisa, was born in the summer.

2001

- I started performing live once a month at Daikanyama Classics (later Koen-dori Classics).
- Started playing live once a month at Namak Café.
  - At this time, I also performed with DJ Kensei.
- I joined Suzuki Cohji's group Zuking.
- I formed Zacro with Joji Sawada, Yoichi Okabe, Naoya Numa, Yuji Katsui, Satoshi Ishikawa, and others.

- I performed with Maha, Akiko Takada, Safi, and other dancers. I bought his first laptop and started using computer software to make and record music.

- My stepfather, Mansour Malekpour, visits Japan and I perform traditional Iranian songs with him.

- Arranged and performed two songs on singer Yae's CD.

- I wrote English lyrics for "Everything Birds Can See" and "We Are a Part of the Ocean," as well as lyrics for "Standing on a Cloud" for the Bosnian singer Jadranka Stojakovic's CD *Moon Will Guide You.*

- My song "1000 Springs" is included in the compilation *Cube 2001—A Healing Odyssey,* released by PolyGram.

- Sound by Noh Play by Zeami

- I wrote the lyrics for the chorus of "Magic Light."

- After hearing the news of the September 11 attacks in 2001, I was shocked and wrote the song "Ghost City."

- *Eurasian Tango* Nos. 1, 2, and 5 were recorded and released on the Swedish label BIS.

Figure 22 Photo with my stepfather, Mansour, and my mother at Shinjuku station.

2002

- Live performances with Kiyoshi Awazu's live painting.
- I formed a trio with Akinobu Imai and Tsunoken.
  - We performed the entire album of Lou Reed's *Berlin* live at several places.
- Composed and played music for Kiyoshi Awazu's "Rock Art Exhibition" and released it as the CD *Stoned*. Jadranka also participates.
- Performed with Shuntaro Tanikawa, Kensaku Tanikawa, Hiromi Ota, and Ma-To at "Rock Art" live.
- I composed a suite of piano pieces entitled *Legend of Alien Zero*; this is now available on ayuo.bandcamp.com

2003

- Started recording with Hiromi Ota. I composed "Aoi no Ue" based on Zeami's Noh play for the theatre of Kyoto University of Art and Design, with *sangen*, *biwa*, *shakuhachi*, electric guitar, and song.
- I composed and composed "I Have a Dream" for recitation and electronics; I then performed it with electric guitar and electronics at Kyoto Art Theatre Shunjuza.
  - Performing with Kazuko Takada and Yoka Nagasu. Dance is by Kim Uni and Pang Hyeonae.
- Taught film scoring (film and video music composition) classes at the Japan Electronics College.
- I composed and performed the music for the film *Borderline* directed by Lee Sang-il, starring Tetsu Sawaki, Ayaka Maeda, Jun Murakami, Ken Mitsuishi, Yumi Aso, Harumi Miyako.

2004

- Tzadik released the album *Red Moon* with Hiromi Ohta under the name of Ayuo/Ohta Hiromi in New York. The album consisted of 10 songs in the style of acoustic rock and electronics. I recorded much of the electronics and electric guitars at home using recording software.
- I composed and performed "Circus," "Tokyo Festival," and "Summer Night in the City" based on three poems by Chuya Nakahara.

- Yoko Ueno, Shuichi Chino, and I performed *A Page of Madness*, a newly composed and improvised music for a silent film of the Taisho era (1912–1926) directed by Teinosuke Kinugasa and titled the same.

2005

- The album *Aoi* was released on the Tzadik label in the US. The album included "Aoi no Ue" based on the Noh play by Zeami.
  - o "A Stranger" and "Oh Light of My Heart" were psychedelic songs played on the Greek *bouzouki* with electronic beats manually played by Ayuo.
  - o *Ulysses and the City of Dreams* was a set of two pieces for the piano.
  - o "On the Morning of March 1, 2005" was the first improvised solo on *bouzouki* that I performed at home that morning.
- I composed a set of songs based on Shuji Terayama's re-telling of *Green Mansions* (based on a story by William Henry Hudson). The film version of this story starred Audrey Hepburn and Anthony Perkins.)[5]
- I coordinated and performed joint concerts with Hiromi Ota, Shuichi Chino, and Zacro.
- I played the *bouzouki* at the Japanese premiere of Oliver Stone's movie *Alexander*.

2006

- I performed with actresses Sayoko Yamaguchi, Kazuko Takada, and Tomoka Nagasu at a live concert to commemorate the release of *Aoi* from Tzadik.
- Together with Yuki Yanagihara, we translated Jennette Winterson's picture book *The King of Capri*, which was published by Shogakukan in 2012.
- The CD *E no Naka no Sugata* (What We Look Like in The Picture) is released from the Zipangu label. This is an album of mainly open-tuned guitar songs.

---

[5]My composition is now available on ayuo.bandcamp.com in the album *At Heart, I Am a Child with No Home*. This was performed on open-tuning guitar, storytelling recitation, and vocals with tabla. Analog synthesizer and rhythm programming were added to the recorded version.

- o I made open-tuning guitar arrangements of Syd Barrett's "Late Night," Lou Reed's "The Kids" and "Men of Good Fortune" from Berlin, among other songs.
- Around this time Ayuo's *bouzouki* solo instrumental was played a few times on an American bluegrass radio program.
- I composed a commercial song for the Shampoo, Yakusodo. I played the Irish harp, medieval *psaltery*, and various other instruments in this composition and Yoko Ueno sang.

2007

- To create music, dance, and recitation performances, I started a performance group called "Memory Theatre" consisting of me, Junzo Tateiwa, Reki Shibata, Yoshie, Ken Awazu, and Yosuke Jikuhara.
- A Norwegian pianist, Elen Ugelvik, commissioned me to compose three piano compositions: *When Illusion Looks Like Reality, Then Reality Becomes Just a Fantasy; Transforming Cells of Memory;* and *Dinosaur's Egg.*
- I composed "The Phantom Night Train" to lyrics by Carmen Maki.
- A one-hour program about me is made for the Belgian National Radio.

2008

- Kiyoshi Awazu's exhibition "Graphism in the Wilderness" at Kanazawa 21st Century Museum of Contemporary Art featured four live performances and a workshop by me.
- I formed the group Ayuo & Seashell with Fumiko Kai, Yoshiko Sato, Takui Matsumoto, and Yuki Oshika.
  - o I played guitar and *bouzouki* and recited poetry with a string quartet.
- Inspired by a book based on the conference between scientists and the Dalai Lama, edited by biologist Francisco Barrera under the title *Sleeping, Dreaming, Dying*, I presented a suite of songs for open-tuned guitar and string quartet.
  - o Many of the pieces presented here appear on my 2009 CD *dna.*

- Started experimental music workshop in Setagaya-ku, Tokyo.
- Formed a duo group, "Temple of Sleep" with Masaaki Aoyama. This was an acoustic group combining hypnotherapy and open-tuning guitar performances.
- I wrote the script, composed the poetry, sang vocals, and played open-tuned guitar for the contemporary dance and acoustic music performance *The Book of Genome*.
- A one-hour program was produced for a New Zealand world music program, including an interview with Ayuo.

2009

- I conducted a sketching and onomatopoeic sound class for kindergarten-aged children and their mothers at Kyoto University of Art and Design.
- Presentation of *dna*. Fumiko Kai, Yoshiko Sato, Takui Matsumoto, Yuki Oshika, Yoko Ueno, and Reki Shibata participated.
- Composed *When I Die*, a suite for string quartet and narration.
  - Script, poetry, vocals, and open-tuned guitar performance for Rumi, a performance of contemporary dance and acoustic music.

2010

- I arranged works by Debussy and Satie for guitar and song.
- I arranged "Nuages" (Clouds) from Debussy's *Nocturnes* for a chamber ensemble including prepared piano, toy piano, and guitar.
- I arranged "Lilies" from Debussy's *Martyrdom of St. Sebastian* for prepared piano and string quartet.
- I arranged Debussy's suite of songs, *L'Ode de Bilitis*, for string quartet and song.
- I arranged Debussy's *The Haunted Palace* (inspired by Edgar Allan Poe's *The Fall of the House of Usher*) for piano, violin, and vocals.
- I arranged Debussy's melodic song "Let's Love and Let's Sleep" for guitar and vocals, making it sound like a folksong.

- I also arranged Ravel's "Ballade de la Reine morte d'aimer" for guitar and song, making it like a folksong.
- I also arranged Genesis' "The Lamia" for string trio and vocals.
- After listening to Genesis' *The Lamb Lies Down on Broadway* in 5.1 mixes, which included "The Lamia," it became clear to me what I wanted to do when I was 14 years old.
- I decided that there were several things I wanted to do in my lifetime—one of the things was to study dance and mime.
- I started taking lessons in jazz dance, hula dance, and beginners' ballet.

2011

- I presented a chamber music theatre based on *Blue Eyes, Black Hair* by Marguerite Duras. It was performed with piano, string quartet, guitar, percussion, two singers, and a dancer.
- I composed and premiered *Hawaiian Mythology Pele* based on my research of Polynesian mythology.
- I composed and premiered *Voices in the Wind—A Prayer for those swept away by the Sea* for string quartet, Irish harp, and song. This song is dedicated to those who died in the tsunami of March 11th of that year.
- I arranged Wagner's *Prelude to Tristan und Isolde* for the string quartet.
- I composed and performed a collaborative work with the poet Keijiro Suga.

2012

- Presented a new version of "Hawaiian Mythology Pele" at the event *Mythical World of the Pacific* at the Academy Hall in the Academy Common of Meiji University Surugadai Campus.
- I performed the role of Izanagi as a dancer in the musical play *Kojiki*, commemorating the 1300th anniversary of the Kojiki—*Records of Ancient Matters*—an early Japanese chronicle of myths, legends, hymns, genealogies, oral traditions, and semi-historical accounts, which was performed on Iki Island, Nagasaki Prefecture.

- I began performing American jazz standards and musical tunes.

2013

- I composed and premiered *Nijinsky*, a short work for recitation and piano or recitation and guitar based on Nijinsky's diary.
- I composed and presented *Abelard and Héloïse*, a work for narrative, piano, and performance based on a poem by Antonin Artaud.
- The British contemporary dance company, the Richard Alston Company choreographed and performed all five of my *Eurasian Tango* compositions on live accordion on their UK tour during this and the following year.
- *Eurasian Tango,* No. 1 was presented in Germany with a new contemporary dance choreography, presented by Bridget Breiner, a prima ballerina of the Stuttgart ballet.

2014

- *Outside Society 1* was premiered by Christopher Yohmei Blasdel, Tatsuo Kondo, Mika Kimura, and me.
  - o The compositions were based on the journals of Donald Ritchie, a film critic and journalist who lived in Japan for nearly 60 years.
  - o *Outside Society 2*, which I later wrote and composed, is based on my own experiences.

2015

- I composed *The Dream Journals of Carl Jung*, a suite of songs and compositions premiered by Akikazu Nakamura, Yoko Ueno, Toshiko Kuto, and myself.
  - o Many of these songs were later recorded on the album *Outside Society*, released in 2019.
  - o We formed a new group, Yumemakura, after this concert with the addition of Junzo Tateiwa on percussion.
- I formed a new group—Genome—with dancer Nashaal, percussionist Junzo Tateiwa, pianist Makiko Seo and bassist Takuyuki Moriya, and myself. We create a new series of performances mixing dance and poetry recitation with music.
- Ayuo's *Eurasian Tango* No. 1 was performed at the Juilliard School in New York City.

2016

- I write "What is life?" and the poem "Existence." These poems are recited with music.
- I organized a David Bowie tribute concert and a Prince tribute concert at Koen Dori Classics. Prince's works were performed with *ukulele*, Middle Eastern percussion, cello, vocals, guitar, bass, and drums.
- *Eurasian Tango* No. 1 was performed and recorded by Ensemble Black Pencil from Germany and released on their CD *Kaiseki*.

2017

- I performed an acoustic live and talk show, *Psychedelic Culture through the Eyes of a Child* at The Tadanori Yokoo Museum of Contemporary Art in Kobe, Japan.
- My arrangement and performance of Toru Takemitsu's "Waltz" from Hiroshi Teshigahara's film *The Face of Another* was released on the *Zipangu* omnibus album.
- My group, Genome, presented a poetry, dance and music show based on the Sufi mystic thinker, Rumi.
- Reunited Zacro with Joji Sawada—this formation is known as Zacro II.
- A song I originally composed for the actress, Saki Takaoka, "Ni-Ya-Oo" is recorded in Chinese by a singer/entertainer from Taiwan—Mickey Huang.

2018

- I perform concerts with my groups, Yumemakura and Epigenetics.
  - Amin Choghadi guested on a few of them singing Persia traditional music.
- The Japanese version of my book *Outside Society* is published. Ken Awazu organizes a party for me to celebrate its release.

2019

- The CD *Outside Society* is released on my label, Ayuo Music Records. The digital version is available on ayuo.bandcamp.com.

- Ayuo tours with hurdy-gurdy player, TOMO Hurdy Gurdy. Performances are held at Yokoo Tadanori Contemporary Art Museum, Kanazawa Jazz Street Festival and other places.
- Amin Choghadi, an outstanding vocalist of Iranian traditional music, frequently appeared in Ayuo's group concerts.
  - We perform band versions of traditional Persian music with poetry by Rumi. Members include Junzo Tateiwa, Takuya Moriya, Eugene Okano, Tomoko Maruono as well as myself.

2020

- COVID-19 interrupts many activities. Music schools and small live venues close down.
- I begin editing, mixing, and uploading unreleased works to ayuo.bandcamp.com.

2021

- I produced the concert *Eurasian Dream* with my group, Yumemakura, with Yoko Ueno, Morgan Fisher, and Amin Choghadi as guests.
- I translated Byung-Chul Han's book *Psychopolitik* into Japanese.
- I wrote articles about philosophy.

2022

- I composed music for the architect Hiroshi Hara.
  - Hara created an *Objet d'art* for the Oku-Noto Art Festival.
- I spent much of this year editing, re-recording, and mixing works to be uploaded on ayuo.bandcamp.com. I intend to create my archive there.
- I also wrote music and film articles and did interviews for the Tower Records' magazine *Intoxicate*.

2023

- I produced a concert with a classical chamber music ensemble entitled *The Painted Bird*, inspired by the novel of the same title by Jerzy Kosiński.
- I performed a solo concert at Gallery Denguri.

2024

- I performed a solo concert at Kiyoshi Awazu's atelier in Awazu House.
- The compilation CD *ayuo.bandcamp.com* is distributed by Disk Union and Tower Records.
- I choreographed and performed a solo dance at Kei Takei's studio, Moving Earth.

I am living alone again.

After the earthquake in March 2011, I thought about going back to New York, but I would have needed to find a teaching job to do this.

When I lived with a Japanese partner, there were Japanese-language magazines and newspapers in the house, and the Japanese-language TV and radio were often on.

When I'm alone, however, it's easier for me to just use English, which I've done since I was a child.

When you're an adult, languages you acquire later will never be as deep as your first language of expression. For everyone, their childhood home will always be the place they call home.

Matt Ridley gives examples in his book *Nature via Nurture* that there is a critical period in language learning during the formative years of a human being. There were kings and emperors in Egypt, Germany, and Scotland, who tried an experiment of depriving newborn children of all human contact except a silent foster mother to find out whether people were innately Hebrew, Arabic, Latin, or Greek—but all they got were deaf-mutes.

Some people in Japan in the 1980s used to tell me that I reminded them of Kasper Hauser. *The Enigma of Kasper Hauser* is the name of a film by Werner Herzog, based on a true story about a boy who lived the first seventeen years of his life chained in a tiny cellar, devoid of all human contact save for a man who came to feed him. Even after years of careful coaching, he could never speak properly. Matt Ridley brings him up as one of his examples in the above book. Ridley writes, "But the most direct test of the critical period in language learning would be to deprive a child of all language until the age of 13 and then try to teach the poor creature to speak."[6]

---

[6]Ridely, Matt. *Nature Via Nurture*. HarperCollins Publishing Inc., 2004, pp. 168–169.

To me, Japanese people in real life as in TV dramas seem to act odd, but I am also well aware of how strange I seem to them. My biggest challenge was figuring out how to express my feelings to people from a different culture.

This is not immediately apparent because I appear similar to a lot of people here, and I am knowledgeable about many cultural features.

I devoted much time to figuring out what to do in such a case. I began to communicate with those I knew in elementary and junior high school in New York via the Internet and social networks. Having friends from middle school still gives me a sense of belonging. They were the first people who encouraged me.

For me, Chinese-Americans, Korean-Americans, and Japanese-Americans who grew up in America have a stronger sense of cultural connectedness than Japanese and Japanese-Americans. They grew up in the same culture and spoke the same language.

In the United States, we are called Asian-Americans. At Stuyvesant High School in New York City—which I once applied to when I was in middle school—75% of the student body in 2018 was Asian-American. When I was in middle school, the Asian-American population was 1.5% of the US population.

Today, according to US official data, 7.3% of the US population is Asian. If half-Asian-Americans are included, the percentage rises to more than 9%.

More than anything else, my experiences have taught me that ethnicity is an illusion. The historian, Yuval Noah Harari, writes in his book *Sapiens* that nation-states were artificially created. It is just one way of grouping people. Religion was another. The term 'borderless' became popular in the 1980s. People often say: 'music has no borders.' But the truth is, there are borders. The boundaries are created by your cultural background and the languages you speak.

People living "on the outskirts of society" or "without a country" are not attempting to become "borderless" by choice. Those people are no longer part of that society because they were raised in different languages and cultures. They have been thrown outside of it. People who are not part of a society, on the other hand, can often look at it objectively.

I normally try to blend in with society as much as possible by wearing a cultural mask. I am aware that the person people see when they see me in Japan is a translated version of who I really am culturally, but I believe that only those who have gone through comparable circumstances can truly grasp this.

For me, my interest in cultural anthropology, philosophy, psychology, comparative religion, modern science, and life sciences is not academic. My own experiences and situations motivated me to look into these topics. If I hadn't been forced into a corner, I never would have researched these topics to find answers.

I was also inspired by the words written by the Japanese-American physicist Michio Kaku; the Chinese-American novelist Amy Tan; the British-Indian novelist Sir Salman Rushdie—among others.

Amy Tan, the author of *Joy Luck Club*, said in her Masterclass video that she realized she was an American after she visited her sisters and her relatives in mainland China. The British-Indian author, Sir Salman Rushdie said in his Masterclass video that he learned how to write well, once he recognized what his cultural identity was. In other words, he is a British-Indian with parents who were Muslims, who moved to Pakistan. These are new identities. Not just British or Indian or Pakistani or Chinese, but of those people from Asia raised in an English-speaking country.

I dream of a future when we can come to understand each other as *fellow human beings of the earth*, although I am quite aware of how difficult that is. I write words and poetry as well as make music toward that era.

I hope my autobiography can help those in similar situations and spread more awareness.

This is the heart of my work.

Figure 23   2011. Ayuo wearing mask. Photographed by Takashi Arai.

Figure 24   2017. Ayuo with guitar. Photographed by Yoshihide Nakano.

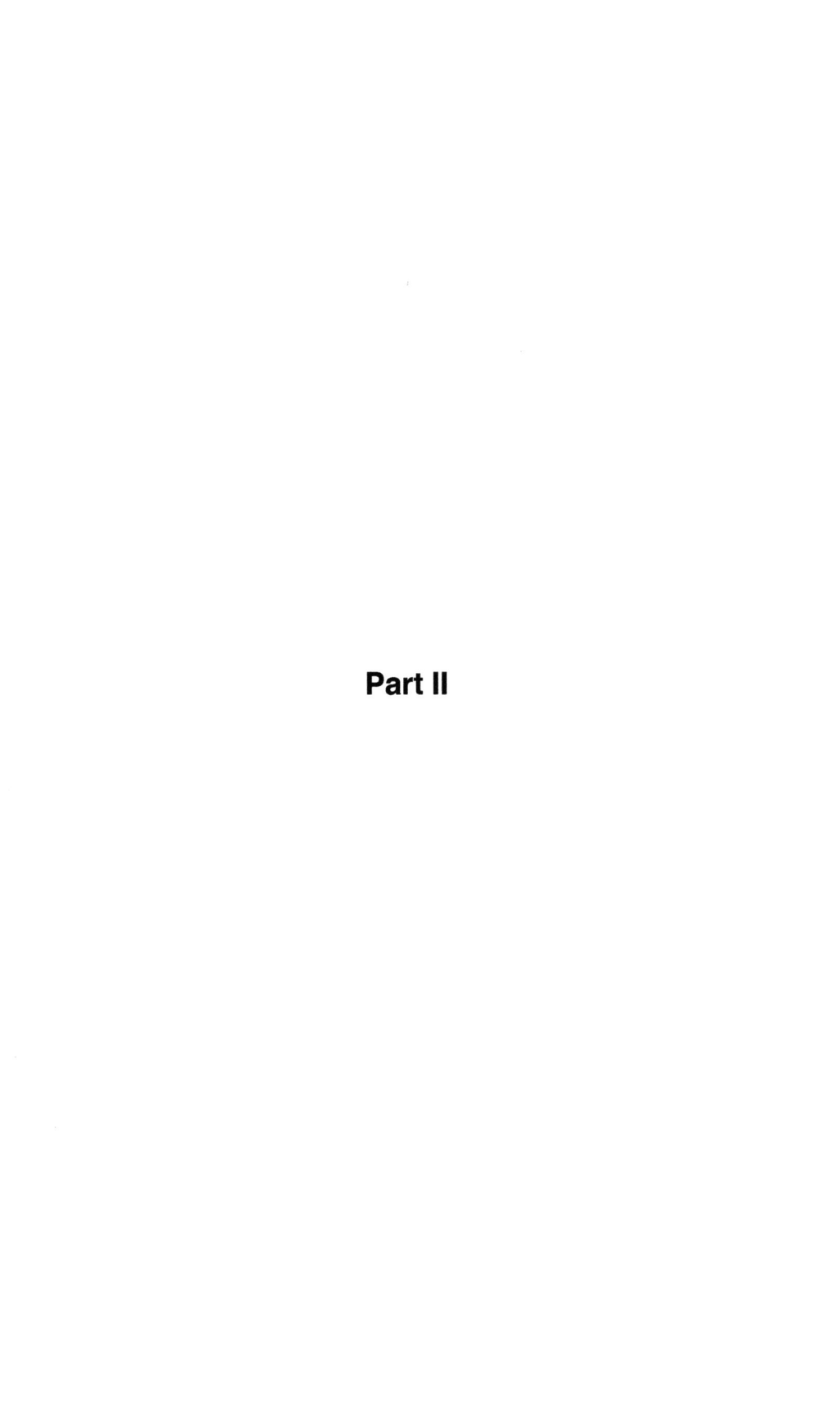

Part II

Rock concerts I saw before and after 1970

The first rock concert I ever saw was the Beatles at Budokan, but the first rock band I saw after I went to New York City was the United States of America.

The United States of America was an American avant-garde rock band, founded in 1967 by composer Joseph Byrd and vocalist Dorothy Moskowitz. They were joined by electric violinist Gordon Marron, bassist Rand Forbes, and drummer Craig Woodson. The group's sound combined psychedelia with the avant-garde experimental music of the time. Byrd had been involved in experimental music as part of the *Fluxus* movement, along with La Monte Young, David Tudor, Yoko Ono, and others.

Byrd's aim for the band was to form "an avant-garde political/musical rock group with the idea of combining electronic sound, musical/political radicalism, and performance art."[1]

I had their self-titled LP at home, but at that time they weren't a successful band. This was before the Moog synthesizer would become a popular commercial instrument, so they were using very primitive electronic instruments with volt-control oscillators and voltage-control filters, such as those used in Stockhausen's live electronics at the time. They added effects such as ring modulators and echoes.

Their lyrics reflected an anti-establishment, leftist political stance. However, they were not real rock musicians.

Byrd later said, "We had played Cage and Stockhausen, African and Indian music, and I thought we could simply bring all that to rock. But we knew almost nothing about the roots of rock and roll.

---

[1]Holm-Hudson, Kevin (2002). *Progressive Rock Reconsidered.* Taylor & Francis. pp. 48–61.

We all improvised, of course, but in a 'contemporary music' style. In retrospect, creating a rock band with no rock musicians was a bad decision on my part."[2]

This is well said. There were many contemporary classical composers who tried to create a new 'people's music' without knowing much about popular music or rock music. Many of them failed, but never admitted even to themselves why they failed.

Today, their only album released on Columbia Records is considered a cult classic among psychedelic and progressive rock collectors. At the time, they were not that successful and broke up after their only album. Other groups that combined experimental avant-garde music with psychedelia and rock would have more success, such as The Velvet Underground, and Can in Germany.

I went to see the United States of America with my father, which was a very rare thing since he had no interest in rock music. I think he had heard about the United States of America from a composer friend of Joe Byrd.

The concert was at the Assembly Hall at Hunter College. The venue was quiet, like at an experimental classical concert. The lighting was relatively dark. It was simple enough to light each member of the band. There was no light show like those that I would later see at the Fillmore East or Electric Circus. They played songs from their debut album. The crowd sat quietly and watched, and clapped their hands politely when each song was over.

Their performance was about an hour.

Dorothy Moskowitz later joined Country Joe McDonald's All-Star Band. She composed theater music, recorded commercials, and later became a music teacher. The producer David Rubinson was already known for producing Moby Grape. He then went on to produce Santana's hit album.

I will interrupt this narrative to relate something that happened much later.

In the 2000s, the president of MIDI Records asked me if I could produce and arrange a CD of my father's piano playing. Hiroshi Ohkura, the president, told me that he liked my father's playing,

---

[2]Breznikar, Klemen (February 9, 2013). "The United States of America | Joseph Byrd | Interview." *It's Psychedelic Baby!* Magazine.

but he was afraid that if he tried to make a record with my father himself, my father might come up with something that could not be commercially sold. He said that he trusts me, Ayuo, as a producer who can come up with a project that would sell. However, my father immediately rejected this proposal. I was not able to persuade him by any means.

Many classical musicians look down on rock musicians, and my father is the same. On top of this, he had been called a musical genius throughout most of his career in Japan, so he's not likely to listen to other people's opinions. His performances can only be arranged by himself.

I remember when Suntory asked my father to make music for a TV commercial. He created something that Suntory thought was unusable as background music for a commercial, but he refused to make any changes. Then his manager demanded that he be paid 10 million yen for the 30-second piece of music, or else he would use his power to fire the man in charge of advertisement at Suntory.

In the late '70s, my father had formed a group with a former studio musician who used to back the popular singer, Toshiko Kato. The group played 'people's music' at left-wing political meetings. However, he and the musician couldn't agree on the direction the group should take, and they broke up after many long arguments. I think it would be hard to make 'people's music' if you look down on the 'people' and see them as ignorant and below yourself.

In 1970, my stepfather, mother, and I were invited to the home of then-CBS producer John McClure. He produced John Cale's first album, *Church of Anthrax* (a joint album with the composer Terry Riley), as well as recorded over 200 albums by Leonard Bernstein, and albums by Dave Brubeck and Peter, Paul, and Mary.

He lived in an expensive-looking apartment in midtown New York City. Upon our arrival, he proceeded to introduce us to Quadrophonic, a four-channel system that he predicted would revolutionize audio in the living room. Speakers were positioned in each of the room's four corners. While lying on the carpet, he asked us all to listen to the thunderous sound of a passing train. It was as if a real train was passing by over our bodies.

After supper, we went to the next room. There was a large synthesizer there; at the time, they were rare and valuable. It was so large that it took up an entire wall, with many wires connected to various devices. There was a keyboard on the desk to control it. He allowed me to play it. Polyphonic synthesizers had not yet been invented, so I could only play one note at a time. I sat in front of it and hit the key. It went "wham, wham, wham." It was exciting—the sounds kept going on and on until everyone in the room had had enough of it. When I twisted the buttons and knobs a little, it made different sounds again. I never got bored of it, and I could play it all night. Imagine an eight-year-old being permitted to make loud electronic noises at a well-known producer's home.

I went to see the Jefferson Airplane concert on March 25, 1970, in Long Island, New York. Grace Slick, the female vocalist, was unable to perform that day due to throat difficulties. The other members performed without her.

At first, I sat in the audience and watched; then I moved closer to the stage and saw them just below the stage. More and more often, guitarist Jorma Kaukonen and bassist Jack Cassidy would start a song by stamping their feet on the stage floor to set the beat. Marty Balin was the main singer that night. That night, he sang in a fast, funky style. Electric blues and funk were especially strong on this night. They played many songs that I had not heard yet; at that time, songs such as "Emergency" and "You Wear Your Dresses Too Short" were not on their official albums. They were only released as bonus tracks after the Jefferson Airplane no longer existed as a band. The audience was very different from the one at the United States of America concert. We were free to walk around and listen to the songs. I felt a sense of freedom in the air.

I saw one of Janis Joplin's final performances, just two months before her death.

This was on August 6, 1970, at the Festival for Peace, a one-day festival held at Shea Stadium in New York City. It was organized by Peter Yarrow from Peter, Paul, and Mary. My mother, stepfather, and I were introduced to Peter Yarrow by Seiji Ozawa.

Peter Yarrow had wanted to work with Seiji Ozawa, but Seiji was not interested. My mother tried to promote her own music to Peter

Yarrow at the time. She had dreams of becoming a singer/songwriter, and so she went to his office with her songs. He gave my mother, my stepfather Mansour, and me tickets to sit in the seats reserved for special guests.

The bill featured Ten Wheels Drive, Johnny Winter, John Sebastian, Steppenwolf, and Creedence Clearwater Revival. Miles Davis was also slated to perform, but he arrived late and missed his set time. He was going around with his then-girlfriend. Mansour said, "Aren't you going to play?" He said, "I came here intending to play, but they stated I wasn't there when it was my turn. So, I'm waiting here to see what happens."

There were already a lot of musicians performing that day, so he never got the chance to perform.

Janis Joplin came out with Big Brother and the Holding Company, her old band. She hadn't played with them in some time. It was a reunion, as well as the last time they would play together. When she came out, the stadium lights were too strong for her. She started yelling, "Turn off the lights!... It's too bright!" When the light-man didn't react, her anger increased. "I can't sing in this glaring light! Don't you understand!" She screamed and started becoming hysterical.

Then the crowd began to demand that the lights be turned off. After a while, when the lights went out, she finally started to sing. She sang mostly soul and blues. The stadium was now quite dark. She sang Burt Bacharach's "What the World Needs Now" as a duet with Dionne Warwick, as well as her own songs. Janis was probably debilitated by drugs and alcohol at the time, and her singing was not as impressive as I remembered her on records.

This festival was just a year after Woodstock, but it still had a lot of the flower-power flavor of that era. The most impressive that night were Steppenwolf and Creedence Clearwater Revival (often abbreviated as CCR). They both played quite late. I'm really glad I got to experience this kind of rock festival.

Steppenwolf had become well-known for "Born to be Wild," which was used as the opening title theme for the movie *Easy Rider*, but in the early days, they were quite an avant-garde improvisational band. "The Pusher," from the album *Early Steppenwolf*, is a 21-minute improvisation-heavy performance. I often thought that it was more avant-garde than King Crimson's "Larks' Tongues in Aspic."

I saw them at the time when *Monster* and *Steppenwolf Live* were released, and they mainly played songs from those albums, with vocalist John Kay standing in the middle of a dark stage. *Monster* was about America, and this ten-minute suite was comprised of a song protesting the American invasion of Vietnam. At the time, the lyrics of this song appeared in the magazine *Hit Parade*. Steppenwolf's stage ended with "Born to be Wild." If you had asked me then what I wanted to be when I grew up, I would have responded, "Something like what this band is doing."

I've always thought that Creedence Clearwater Revival's masterpiece is their album, *Cosmos Factory*. This album has a good blend of blues-rock elements and long jam improvisations. The guitarist/singer John Fogerty had an incredible voice; even though he was white, he could sing like a black gospel singer. I was impressed by John Fogerty's powerful singing over simple chord progressions and funky rhythms.

When I saw a video of his performance in 2016, he still had the same voice as he did back then, which is very impressive. It's rare to find someone from this era performing so well today. He was influenced by black vocalists like Howlin' Wolf and Wilson Pickett and studied how to sing with such a voice.

CCR only existed for four years, from 1968 to 1971. John Fogerty often told the following story in interviews:

When they were playing as an opening act in their hometown of San Francisco, after their first album was released, they were only given ten minutes for a sound check before the doors opened. John was strumming one chord and singing "woohoo" when the PA crew suddenly unplugged them and said, "The doors are open! Stop it! People like you will disappear anyway." He got mad and said, "Well, we'll see what happens in a year!" A year later, Ike and Tina Turner had a huge hit with his song "Proud Mary," which charted high on the R&B chart.

The main part of this tune is built on a single D major chord. The chorus likewise consists of one D major chord, with other chords appearing only in the intro and bridge. The rhythm of the English words, as well as how they are sung are the charm of this song. The song is in a major chord and appears cheerful on the surface, yet there is a dangerous shadow behind his voice. I have often felt this when listening to many classic blues tunes.

During the two weeks of winter vacation in 1970, I went to see my father for the first time in many years in San Francisco. It was probably the first time since 1968 that I saw him for more than a few days. He had just married an Irish-Polish American named Karen. When your parents are divorced and live in different cities, it is nice to see them after a long time. They tend to be kinder than usual because they don't see you as often.

My father, my stepmother Karen, and I went to the show, but Karen gripped her ears tightly and appeared to be in pain when Edgar Winter's band began to play. Then she left in the middle of the show—she couldn't stand the loud volume. Edgar Winter's shows at that time played mainly black soul music with a big band consisting of white musicians. They called the band White Trash. It was very different from the music of Emerson Lake and Palmer, but bands were often booked together regardless of the difference in their genre. Edgar Winter later became widely known for his instrumental composition named "Frankenstein," which he played mainly on an Arp Synthesizer. That song became a hit, and I would listen to it a lot. But their performance on that day in Berkeley was not that impressive.

Emerson Lake and Palmer just released an album titled *Tarkus*. It was the second time I got to see this band. Last time, they played an arrangement of *Pictures at an Exhibition* in the first half of the show, but this time, the setlist was "The Barbarian," "Take a Pebble," "Tarkus—Lucky Man—Epitaph," "Knife Edge," and encore "Nut Rocker," a rock version of the march from Tchaikovsky's 1892 ballet *The Nutcracker*.

Tarkus was a suite that lasted more than 30 minutes in a live performance. In the middle of this song, Keith Emerson pulled out a very long wired stick from his Moog Synthesizer, and every time he swung it around, a piercing electronic sound would go up and down. During drum solos, Carl Palmer frequently removed his shirt and undressed all the way to his bottom half. He was popular among gays at the time since he had a really pretty face.

Figure 25 Photo from 1970. In San Francisco with my father, Yuji Takahashi, and my stepmother, Karen.

I don't think my father enjoyed the concert. "The Barbarian" was based on Béla Bartók's 1911 piano piece *Allegro Barbaro*, and Keith Emerson was a good classical and jazz piano player, but my father didn't seem to like the rock beat and the showmanship. As I watched the show, I marveled at how the three of them were able to achieve so much with their musical performance alone. There were no light shows or costumes, or any other visual effects.

There was also a concert that Terry Riley organized for the singer of Indian traditional music, Pandit Pran Nath. It took place in what looked like a large living room in a normal residential apartment building.

A man with long black hair spoke to Karen at the entrance. "I'd like to go to the concert, but I don't have enough money," he said.

Karen gave him a dollar.

"Why did you give him a dollar?" I asked.

"Because he said that he wanted to go to the concert, but he probably won't come. I think he just wanted a dollar."

There were many cases in those days where people could somehow get in without tickets or money at these kinds of concerts. The feeling that people could trust each other had been stronger in San Francisco than in New York since about 1966. There was an atmosphere of those who 'have' should share with the 'have-nots.' I entered a room full of hippies who had come to listen to Indian music. The guy who asked for the dollar earlier was there too.

The Indian singer, Pandit Pran Nath, was staying at Terry Riley's house. Terry's wife had told Karen that she was tired of the Indian telling her too many rules, such as not to eat this kind of food or do such and such thing. She told Karen, "If that Indian doesn't leave, I will leave myself."

Without a PA, Terry Riley and his daughter began to accompany the Indian vocalist. Terry's daughter played the *tamboura*[3] all the way through the performance.

Terry Riley's daughter and I played jump rope once when I was eight years old in New York City. I recall that she was in the fourth grade when I was in the second grade.

Pandit Pran Nath later released a solo album, *Ragas,* on the French label Shandar, produced by La Monte Young.

We had three tickets to the Grateful Dead's New Year's concert on December 31, but Karen didn't want to go, and my father wasn't that interested either. I ended up going with Paul Chihara, a Japanese-American composer who was living in San Francisco at the time, as well as Karen's friend Margie.

The bands that performed at this concert in Winterland were, in order of appearance:

Stoneground

New Riders of the Purple Sage

Hot Tuna

Grateful Dead.

The crowd in San Francisco was rowdier than the crowd in New York. The guy sitting right next to me was completely tripping out on LSD and laughing his head off. I asked him a few times, "Are you alright?"

The lineup of Hot Tuna was the same as on their classic album *Burgers*: Jorma Kaukonen on guitar, Jack Casady (from Jefferson Airplane) on bass, Papa John Creech on electric violin, and Sammy

---

[3]A *tamboura* is a stringed instrument that accompanies a raga by playing the root note and its fifth degree and octave as a drone without holding anything down.

Piazza on drums. I had seen Hot Tuna four times in total; I had also seen them as an acoustic band at the Fillmore East before this, but this New Year's concert was the most powerful I remember of theirs. This was my first time seeing Papa John Creech, the black violinist, who performed powerful blues phrases that I had previously heard only on an electric guitar. This day's performance was mainly electric blues songs such as "Candyman" and "Come Back Baby."

The countdown from 1970 to 1971 began, with "3, 2, 1, 0… Happy New Year!" spoken aloud, and the Grateful Dead began to perform. Jerry Garcia, Bob Weir, and Phil Lesh were all smiling happily on stage.

A huge party ball on the ceiling opened, and confetti began to fall from it. The audience was ecstatic, shouting and yelling. The band started with "Truckin'." I thought the Grateful Dead performed far better live than on their studio records. The crowd had come together as one, and the venue was buzzing with enthusiasm.

In the summer of 1973, I went to see a show at Gaelic Park that featured three bands: Humble Pie, Edgar Winter, and Ramatam.

The press promoted Ramatam as a new supergroup with several musicians, including drummer Mitch Mitchell of The Jimi Hendrix Experience, bassist Rick Grech of Blind Faith, female lead guitarist April Lawton, and singer Mike Pinera, who had previously been with Iron Butterfly. Rumor had it that April Lawton didn't sing but was beautiful and played hard blues rock guitar just like Hendrix. The experimental improvisational elements heard in *Electric Ladyland* by Jimi Hendrix were present in Ramatam. Since there are millions of people all over the world who wish they could be the next Hendrix, their sales point was that they had Mitch Mitchell. They opened the concert show.

Edgar Winter played second. This time, he was playing a synthesizer that was slung over his shoulder. The music was very different from the white soul music he had previously performed; his synthesizer became the main instrument of the band, and the instrumental "Frankenstein" achieved significant commercial success. The live performance exhibited a distinct prog-rock inclination during that period, rendering it considerably more captivating than my initial encounter with him.

Lastly, the headlining act, Humble Pie, performed. I saw them live around the time of the *Smokin'* and *Eat It* albums, but in my opinion, *Rock On* and *Rockin' the Fillmore* are the two greatest works by Humble Pie. Some of the most incredible rock music of the era was performed on those albums, with a lineup of Peter Frampton on lead guitar, Steve Marriott on guitar vocals, Greg Ridley on bass, and Jerry Shirley on percussion.

The 25-minute arrangement of "Walk on Gilded Splinters" featured a dynamic interplay among the band members that was almost suggestive of a telepathic energy. Although Jerry Shirley's percussion adheres to the rock style, he possessed the same ability to alter the tempo and rhythm as Tony Williams did in the Miles Davis Quintet.

Peter Frampton had already left by the time I saw them, and Clem Clempson was playing the guitar. The band had evolved into Steve Marriott's band, and there was less improvisational interplay between the members than there used to be.

Eat It wasn't released yet, but they had already performed songs from the album at Gaelic Park, including "Up Our Sleeves," "Honky Tonk Woman," and "Roadrunner." When the band started playing "I Don't Need No Doctor" as their final song, the crowd in the crowd created a huge wave by clapping their hands and swaying in time with the music.

The next time Humble Pie came to New York, they played at Madison Square Garden, which seats 20,000 people. They enlisted three black female chorus singers as backup musicians. It was called the *Eat It Tour*. I was really delighted by Steve Marriott's funky organ playing on their single "Hot 'n' Nasty" from their album *Smokin'*, which they performed as an encore.

Humble Pie was a band that deserved to be as popular as Led Zeppelin. But this was their peak—they recorded two more albums before breaking up. The last time I saw Steve Marriot's band, they were performing in a London pub in front of 20–30 people. From 20,000 to 20 in the audience—it must have been a psychological shock for him.

Every Friday night, beginning in 1972, two TV shows aired featuring rock bands—these programs introduced me to a variety of bands. *In Concert* began at 11:30 p.m. and ended at 1 a.m., where the *Midnight Special* took over programming until 2:30 a.m. *Midnight*

Special introduced me to the band Steeleye Span. I went to the record store to buy their most current CD after seeing the female vocalist, Maddy Prior, in a 19th-century Victorian dress, throwing flowers to the audience while singing "Cam Ye O'er Frae France." It was the first time I'd ever heard an electric rock band perform a song in the medieval European style. To me, it sounded like a Middle Eastern or Asian scale. Modal melodies had the most influence on me while I was in my mid-teens.

Genesis played "Watcher of the Sky" and "Musical Box" on *Midnight Special*, featuring Peter Gabriel's costume and mime routines. *In Concert* was more of a live concert broadcast than a television show. When the Allman Brothers appeared on *In Concert*, they would perform 20 minutes of improvisations interspersed with TV ads.

The Third Ear Band was known for their work on Roman Polanski's film *Macbeth*. This was another band that based their sound on medieval music that I discovered around this time. The band consisted of oboe, cello, violin, electric guitar, and ethnic percussion, and their music was a natural combination of medieval music and psychedelic improvisation that still sounds fresh to this day.

Around 1971, the Academy of Music, a 3,400-seat auditorium, was the primary venue for rock performances in New York City. It was located at East 14th Street and Third Avenue, near Union Square. This was within walking distance from my apartment on Horatio Street. On weekdays, it operated as a movie theatre. When I was in junior high, I would occasionally stroll there by myself; the audience there was predominantly from junior high school to college age. Typically, three bands would perform each night, shrouded by clouds of marijuana smoke.

The loudest band I saw at the Academy of Music was Argent. The band consisted of four members, led by keyboardist Rod Argent. Rod Argent composed the hit song "Time of the Season" while still with The Zombies in the 1960s. I saw Argent just after they released their progressive rock album *NEXUS*.

They began with the first instrumental piece from *NEXUS*, "The Coming of Kohoutek," but the music was so loud that when the drummer slammed his drums, my stomach felt like it was punched with a fist. Perhaps something happened before the concert or during the sound check. The band members had an odd expression on their faces as if they were saying, "Take this, this, and this!... Give them hell!" I was with my mother and stepfather, Mansour, when Mansour exclaimed, "This is crazy!" and sprang from his seat. He would return to our seats several times during the concert to inform us that we should leave since it was damaging our hearing. No other band, including Led Zeppelin and other hard rock bands, has ever been so loud. The bass player and drummer from that period eventually joined The Kinks in the 1980s, and I saw them live a few times, but never this loud.

The hits "Hold Your Head Up" and "Time of the Season" were performed at the end of their program, which was mostly made up of *NEXUS* songs, but "Hold Your Head Up" was performed with extensive improvisations. Rick Wakeman of Yes subsequently said that Rod Argent was one of the best organ musicians of his time, and these performances demonstrated why.

Tranquility was one of my favorite lesser-known bands. They have performed as the opening act at the Academy of Music on several occasions. They released only two albums, which are now available on YouTube.

The manager of the British folk singer, Donovan, founded the band Tranquility. The band had a British traditional folk flavor that was nicely mixed with Beatles-style pop color but unfortunately vanished following an incident in which all their equipment was stolen. Terry Shaddick, the band's leader, eventually made a fortune by writing the song "Physical" for female singer Olivia Newton-John, which became a worldwide hit. The lead guitarist, Berkeley Wright, later appeared on an album by Pascal Comelade, a French experimental avant-pop musician.

Tranquility had a distinct sound, and I still occasionally listen to their records. It demonstrates how good bands can slip from history if luck is not on their side.

When I look at their photos from those days, I get the feeling that they were allowed to appear that way because it was around 1970, the time when Glam Rock was popular. Terry Shaddick wore black lipstick and had his fingernails painted in an eye-catching color, along with various necklaces and women's attire, but his face was incredibly masculine, giving him the appearance of a weird monster.

However, his tunes and voice were excellent. Their sound evokes a sense of innocence, comparable to that of Fleetwood Mac when Danny Kirwan was their guitarist and main songwriter.

10cc performed as the opening act at a performance headlined by Rory Gallagher. The event took place on March 9, 1974, at the Academy of Music. The concert began with a tape recording of a dialogue spoken by Vincent Price from *The Devil's Triangle*, which went: "Ships don't just disappear in the night, do they?" At this point, 10cc starts playing "Ships Don't Disappear (Do They?)." Paul Burgess performed as an additional drummer in a supporting role. He drummed alone when Kevin Godley, the drummer of 10cc, sang "Fresh Air for My Mama" in front of the stage. Kevin Godley's vocals were great, making him the standout vocalist in the band. Although only their debut album was available in the United States at the time, they performed "Worst Band in the World," a song intended for their upcoming album, which later became a minor hit. They concluded with "Rubber Bullets," a major hit in the United States. Despite being the opening act and having a brief time slot, they delivered the finest performance of the day.

Rory Gallagher's performance did not make as significant an impact on me as 10cc's did. Sometimes, a good band can steal the show.

I saw several live performances by Peter Frampton with his band Frampton's Camel after he left Humble Pie. His guitar playing was lyrical and mesmerizing. He performed extended guitar solos reminiscent of his time with Humble Pie, and similar to other jam bands from that period.

By the time of the release of his most successful album *Frampton Comes Alive!* in 1976, he transitioned to a more mainstream and popular style. However, I liked his guitar playing in the performances leading up to that time and during the Humble Pie period.

The only concert I saw at the Academy of Music that became so boring that I wanted to leave halfway through was Alvin Lee's solo live show. Gentle Giant was the supporting act.

Gentle Giant appeared on the television show *In Concert*. At the time, they were performing a medley of songs from their *Octopus* album, and their intricate rhythmic interaction was fascinating to hear and see. I was to learn later that these rhythms were similar to those of the medieval isorhythmic motet. At the concert, they mostly performed songs from their then-new album *In a Glass House*. They did not play for very long. I felt that they didn't have a strong personality like Genesis, ELP, or Yes, but they were nonetheless good in their own way.

Alvin Lee looked amazing and cool when he was playing hard rock blues with Ten Years After, but on this tour, he performed mainly laid-back acoustic folk in his clogs (Dutch sandals) in front of a large backup band. The band's performance was monotonous. I paid to see them but found it boring and I didn't feel like staying till the end. Although many people can express themselves great in an unplugged acoustic setting, Alvin Lee with this band was not one of them. The band just didn't gel.

In contrast, Traffic sounded great with a big band.

It was around the time of their album *Shoot Out At The Fantasy Factory*. The main members of Traffic were Steve Winwood, Jim Capaldi, and Chris Wood, but this album was recorded with four members of the Muscle Shoals Rhythm Section: bassist David Hood, drummer Roger Hawkins, keyboardist Barry Beckett, and guitarist Jimmy Johnson. These were a group of American session musicians based in the northern Alabama town of Muscle Shoals. Except for Johnson, all the recording members were on this tour along with Ghanaian percussionist, Rebop Kwaku Baah.

There were seven of them on stage: Steve Winwood was the leader, singing and playing both keyboards and guitar very well—I especially like his electric lead guitar solos. Even though Eric Clapton was the more popular guitarist in the band Blind Faith, Steve Winwood has a unique psychedelic style of playing different from the more blues-based Clapton. The song "Dear Mr. Fantasy" by Traffic has been covered by the Grateful Dead for many years, but Steve's guitar solo on this song has a unique color all its own.

Drummer Jim Capaldi was not playing drums on this tour but hitting a tambourine and singing along. He co-wrote many of the songs with Steve Winwood. Chris Wood on flute and saxophone was an alcoholic by this time and wandered around the stage looking very drunk. Wood had introduced the British traditional folk song, "John Barleycorn" to the band and was a major contributor to their music, by at this point his drinking seemed to be a problem. In 1983,

Wood was to die of liver disease, said to be caused by his drinking.

The songs were getting longer and longer, with a duration of 10 to 20 minutes each; this allowed for a very free feeling in the music that you can get from a good psychedelic jam session. Even when listening to it today, one can still feel the sense of freedom that existed in the early 1970s.

Steve Winwood became a much more successful artist in the 80s, winning Grammys in this period, but I personally liked his recordings better from the Blind Faith period to this period of Traffic.

I also saw many other bands like Renaissance, Nektar, King Crimson, Wishbone Ash, and Caravan at the Academy of Music in the early 1970s. The record shops started to stock European rock bands like Gong, Can, and Tangerine Dream, and I became interested in these bands.

I saw Hawkwind twice—during the *Space Ritual* tour and *The Hall of the Mountain Grill* tour at the Academy of Music.

The record company did a lot of promotion for *Space Ritual*. In a full-page newspaper advertisement, there was a picture of a young man wearing broken glasses and big black letters saying that they had sent a young man from America to England to preview the *Space Ritual* show and that he had come back with his glasses all shattered and looking like he'd lost his mind. This made people wonder what it was about; at the same time, it made people think that it must have been great. They were also introduced as "the last psychedelic band." However, the review in the magazine *Circus* said, "It sounds like you've stuck your head in a washing machine." At that time, Hawkwind, and the German bands, Amon Düül and Can were often criticized like this in the press. There was a one-word review of Can in *Circus* which simply wrote "Can't"—but these criticisms did not have a negative effect. On the contrary, it made people wonder what they sounded like. Reading these kinds of criticisms was how I got into these bands. It made me feel that they could be interesting.

When Hawkwind did the *Space Ritual* show, a Welsh band called Man opened the show.

Man had just released an album called *Be Good to Yourself at Least Once a Day*. They were a jam rock band with a lot in common with the Grateful Dead, playing with a light show that made their shadows appear like flashes on the white screen in the back of the stage. After about 40 minutes of Man, they changed the stage set-up, and Hawkwind started playing. With the sound of a spaceship leaving the Earth to go out into space, they began with the song, "Born to Go." Their light show was more elaborate than in the psychedelic era of the '60s, mixing moving images of space projected onto the stage backdrop screen. It felt like a rock planetarium. Stacia, a female dancer, was dancing on the left side of the stage. Each song was about 10 minutes long, and all the sounds except for the drums and bass were filled and went through the effects of the echo machine.

In between songs, Bob Calvert read some spacy poetry. During the reading of "Sonic Attack," two searchlights were rotated from the left and right side of the stage toward the audience. It was very effective.

The music, lights, and dance all came together to make this psychedelic show effective.

For *The Hall of the Mountain Grill* show, I was in the second row from the front, facing the left side of the stage. Stacia, the dancer, and Nick Turner, the saxophonist, were right in front of me. Nick Turner was dancing with Stacia the whole time, wearing a frog costume. Stacia noticed a customer in the first row, smoking marijuana, so she bent down, took it from the audience member, and smoked some. The audience member in front of me was listening with her cat on her shoulder. The cat was also listening to Hawkwind. An animated image was also projected behind me. The song "Wind of Change" sounded like the ending of Pink Floyd's "Saucerful of Secrets."

There were changes in the lineup from the last time: Bob Calvert was gone, and a former member of the Third Ear Band, Simon House, joined them on keyboards and violin. The rhythm section of Lemmy and Simon King, who later formed the first incarnation of the heavy metal band Motorhead, was great.

Truthfully, by the time the reputation of these bands arrived in the US, these bands had already broken up or changed their sound. By

1975, the culture of the new liberal and free society that had begun in the late 1960s was crumbling and falling apart in the Western countries of the US, Western Europe, and Japan. Many bands became more commercial and accessible.

Before I knew it, the atmosphere had changed completely. In the late 70s, disco, fusion, and punk took over the major scene—and this was to be the mainstream for the rest of the 1970s.

The Kinks

In the mid-1970s, rock concerts began to transform into larger-scale entertainment events. The Kinks created two rock musical productions; Mott the Hoople played a one-week engagement at the Broadway Uris Theatre; Queen was the opening act for Mott the Hoople's Broadway shows. David Bowie also performed at New York City's Radio City Music Hall, which is well-known for its musicals.

Every band appeared to be vying with one another to produce a more noteworthy musical performance. I saw many of these shows.

I thought the Kinks' musical act was particularly fantastic. I'm not sure how they pulled off such a large-scale production. With a complete brass section, multiple chorus singers portraying various roles, and a rock band, the *Preservation* show had all the makings of an authentic Broadway production. Having that many people on tour must have been costly and challenging. They might have lost money traveling around the United States with so many people. Since this tour, The Kinks have never performed a show quite like this, but it was fun to watch. Looking back, I'm sure that Ray Davies of The Kinks was quite influenced by Kurt Weill's musical *Happy Ending*.

It was through these live shows that *Preservation* truly came to life, not on the record. Great tunes were on the albums, *Preservation Act One* and *Preservation Act Two*. They have some of my favorite songs by Ray Davies. But just listening to it on record was like listening to a soundtrack album. The real impact was in watching the stage performance.

The show began with "Daylight." It was daybreak in the quiet town of Village Green. Every villager begins their day. Then, a gangster named Flash arrives to town and buys up properties all across town, rebuilds them, and resells them for a higher price. Flash is a man who started in the working class and worked his way up. He will not accept any laxity. *"We'll buy up all the towns, and we'll knock them all down/Build a brand new world of our own,"* he sings.

Lead singer Ray Davies plays the character of Flash on stage. He performs his character, delivers his lines between songs, and even addresses the audience with *"Isn't that right?"* to elicit audience participation.

The political revolutionary Mr. Black stands in stark contrast to Flash. Mr. Black sings of saving the people from corrupt politicians and says, *"Every woman, every man, stand together."* He also promises that one day he will lead the people to freedom. Ray Davies portrays Mr. Black in a black and white film that is shown on screen, so he was playing two roles—one in a black and white film, the other being Flash, the charismatic leader on stage.

The majority of the songs at a Kinks concert are usually sung by Ray Davies; however, in this *Preservation* musical—as in other musicals—other vocalists took on the roles of the other important characters and sang their songs. Even the hit single "Mirror of Love," which was sung by Davies on the album, was sung by a female singer playing the role of Flash's girlfriend.

Some old-school Kinks fans may have been disappointed because Ray Davies didn't take center stage on all the songs. But this was the rock musical at its best, and this was my favorite period of The Kinks. I especially like "Nothing Lasts Forever," "Mirror of Love," and "Oh Where Oh Where Is Love."

Ray Davies sang, in the song "Oh Where Oh Where Is Love," on how the fairy tales and picture books we were encouraged to read as youngsters gave us a false view of reality. How can you be honest in a world rife with hate, anger, and resentment? Where is the kind of love you read about in fairy tales and picture books?

Every night, when you close your eyes and you ask the stars above, "Where is the love we read about?" There is no room for love and passion in a society full of deception, murder, and suicide.

How can you be honest in a world of rape, hate, and resentment? There is no place for love and romance in a world of phony stories, murder, and suicide.

And every night when I close my eyes, I ask the stars above:

"Oh Where Oh Where Is Love?"

Where is the compassion or trust? Where is all the stuff I've heard people used to do in the old days?

Does the joy for simple things still exist?

Towards the end of *Preservation*, Flash's conscience informs Flash: "*You said you were doing everything for your country, for your people, but you were only doing it for yourself.*"

Flash weakens as he begins to question his own deeds: he is no longer the charismatic gangster; his girlfriend leaves him; Mr. Black has captured him and created a new country for the working-class people. Mr. Black begins to monitor everyone's brains. He creates a new artificial man with a body like Tarzan and a beautiful face like Cary Grant.

The chorus sings that while people may be enduring difficult times now, we should not dwell on the past, for a brave new world has dawned. The chorus sings that we should all join hands and march into the future.

Preservation was probably produced at a loss. Ray Davies created these performances because he wanted to spread his message through his musicals. He was prepared to lose money for his work. The Kinks have never toured with such a large spectacle since then. Perhaps it was only conceivable in the early 1970s. But it was wonderful to witness it.

On the Kinks' next tour, they did a miniature musical show with a smaller cast, called *Soap Opera*. In the first part of the show, they played songs from the *Preservation* musical.

The second half of the concert featured a performance of songs from *Soap Opera*, together with written dialogue from the plot. This time, there was only one guest, an actress. The plot revolves around Ray Davies, a rock singer and producer, who tries out the life of a 'normal' 9 to 5 job as an accountant. Finally, his wife informs him that the contrary is true and that the accountant has a fantasy of becoming a rock star. Ray Davies announces: "*Lies, I'm a rock star*" and begins playing all of the classic Kinks' hits, much to the pleasure of the audience. However, the story concludes with the discovery that he was simply a regular guy, not a rock star after all.

This concert was interesting, but I preferred the *Preservation* show.

Figure 26 1973. Photo of The Kinks show at the Felt Forum, New York. Photographed by Ayuo.

About Yes

Yes was a very innovative group in their early days.

They started out by covering a wide range of different music: soul music, classical music, film music, musicals, folk, and television music; they mixed it all. Pete Banks, their original guitarist, wrote in the liner notes of their early live performances that it was similar to the way people use samplers to take parts from different music and use them in a new context. Bill Bruford, their original drummer, talked of how the theme from the Western TV show *Bonanza* was taken and transformed to become the opening for the song "Yours is no Disgrace."

As a progressive rock band, their peak was around their albums, *Close to the Edge, Tales from the Topographic Oceans,* and *Relayer.*

This was around the time that I saw them live in New York City.

The first time I saw them was at Gaelic Park, an outdoor park in the Bronx, New York, on August 16, 1972. It was a dirty park, and near the exit was a pile of trash and broken bottles. The producers of this concert might have had in mind a summer outdoor event like Woodstock, but there was no lawn in Gaelic Park, so everyone had to sit on the concrete.

I was with my mother's distant relatives who came from Japan that day, and we were watching them at the front of the stage. Their drummer, Bill Bruford, had suddenly left before this tour began, and this was one of the first concerts without him. Bruford was responsible for introducing a lot of rhythmic influences from jazz, making the music sound more progressive in the process. Bruford also played keyboards and came up with parts of the music for songs like "Heart of the Sunrise," "Siberian Khatru," and "And You and I."

It was the combination of different music genres that made Yes sound unique. They had harmony vocals like The Byrds, Crosby Stills Nash and Young, and The Beach Boys. The keyboards were played by Rick Wakeman, a classically trained ex-studio musician, who introduced classical music elements and melodies. The band was originally formed by singer/lyricist Jon Anderson, and bassist/composer/arranger Chris Squire.

Chris Squire was an experienced chorister from the time he was a child and came up with the vocal arrangements. He was influenced by John Entwistle in his bass playing and played a very melodic bass, which many would have associated with the lead guitar. Jon Anderson wrote stream-of-consciousness lyrics and sang in his natural alto-tenor range. Sometimes his critics would write that Anderson's lyrics don't make sense, but they often sounded wonderful sonically.

During the first half of the concert, the audience in front of us was standing, and there were angry shouts from behind. The vocalist, Jon Anderson, told the audience, "We're here to play music. It's not our job to tell you what to do. But if it's good for everyone, you should all sit down." The crowd up front still wouldn't sit down, and the chants of "Sit down!" got louder. So, Anderson said, "Okay, stand up," and the whole audience stood up until the end of the show.

The setlist was as follows:

Firebird Suite/I've Seen All Good People/Siberian Khatru/Mood for A Day/Heart of The Sunrise/And You and I/Wakeman Solo/Roundabout/Yours Is No Disgrace.

I had recorded it all on a cassette recorder at that time, but I lost it when I lost my home in New York in 1975. I later found a pirated copy of this same performance later on. It was the first tour with Alan White and he hadn't fully settled in yet, but he did a good job. He was a professional studio musician who had played with John Lennon, among others, and you could never tell that he had just joined. Sometimes the bass player, Chris Squire, would give him cues, while jumping up and down with the rhythm of the music, wearing a black cape.

In 1973, Yes released a two-record set with four side-long tracks ranging between 18 and 21 minutes, as if it were a 19th-century classical symphony like those composed by Mahler. It was their first studio album with Alan White, but I liked his contributions both as a drummer and as a composer. He is credited on "The Remembering" and "Ritual" for coming up with the music for parts of the song.

Their *Tales from Topographic Oceans* tour from 1974 sold out Madison Square Garden, a 20,000-seat venue in NYC. I went to both shows on February 18th and 20th.

I had a friend at school named Dave. He had bought two tickets for us to go. These Yes concerts were on Mondays and Wednesdays, so after school Dave would come over to my house and we would play Monopoly, a property-buying board game, until it was time to go.

This concert was longer than the previous Yes concerts.

The set list was as follows:

Firebird Suite/Siberian Khatru/And You and I/Close to the Edge/ The Revealing Science of God/The Remembering/The Ancient/ Ritual/Roundabout.

They did all the songs on "Close to the Edge" and "Tales of Topographic Oceans" in their entirety. Their concerts were getting bigger and longer.

"The Remembering" was especially good. Rick Wakeman took a very long and emotional solo on the Moog synthesizer. Truth be told, he didn't like the songs on *Tales of Topographic Oceans* that much. Most of the songs were composed by Steve Howe on the guitar with other members adding additional parts. Chris Squire later said that he felt he had come up with some of the most intricate parts so far in his career; but since the music was so guitar-centric, there was often very little room for Wakeman's keyboards, and he wound up playing a lot of padding behind the guitar parts. So, his solo on "The Remembering" was a spot where he could really shine, and I think he really let go in this part.

Rick Wakeman took a very long and emotional lead solo on the Moog synthesizer, which was quite different from what he played on the album. Some of the other members of Yes did not like him doing that and apparently told him as such, so he quit playing with Yes for a while after this tour. His solo career was taking off anyway.

Wakeman didn't enjoy playing the jazz fusion-influenced parts in "The Ancient" or the songs Yes wrote for their next album, *Relayer*. Jon Anderson, with whom he had a brotherly relationship, sent him the song, "Wanderous Stories," in 1976 to entice him back to Yes for the recordings of *Going for the One*. This album also has "Turn of the Century" written by Anderson with Alan White and Steve Howe. "Siberian Khatru," "Close to the Edge," "The Remembering," and "Turn of the Century" are my favorite songs by Yes.

I used to cover both a part of "Close to the Edge" and "Turn of the Century" in my live shows.

On November 20th, 1974, Yes played the *Relayer* concert at Madison Square Garden. The opening act was Gryphon; they got a lot of attention for using European medieval instruments such as crumhorns and recorders, and for playing Renaissance tunes. Gryphon's short set ended with a fun European medieval song.

The set list for this Yes show was as follows:

Firebird Suite/Sound Chaser/Close to the Edge/To Be Over/Gates of Delirium/And You and I/Ritual/Siberian Khatru/Roundabout.

This time, there were a lot of stage props. First of all, each member appeared from a tube that looked like something out of a sci-fi movie. These kinds of stage props were parodied in the film *Spinal Tap*, a comedy parodying the excesses of prog rock and hard rock bands in the 70s.

A new keyboard player—Patrick Moraz—who could play jazz and avant-garde, joined the band to replace Wakeman. Speakers were placed all over the venue to create a surround sound effect, and they made the sound go all over the whole venue.

This was quite effective with a song like "Sound Chaser" where a Balinese chant suddenly pops up from here and there. I was lucky I was in the front, but the people in the back seemed to be startled by the sudden loud sound coming from a speaker near them.

The front of the auditorium was filled with the smoke and smell of marijuana. By the time they played "Ritual," I was feeling very good. There were a lot of junior high and high school kids in the audience. Everyone was out of their seats, sitting on the floor, surrounded by marijuana smoke, and they all looked stoned. The performers were probably high, too.

Perhaps you could say that this 'peaceful atmosphere' was just an illusion, but this was what many wanted in this age right as the Vietnam War was ending. It was certainly peaceful.

After this period, the band started to fall apart. Members wanted to do different things: Jon Anderson left. Rick Wakeman left. They got Trevor Horn to replace Jon Anderson. Trevor Horn was to become one of the best music producers of pop music in the 1980s, but as a singer, Trevor Horn didn't work out very well in Yes. The audience was expecting Jon Anderson and his unique alto voice.

Trevor Horn said that when Yes was touring Britain, during a very quiet moment in the middle of a song, an audience member yelled "Fuck off," and he wanted to stop singing. Trevor Horn's wife and manager, Jill Sinclair told him that if he pursued production, he would become the best in the world. And from the early 1980s, he began a successful career as a producer.

As I have written elsewhere, I did not like much of the pop music in the early 1980s. I liked Prince, and I would discover Siouxsie and the Banshees and The Cure later. However, some of the records produced by Trevor Horn were very innovative. They were some of the best from this period. He would come up with unique ways of incorporating samples that no one had done before. In a 12-inch single, he produced for the group Propaganda, there were snippets of orchestral cluster music that sounded like Penderecki or Xenakis.

Since he was still friends with Chris Squire of Yes, he was asked to produce a new album of what was to become *Yes* with the South African guitarist Trevor Rabin. Horn said that people around him told him that Yes was no longer relevant and that he should no longer work with them. But Horn was determined to re-make their sound to fit the 1980s. And he succeeded in doing so.

From 1981, Horn formed a production team featuring programmer J. J. Jeczalik, engineer Gary Langan, and keyboard player/string arranger Anne Dudley. In 1983, while Horn's team was working on the Yes comeback album *90125*, they began recording on their own. The Red & Blue Mix of Yes's "Owner of a Lonely Heart" single, showcased the prototype sound of the group that came to be known as The Art of Noise. They joined forces with music journalist Paul Morley as a provider of concepts, art direction, and marketing ideas.

They produced some of the best avant-garde synth-pop of the time. But my personal favorite of theirs is their comeback album *The Seduction of Claude Debussy*, released in 1999, and their live recordings from 1999 and 2000, which were released on CD as *Reconstructed* and on DVD as *Into Vision*. Lol Creme, formerly of 10cc had joined them. Their arrangements and reconstruction of Debussy's music were unique and wonderful. They crafted new arrangements of "The Songs of Bilitis" and Debussy's opera *Pelléas et Mélisande*. These are not the more popular pieces by Debussy that most people know such as *Clair de lune, La fille aux cheveux de lin, Rêverie,* and *Deux Arabesques.* They chose the more obscure but deep works by Debussy and made arrangements that showed their beauty. It is too bad that many people do not yet know of these albums.

For some reason, progressive rock fans tend to be quite conservative, and most are not fans of Art of Noise, even though I think that Art of Noise was truly 'progressive' in the real meaning of the word for some of their early work and their album of Debussy. "Progressive Rock" became a genre, and its fans tend to want those bands to continue playing the same kind of sound. Trevor Horn's production in Yes' songs like "Leave It" was also revolutionary, especially if you hear the acapella version.

I also like Jon Anderson's lyrics, not just for Yes, but also his solo songs such as "Animation," "And When the Night Comes," and "Deborah" on the Jon and Vangelis' album *Private Collection*. He has said in interviews that he was influenced by Joni Mitchell, and his stream-of-consciousness lyrics seem to show some similarity.

What made bands like this interesting was that musicians from very different backgrounds could gather and make unique music by mixing all their influences.

This was how I got to interview Bill Bruford, who was one of my favorite drummers.

Bill Bruford interview

For many people of my generation, Bill Bruford is a legend whose drumming we grew up listening to in bands like Yes, King Crimson, Bruford, Genesis, UK, and many others. He contributed important compositional ideas to the albums regarded as Yes' masterpieces: *Fragile, Close to the Edge,* and *The Yes Album.* He then went on to further consolidate his drumming style in King Crimson, before composing and making his own more jazz-oriented albums from the late 70s onward.

He first formed Earthworks with Django Bates, Iain Ballamy, and Tim Harries. After rejoining Yes and King Crimson in the early 90s, he recorded a jazz trio album with Ralph Towner and Eddie Gomez in 1997, and since then he has returned to a more acoustic jazz style.

He reformed Earthworks with new members in 1998; in passing remarks, he felt the new Earthworks would be positioned somewhere between Bill Stewart (ex-drummer for Pat Metheny, whose *Snide Remarks* Bill regards as a big influence) and the Dave Holland Quintet.

The chance to interview him was very important.

This interview was taken when he came to play with his group Earthworks for three nights in Tokyo in February 2001.

EARTHWORKS' NEW CD *The Sound of Surprise*

Ayuo (A): I think your playing has evolved and changed recently.

Bill (B): Yeah, more jazz. It's more acoustic. Freer. Looser in some ways.

A: Your music always has something happening. It is constantly changing, and you're watching and giving out directions. And the music is exciting in the way that early jazz was at places like the Village Vanguard.

B: Well, I hope so. Should be exciting. It's the classical jazz quintet sound, which we all know very well. So, the interest becomes in how you arrange for that and what can you bring to it that's a little different. I think I bring some odd meters and rhythmic material that's unusual in that genre.

A: You've always had a distinctive style in drumming. But your style has changed from the first period with Earthworks. At that time, there was more emphasis on the rhythmic groove. And you would put in very distinctive fills. There was more funk groove.

B: Yes. True. But the big difference is that the first band used electronic drums. The electronic drum kit forces you to play in a certain way, which is interesting. But for many years, I've played with that, and now I just want to do acoustic.

A: At the same time, you are playing in a very melodious way.

B: Yeah.

A: Is there an influence from playing electronic drums?

B: Absolutely. I love the idea that the drummer had the melody. I always heard, from my early days, the melodies in the drums. Particularly with Max Roach. I liked all that. Electronic drums enabled me to really play tunes. So, on the band's first 3 CDs, the drummer carried the harmony by playing chords from the pads. "Bridge of Inhibition," "Stromboli Kicks," "Pilgrim's Way." Some of these tunes. So, I really was playing the tune and I loved that. I thought that was great. But the technology was very old-fashioned. Very difficult. Very expensive and unreliable. A real headache. So, now, I write the melodies that I want in the compositions and play them that way.

A: "The Bridge of Inhibition" is kind of like Balkan Gypsy music.

B: It is. Yes. Central European. Very rhythmic. Great dances, they have.

A: Your playing has never been this detailed. There are so many things going on like percussive elements.

B: It's all recorded in one pass on the CD. There is no overdub. But yes, I treat each tune as a little drum composition.

ON COMPOSING

A: I notice that more of the music is credited to you, whereas in the early days of Earthworks, a lot was credited to Django Bates and Iain Ballamy.

B: Django Bates and Iain Ballamy were really very good writers. In the early days, I would make some rhythmic confection with a Simmons electronic drum kit and say "I'm gonna do this. You guys do whatever you want." So, they would write a tune on top. Now we have no Simmons kit, and now I pretty much write all the music all the way through. And if it needs improvements or corrections from Steve Hamilton, he gets credited for that. But now I find I'm good with the rhythm. Great rhythmic ideas. Okay with the timing. I like tunes. I think there are some very strong tunes on *The Sound of Surprise*. My harmony is okay, but sometimes Steve will re-voice the harmony to a more sophisticated harmony. Particularly on ballads. To more sophisticated jazz harmony. So that's my weak spot.

A: I remember in the liner notes to your first solo album, *It Feels Good to Me*, you wrote that they were the first pieces that you actually sat down and wrote on the piano.

B: Yes, that's correct.

A: And it took a long time.

B: Yes. Not good at piano, but getting better.

A: Are you still writing on the piano?

B: Yes. All the music on the new CD, *The Sound of Surprise*, was written from the piano. And then I do a terrible little demo on the MC-500. And I mockup the tune just so the others can hear it. And then I interface that with the computer, to Sibelius [music software]. And that prints the chart. And then we have a rehearsal. We take some comments and maybe make some changes. Print out again a second draft. Another rehearsal. More input from other musicians. Third draft. Finish. Rehearse. Go on tour. 20 cities in England. And make the CD in 3–4 days.

A: What is the British jazz scene like at the moment?

B: The problem with the British jazz scene is the problem with the British. I think so many musicians still think of themselves as inferior, and they don't need to. They are world-class players. But sometimes they're rather small-minded. We're in a small island like Japan. And sometimes we live in the shadow of the United States, musically. It's a small scene. Not much money. People like to sit around and bitch and complain. Whereas the great attraction of Earthworks is that I can get them out of England and give them a platform in which to improve themselves. Tokyo, Los Angeles, Rio de Janeiro, and everywhere else and that opens their ears. And they become bigger players as a result. So, they like to be in Earthworks. And I like to work with young musicians, who are not too formed in their ideas. So, it works well.

WORLD MUSIC AND EARTHWORKS

A: I noticed that you have a number of pieces with Balkan Gypsy melodies, like "The Bridge of Inhibition" that you played last night from Earthworks' self-titled CD, and also the composition you played from the new CD.

B: Exactly. "The Wooden Man Sings and the Stone Woman Dances" on the new CD. The jazz musician and the audience have always connected through the dance, but now the dance is a Rumanian dance.

A: So, you've listened to quite a lot of Rumanian Gypsy music?

B: Yes, but I'm no student of any one thing because you hear so much music. Taiko drumming here. Brazilian samba here. Rumanian Gypsy here. Art-rock here. It's all Earthworks. We take music from everywhere. And the only good thing about being British is that we have no rhythmic culture of our own. The British in rhythm are terrible. So I take all my rhythm from everywhere else. I steal it like a bird that takes from here and there and builds a nest. That's also the story of jazz. It started out as African-American music. But that in itself was a fusion of Spanish, African, and other elements. So that was a mixture too. And now jazz is an international sport. Now we take influences from everywhere. Earthworks.

A: I think a lot of Balkan music is interesting these days. A few months ago, I met a Rumanian Gypsy clarinet player who was touring here. He was talking about wanting to do more jazz. But it's often better to sell the music as music from your own roots. A Japanese Clarinet player who toured Europe also promoted his music as Japanese Chindon music, although it also contained jazz and rock elements. I think the next step for world music is after people recognize their roots, they can be more free to do what they really want to do.

B: I think that's very true. I think the influence of world music and the permission to mix it all up has actually liberated so many of us. We can fly from London to Los Angeles to Rio and back again in two days. The world is getting small. Very rarely do you find someone who insists that the music has to be done this way only. Most people would say: "Ah, that's interesting. Wow, you put that with that, and got that. That's great."

A: Will you be doing any projects with musicians involved in various music of the world?

B: Yes, if I can find them and when they arise. For myself, I can't initiate any more work. I have so much on. And you have to focus. And follow something through. And I'd like to follow Earthworks to wherever it leads me.

YES, KING CRIMSON, GENESIS

A: In ABWH (Anderson Bruford Wakeman Howe), I noticed that the style you were playing in was similar to that of *Earthworks,* even though the music was very different. It was also very different from the early days in Yes, when you were playing the same songs.

B: *(laughs)* Yeah, well, maybe. That was like a vacation for me with old friends. There was nothing particularly creative about it. We were playing music that was already written. But for about a day or two, there was a possibility that that group ABWH could have really become quite good.

A: One of the songs on the new CD actually reminds me of King Crimson.

B: Maybe. Which one?

A: "Half Life."

B: It's kind of got a rock feel. King Crimson is a big influence. Robert Fripp was a big influence. It's a terrific group. I think it's maybe that I have to leave something I really love in order to do something I love even more. And I don't think I can be in King Crimson and do what I want in Earthworks. But there is a lot of influence from King Crimson. Often, I hear myself saying, in Earthworks, many of the things Robert would say, or that was said to me in a King Crimson rehearsal room. Many philosophical ideas about music. Jazz? Rock? It doesn't matter. One's played with amplifiers, and one isn't. That's the only difference. It's more of an attitude to music.

Don't play unless you have to.

Don't play until you hear something you want to play.

If you don't hear anything, don't play.

A: In an interview, I read somewhere, you mentioned that journalists often lump King Crimson, Yes, and Genesis as the same thing, but that you've been in all three and you couldn't think of three different bands that do things in three completely different ways. Can you cite an example of that?

B: Yes was and still is a vocal group modeled on the Beach Boys. King Crimson essentially was an avant-garde jazz group, much more interested in the music than the singing. Yes would use a diatonic scale. King Crimson would use a whole tone scale. Yes had its basis in American pop music like the Beach Boys, Fifth Dimension, Vanilla Fudge; while Crimson had its basis in the European avant-garde.

It's a completely different way of working.

In a rehearsal room with Crimson, there is very little talk and a lot of playing. With Yes—a lot of talk and no playing.

The philosophy is different. And Genesis? In Crimson and Yes, we thought that Genesis were copying us. They just seemed to be doing everything that we did. We thought they were really too late. Of course, they became the mega-stars. And when I played with them, that was the first time I played somebody else's music, where I had no compositional input and therefore felt no emotion for. With Yes and King Crimson, I was intensely into the music. With Genesis, I was just the studio guy. I was very badly behaved. But it wasn't their fault, it's my fault entirely. I was very young. It came at a very bad time for me. I knew I wanted to be a band leader and a writer but didn't know how to get there. So, I was marking time in Genesis.

A: You are credited as a co-composer in songs by Yes such as "Heart of the Sunrise." How did you take part in the composition of it?

B: In those days—and this is the problem with rock music—everybody would sit in the rehearsal room, waiting to find out what to play. With nothing on paper. Nothing written. And this takes hours. Somebody has a bass riff. And the other guy says "Oh, that's good, I'll play the keyboard like this." And the other guy says "I hate that. Let's do this." Then there is an argument. And then you start again. And people would contribute ideas.

So, for "Heart of the Sunrise," I would've come up with some bass riffs. *(Bill sings the first lines in "Heart of the Sunrise.")*

I came up with many bass ideas in Yes because I'm a drummer, so the next thing I hear is the bass. Then I hear up, up through the music. Drums, bass, chords, melody. So, I come to melody last.

Years later, in *ABWH*, there was a possibility for a short while that that group could have really become quite good—but market forces insisted that it had to become Yes and that we had to cooperate with Chris Squire and Trevor Rabin. And the whole thing turned into a horrible mess.

A: The CD, *ABWH*, begins with the words "Be gone you power play machine, we don't need your gold (and money)."

B: But that's Anderson. The next thing you know, he's got a big contract. He needs the power machine. But he's a crazy man, a good crazy man. He's crazy, but good.

A: In a recent interview, Phil Collins said that he was very much influenced by you in his early days. He used to go see Yes all the time and learned all your drum parts.

B: Yes, he did. Phil's a great drummer. Genesis was very influenced by Yes. And I was influenced by King Crimson. So, it's quite different. It's all called "Progressive Rock," but the philosophies were all different. And it shows now because really the most artistic group now is King Crimson. The one with its heart in the right place. Yes is now a parody group of itself. It's like watching a cover band playing their own music. Like an imitation of the real thing. So, Yes is a tribute band. Genesis became a very commercial pop group, but maybe it's now broken up. But King Crimson still has life and ideas because it was brave enough to change.

Don't you think so?

A: I haven't heard their new CD.

B: I don't like their new CD, but that's not their fault.

A: I liked the mini-CD *Vroom* more than the CD that came afterward (*Thrak*) because I thought there was more excitement in *Vroom*. *Thrak* was more organized. Then I went to the live show.

B: Was that effective?

A: Well, I enjoyed your playing.

B: Maybe you didn't see why there were six people.

A: No.

B: Well, I didn't either.

A: I would have enjoyed it more if it was you alone on the drums.

B: So would I, but Robert Fripp said this guy's gonna play drums, do you want to play drums? I said sure. I worked with Pat and we made interesting rhythmic ideas locked together. There's a tune called "Sex, Eat, Drink, Sleep, Dream." This middle section of that is amazing rhythmically. It's terrific. "Baboon" was a duet that we did that was really good.

But this was a situation forced upon me, and I said "Okay, I'll make it work." And I did make it work.

But enough now.

A: So, the period after that is when you started to evolve into your present style.

B: Sure, since 1998, I've been working on Earthworks full time. Getting looser in my playing. More jazz-like. Better with dynamics. Becoming a better musician. A better composer. A better band leader.

Figure 27　Photo of Ayuo interviewing Bill Bruford.

I met Andy Warhol when I was in the fifth grade

I met Andy Warhol when I was in the fifth grade.

In the 1960s, he was at the center of one of the most important gathering places for patrons of the arts. He had a workplace, which he named Factory, that was covered in silver aluminum foil and painted with silver spray paint; he allowed people from all walks of life to gather there.

However, after being shot with a pistol by Valerie Solanas, a radical feminist who came to pitch a film script in 1968, he moved to a new workplace—which he named The Office—and began making what he called Business Art.

I went there alongside Hiroshi Teshigahara, my mother, and Claude Picasso (Pablo Picasso's son). Claude Picasso was dressed like a hippie with long hair at the time. Claude introduced me to the music of Syd Barrett and Dave Gilmour of Pink Floyd, who were his friends in London.

When I walked into The Office, it was like walking into an experimental playhouse. Holly Woodlawn, a transvestite with long curly hair, was sitting on top of a table. She started laughing like a weird ghost monster with her mouth wide open. A couple of people were hanging outside the window, with just their hands holding on to the windowsill. Andy was walking quickly around the office with his camera, taking pictures of the visitors.

Actually, it was a ruse—what actually happening was that they had decided to play a trick on the visitors by acting a bit mad. It was simply a performance. Not the way they would act normally at The Office. When I approached the window where some people had been hanging out of, the people in the office suddenly reverted to being normal.

"It's dangerous," one of them warned me.

Andy was constantly working. He would turn many daily objects around him into art. He painted images of Campbell's Soup because he ate a can of Campbell's Soup for lunch every day when he was young, because he couldn't afford anything expensive. He also made an action painting series, which he named *Piss Art*, using his own urine as the medium. He was a shy boy when he was young, unsure of his face and figure; but when he became an artist, he started transforming himself. He'd wear a jacket like what Marlon Brando would wear, sunglasses, and a silver wig that looked plastic. He created his own character as a work of art.

I think it must have started with him realizing that we were all playing a role anyway, without even being conscious of it.

Andy Warhol once said, "If you want to know more about Andy Warhol, you just need to look at the surface of my paintings and films and me and there I am. There is nothing behind it."[1]

Lou Reed, in contrast, just said: "If you want to know who I am, just look at the surface. I'm behind it."[2]

These two quotes seem similar, but you can see that what they are talking about are different things. But Lou understood Andy's way of thinking very well. If you listen to *Songs for Drella*, a CD and concert about Andy's life and philosophy, Lou's lyrics convey different aspects of Andy's way of thinking.

Lou Reed has often said that he learned many things about life just by talking to Andy. In the early days of glam rock, when he started wearing heavy makeup and playing rock and roll, Lou said, "You can be anything you want to be—I learned that from Andy. I think that's one of the most important lessons of life."[3]

---

[1]Andy Warhol; from a 1967 interview quoted in Kynaston McShine, *Andy Warhol: A Retrospective*, New York: Museum of Modern Art, 1989.
[2]Lou Reed. 1975.
[3]BBC POP HISTORY #8 "Glam Rock 1970s." feat Velvet Underground/LOU REED/ JOHN CALE/DOORS/JIM MORRISON/IGGIE POP/Stooges/Alice Cooper/DAVID BOWIE/KISS/ NEW MERSEY BEAT. DVDR060359-2.

The school I went to in New York City

I went to the Little Red School House in New York City, which is on the corner of Bleecker Street and Avenue of Americas (Sixth Avenue). All of Bob Dylan's kids went there as Bob Dylan was a member of the school PTA, and Mary Travers (of Peter, Paul, and Mary) graduated from there. Patti Smith eventually became a member of the school's PTA, and the children of other PPM members also attended this school. I had known Peter Yarrow since I was a child; Maria Dylan, Bob Dylan's stepdaughter, was in my class. At school, we used to play games together.

Maria was a good student, and her notebooks were filled with pages and pages of detailed reports written in very tiny handwriting. I was influenced by this way of writing reports; it looked cool to me. Later, when I was in high school, I started to write essays with small, hard-to-read letters that filled up the entire page.

Maria was a popular girl in her class, but she also enjoyed playing practical jokes. She would gather other girls in class and make prank calls to strangers. Numbers were often chosen at random from the phone book. She didn't mean to be bad. One day, she and other classmates made a prank call to a random number, and a nice Italian lady answered the phone. She said, "We are just three children at home alone, and we are very hungry." The lady felt sorry for them and over the phone taught them an easy way to make pasta.

Bob Dylan was to act in the film *Pat Garrett and Billy the Kid* while we were in the sixth grade, and Maria was to accompany him to Mexico along with her family for the shoot. My classmates received a letter from Maria in which she said that she had also appeared in one scene in the film, so when the movie came out, I went to see it.

"Knockin' on Heaven's Door," a song Dylan wrote for the film, became a tremendous hit.

Many folk singers, including Judy Collins, Joan Baez, Bob Dylan, and Joni Mitchell—performed early in their career at The Bitter End, a famous nightclub that was about a block away from our school. I went to see several performers live there, but by the time we were in junior high school, rock music had become a much stronger influence on all of us at school.

Gil Evans (the famed Miles Davis arranger) and Pete Seeger both came to conduct a music workshop at the Little Red School House. Gil Evans shared an apartment complex with my classmate and junior high school friend, Jason Rosen, where we also met. He was residing in an apartment that housed persons on welfare from the city of New York at the time.

Make no mistake, this was not a school for the wealthy. It was a school for the children of people who desired an intellectually progressive education. It was well-known for its progressive educational system, and students came from Harlem, Chinatown, and many other neighborhoods. I received a school scholarship.

Bill Walters, the American history instructor, was the principal of this institution at the time. He, as a black man, argued that America was not founded on the freedom of all men. Thomas Jefferson, who wrote the Declaration of Independence, owned 200 slaves, and his writings reveal that he did not believe black people and white people were equal.

Bill Walters taught us that there are many people with different viewpoints on major events in history and that the most important thing to do, when thinking about these events, is to look at them from every angle you can think of. Make your own judgments, he instilled, not whether they were right or wrong. He also taught us to think for ourselves instead of following other people's opinions.

This environment had a profound effect on my music and thinking.

Winter 1983

When I was 23, I was walking near the Hachiman Jingu shrine in Kamakura when I was suddenly hit by a car. I received compensation, and with it, I was able to go to New York City for the first time in eight years. Back then, a round trip to New York cost at least 200,000 yen, making it difficult to visit the city without a significant amount of money. My monthly living expenses back then were around 50,000 yen.

I called an old friend in New York, whom I hadn't seen since eighth grade.

"Hi Bill, how are you? I got a letter from you at the end of junior high; I'm sorry I didn't write back."

Bill was a black man who was also in my middle school class. We used to study at the library together. I knew his family had long been Muslims. Black American Islam was not tied to Middle Eastern Islam, but rather a new religion that had spread among blacks who felt discriminated against in northern American society. White folks were the devil in this Islamic sect. But Bill was a serious young man who welcomed individuals from all walks of life.

"What? Eugene? Where the hell have you been?"

When I lived in New York, I was known as Yuji. My real name is "Yuji Takahashi" on my birth certificate. At first, I was named "Yuji" (with the same kanji [Chinese characters] as my father), but because the kanji "Yu" could no longer be legally used as a personal name at the time, it was put in the family register as "Yuji" in hiragana (without Chinese characters). Eugene is close to how Yuji is pronounced, so some people called me that.

"I went to Japan for a summer vacation and planned to return to New York City, but circumstances prevented me from doing so," I replied. "But how are you doing, Bill? What are you up to now?"

"Right now, I'm home with my family for Christmas vacation, but I'm studying law in Washington. I'm studying to be a lawyer."

"Really. I make music. Epic-Sony is putting out my first solo album."

"Oh, so you're a rock star. huh?"

"Not really. My album is going to be released as a New Age album. Although Michael Jackson's *Thriller* is the biggest seller on Epic-Sony right now."

"Yeah? Then, why don't you release your next one as *Michael and Eugene*? Then maybe it will sell."

"Now that I'm back in New York City, I'd like to see some of the people I used to know," I said. "I'm going to try to get in touch with some of them. Would you like to meet up?

"Okay," Bill replied.

"Do you keep in touch with any of the people from back then?" I asked Bill.

"No, I don't. I'm in Washington D.C., after all. Sometimes I hear rumors. But from high school onwards, our former classmates all went off to different places."

"Do you know what happened to Michael, or Sarah, or Dan, or Naomi?

Michael was a Jewish classmate of ours. According to Judaism, a person becomes a man when they are 13 years old. The coming-of-age ceremony is called a bar mitzvah and is held at a Jewish temple in the ancient Hebrew style. Anyone who went to the party with their friends, Jewish or not, would wear a kippah (a Jewish round hat).

Sarah and Dave were both childhood friends of Bill. They had been in the same class since they were in kindergarten.

"When Michael turned 13, to celebrate his Bar Mitzvah, you, Dan, and I bought him a year's subscription to the rock magazine called *Circus*. Do you remember that?" I inquired. Bill remembered those days well.

Bill told me what he knew about our former classmates, and what was currently happening in their lives.

"Michael helps his dad with his business by kicking tenants who don't pay their rent out of their homes. Sarah went to Paris to study dance. Naomi went to Texas that summer and I never heard from her again. Dave went to high school in Brooklyn after that. I'd see him around every once in a while."

Naomi and Dave were also former classmates of ours. Both Dave's parents came to the United States from Ukraine, but people often thought he was Puerto Rican because of his frizzy brown hair. He had a brother in a rock band.

Naomi was half-Japanese and half-Scottish. She had very white skin, but her face looked very Japanese. She wore the same style of clothes all the time and had long black hair. She spoke Japanese better than I did, but she didn't want to talk to me in Japanese.

She seemed to be pretty good at Japanese when I heard her talking with her mother one day. I spoke a little Japanese with my mom, but I mixed up English and Japanese words all the time, like when I said, "*Kyo wa*[1] working late." The Japanese I spoke at the time wasn't really Japanese; I didn't know enough vocabulary and wasn't aware of the grammatical difference between English and Japanese.

When we wrote reports on countries around the world at school, Naomi was always in charge of Japan. My stepfather was Iranian-American, so I was often in charge of the Middle East. I once told my teacher that I wanted to work in Asia, but the teacher said that Naomi wanted to work alone and that she knew more about Asia than I did, so he put me back in charge of Iran and Iraq.

Maybe she was embarrassed to have a failed Japanese like me in the same vicinity as a 'Japanese' like her.

"Remember a guy called Lester, right?" Bill asked.

"Oh yeah."

"He died. I think it was a heart attack."

I asked what happened.

"He was too fat."

"Was that the reason for it?"

"It's possible," Bill demurred.

---

[1]*Kyo wa* translates to Today [is].

He reflected on a few more classmates: "After that, Jesse died in a car crash. He was going somewhere when a truck hit his car. That was a long time ago."

"Where did Christine go? Last I heard, she went to Elizabeth Irwin High School."

"Yeah, but she was caught with drugs so many times that she got expelled from school."

"She was always telling everyone at school that I must be doing drugs every day. Do you know how Lionel is doing?"

Lionel was a black boy from Harlem, which is way uptown, and went to our school in the Village. He liked to make people laugh with his jokes. He would joke around a lot of the time and our teacher would sometimes tell him to go stand outside.

"He got a girl pregnant in high school, quit school, and went down south to become a cop. But the other day, I heard that he got killed."

I fell silent when I heard these words.

I remember Lionel well. The last time I saw him was at Cathy's house when we all smoked pot together. Cathy was a Jewish girl in our class. She and her mother lived in a big apartment right in front of Washington Square Park. Her mother worked for television. Cathy always had marijuana with her. She was always asking her mother: "Hey, Mom, can I take some grass to school?"

I went over to her apartment a lot when I was in eighth grade. She played the guitar then. At school, she always had her guitar case with her; we were still the only few in our class who could play the guitar. Every time I went to her apartment, there were records by Crosby Stills Nash & Young, David Bowie, and Joni Mitchell. We smoked pot while sitting on the carpeted floor with Lionel, Danny, Sarah, Michael, and Wendy. Dave started going out with her by the end of junior high.

Cathy, Wendy, and Sarah embroidered on wool, while I improvised on the guitar. They would tell me how good I sounded since some of my friends couldn't improvise yet. Sarah and Michael kissed and hugged each other. At the time, we were 13 or 14 years old, but by the end of junior high, we began to become aware that we were becoming men and women. But we were still shy. That's where the marijuana came in. It's easier to get to know each other when you smoke it and listen to music. There's a sense of peace in the air. We just enjoyed being together while listening to music. There was no hassle. We were all still naïve. This last period of junior high school was the most enjoyable time for me with my friends.

Later, I called Dave.

"Hey, it's been a while. Is that really you, Eugene?" He answered, with warmth and a lot of feeling. I responded in the affirmative and carried the conversation further.

"I'm living in Japan right now, and I'm only going to be in New York this winter break. I'd like to get together with my old classmates. How about the night of December 28th? So far, Dan Taub, Christine, and Bill are coming. The rest are either not in New York, or I don't know where they are."

"I can't make it that night. I can come by a little earlier in the afternoon."

I could tell from the way he spoke that he didn't want to see the others.

"What are you up to these days?" I asked.

"I've been painting for a long time. I'm trying to find a gallery that will exhibit them. So, I'm choosing which works to show and putting them in frames. That night, I also have a friend coming over to help me."

"I'd like to see your works. I didn't know you painted. Were you painting while we were in middle school?"

"I used to spray gun graffiti on the subway all the time. My drawings are an extension of that. Come over to my house and I'll show you."

"What happened to your Russian folk dancing?"

"I got hurt once. I can't move like that anymore, so I had to stop dancing."

"Where's your brother?"

His brother was of the hippie generation, and he had gone to the original Woodstock festival.

"He became a junkie. We had to put him in the hospital for treatment a few times. He'd come out and then he'd get addicted all over again. Just the other day, he broke into my parents' house and stole their money. So, I had no choice but to call the police and have them arrest him. I didn't like the idea of having my brother arrested, but when it went that far, I didn't know what else to do."

Dave was proud of his brother when he was in middle school. His brother, who played lead guitar in a rock band, had met the manager of the Allman Brothers at some point and there was the possibility that his brother's band could be the opening act for the Allman Brothers. I guess things didn't work out the way he wanted.

Back then, Ukraine was part of the Soviet Union at the time. Dave had an uncle who still lived there, and he had visited him.

In the 1950s, two of his parents' friends were executed for being Soviet spies, which was later shown to be a mistake. There was a 'Red Scare' at the time, and Russian, Ukrainian, and other immigrants were frequently targeted. Dave had been raised to believe that all humans were violent. He had serious reservations about anyone who denied or concealed it.

His parents both worked at the school we attended. His mother was a fourth-grade homeroom teacher, and his father was a gym teacher. And yet, Dave was famous for his bad language. He'd been saying things like "fuck you" since kindergarten.

He spoke phrases like "motherfucker" and "shit." Those around him were saying, "Where did he learn that kind of language, and how can he be saying that when his parents are schoolteachers?"

Dave was a big fan of Bruce Lee at the time. He bought and owned nunchucks and brass knuckles—a weapon that fit on all four fingers. He also worked out. He liked to show off his strength.

He told me one morning, "I was strolling yesterday when a gang of four high school students approached me and demanded money, so I took my brass knuckles and pounded the tallest one till he bled."

He said to me quietly one day at school:

"I killed a man once."

"It's not true. I don't believe you."

"No, it's true, I was ten years old. I was in the mountains, and this guy I didn't like was standing right there on the cliff. So, I pushed him down. I told everyone it was an accident. I don't think anyone's going to get to the bottom of that now. But it's true."

You should never lower your guard just because you are facing a child. When I was in elementary school, there was an incident. As I walked, a pair of pliers fell from the top of a nearby building. I looked up and saw an elementary school student exclaiming, "I missed." There was once an ambulance parked in front of my apartment building, and everyone was pointing to the top of the building. A heavy object landed on an unfortunate man's head. I wonder if he was all right.

I felt very safe walking around with Dave. If we were strolling together and some weirdo approached us, he'd scare the crap out of them by saying, "What are you doing to my friend?"

In eighth grade, I, Dave, a half-black, half-Jewish friend named Jason, and a white guy named Donald Brock used to sit at the same table; we all loved rock music. As an adult, Dave worked as a road manager for the black punk band BBs and subsequently as a rap producer. Jason grew up in the same flat as big band jazz arranger Gil Evans and was friends with his son, Miles Evans, who he formed a jazz funk band with as an adult. I remember saying hello to Gil Evans when I visited his house in junior high.

Around this time, Donald Brock and I went to see Yes at Madison Square Garden.

I'm not sure what happened to him in the years that followed.

In seventh grade, Dave and I both wrote book reports on the same topic for our history class.

It was a report on a collection of poems by Vietnamese revolutionary Ho Chi Minh. I mostly wrote about how the poems were expressed. He expressed his thoughts on Ho Chi Minh's life as a revolutionary without commenting much on the poetry itself. The teacher gave me a *Very Good* grade and a bad grade to him. I did not read his report, but I suspect he may have been critical of socialism.

Our teachers were primarily of the leftist generation who were active in the student movement. Our history instructor had gotten the school to import a book on Mao Zedong directly from China, and we spent half a year in class reading a book on the history of the Chinese Revolution. The title of the book was *On the Long March with Chairman Mao.* Even now, when I hear phrases like those written there, I get nostalgic, even if I don't agree with some of the viewpoints that are expressed in them.

The Chinese influence in my music reflects nostalgia for this era. It's not a fascination, longing, or cultural exploration of "Asian culture." It's an element of the Asian culture I was familiar with in New York.

My class included three Chinese girls, all from different backgrounds.

Huang was the People's Republic of China's first overseas student.

Everyone in our class at first thought she was a boy. She had very short hair and dressed in the Maoist people's clothes of the time. 1973 was the year after President Nixon visited China to reestablish diplomatic relations, but China's cultural revolution was far from over. Every morning, she was driven to school in a Cadillac from her apartment near the UN building.

She brought a lot of Chinese propaganda materials to school. She used to smile when she saw other East Asians, including me, because at first, she assumed I was an overseas Chinese. But I began to suspect that she did not like me or Dave. I believe she also wanted me to learn more about the Japanese aggression during the Sino-Japanese War. Dave thought the concept of communism to be ironic. We knew relatively little about the Japanese Imperial Army's massacres in China and other regions of Asia at the time. Many Japanese felt they were victims of the first atomic bomb, but they never investigated what led up to that during the Pacific War.

Karen, another Chinese-American girl, was in our class. She was from the South and spoke English with a Southern American accent. She had shoulder-length hair, wore spectacles, and was frequently angry. Lester, a classmate, used to make fun of her by imitating her Southern accent.

Perhaps she was mocked and called a "chink" in the South. As a result, emphasizing her Americanness became more than natural. But in this New York class, she was mocked for being an American Southerner.

She didn't seem to like it when Huang came to our school. She took the attitude that she did not want to be seen as being similar to Huang, that the two were different. From different cultures. In music class, she even told the teacher that she didn't want Huang to sing because Huang's English had a Chinese accent. Everyone else told her that she was being mean. Those three were very different from each other and didn't necessarily get along.

Cissy grew up in Manhattan; however, she had family in Hong Kong. She was tall and had long black hair. She went to our school from the time she was in kindergarten. She began playing guitar in junior high, learning songs by Judy Collins and Joni Mitchell. She sang "Both Sides, Now" and other songs in the school talent show with a Jewish girl in his class named Mandy, who played the piano.

Cindy's father frequently visited her at school. He always dressed in white traditional Chinese clothing. His looks and clothing reminded me of a photograph of the writer, Lu Xun. When he saw me, he always smiled.

I often spoke to Cissy since we shared similar interests. At our junior high school graduation, we accompanied the class on guitar, and we sang "Changes" by Phil Ochs together. Phil Ochs rose to prominence in the 1960s for his anti-Vietnam War lyrics. However, his commercial career flagged three years after the war ended, and he committed suicide.

Cissy enjoyed teasing me. On our way home from the park with the entire class, she would suddenly grab my hand. I almost ran away, but she laughed and said, "You have to walk holding hands with me from now on."

I also called Cissy. Her brother picked up the phone.

"She just went to Arizona yesterday, so you just missed her."

"What? Arizona?"

"Yes, to learn acupuncture and traditional Chinese medicine."

I was unable to inform my former classmates that my mother and stepfather had divorced. Since the last time I had seen them, my family genealogy became too complex to explain. Besides, no one seemed to be happy about it back then.

"I was robbed of my wife by a man named Robin Martin, but she came back with a different man named Martin as the first name," my stepfather, Mansour, said. At the time, my stepfather had a young black girlfriend. But he was seeing another woman, and she was seeing several men at the same time.

In my heart, I was deeply disappointed with how life had turned out for us. We were still dreamers when we were young, but life turned out to be very different.

I dropped by Dave's place to see him. He was arranging his drawings, as he had told me over the phone. His assistant was someone who had attended the same junior high school as us in another year.

"Hot Tuna's playing a concert for the first time since the 1970s," his friend told Dave as he worked. "Wanna go see them?"

Hot Tuna was the guitar and bass duo from Jefferson Airplane, a band I had admired since elementary school. As a child, I saw Jefferson Airplane and Hot Tuna four times. They were a key figure in the 1960s psychedelic scene in the United States.

"Right. Let's go when we're finished," Dave said.

The drawings were like graffiti. Some of them reminded me of Keith Haring, but the majority of them represented humanity's violent side. One of them depicted a Klu Klux Klan lynching.

Dave went on to work in the music industry as a rapper, music producer, and manager. He also continues to paint, and I can view some of his work on the internet.

That night, a handful of my former classmates showed up.

Dan Taub was the first to arrive. When I saw him, I was a bit surprised. He donned a long beard and looked very Jewish. In my class, he was an honor student. He, like myself, enjoyed writing short stories. We went to the movies and studied together.

Christine, the next person to come, is also Jewish. She had been in all of my classes since third grade. She had long brown hair and appeared to be taller than she was in junior high. She was training to write scripts for TV shows while she worked at a sports magazine. She asked me to read over her scripts.

Bill appeared next, exclaiming: "Hey, where's the rock star?"

I put *Court and Spark* by Joni Mitchell on the record player. It was a huge hit in 1974, our final year of junior high school. This record was formerly in my collection, and I kept it at my stepfather's place. It was still there.

"I called Cissy the other day, but she wasn't there, so I spoke to her brother. Apparently, she went to Arizona to study acupuncture and traditional Chinese medicine."

Christine said, "Have you seen Cissy's brother? He's got a body build like Bruce Lee. Cissy was in my class in high school, and she fell in love with a Jewish guy named Henry. But because Henry was usually messing around and had other girls, Cissy was always sad. I think she's unhappy."

We all talked as if we were back in middle school once again. This was strange. But it must have been strange for them to see me playing only records that were once popular back in the early 1970s.

When my classmates invited me to meet them in Midtown Manhattan, where the privileged reside, they assumed I was wealthy. When I informed them that I was going to release an album on Epic-Sony, I could tell they thought I was doing extremely well, even though they didn't tell me so. The truth is that I was sleeping in the closet of my grandmother's little six-tatami mat room in Kamakura at the time.

That night, a completely fake and fabricated image of myself was created. But I couldn't show them my true, battered inner self. Even if I did, they might not be able to comprehend it. It would take some time to convey what had occurred to me since the last time I saw them.

The protagonist in Martin Scorsese's 1985 film *After Hours* is rescued by a woman and taken to her apartment, where he discovers nothing but 1960s clothes; psychedelic patterns floating in liquid, which were formerly a popular adornment; posters from the time period; a colorfully designed cup that used to be sold in hippy shops in the 1960s. "Hey, do you want to listen to this?" the woman asks and plays Joni Mitchell's 1968 classic "Chelsea Morning."

The protagonist makes an odd expression as if to indicate: "There's something strange about this person." He inquires as to why she surrounds herself with items from the past. Why can't she move on with the times? The woman starts to lash out in anger because she doesn't want her illusion to be destroyed.

"Get out of here," she says. "Get the hell out of here. Get the hell out!"

She screams and throws things at him.

The protagonist flees and informs someone he meets on the street that there is a weird woman living there, to which the person responds, "Oh, she's known by everyone as '1962.'" Something happened to her, and she's still stuck in that era.

Everyone there had lived in and around New York all their lives and experienced all the changing times together. Everyone except me.

I wondered what would have happened to me if I had been able to stay in New York City.

If only it had lasted like the spring of 1975.

"Here We Go" by Ayuo
(Composed for the set of songs in *Silent Film*)

Here we go
The whistle blows at last
The train moves us forward
To lands scattered in space

Stars against the sky
Turning in spirals
We're leaving in shadows and stars
Passing through deserted lands

O the time we left as in a film
The dreams we felt in your memory
I hold the cup that binds us
While we revolve upon the wheel

Stars against the sky
Turning in spirals
We're leaving in shadows and stars
Away from the home we loved so well

Past memories
Are clouds floating by
You cannot trap them in a cage
Like a child with a butterfly

Stars against the sky
Turning in spirals
We're leaving in shadows and stars
Away from the time we loved so well

Copyright owned by Ayuo Takahashi.
Registered @JASRAC.

"Here We Go" by Ayuo

(Interpretation of the lyrics by Ayuo)

Time for the train to leave. The whistle is blowing.
Where is this train I'm on headed?
I looked out the window.
The desert continues forever. The stars are spiraling. Weaving between the stars and their shadows
A time left behind like a movie, a memory from a dream.
I still hold the cup that connects us. Even though the seasons of time have turned over the years.

Stars shining in the sky, drawing a spiral.
Weaving between the shadows and the stars.
I'm leaving the home I loved so much.

The past, they pass by like clouds.
You can't lock them in a cage like when a child is playing with a butterfly.

Stars shining in the sky, drawing a spiral.
I am leaving that era that I loved so much,
Leaving with the night clouds, far behind me.

End of Earth

Before recording began at David Lord's Crescent Studios in July 1986, I took a short journey to the south-west of England. I brought a *psaltery*, a little steel-stringed instrument dating back to medieval times. I first went to Glastonbury, then to a small town called Wells. There were actually a lot of wells in Wells—this is how the town got its name; some old English towns get their names in this way. There is also a street there that is thought to be Europe's oldest preserved street. It's been around since the 13th century. To me, it looked like an old illustration from a book of European fairytales.

The owner of the inn where I stayed was originally from Italy and spoke with a thick Italian accent. Based on my impressions of the town, I composed an instrumental called "Silent Springs" in my room. The next day, I took a bus west to Cornwall, England's southernmost province. The bus was on its way to a seaside town near Tintagel. This was the bus's final stop; Tintagel had no direct bus service. The people's faces were rough, probably from the salt wind. There were no trains running south from this town—only one bus, every day, and it left at ten o'clock in the morning.

I knocked on the door of a cheap bed-and-breakfast inn beside the shore and inquired about available rooms. He glanced at me with interest, knowing I was an East Asian, and replied that there was a room available. The cost of accommodation, including breakfast, was 8 pounds 50 pence, which was less than 2000 JPY. It was already past ten o'clock at night, so I quickly took a shower and went to bed.

I awoke the next morning to the sound of shrieking seagulls. One was tapping its beak on the wooden window frame where I was staying. I have never previously or since heard birds cry so loudly.

After breakfast, I inquired about the bus schedule, paid for the inn, and hurried out. On a sunny, summer day, this place was gorgeous. The woods and forests were lush, with small historic settlements and waterways dotted throughout.

We arrived in Tintagel after a few hours of driving.

At the edge of Tintagel, facing the sea, are the ruins of an old castle. It is said that King Mark of Cornwall welcomed the Irish princess Isolde as his queen here in the sixth century. This is where the legend of Tristan and Isolde, immortalized in Wagner's opera, is said to have originated.

The story has been told by minstrels for hundreds of years. Former singer and founder of The Incredible String Band, Robin Williamson, recorded a rendition of this medieval minstrelsy (or minstrel show) in a manner that may be most similar to the way minstrels performed it in the Middle Ages. The performance can be seen in his video "An Evening with Robin Williamson."

Another group, Ensemble Parsifal, which recreates medieval music on old instruments, recorded a medieval retelling of the story of Tristan and Isolde.

Most of the castle had already crumbled, yet there was something mysterious about it. It faced the sea, and there were a lot of seagulls soaring around in the breeze. There was an old church and a graveyard nearby.

There were no more buses and no other modes of transportation when sunset approached, so I decided to hitchhike. I had no other choice. I walked to Camelford, the next town, since no one stopped for me. It was supposedly the fabled site of King Arthur's castle, Camelot Castle, but it was just a rural town. A group of adolescent delinquents were smoking cigarettes and listening to hip-hop on a boom box on the outskirts of town.

"You all right?" one inquired.

I nodded and continued. The stores and banks were all closed. I had nothing but traveler's checks and virtually no regular cash.

A car with two men pulled up and offered me a ride. They met in the British army, and still traveled together every year. They agreed to give me a ride because they were intrigued by the sight of an Asian man standing alone on the road with his luggage. They bombarded me with questions out of curiosity. It wasn't long to the next town, where a bus was waiting, so I left them and went in search of a place to stay. I was tired of walking.

I stayed in a modest hotel, which cost me £15 including breakfast. After paying for my lodging, I stepped outside to check the bus schedule for the following morning.

The bus stand was completely dark.

A lone woman sat on a bench at the stop. Her hair was long, and she was wearing heavy makeup. I didn't get a good look at her face, but she seemed to be in her thirties. She appeared calm.

"Where are you staying?" she said, as I checked the bus schedule.

"I'm staying in Kent. And I have to go back, so I came here to check the bus time," I answered honestly.

"So where are you staying?"

"As I said, I'm staying in Kent. This is the bus timetable, isn't it?"

"The bus isn't going to be here tonight."

"I know. I'm checking what time I need to be here tomorrow."

After checking the time, I prepared to return to my hotel room. The woman still sat at the bus stop; she had a look on her face that said that it was hopeless to make me understand.

She couldn't get anything through to me.

A few months later, I saw a British movie in Japan. The film contained a scene in which a prostitute wearing heavy make-up propositioned a painter. As I watched this scene, I was reminded of that encounter at the dark bus stop, and I finally got why she kept asking, "Where are you staying?"

There wasn't much to see in this town, and the sole tourist gift available was a book about a murder that occurred here 100 years ago. The next day, I took a bus to Exeter, a large city in the south of England. From there, I traveled to the Bath studio via Exeter, and then back to Kent, where I was staying.

I was staying with the parents of my mother's then-partner Martin. Something unexpected had happened when I returned from this little adventure. Martin's mother informed me that my mother had left him in New York City. My mother had heard a message for Martin on their answering machine from a woman she didn't know while we were in England, and she learned about an affair that had occurred a few months before. That's how it all began.

Martin's mother went on to say, "Can you try to talk to her and see if you can somehow make things right?" When I phoned my mother, she told me that she was leaving Martin and that I ought to leave the house right away and return to New York City.

Even before they married, no one could predict how long their marriage would last, since Martin was only three years older than I was.

I stated that I was due to begin recording the next week, that everything was going great, and that I was here for work. I couldn't just stop.

She didn't give up. She called me again at the recording studio while I was singing "Across the Seasons" to tell me to stop what I was doing and to come to Hawaii, where she had moved, as her brother had business and a place to stay. I told her again that I was in the middle of recording and couldn't do that.

The next day, I penned the lyrics to a new song inspired by both this incident and the origin of the name of a town in Cornwall.

Cornwall's most western town is called Land's End. The name refers to the end of the land, and like its namesake, this town was the departure point for many ships. Before Columbus, it was thought that the earth was flat, not round. If you traveled too far from the end of the land, you would wind up where the earth ended. According to mythology, where the earth ends, dragons await, and if you pass them, there is a huge waterfall, and the water will carry you down off the edge of the earth.[1]

"End of Earth"

(Words and Music by Ayuo)

A human creature, he's a drifter, isn't he?
What he imagines as home,
falls through your hands like sands.
And what seemed to be stable,
is like a loose pillar,

---

[1] I remember my fourth-grade teacher in NYC telling me this when I was nine years old. Dragons in Western literature are evil, destructive creatures, as in Beuwulf.

ready to come tumbling down.
And what you call your people,
who are they?
A bunch of tribesmen,
who gathered into villages.
Who wanted to belong.
Now they gather into larger groups
but you know when our modern technology fails,
you'll get warring tribes all over.
And self-proclaimed kings and princes,
of this and that land.

Now listen to this dreamworld:
there is a new nation somewhere,
not of any particular borders
nor of any set of peoples
but with a tradition
a way of doing thing –
they bought a piece of land,
to make concrete, their existence,
and they proclaimed a ruler.
And a land of freedom,
a paradise on earth, they call themselves,
the "end of earth"
to justify that it is the final solution
to all existing problems.

Their symbol is that of three dragons,
at the edge of the sea.
They have rulers making speeches on t.v.
who are but comedians,
who talk in riddles.
They gather new comers by checking their d.n.a.
to keep out elements of failure.
But one day, they will be ready,

at a time when the world is in decline.
They will come by ships, planes, and flying saucers.
And you will see,
a new world,
and the end of earth.

Copyright owned by Ayuo Takahashi.
Registered @JASRAC.

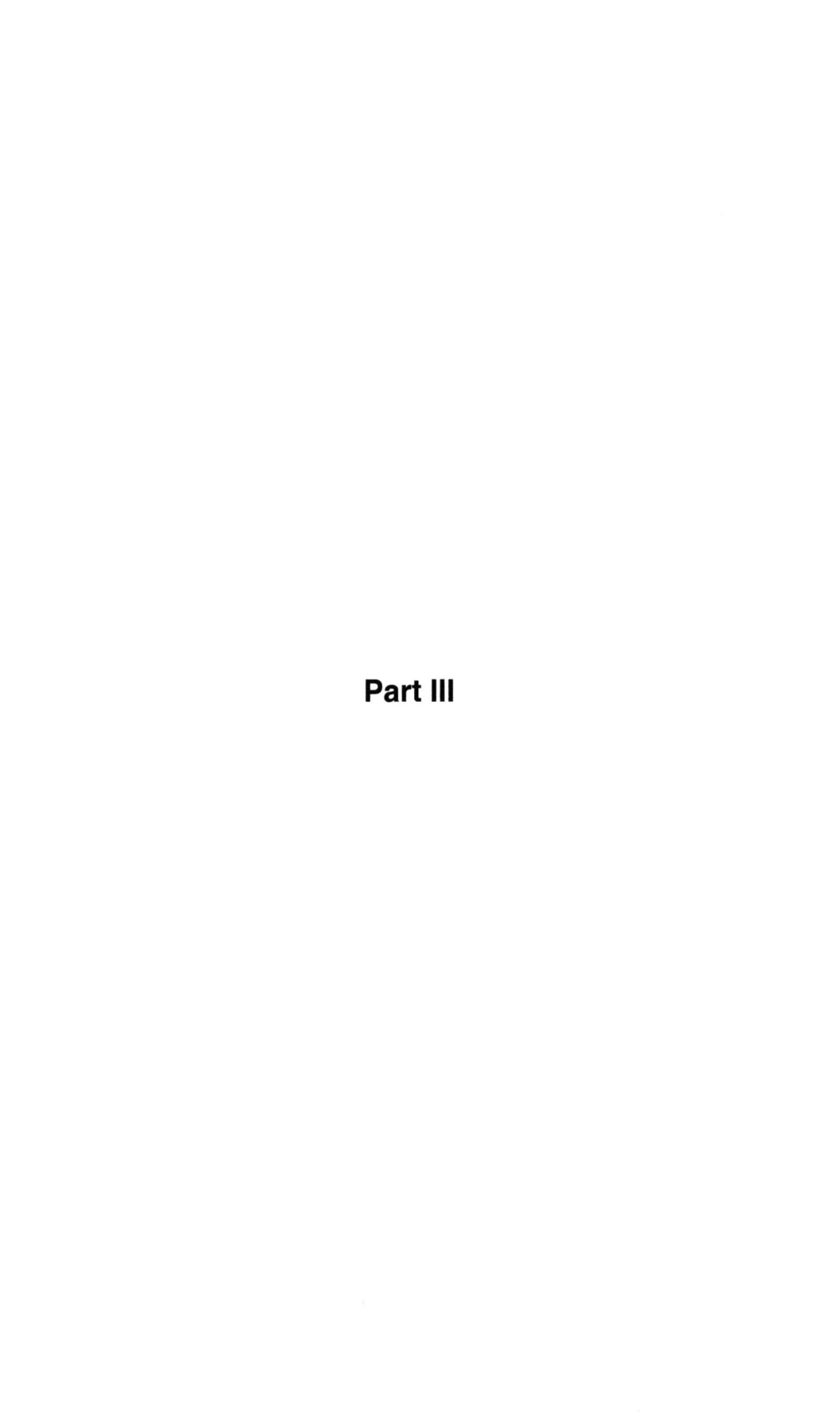

Part III

I don't understand the Japanese

I had a number of different possibilities for myself until 1975. What would have happened if I had stayed in New York? What would have happened to the people I knew?

The 'me' who lived in New York was a different person from the 'me' in Japan. I was seen as a different person and lived as a different person. However, I've always felt that the 'me' who was seen in Japan was not the real 'me.'

When I lived in New York, I saw the political movements in the United States at the time as related to my future. I liked rock music and was often daydreaming, so people used to ask me if I was on drugs. I liked to write short stories and read them in front of people. My classmates were often waiting for my next story. Some of my friends had grown up on the streets of New York City and later became funk musicians or music producers and managers.

And all of a sudden, I was left in a town with a totally different culture. In Japan, the way I spoke the language was considered stiff because I had never even been to a Japanese school. And then, unlike in New York City, I didn't grow up hearing the street language of the city, so people often thought I had a sophisticated elite upbringing. The truth is, I just didn't know how to speak properly. When I spoke, I was often misunderstood.

Later I found out that a lot of misunderstandings came from the fact that I didn't know how to use the language. It didn't come naturally to me. And most people don't have the time to realize why I was using the wrong words. I couldn't get my point across to people. I couldn't communicate properly.

You probably don't know what this is like unless you've experienced it yourself. But if you stay in such a state for a long time, you become crazy and neurotic and are likely to wind up in trouble.

One of the reasons why I featured the theme song from the movie *The Face of Another* directed by Hiroshi Teshigahara and written by Kobo Abe on my CD *What We Look Like in the Picture* is because I thought that the situation of the protagonist in the novel was a little bit similar to myself. If you live your life wearing a mask as a different person all the time, no one will know your true feelings or what you are really thinking, and in the wrong situation, you could wind up becoming a criminal.

Culture is about the society or the community you grew up in. It is not just about race or ethnicity.

Just because your mother or father is a Japanese does not automatically make you understand Japanese culture. If you grow up as a minority and there exists racism in that community, the scars of growing up as a discriminated person remain for the rest of your life. And that consciousness is engraved in your mind for the rest of your life. Just as a black person in America is not an African even though he may be of African descent.

That consciousness will never go away because it becomes a part of your cultural consciousness. The world is becoming more and more global in a way, so I've always wondered why these cultural matters are still not understood.

I feel especially sad when many people who work in the arts and cultural fields don't understand this at all.

However, I always liked reading and researching alone, and I didn't really like drinking and socializing with people. On top of that, trying to find friends in a country that I didn't know at all, without even going to school, was much harder than most people can imagine. I didn't know anyone, and I didn't know what kind of culture they had and their way of thinking. I could hardly read the language, and I couldn't speak it well enough to be understood. If my language or reactions were a little slower than those of people who grew up in Japan, I was often asked, "What country are you from?"

I didn't know what kind of culture people of my age had grown up with, but it certainly was different from what I knew.

When I lived alone for the first time, a policeman would often come to my apartment and ask 'What country are you from? When I told them I was Japanese, they looked at me in total disbelief.

I thought he probably thought I was Korean, Chinese, or someone from another Asian country.

A musician I met around 1989 named Tsuneyuki Suzuki said that my way of speaking reminded him of the Koreans in Japan when he was a child. At that time, if you dressed in a fashionable American style, people thought you were cool, if they saw you as a weird Asian, they looked at you very suspiciously.

However, that did not mean that I could befriend people in the Korean community. They have their own identity in Japanese society and their own community. Those who are left alone as loners have no such community. They become completely isolated.

Of course, some people have an extraverted personality to manage with such handicaps. I was not one of them.

If you have divorced parents who only see you a few times a year, they don't really know you because they didn't see how you grew up. This is where having divorced parents causes problems. When they find you different, your mother will compare you to your father, and your father will compare you to your mother. In other words, you are told by both parents that you are different. And I was told to go off to do my own thing somewhere else because I was different from them and therefore NOT a part of their family.

Before the Vietnam War, the student movement and protests in America began as a struggle for civil rights. It began with numerous American-Jewish folk singers and blacks speaking out against racism. Of course, as an Asian, I was frequently called "chink, chink," and the typical Joe on the street assumed my parents worked in the Chinese laundry industry. This was because many Chinese and Japanese immigrants to the United States since the early twentieth century worked as cleaners or house staff. Anyone who went to public school in elementary school would have witnessed white folks racing around with their index fingers raised over their eyes to make it look like slanted eyes, saying, "Here comes the chink, here comes the chink."

So, people like us are very sensitive to such racial discrimination.

Instead of saying, "Aren't we all the same inside," Japanese and other Asian nationalists would say, "We're not like you. We're different." Such nationalists appeared insane to me. When you grow up in NYC in the 1960s with an English-speaking family, it's natural to grow up feeling the culture around you in America as your own society. You could look different, but you are the same inside.

I feel that abnormal nationalism and racism can only lead to war in the end, like the Second World War. What has been done to you must be done again to make you feel better. Anger turns people into the same kind of people as their enemies before they know it.

It was during this period that I met a certain Japanese composer. At first, he asked me to teach him English. So, I went to his house. I used to teach him English and then his wife would serve us dinner and we would talk.

When I first met him, he had long hair and was dressed like a hippie. And he was listening to Pink Floyd and progressive rock music. On the surface, he seemed friendly to me.

But many things lurk in people that we don't understand when we first meet them. You can't tell just by appearances.

He also taught composition, but when he got to college, the left-wing student movement had just gotten so intense that the college was in lockdown. So, he only took classes for about a month and then dropped out. He only had a sense of what he could make, and he never studied much theory. He could only say what he liked or disliked and had no ability to teach. He was once hired at a music school after being introduced by a well-known music teacher, but he was fired soon after. In terms of music, there was nothing I could learn from him. He was unable to do solfège, harmonic music, or orchestration. Composers often write sketches and then start work, but he couldn't do that. When he composed, he would check each note carefully on the piano and write it all out in a notebook. His wife had studied classical music composition properly at a university and helped him put his pieces together.

His teaching consisted of looking at the pieces his students had written and telling them what he liked and disliked. He didn't know the methodology, and he had no logic or theory. He couldn't analyze a song.

He was said to be a bit of a right-winger. His father was said to be a hero during the Second World War. His father's hobby was to capture Chinese people off the street every day and cut off their heads. He didn't do it because he had to do it. He did it because he wanted to enjoy seeing the horror before people were killed. So, he used his position at the time to make his sadistic fantasies as real as he wanted. They said that after the war he was supposed to have lost his mind, and he was never caught as a war criminal. If it had been in Germany, he would have been put on trial by the Jewish people. Because such killings and other perverted crimes are still being covered up, Japan's issues with China and Korea remain unresolved.

He told me that people were a continuation of their own parents, so he knew how his parents thought. (He had sadistic tendencies too. His sadism became visible in the way he spoke and acted.)

At first, he seemed gentle and kind, and spoke softly. However, after drinking, his manner changed. He began to speak in the manner of police interrogation. When they interview criminals and break them down, leaving them confused about who they are. His eyes had the look of a man who enjoyed killing rats and small animals little by little. I could imagine how his father enjoyed killing people. I began to think that many political prisoners must have been interrogated and killed in this way. Some of the musicians I knew said he gave them the creeps because clearly there was something wrong with him.

I don't know why he asked me to teach him English. He was still in his late twenties at the time. He was still making connections with various people in the music business. I was interested in Chinese literature and music at the time. In truth, the Asian culture that I was most familiar with in New York was Chinese, so there was nostalgia for me. However, he assumed that I was interested in China because of my father's left-wing influence. My father was often writing about left-wing politics at the time. Maybe he thought that my involvement with him would do him some good. At first, when I met him, he spoke politely. But after a while, when he didn't see any benefit in going out with me, his attitude changed little by little. And he stopped learning English from me.

His complexes started to come out more and more. Later on, I think that my very existence might have made his complexes come out. He would immediately start talking about how Japanese people are like this and like that. He was also a nationalistic person. He used to say that Japan was right in doing what it did in the Second World War. And he would say, "You don't understand anything." I still didn't know what the average Japanese thought and felt. If I asked him what he meant, he would have no ability to answer. He just put on a mysterious look on his face.

There is something mysterious about encounters between people. Complexes and shadows can be found in places where people normally can't see them. If you trigger them without meaning to, something unexpected may happen.

For example, in Truman Capote's non-fiction book *In Cold Blood*, Capote writes about a young man of American-Indian blood who meets a young white man, and what is supposed to be a robbery turns into a murder. It would never have happened if these two people had not met and had not had their complexes stimulated deep within them.

One time he said: "All Western philosophy is bad."

Me: "Why?"

He: "Because philosophy is for people who want to be happy. See, they're not happy."

He always wanted to say that Japan was better. There was no logic to it. There was only emotion. All Westerners were *Renchu* (an impolite way of saying 'those guys') because he saw them as the enemy of the Second World War.

He: "Shakespeare is sometimes compared to Japanese Noh, but Japanese Noh is far superior."

He read comic books all the time. Everything he didn't understand was *Baka* ("stupid") to him. Maybe it was a way to escape from the things he didn't study. He liked to talk about sex. When he saw that I didn't respond well to it, he wanted to talk about it even more. I eventually got into the habit of laughing it off with embarrassment. He started talking about his love life and sex. He drank alcohol every night. He really liked Enka (traditional Japanese ballad) music, but he was making experimental music and classical contemporary music. But every time his work was performed, he would say bad things about the performer.

He became friends with the editor of a magazine called *Ongaku Geijutsu* (Music Art). He introduced me to him at his house. But he said to me: "The only reason I am socializing with a guy like that is because he has the position as the editor of *Ongaku Geijutsu*. Otherwise, who would converse with a guy like that? He's an idiot."

He began to use rougher and rougher words when he talked to me. Those who know how to use Japanese properly use polite language for those in a certain position and rough language for those who are younger or not in a certain position, but as someone who was not raised with the Japanese language, I can't tell the difference. The language I hear will be the language I use. But when I spoke using those words I heard, people often told me they weren't the appropriate language to use.

I helped him write several letters in English. And he would treat me to dinner. He was trying to sell his work to foreign countries. I helped him a lot with the letters and forms, so he could go to New York City. He never helped me with my music. Instead, he started saying bad things about me to other people. By saying to people, 'I'm trying to teach him, but he doesn't get it yet,' it made him look good and it made me look bad. He often didn't make eye contact with the well-connected or the elite, and he would often lower his gaze when speaking to a well-connected person.

When you get too close to people, you will start to see all sorts of dark nasty things about people.

Ultimately his work was well received in the United States. Some of his works have a New Age sound to it. Perhaps it was his mysteriousness that made him so popular in the West. And his music was not without a message. He had a haunting atmosphere about him, partly because of his father. The American writer Nathaniel Hawthorne was also haunted by his grandfather's execution of several innocent women during the witch trials of Salem and went on to write several novels about the horror. In the same way, when I talked to him, I could feel there was fear within him that one-day people might take revenge for his father's murders during the war.

The more I talked to him, the more neurotic I became. He was also a bit insensitive. He couldn't see the subtle changes in people or the way their faces changed. Sometimes he was drinking so much that he lost all sense of time, and the conversation would go on and on.

When I told people about this later, they all said it couldn't be helped because he was drunk. It was a mistake to try to communicate with a person who, no matter how much I talked to him, would always end up misunderstanding everything.

Why can't they understand what I'm saying? And when I try to explain it to them, all they can say is that I don't try to understand what they are telling me. That I am being self-centered. Individualism doesn't exist in traditional East Asian society, so if you express your own opinion, people would call you self-centered and individualistic like an American which they often see as a curse.

The reason why I was meeting him was originally because he wanted to learn English. I was also looking for someone older who was already composing and doing music as a possible guide and mentor. However, I wasn't really impressed by his music. If my father had taken that role, I wouldn't have had to look for someone outside my family and relations, but my father was also against the academic school system and couldn't teach people.

Society bounces back at you as a mirror. When society bounces something back at you that is different from who you really were, you know that you are seen as a different person from what you were. This also changes you superficially. But only superficially. There is a kind of mask over your face. The real you still exist there underneath. But the person sitting in front of you doesn't see it.

It was at this time that I looked at myself in the mirror and was surprised. I saw a different person in the mirror from the person I was a few years before. The person I saw in the mirror was someone I hated. I wondered why I looked like this.

In his autobiography, Miles Davis said that all black people play the role of "black" characters in American society. 'We have to act that way because that's the way society looks at us. That's why I wear the mask of the Negro.' The same thing is said in Kobe Abe's novel, *The Face of Another*.

All the people I met at his house also became people with whom I could not communicate. I even started teaching English several times to the editor of *Ongaku Geijutsu* (Music Art) magazine. But one day, when I was talking to him about my parents' relatives, he told other people the exact opposite of what I said—180 degrees different. I was shocked by this. This had never happened to me before in New York City. For a brief moment, I reasoned that it was because, in Japanese grammar, a negative term comes at the end, such as 'because something it is not,' and if you don't speak effectively, everything sounds upside down. Regardless of how many times I informed him that I had not said such a thing, he stubbornly insisted that I had. Eventually, I recognized that much of what I said was delivered to people in ways that were diametrically opposed to what I intended to express.

It is true that my Japanese was terrible. I never went to a Japanese language school, and no one ever taught me how to speak properly. My father's everyday use of the language is also a broken type of Japanese and not formal Japanese. So was the spoken language of the composers I met. If you know the correct way of speaking Japanese, you may be able to understand it, but if you don't learn it properly, you can't speak it, because language is something that is NOT naturally transmitted through DNA. I didn't know Keigo (polite language) at all. I couldn't write in Japanese at all. If you don't learn these things, you simply can't do them. He just started yelling at me, "What is that way of speaking? That is not the correct way of talking to your own parents?"

It's natural that I can't speak the language. You never taught me. My mother never taught me. I never went to school. How can I learn if you prevent me?

I kept telling him that I needed to go to school. I was told that school only brainwashes people to believe in the government. However, I always felt that school was not just a place to go to take lessons, but also a place to find friends and have discussions. Maybe the Japanese schools during the 1930s and the Second World War were places where no discussions were allowed, and the students were forcibly taught to obey the government and the military.

I had one more big problem. I didn't have a name. My parents thought I was going to be born a girl, so they only thought of a girl's name, Ayu. When I was born as a boy, my father wrote his name on the birth certificate. It was not that I was named Jr, but it was the same name. People around him warned him that this would cause problems in the future, but he never changed it. At first, we used to call him "Yuji-san" and me "Yuji-kun" at home. People often use "San" to show respect; it means the same thing in Japanese as "Mr." or "Ms."

in English. "Kun" often seems to be used for addressing young males and can also be used among friends or social equals.

This wasn't a problem when we lived in New York. My biological father was not living with me. But when I entered Japanese society, I not only realized that my identity was different from the person I had been in New York, but that I didn't even have my own name. And I had no one around me who knew anything about my upbringing, no photographs, no written documents, etc. I had become a person without a past. And people would develop a completely different image of me on their own. I felt as if everyone was talking to someone who didn't really exist. I had become invisible. A new image of myself had been artificially created.

You'll be someone who's right in front of you but doesn't exist.

I told my father about this and tried to get him to understand, but he didn't. He told me that back in America, they only see all Orientals (East Asians) as monkeys. He told me that was the way it had always been and that it would never change. He said it would be better to be seen as odd than to be seen as monkeys.

At this point, there was not a single person I could communicate with. I didn't even know what the correct Japanese was. I knew English grammar, but I didn't know Japanese grammar at all. I didn't even know the basics of where to put a noun and where to put a verb. Every word I spoke would end up in a misunderstanding. And even if you try to explain to the other person that it's a misunderstanding, they don't understand. With certain people, I might be able to say that I don't understand what was being said, but with many, this was not possible. After all, I have the same face as many Japanese. Why would I be different inside?

I hardly spoke to anyone for months. I couldn't even talk to anyone because my speech sounded 180 degrees opposite to what I was saying. Soon, my Japanese became even more messed up. I only opened my mouth when I went to a restaurant and asked for something. I continued to read books by myself. Colin Wilson, Kurt Vonnegut, Dostoevsky. But strangely enough, no one noticed that I was becoming thoroughly deranged. Whenever I opened my mouth, I was misunderstood.

At this point, I was almost broken. I can't forget this feeling of fear even now. This fear is greater than when I was in a car accident.

Even if there is a person in front of me, it is a feeling of fear like being put in the middle of a deserted island. Eventually, people don't even look like people anymore.

And in the middle, there is me, living a complete lie. It was like I had a mask over me at all times. I can see what people are doing, but I can't answer them. Even if I answer, the meaning is not understood, and I know that the other person misunderstands what I am saying. I can see their eyes and subtle facial movements. I want to answer them, but I can't. I felt like an alien who couldn't speak the languages of the earth.

It might not be noticeable to people who speak Japanese well, but even a small mistake in the words that link them can be taken to mean something totally different.

I used to be argumentative because I liked having discussions and participating in debates in high school. I soon discovered, though, that I was unable to communicate with the other individual. Japan had no history of debating. Subsequently, I developed the strange practice of trying to laugh it off by making an embarrassed expression and muttering, "Heh, heh, heh." I hated doing this, but I didn't know what to do. I reasoned that since everyone behaved so respectfully and never challenged anybody else, I should follow suit. But by then, I'd lost all control of myself.

I met no one. I completely stopped cleaning my room. I stopped taking baths. I didn't do my laundry. I kept wearing the same clothes. Bugs started to appear more and more from inside the room. However, it was so dirty that even the insects died rapidly. The dead bodies of the insects were still there in the corner of the room. The refrigerator had rotten food in it. The refrigerator itself was broken and rotting. The room had become a pile of garbage, like a garbage dump, there was no place to walk. It was a complete mess.

I had no one to talk to. There wasn't a single person I'd known for a long time. I had never been in a setting like this. There was nothing I could do. Because nothing could be communicated.

As for my father, I didn't see him at all. He never contacted me. I wasn't interested in the anti-American political meetings he went to. And since we rarely lived together, to begin with, it was no surprise to me or him that we only saw each other two or three times a year.

When this occurred, I realized that I needed to demonstrate what culture means using my situation as an example. Many people have families. I did not. I was an honor student once—and I now behaved as though I had a mental illness.

There was a Korean living in Japan who repeatedly said to me as if he was neurotic, 'Don't say Paka about Poku. (Koreans often used to pronounce Baka as Paka because of difficulties in pronouncing the letter B. Baka means stupid in Japanese. Boku is a boy's way of saying the word, 'me.' The sentence means "Don't say I am stupid," however the words are spoken incorrectly. This seems to be something that some bigoted Japanese used to say about Koreans in the past to mock them, but since I was not in Japan, I had never heard it before.

When he realized I was Japanese, he started saying it to me. It reminded me of white folks in America who go around with their index fingers raised over both of their eyes, making them appear slanted, saying, "Chink, here comes the chink." What happens if you do this to someone like me, who is already sensitive to cultural issues? Why were they unable to see what they were doing?

People from all over the world gathered in the 1960s, but they were unable to communicate with one another and ultimately destroyed one another. Why? I wanted to know the answer.

Different cultures think differently. Language itself reflects the way we think, so those who speak different languages think differently. People who grew up in America cannot deny the culture they grew up in, no matter how superficially critical they may be of America. It is because they would be denying themselves as well.

My father used to tell my stepmother and me that we couldn't understand different ways of thinking. But did he himself understand any other way of thinking but the one he was raised with?

Humans should be able to understand each other.

However, we all live our lives with our complexes outwardly buried but hardened so as not to be discovered. And kids learn racism and other prejudices from society. In the middle school I went to, Jews, Russians, Chinese, Japanese, Blacks, Hispanics, etc. all grew up as people of the same single culture. I was fully aware that there was prejudice against Orientals (East Asians) and Blacks in American society outside of our school, but we seemed to be able to create a society among ourselves that wasn't prejudiced. But then I found out that prejudice is actually learned from history.

It is often written that in Africa there are people called Albinos who are sometimes born with white skin. In black society, they were considered disgusting if they had white skin. They were discriminated against in black society. There is a theory popularized by black Muslims that whites are the descendants of the albino people who were discriminated against and left Africa.

All human beings of the homo sapiens species came from Africa. And the consciousness that they were once discriminated against creates the next discrimination. And as the human race spreads to Europe and Asia, it breaks up into new "ethnic groups" and new discrimination is born from there. The discriminated people want revenge even if they deny it superficially. And violence is passed on to the next generation as if it were part of tradition.

In Colin Wilson's study of murderers, he writes that there is a combination of human types and backgrounds that if certain two people had never met, the murder would never have happened.

Around 1980, I recalled a nightmare I had in junior high school. In that dream, I was wandering around the streets of Shanghai by myself. I didn't know anyone. The city was full of Chinese characters I couldn't read. I was walking around peeking into shop windows to see what was there. The feeling of not being able to communicate with people was the loneliest thing I had ever felt. Shanghai was still in the middle of the Cultural Revolution when I had the dream. However, I realized that the feeling I had in the dream was the feeling of living alone in Tokyo in the early 80s. I thought to myself, "Oh yeah, that was really Tokyo."

I wanted to get out of this hell. I wanted to go to college. My father was still against it from the beginning, but I managed to convince him at first, and I was going to stay at my grandmother's house in Kamakura for a few months and take all the exams to go to university. I passed all the scores on all of my exams. I had two years of high school left to go before I graduated, but my high school history teacher wrote a letter of recommendation to the university saying that I was the best student he had ever met at the school. When everything was arranged for me to go, my father told me that he still couldn't afford to help me. He often changed his mind at the last minute.

Being a lone wolf is a dangerous thing. I could have easily created trouble out of frustration. My saving grace came in 1983 when I was suddenly offered the chance to do an album with Epic-Sony. I don't know what I would have done if I hadn't had that offer.

The perpetrators of the 9/11 attacks in 2001, as well as many fundamentalist Islamic terrorists, received their education in Europe. They had also met discrimination in Germany and the United Kingdom. They were significantly angrier about discrimination than the people from the Middle East. They were more likely to join religious and political groups that allowed them to express their anger. I was in that state of mind myself. In a society that demands identity, no one is more likely to turn to terrorism than someone whose identity is blurred. If we pursue more accurate research on how culture and the society in which we grow up affect us, we should be able to learn more about these things. In my case, I realized that no matter who I met, I couldn't get anything across because my cultural background was blank except for the New York culture of the 60s and 70s where I grew up. Even the same-looking Asians didn't understand me culturally. They didn't understand what this pain was like.

I once read an interviewee of a British skinhead who said that many white European right-wingers and neo-Nazis have no culture or anything to be proud of, only that they are white. For young British urban working men, culture is usually not around them, as they enjoy drinking in pubs, soccer (called football in the UK), and sports newspapers with gossip and nudity. The more ambiguous their identity, the more they want it, and the more they want the illusion of patriotism and nationalism.

In 1986, when my album *Nova Carmina* was released, a writer wrote: "When I first heard it, I was disgusted, thinking that Ayuo was a Japanese pretending to be a European. The writer wrote, "Why is a Japanese guy doing European music? I guess he's just a dork from a good family. Then I read in his profile that he grew up abroad with a father performing classical music, and I hated him even more. However, the more I listened to him, the more I began to think that this was not the sound of a Japanese, but the music of a Japanese-American."

Another French disc jockey living in Japan said after listening to this album: "It's not Japanese music, it's not American music, it's not German music. He doesn't belong to any culture. He's going to have problems getting understood."

It's one thing to be called borderless, it's quite another to be called music that doesn't belong to any country or ethnicity.

I never set out to make 'borderless' music. I just wanted to express myself naturally. And when you live naturally, your culture comes from the social environment researcher that you grew up in. I didn't understand why this was so difficult to understand and why people misunderstood it.

The consciousness of having an enemy begins with being conscious of belonging to a certain ethnic or religious group. Because the ethnic consciousness always comes from the consciousness that 'we' are different from 'you,' that we are special. If you look at the Old Testament, Jehovah says, "The God of the Jews has given you a land called Israel." Jehovah goes on to tell them to kill all the men of the Canaanites who are living there now and take all the virgins who are able to bear children and make them bear Jewish children to increase the population. This is the essence of tribal nationalism and the roots of war. This is what led me to make what is called world music. I wanted to express the results of my research into how culture and society affect people. I needed to do that for myself, and I thought I could express something that others could learn from. In this way, I see myself as a researcher as well as a performer.

With the discovery of new biological sciences such as the study of the genome and DNA, things that were previously shrouded in mystery are coming to light, and people may realize that all human beings are connected from centuries ago and be able to show how nationalism feeds hatred and create wars and discrimination. The answer can come from within us.

And this can be expressed in new forms of literature, music, and art.

Society can be born anew.

Why I don't understand the Japanese

Many Japanese communicate with one another through nonverbal communication.

There are words such as *Haragei, Ningen Kankei, Ninjo, Omote* (front, the polite attitude one shows on the surface, often superficial) versus *Ura* (back, the real feelings); *Tatemae* (front face, what is presented) versus *Honne* (true feelings privately held); and many other defined concepts.

I was not aware of this. No one ever told me.

Haragei means belly language and stems from the word *hara* (stomach). It is nonverbal and is used to convey one's true intentions.

Throughout my life in Japan, I have been told that I do *not* speak from the *hara*. This means that since I am not using the proper body language, people don't know if I am sincere or not. Since this seems to be a behavior learned from childhood, I have no idea how this nonverbal communication is done.

Japanese people often say one thing but do something else.

I later learned that this kind of attitude may come from *Bushido*, a Japanese style of Neo-Confucianism.

If I don't catch what they are conveying without using words, I am often accused of *not* paying attention to what they are trying to say. Yet, they do *not* express their true intentions in words. Only people who grew up in the same culture can tell what such things could mean.

Most Japanese are not even aware that they communicate using nonverbal communication most of the time. It's like a fish swimming in a bowl of water. The fish are often not aware of the water.

There is also the term *Kuuki wo Yomenai*—where one "cannot read the air."

For most people raised in Japan, these behavioral displays are as common as the air they breathe. They don't realize that people who are raised outside of Japan cannot understand these nonverbal communications.

I thought at first that some people were using some kind of telepathy. Just learning the language and the vocabulary isn't enough because these kinds of cultural behaviors don't exist anywhere else.

I was virtually illiterate in Japanese, excepting some hiragana, when I was told to live in a Japanese society. I was already 18 years old by then, so I never adopted Japanese as my language. My father told me that Westerners communicate mainly with words, but the Japanese communicate more with body language. I could not read this body language. Only people who grew up in Japan with both Japanese parents can understand this kind of communication. To me, it looked like either telepathy or some kind of animal language. Animals communicate like this.

My father also told me that discussions and debates are Western customs. In Japanese schools, people obey their teachers according to traditional disciples and do not discuss things further. I grew up in NYC where we had discussions every day.

When I was signed to MIDI Records, the company director told me that no one in MIDI Records wanted to talk with me; the things I am interested in—philosophy, cultural studies, and history—are of no interest to the average Japanese.

Recently I was re-reading a book by Edward T. Hall called *Hidden Dimensions: How to Do Business with the Japanese*. This came from a series of books about how to communicate with people from other cultures. I used this book as a guide to speak to the Japanese for many years. Japan is for me a foreign culture, even though I have lived here longer than anywhere else.

In the US media, I often read how individualism is disregarded in China because of communism. This is *not true*. Similar customs exist in Japan and many East Asian countries because of Confucian tradition, also called *Bushido* in Japan.

Many Westerners often cannot tell the difference between Communism and Confucianism. For example, to many Asians, North Korea might seem closer to a traditional authoritarian Confucian kingdom than a socialist republic. A Russian musician once told me that East Asians don't understand socialism or communism because they come from a collective rice-growing culture, whereas communism in Russia developed from Christianity.

Recently, I saw *Lee Kuan Yew & Robert Kuok's RAW Insights on Japan* on YouTube, in which President Lee of Singapore says that it is the foreign-raised Japanese that face the most difficulty and discrimination in Japan. Japanese-Brazilians were once invited to work in Japan in the 1990s, but many companies would not hire them because even though they looked Japanese, and had 100% Japanese DNA, they did not understand Japanese culture, language—and above all—Japanese behavior. I heard a Brazilian student say that the Japanese-Brazilians were gathered and kicked out of Japan three times. No one would hire them, and they had to rely on welfare until the government finally threw them out of the country, causing an international problem.

Lee Kuan Yew says that Chinese and Korean workers can work better in Japan than foreign-raised Japanese because they understand Japanese culture better than Western-educated Japanese. The Chinese and Koreans have more similarities in their cultural backgrounds.

There is an interesting animation in this video, where a man is just saying "*Um... Un... Um...*" It sounds like pigs grunting; the Japanese are supposed to understand the meaning of this.

People who live secluded for many years in a tribal society often develop a form of communication that is incomprehensible to everyone else. Perhaps this is what happened during the years of seclusion (*Sakoku*) during the Edo era. There are many people in Japan who feel that Westerners see the Japanese as yellow monkeys. They assume it's racism, but I think there is something else involved here. They communicate completely differently from Westerners. I would even say that it is animal talk if they don't rely on language. It is like the way apes in a tribe communicate.

How can anyone understand this kind of communication if they come from abroad?

A Japanese who was educated in the United States recently presented a video on YouTube saying that "*Bushido* has the roots of all social problems in modern Japanese society." This YouTuber explains by referring to a book by Toshio Yamagishi titled *Japanese, Uso* (The Japanese Lie). He talks about how the Edo period further strengthened the Japanese idea of "group" through social syncretism.

The following rules were established during the Edo period: a registration system was established so that people could not easily leave the land of their birth; class determined where they could live; foreign trade and travel were restricted, and the Sung-Ming school (neo-Confucianism) introduced from China strengthened the system by making those of higher status stand out.

What kind of society was created?

(1) A society where social harmony is more important than progress and development.

(2) People judged relationships with an animalistic sense of "reading the air."

(3) People are superficially polite and discrete. They hide their true feelings and intentions.

(4) People trust those within their community because there is no merit in disrupting the social order.

(5) They do not include people outside of their society in their circle of friends. This is because the common rules of that society cannot be applied to others.

The morals that *Bushido* fundamentally teaches are as follows, according to this book:

(1) Observe traditions and rules.

(2) Be a follower of those who are stronger than you and follow them faithfully.

(3) Shut out strangers and those from elsewhere.

(4) Hold grudges. Plot revenge on your enemies.

(5) Lie if necessary! (You do not have to speak the truth.)

These laws were created in the Edo period to ensure the sanctity of the society that was created.

Many Japanese people mistake this idea of "reading the air" for democracy, but it works rather like the opposite of democracy in Japanese society. It means to be in harmony with everyone else.

In a society where rice is the staple food, if one person acted on his/her own, the balance of the whole community would be upset, because everyone shared the water to grow rice. Democracy is a society in which everyone has a say. This is how it was explained in *A Study of the Air* by Shichihei Yamamoto, who wrote *Nihonjinron* (Theories of Japanese Uniqueness) after the Second World War.

Bushido became intertwined with Japan's nationalist expression in the mid-1800s. The victory of Japan over China in the Sino-Chinese War in 1895 restored a feeling of pride in *Bushido*, which was considered the "origin of military success." As a result, it became the propaganda tool by the government and military, who doctored it to suit their needs. *Bushido* regarded surrender as cowardly. Those who did forfeit their honor, and lost dignity and respect. *Bushido* therefore explains why the Japanese Imperial Army so mistreated POWs in their custody, murdering them by shooting, beheading, and drowning. These acts were excused by the government since they involved the killing of men who had forfeited all rights to be treated with dignity or respect. This attitude spilled over to their treatment of civilians.

The *Bushido* code still affects corporate behavior in contemporary Japan today. It structured the capitalist activity in the 20th century and is still the ideology of modern Japan.

I believe some kind of 'de-Nazification' should have taken place after World War II.

In the United States, people are taught that it is good to speak up for yourself, but if you speak up and state your opinion in Japan, you are often labeled as a "self-centered" person. There is a deep sense in Japanese society that one must be the same as everyone else. This stifles creativity.

The truth is that the more superficially polite a person is, the more self-centered he or she really is inside. The social system and traditional manners hide this.

During the Edo period (1603–1867), people who traveled abroad and attempted to return to Japan were put to death. Even though this is not the case today, Japan is still a country where social customs of seclusion still remain.

Notes for "Theme for a Stateless Wanderer"

Below are the notes to a composition I wrote about people who traveled abroad in the 16th century and were not allowed to return under the threat of execution.

This composition was originally the theme song for Jiyu Kobo's documentary film *The Story of Kadoya Shichirobei: A Japanese Town in Vietnam* (1995), about a young man who went from Japan to Vietnam to trade in the 16th century.

Shortly after he crossed over, the Tokugawa Shogunate unified Japan and closed the country to the outside world, issuing a decree that anyone who returned would be put to death. He resided in a Japanese town that was developed next to the Chinese town. The Chinese quarter still exists, but the Japanese residents that lived there blended in with the Vietnamese.

While writing the theme music for this documentary film, I was thinking about the following things:

Unlike Europe, Japan does not have the historical tradition of creating a nation-state. Therefore, the concept of a nation is also different from that of Europe. It was not a modern *nation-state* that emerged naturally from tradition, but a *nation-state* that was created in a hurry when it could have been dominated by European powers in the 19th century. Newspapers, education, and later radio were used to propagate an image of a nation that people could have some common attachment to. However, this did not include the traditions of individualism and democracy that emerged from a European tradition. Such ideas were created from Western Europe's history of domestic wars and resistance. When they are artificially created, as in Japan, they deviate from the European model into something different.

There were always individuals in every period and culture who were unable to integrate into their society. When a country closes down and becomes isolated, individuals who are aware of another culture become outsiders and enemies. Those who came from another culture were executed during the Edo era. I grew up in the

American culture of New York City in the 1960s and have always felt culturally shut out of this Japanese society.

My title for this composition is "Theme for a Stateless Wanderer." The word "stateless" here does not have a happy image. It refers to people who are shut out of society. This composition is from *Music for Harp, Bouzouki, and String Instruments*, released on June 28, 2022, on Bandcamp.

It is also on *Compilation Part 1 Ambient and Classical Music*, also on Bandcamp, and the piano solo version is on *Piano Compositions by Ayuo* as performed by Yuji Takahashi.

Now, let me explain how nation-states and nationalism came to be:

Nation-states are an artificial creation.

There was no word for a nation in either Chinese or Japanese before the 19th century. Instead, the concept of nation-states was introduced by Western countries. The word *minzu* in Chinese and *minzoku* in Japanese had to be invented.

The Israeli historian, Yuval Noah Harari, points out in his best-selling book *Homo Sapiens* how the concept of a nation-state was artificially created in the 19th century.

One of the greatest discoveries of the late 20th century is the study of genomics. Today we can see that the scientific connection of how human beings traveled out of Africa and reached the four corners of the earth. We can see that people who originated such in close areas such as the islands of Shikoku and Kyushu in Japan have different DNA. People from Shikoku have more DNA from the Yayoi people who came to Japan from the Korean peninsula, compared to people from Kyushu. Kyushu people have a mixture of different tribes and nationalities who came at different periods in time. They include Polynesians (Austronesian), Siberians, and people who came from mainland China at different times, including people who have similar DNA to the Ami nationality in China.

People in Northeastern China and Southeastern China are both considered Chinese but have different DNA. The state of Israel requires government permission to check one's DNA. Many believe that it is probably because it will bring out scientific evidence that many rulers of modern Israel have a significant amount of European DNA, while the Palestinians have DNA that goes back to the time of the Canaanites. The linguist and political activist Noam Chomsky said in recent interviews that DNA isn't what makes one Jewish. People who are raised in Jewish culture are Jewish, whether their genes come from ancient Israel or not. Chinese is a culture, not a race. The same applies to Japanese. What happened in the 19th century muddied many cultural developments and resulted in modern nationalism.

Modern nationalism is very much like racism.

Let's look at what happened to Japan:

In the late 19th century, the military from Satsuma in Kyushu and Choshu domain (in the southern region of Honshu Island) formed a military alliance to overthrow the Tokugawa government, which they felt was too weak to defend Japan. They brought in an 'emperor' who was virtually forgotten and created the modern religion of *Shinto*.

Until then, *Shinto* was a set of folk beliefs. It was believed that there were gods everywhere. For example, if you made a mess in a toilet, the god of the toilet would become angry at you.

Japan was still a medieval feudal society. The new rulers wanted to create a strong, centralized culture defining its national identity. Until the so-called Meiji Restoration, few people knew of the existence of an ancient emperor. Most people were not allowed to travel outside their province unless they had specific permission from their rulers. The government established a dominant national dialect called "standard language" (*hyōjungo*) that replaced local and regional dialects. They also unified the modes used in folk songs. Many areas in Kyushu, which were close to Korea, had the same modes or even the same melody as folk songs in Korea. When folk songs were played on the national radio, the melodies were changed to fit the Edo (Tokyo) mode. Having a centralized religion and an 'emperor' was thought to give the people a sense of a unified culture; after all, the Catholic church had a pope. The Yasukuni shrine was built in 1869 as a shrine to honor those who died fighting for the emperor. It is not an ancient shrine, but a propaganda tool for the imperialist ambitions of the Japanese Empire. The shrine played an important role in boosting the military and civilian morale during the war as a symbol of devotion to the Emperor.

The fact that such things remain to this day is the main difference between Germany—which went through a de-Nazification program—and Japan, which was allowed by the United States to retain such propaganda tools from the Pacific War.

In my opinion, these outdated instruments of imperialism ought to be exposed for what they are.

Yuval Noah Harari believes that even though nationalism was artificially created, it is still useful to unify people as a tool. I don't think this is a good idea. The main tool of propaganda used in many of the 20th century's wars was nationalism. Nationalism became closely linked to racism, and much of racism is based on scientific lies.

Turkey advertises that their people came from Central Asia. They show the Uyghur Empire, which used to exist above the Tang Dynasty of China as the country that they originated from. However, DNA shows that at least 93% of their DNA is that of the people who lived in the Byzantine Empire as Greeks, Kurds, Armenians, Slavs, and many others. Conquerors are usually men who force their culture and language on the people they conquer. Turkey continues to say that Kurds don't exist in their country. Yet are the Uyghurs the same as the ancient Uyghurs?

DNA research shows that when the Uyghur Empire was overthrown, the rulers escaped to the areas in western China, where they live today, and mixed with the Persian-speaking population that lived there before. DNA research into every country brings up something similar. Usually, it will show groups of men conquering people who lived in that area. Often, the female DNA will show those of the original inhabitants, while the male DNA is that of the conquerors. This seems to be the case in many European countries.

A utopic future would have all nationalities and nation-states break down, where people of all nationalities can group in more peaceful communities.

I also believe that there should be one global language that everyone in the world can understand. Language is the basis of culture. Having one language that everyone can understand will prevent a lot of misunderstandings that I faced in Japan. In medieval Europe, all scholars and academics learned Latin as the universal language. Students were able to attend universities in any European country because the courses were taught in Latin. I would propose a return to having a universal language.

A Universal Language

I would propose English to be that language; not just because I was raised in that language, and not because of US imperialism, but because it is simple to learn and is a living language. This is unlike Esperanto, which was a language that the Soviet Union proposed to be the universal language. Many people in the world already understand English since it is employed often in business discussions and science. The Japanese-American physicist, Michio Kaku, has also proposed that English should become the global language of planet Earth. India has proposed that English should become one of the standard languages of BRICS, an association of countries that rivals G7 and the US allies. This is because Chinese or Russian would be more difficult to acquire.

The only reason that Japan became an economic giant after World War II was because the United States needed Japan to make radios, cars, and jeeps to use in the Korean War and the Vietnamese War. In the late 1980s, the United States felt that Japan was making too much money from their cars and electronics; as a result, they developed agreements that brought down the Japanese economy. Many Japanese businessmen who remember this from the 1980s are still angry and blame the United States for its economic downfall.

The United States began to turn its attention to China as its main trading partner in the 1990s but started to implement trade restrictions once it felt that China was becoming too strong.

Hawaii has an interesting bilingual culture, and I like the way both English and Hawaiian are used in its music and poetry. Learning two languages is good, not only for trade and commerce but also for the brain. People would be able to understand more of what is going on in the world if people could read and communicate with one another from an early age. The educated people in countries like Singapore and India grow up learning English.

It may not solve every problem in the world, but universal understanding is a step toward building a utopian future.

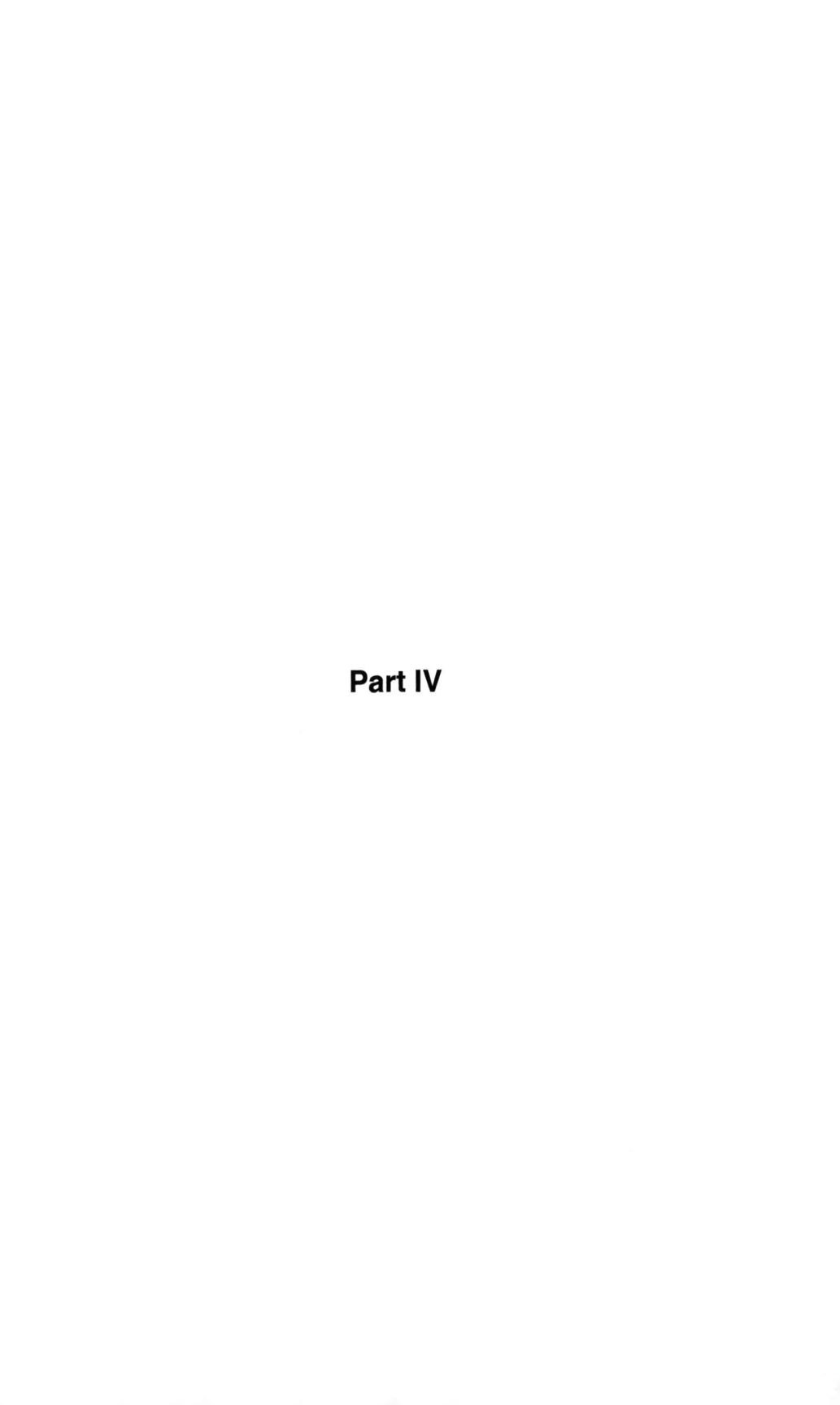

Part IV

Tokyo and my mother in the 1950s and early 1960s

My mother grew up in Setagaya, Tokyo. Her father, Kyosei Akemoto, was a well-known composer in his days, and even today he earns more royalties than any of my relatives. He also wrote prefectural songs for Aomori and Saitama prefectures, and most Japanese people must have heard some melody composed by him at some point.

The graphic designer Makoto Wada and the composer Toru Takemitsu lived nearby. In the postwar era of the 1950s, there was a feeling in the air that many things were about to change. When my mother rode her bicycle around the neighborhood, she used to see groups of people from the experimental music and art group called *Jiken Kobo* (Experimental Factory) gather at Toru Takemitsu's house.

Makoto Wada introduced my mother to various new artists. Those included Tadanori Yokoo, Kishin Shinoyama, and Mutsuo Takahashi.

Toru Takemitsu later told me the following story about my mother: when he was composing on the piano at home, my mother, who was passing by on her bicycle, would often shout, "*Heta Kuso* (You play like shit)!" from the outside and quickly run away on her bike. She must have been about 15 years old at the time.

One of my mother's high school classmates was Seiji Ozawa. When Mr. Ozawa visited my mother's house, my grandmother thought that my mother had brought a juvenile delinquent to their house, because of his disheveled hair, and she put up a broom upside down in the house. This seems to be a silent way of saying that we don't want you here in our home—a way of asking people to leave without uttering a word. I was told the meaning behind those Japanese old customs years later.

Japan seems to have many of these silent languages that people who aren't raised there would never understand.

Figure 28   Photo from 1969. With my mother.

My mother went on to study composition at Tokyo University of the Arts. She worked as an arranger and piano accompanist for the chanson singer, Yoko Kishi. At the site of one of her part-time jobs as a piano accompanist for an opera company, she met my father. At that time, my father was kicked out of his home because he could not get along with *his* father, and his father threatened to disown him.

Around the beginning of the 1960s, new movements in Japan bridging together art, music, and film began forming. They were inspired by the new artistic movements in Western Europe and the United States.

The post-war generation was previously not exposed to these movements because of the heavy censorship of the military dictatorship in Japan, and the war, which prohibited freedom of speech and expression. Many people knew nothing of what was going on in the world, or even of what the Japanese government was doing. A lot of these new art movements were led by people who had been around my mother and father.

Composer Toshi Ichiyanagi and his then-wife, Yoko Ono were there; they had just returned from New York. Ichiyanagi and Ono spread the news about the new art and music scene in New York City. This New York scene included John Cage and members of Fluxus, and would later include John Cale, Kuniharu Akiyama, Nam Jun Paik, and Takehisa Kosugi.

In the '60s, after life had settled down at last after the end of World War II, people were experimenting with new ways of thinking and living. The aim was to encourage people to question what they had previously taken for granted, to expand their thinking, and to realize a new way of life that had not existed before. New art and music were born out of this. In music, it was not only the avant-garde that was expanding at the time but jazz as well. Composers Toshiro Mayuzumi and Joji Yuasa; graphic designers Kiyoshi Awazu and Tadanori Yokoo; and filmmaker Mako Idemitsu—all were also involved in this new art movement. Violinist and composer Takehisa Kosugi also began performing here.

At this time, the Sogetsu Art Center in Tokyo became the center for Japanese avant-garde art, music, and dance. This was possible only because Sofu Teshigahara, who was the *Iemoto* (head of Sogetsu flower arranging school) was there to support this movement.

Electronic music and *musique concrète* by Toru Takemitsu and Kuniharu Akiyama were created there. Takehisa Kosugi began performing there. Hiroshi Teshigahara's films, *Woman in the Dunes* and *The Face of Another* were also made with people who were active at Sogetsu at the time.

John Cage and Merce Cunningham's first performances in Japan were also held at Sogetsu Hall. Hiroshi Teshigahara, Sofu Teshigahara's son, planned and produced the first Yoko Ono performance in Tokyo. It was called "Yoko Ono Recital." My mother also played at this performance. She told me that she had once asked Yoko Ono to babysit me before I was three years old. I have no memories of that time in Tokyo myself, but I do have some photos from that time.

The world of that time from her point of view is described in her autobiography entitled *Cosmic Family* (Film Art Inc.)

After I started to learn the guitar in 1968, my mother suggested that we practice playing Beatles songs together so that I could study ensemble playing at home. We started with "Hey Jude" and in the early '70s, we played David Bowie's "Five Years" and "Space Oddity" together. When we had parties at home, my stepfather, Mansour, would sing Iranian classical music and my mother and I would play Bowie songs. Some of our friends from Japan were at these home parties, as well as people who worked at MOMA, successful New York hair stylists, film critic Donald Richie, and Porter A. McCray.

My mother was not suited to become a housewife. In the early 60s, she worked with *chanson* and jazz singers and had many friends. However, it was difficult for women to get much recognition because they were always in the shadow of men. She even tried to become a painter in the late 1960s, and Hiroshi Teshigahara organized an exhibition of her paintings in Ginza, Tokyo in 1970. She then tried to become a singer and songwriter in the early 70s. She wrote a lot of songs at the time.

She started reading a lot of books about spiritualism in the 1970s. She ran off with a dancer, the summer before I turned 15 years old, and with that, our family life ended.

She became a member of the American Astrological Society in 1990 and started doing professional horoscope readings as a job.

Then, she moved back to Tokyo in 1991, after living in Europe, New York, and Hawaii. She became more relaxed in her thinking in her later life.

Questions of identity in Hiroshi Teshigahara's films and Kobo Abe's novels

Around 1970, I was in the fifth grade when I first saw the film *The Face of Another*. I was sitting next to the director, Hiroshi Teshigahara. Donald Ritchie had helped to present a film festival of his works at the Museum of Modern Art, and he had flown to New York to attend. He was speaking in a whisper throughout the screening of *The Face of Another*. It was as if he was remembering himself at the time he made the film, saying things like, "I should have cut out this scene." But for me, this film is a masterpiece, no matter how many times I've seen it.

I knew Hiroshi Teshigahara from the time I can remember because my father participated in composing and performing the music for the film, *Pitfall*. He was friends with my mother, my stepfather, my father, and my stepmother. My mother worked as a coordinator for him at one time, taking him to meet people like Andy Warhol. I remember when he came to New York and wanted to see some new arthouse films that weren't shown in Japan, but I suggested an American comedy movie just because there was a gorilla on the movie poster. He took us to the movie, even though it wasn't the kind he wanted to see.

At the time, many artists and musicians from Japan would look forward to seeing artistic films in NYC, especially as they were not yet available to watch in Japan. Toru Takemitsu would spend days just going from one movie theater to another. Teshigahara's daughter, Kiri, would come often to my mother's apartment in New York City, and our family would take her to see rock concerts by The Kinks, Hawkwind, and Genesis. We also visited his pottery workshop in Fukui prefecture in Japan, where I made some pottery of my own. He sent us invitations to the premiere of his films.

Figure 29   Photo from October 1970, when I visited Tokyo with my mother and stepfather; Hiroshi Teshigahara organized an exhibition of my mother's paintings at a gallery in Ginza, Tokyo. We stayed there for a month. During this short stay, I met the novelist, Yukio Mishima, at another party; this was shortly before he committed suicide. (Hiroshi Teshigahara, far right; Kishin Shinoyama, far left.)

He came to see a theater play for which I did the music. I also composed some music which was the background music to an experimental film by Mako Idemitsu, which played at the entrance of Hiroshi Teshigahara's *Ikebana* (flower arrangement) exhibition. Knowing him was very important in my artistic development.

However, it was after I spent many years in Japan that I began to understand the problems of identity that Kobo Abe writes about.

The Face of Another stars Tatsuya Nakadai, who is well-known for his roles in the films of Akira Kurosawa; it also stars Machiko Kyo, who is well-known for her roles in *Rashomon* and *Ugetsu Monogatari*. The film is based on a novel of the same title by Kobo Abe, which deals with the issues of human identity. The protagonist is an engineer, Okuyama, who suffers a serious burn on his face in an industrial accident.

The film begins with Okuyama consulting a psychiatrist because he feels that he was rejected by everyone—including his wife. His psychiatrist makes a prosthetic mask for him to wear as a new face, so he can feel confident again and enjoy life again. His psychiatrist warns him that his personality may change; he may become a different person because he is seen as someone different—which does happen. This is a common phenomenon among people who have grown up in different environments. When he is seen under a different lens, he takes on that persona. He becomes different.

I know this from personal experience—from observing the way I was seen and treated in New York, and the way people saw me in Tokyo. I was seen as a different character. In reality, people cannot change from within. If your character has fully developed, you will always carry the same identity with you.

But the way people see you and treat you makes an enormous difference.

Later in the film, Okuyama tries to seduce his wife, pretending to be another man; but he gets upset when she accepts him too fast. However, when he tries to reveal his true face, she tells him that she knew it was him all along. She was only pretending to go along with his act. He tries to persuade her to give their relationship another chance, but she tells him that it's over.

In the last scene, the protagonist and his psychiatrist are walking in the nightly streets together, where they see that everyone on the street is wearing a mask. This is a metaphor.

Who are we in reality? Aren't we all wearing masks in our everyday life?

In the film version, there is a different, parallel story that is interwoven throughout—a young woman whose face was once beautiful, but who suffers from a severe disfigurement on the right side of her cheek and neck. The young woman works in a psychiatric ward whose inmates include many World War II veterans. She keeps asking her brother if he remembers the sea in Nagasaki, suggesting that her scars came as a result of the atomic bombing of that city. She feels just as isolated as the main protagonist.

The role of the young woman was played by a model, who later became Mrs. Vera Ozawa, Seiji Ozawa's wife. She was not a professional actress, and in later years, Teshigahara regretted having her play that role because he felt that she still walked like a model instead of the character she was supposed to be. She is credited as Miki Irie in the film.

Teshigahara had many of the best visual artists in Japan participate in the film. The film titles were designed by Kiyoshi Awazu, who also designed the poster. The architect, Arata Isozaki, designed a blank space with glass partitions for the psychiatrist's office. Large and small severed ears, which appear in a few scenes, were designed and sculpted by Japanese sculptor Tomio Miki.

There are many dream-like surrealist scenes: Teshigahara also used the technique of shooting the same scene twice, once with the protagonist wearing a mask, and another with his new face to highlight his double existence.

The music for this film is by Toru Takemitsu. I often play the waltz he wrote for this film in my own arrangements. When you listen to my version of "A Face of Another Waltz," you'll first realize that I'm doing it in a late 1960s psychedelic rock arrangement. It's like a snapshot expressed through music.

Back then I was listening to Jefferson Airplane, Velvet Underground, The Doors, Grateful Dead, etc. and these influences are there in my arrangement.

The dialogue in the script is often like quotes from a book of philosophy or psychology. Carl Jung seems to have been an influence on the writer, Kobe Abe. Jung's analysis of faces is used in the novel. Many quotes in the dialogue also seem to show Jung's influence on Abe.

Let's take a look at a few examples:

"In love, people try to unmask one another."

"That's why I put on so much makeup, so we would be both wearing masks."

"I have so many selves, I can't contain them all."

"I wonder if losing one's face deranges one's senses."

"There are monsters who act like people and people who act like monsters."

"It's always lonely being free."

(Lines taken from the English subtitles of *The Face of Another*, as provided by Janus Films.[1])

In the book version, how the protagonist identifies himself as an object of prejudice is even more evident:[2]

> "I had almost nothing in common with the Negroes, except for being an object of prejudice. The Negroes were comrades bound in the same cause, but I was quite alone."

> "Perhaps, seeking points of similarity between myself who had lost my face and Koreans who were frequently the objects of prejudice, I had, without realizing it, come to have a feeling of closeness with them."

> *(On the personality of the face the protagonist chooses.)*

> "According to Jungian psychology, this would be an ambitious face, capable of action, or a hostile, extraverted one."

The reader may or may not agree with how the protagonist is thinking. The important thing is that it makes you think about these problems.

What is oneself?

How does your personality change, when the environment in which you live changes?

What happens to you when people start to look at you differently? And what happens to people with ambiguous identities?

It is often people with ambiguous identities who are more likely to be lured into extremist political groups and radical cults. This is the same whether he is a working-class white skinhead who says that he has nothing, but is proud to be British or a British-Pakistani who was raised in Britain without much education in traditional Islamic culture. People who talk loudly of nationalism or patriotism often turn out to be people who have not received much cultural education and are both more vulnerable and afraid of being influenced at the same time.

The original novel by Kobe Abe brings up these questions of ethnicity and race. How did Kobe Abe come up with such a masterpiece about human identity?

---

[1]Teshigahara, Hiroshi (Director). *The Face of Another* (film), Sogetsu Foundation; Toho, The Criterion Collection (DVD), 2007.
[2]Abe, Kobo. *The Face of Another*, trans. E. Dale Saunders. New York: G. P. Putnam's Sons/Perigee Books, 1980.

Let's look at his background.

Kobo Abe was raised in Mukden (now Shenyang) in Manchuria. John Nathan, an eminent translator of Japanese Literature, once called Manchuria "No Man's Land." Abe was already past twenty years old, when he first came to live in Tokyo, Japan.

Abe told Nancy Shields in a 1978 interview, "I am essentially a man without a hometown. This may be what lies behind the 'hometown phobia' that runs in the depth of my feelings."[3] He often said that his experiences in Manchuria imprinted terrors in his mind, which became the surrealist images in his works.

From 1962 to 1968, Hiroshi Teshigahara and Kobo Abe collaborated on four films: *Pitfall* (1962), *Woman in the Dunes* (1964), *The Face of Another* (1966), and *The Man Without a Map* (1968). The questions of identity are the most important theme in these works.

In the novel and film *Woman in the Dunes*, the male protagonist is someone who feels he does not belong in society, but he is held captive in an environment surrounded by only sand. He longs for freedom, but his previous life as a schoolteacher was not that pleasant either. He has no identity except his birth certificate, insurance papers, and other legal documents.

The Man Without a Map is the story of an unnamed detective, who is hired by an alcoholic woman, to find clues related to the disappearance of her husband. The impossibility of finding clues in order to solve the mystery leads him to have an existential crisis, in which he winds up identifying with the man that he was supposed to find.

In Abe's *The Box Man*, an unnamed man gives up society and lives in a box. Teshigahara did not adapt this book, though the thematic similarity between this and his adaptations is evident.

Why were such novels written and such films made in Japan at the time? Toru Takemitsu often said that because of World War II, the dislike of all things Japanese continued for some time. The generation after World War II was thinking of a new cultural identity. There is the problem of figuring out one's identity, as well as

---

[3]Shields, Nancy. *Fake Fish: The Theater of Kobo Abe*. New York & Tokyo: Weatherhill. ISBN 9780834803541. 1996.

trying to figure out a social identity. This is what makes many films and works of this period interesting.

Ian Buruma is an important journalist to note when reading about Japanese art, culture, and identity. He was originally from the Netherlands, and he came to live in Japan in 1975, after becoming a fan of Shuji Terayama's Tenjo Sajiki Theater Company. He made friends with many of the artists in Japan, including Kiyoshi Awazu and Tadanori Yokoo, and became an actor in Shuji Terayama's theater, as well as in other theater companies. He wrote many books about Japan in the 1970s. They are a great introduction to what it was like at that time.

He would later write books, such as *Taming the Gods* and *Murder in Amsterdam,* in which he would analyze why and how many of the Islamic fundamentalist terrorist incidents—which occurred in Europe—were caused by second-generation immigrants from the Middle East. These terrorists, who were raised within Western culture, watching Western television and listening to rock 'n roll, yet had ambiguous identities. They were unlike their parents—first-generation immigrants—who came to Western countries when they already were adults of their own free will. The second generation was raised in Western cultures but often found that they were being discriminated against. Their ambiguous identities made them targets for some rich Middle Eastern religious fundamentalists to brainwash them to join extremist religious cults.

Ian Buruma's experience in living and experiencing other cultures as an actor made him one of the best journalists to analyze this important situation. In an article for the New York Times about the exhibition "Tokyo 1955–1970: A New Avant-Garde," at the Museum of Modern Art, New York City, November 18, 2012 – February 25, 2013, he wrote the following:

> To me, the most fascinating thing about Japan at that time was the rediscovery of neglected aspects of Japanese culture, more in tune with the carnivalesque happenings: the subsoil, as it were, of Japanese tradition—the erotic side of Shintoism, the matriarchal cults of rural life, the low life of Japanese cities, the popular expressions of sex and violence that once produced the Kabuki theater—in short, the very opposite of fine art and high culture, traditional or modernist.
>
> One of the most prominent, Kiyoshi Awazu, a native of the northeast, described his role as a designer as that of a wandering outcast. The

designer's mission, in Awazu's words, was "to extend the rural into the city, foreground the folklore, reawaken the past, summon back the outdated, and confront the most belated 'rear-garde' with the city."

The unashamed use of popular art and entertainment, even the embrace of commercial art, seems to bring out the best in Japanese artists, perhaps because of the long tradition of what might be called refined popular culture.[4]

Ian Buruma noted very well this difference between Western and Eastern art. This is further illuminated in the Korean-German philosopher Byung-Chul Han's essay, "Satori," in his book *Good Entertainment*:

> (In the West,) The construct of true or serious art, strictly separated from mere entertainment, arises in concert with a number of dichotomies characterized by internal tension: reason/mind versus the senses.... Far Eastern thinking, on the other hand, is oriented toward complimentary principles.

> The dichotomy of mind versus the senses, which grounds the concept of a low art addressed only to the demands of the senses, never developed in the Far East. Nor does Far Eastern culture recognize the idea of artistic autonomy or the conflation of truth and art.... It is primarily concerned with affirmation and entertainment.

> Undoubtedly, Confucian morality has also exerted an influence on the art of the Far East.

> Japanese ukiyo-e woodcuts famously exercised a powerful fascination on many European painters of the modern period, enthralling even Paul Cézanne and Vincent van Gogh. Yet ukiyo-e is anything but high art. It was deeply embedded in the entertainment industry that flourished in the Edo period. A popular motif in ukiyo-e was the pleasure quarter of Edo Yoshiwara with its beauties, jesters, tea houses, Kabuki theaters, and actors plying their trades. Ukiyo-e was a part of this pleasure quarter. Its popularity led to mass production. Portraits of actors in particular sold like mad. Ukiyo-e was a mass culture, intended to entertain.[5]

Historical differences, traditional differences, and differences in beliefs; all signify that art will carry different connotations in different cultures.

---

[4]Buruma, Ian. *The New York Review of Books*, January 10, 2013. Reprinted in Buruma, Ian, *Theater of Cruelty Art, Film, and the Shadows of War.*

[5]Han, Byung-Chul. *Good Entertainment: A Deconstruction of the Western Passion Narrative* (2019), published by Massachusetts Institute of Technology.

Christianity is a Western way of thinking that influenced all art, philosophy, and even political systems in the West. In the East, no matter what it seems superficially, the traditions of Confucianism, Buddhism, and Taoism remain strong in how art is perceived and created.

It is the same in politics. In East Asia, socialism is not the same as socialism that developed from Christian beliefs in the West, but more akin to "socialism with Chinese characteristics." This is why many Russians would say that Asians developed a 'Rice Collective' society instead of the socialist society that they had in Europe.

A novel based on the problems that arise from cultural identity, which I felt was important to note, is *Shame,* written in 1983 by the British-Indian author Sir Salman Rushdie. Rushdie based his main character in *Shame* on a murder incident that took place in the East End of London, where a Pakistani father murdered his only child, a daughter, for going out with a white boy. All his friends and relatives refused to condemn his actions and went on supporting him, even when it turned out that the girl had never actually 'gone all the way' with her boyfriend. Her character, Sufiya Zinobia, grew out of the corpse of that murdered girl:

> In my imagination she spoke with an East London accent but wore jeans, blue brown pink... lively, no doubt attractive, a little too dangerously so at sixteen. Mecca meant ballrooms to her, rotating silver balls, strobe lighting, youth. She danced behind my eyes, her nature changing each time I glimpsed her: now innocent, now whore, then a third and a fourth thing.... But finally she eluded me, she became a ghost, and I realized that to write about her, about shame, I would have to go back East, to let the idea breathe its favorite air. Anna, deported, repatriated to a country she had never seen.[6]

Also of note was some dialogue from *Woman in the Dunes,*[7] showing the 'outsider' (the school teacher) talking with the woman in the dunes; then, the villagers, and then with the woman again:

"Here we are ruthlessly exploited, yet happily wagging our tails."

"What'll you do now?"

"Hey, mister, working hard?"

---

[6]Rushdie, Salman. *Shame* (1983), published by Picador USA.
[7]Teshigahara, Hiroshi (Director). *Woman in the Dunes* (film, 1964), Sogetsu Foundation; Toho, The Criterion Collection (DVD), 2007.

"But you'll live like this forever, if you don't speak up."

"Then demand your rights."

The way the schoolteacher is trapped by villagers is treated reminds me of the critical saying "You can't read the air." Being unable to "read the air" is often used against people who are not able to read the thoughts of others, unless they are told verbally. People who grew up in the same culture are expected to understand each other without the use of words. The saying comes from a time when water had to be shared by everyone in the whole village to grow rice. Speaking differently from others was taken as an assertion of oneself—of self-centeredness—and individualism was frowned upon in such a society. People who expressed individualistic thoughts could be killed by the whole village. Reports of such customs existed even during World War II.

Ken Awazu, son of Kiyoshi Awazu, told me that his father often made illustrations of 'faces' without eyes and noses, not just for Kobo Abe, but in many of his creative works. There is a tradition in Japan of drawing faces without specific identities. They could be anyone. The poster Kiyoshi Awazu drew that has the title "Antiwar" is one such work. They make you think about what 'identity' really is.

This is similar to the fact that in many of Kobo Abe's novels, the protagonists are unnamed. They have no name. They have no specific identity.

Kobe Abe's books were one of the first by a Japanese author to have sold internationally. His books were more popular than Yukio Mishima or Kenzaburo Oe (who had won the Nobel Prize in literature). Hiroshi Teshigahara's adaptation of *Woman in the Dunes* was the first film by an Asian film director to have been nominated for an Academy Award in the US. He was also nominated as best director of the year. Andrei Tarkovsky, well-known for directing masterpieces like *Solaris*, considered this film to be one of the 10 films that influenced him the most.

In the US and the UK, many journalists and writers—such as the novelist and screenwriter, David Mitchell (known for *Cloud Atlas* and *The Matrix Resurrections*)—as well as the feminist, Andrea Dworkin, had begun to explore Kobe Abe's works because of their treatment of identity issues, which has become even more important in recent years.

Steven Severin, of Siouxsie and the Banshees, has a solo album out entitled *Woman in the Dunes* with music for its theater production. Yoko Ueno, a musician I often work with, also created an entirely new score for a theater production of *Woman in the Dunes* in 2021.

Both the novels and the films have become recognized classics both in the East and in the West.

Figure 30   My stepfather, Mansour, with film director Hiroshi Teshigahara.

Toru Takemitsu's ear for sound

Toru Takemitsu had a sense of "sound" that is rare to find in other human beings. He was sensitive to each sound and understood what effect it could have. This was a different talent from Toru Takemitsu as a composer. Many film directors could not have added "sound" in the way he did.

The films for which Toru Takemitsu oversaw the music were not necessarily composed by him alone. Magical Power Mako, known for progressive rock in Japan, provided the rock elements in Masahiro Shinoda's *Himiko*; Kuniharu Akiyama provided some electronic music in Masaki Kobayashi's *Kwaidan*; and Toshi Ichiyanagi and Yuji Takahashi composed music for piano in Hiroshi Teshigahara's *Pitfall*.

In Masahiro Shinoda's *Double Suicide (Shinju Tenoamijima)*, directed in 1969, he used Balinese gamelan, Turkish festival flutes and drums, and Japanese shamisen in a completely unexpected way, showing how brilliant he could be at adding sound to film. When Joe Strummer of the punk band The Clash was asked by Alex Cox to compose music for a film, they studied Toru Takemitsu's music for Akira Kurosawa's *Ran* together before even shooting the film.

Here are some excerpts from an interview I conducted in 2002, with Alex Cox talking about the music of his films and his influence from Kurosawa. This interview was published in Tower Records' *Intoxicate* magazine:

Ayuo: Let me ask you questions about your use of music in films, especially those you have made with Joe Strummer making the film score.

Alex Cox: I had made three feature films, in which the music and songs were shared between different composers and Joe Strummer was involved in two of them. When I started *Walker*, I was thinking Joe could provide some music, but Joe said "I should write all of it." And because I'm not really musically educated, I said "okay," thinking that if it does not work out, we could get more music from elsewhere.

But he wrote the score for all the scenes. Amazing soundtrack.

Most of the arrangements were done by his musical partner at the time, who does the same kind of things you do: Zander Schloss. He was a guitar guy. He had a bouzouki too. I think the idea of the *Walker* score was that they would only use instruments that existed in the 1850s. Nothing synthetic. I think that was the intention originally. All the authentic acoustic instruments.

Ayuo: In your films, do you tell the musicians what you want or do you allow the musicians to be inspired by the scenes?

Alex: Yeah. Inspired by. Because I don't really have strong ideas for music.

We went to see *Ran* many times. Saw how very sweet music was used in the battle scenes, so we wanted something similar. We talked about that before we started shooting.

Ayuo: What interested you about Kurosawa?

Alex: It was technical, rather than the message. The philosophy was fine. The ideas were fine. But in a way, I'm less of an individualist than he was. More than the triumph of the individual, I'm more interested in group action.

Ayuo: But Japan is a much more group society than England is.

Alex: Yeah. But I like the idea of group action. Of working together in a group. As you do in filmmaking. But technically, I think Kurosawa is the greatest filmmaker ever, in terms of his technique and his ability. He comes close to perfection. I couldn't do that because I'm not such a perfectionist myself, but I admire that ability. I admire that perfection.

Toru Takemitsu's film music attracted worldwide attention, especially for the films directed by Hiroshi Teshigahara. *The Face of Another* begins with a melancholic theme played by a string orchestra. It is followed by some electronic music, made from the sounds of rubbing the rim of wine glasses—a technique often called glass harp, musical glasses, or singing glasses. In the bar scene, a singer with a bar band sings one of Toru Takemitsu's masterpieces, "Waltz." This song has such a unique charm that it is hard to say which genre it belongs to. It is one of my favorite songs. I have sung this song in a psychedelic folk-like arrangement with a Middle Eastern rhythm; this arrangement is available in both my compilation album and the album *Film Music of Toru Takemitsu* on ayuo.bandcamp.com. Even in this one film alone, we can hear the different aspects of Toru Takemitsu's music.

Some of my favorite music by Takemitsu are those he composed for film. He could make the viewer see the visuals objectively if that was what the director wished. Many times, when I was hired to make music for visuals including TV commercials, I would often be requested to come up with sounds that would make the viewer feel emotional. Unfortunately, this is what many composers for dramas are requested to do—provide sounds to make the viewer more romantic or sad or to create tension as if it were brainwashing using music. Toru Takemitsu was a pioneer in creating new ways in which sounds can be used in films.

Woman in the Dunes (1964), directed by Hiroshi Teshigahara, has music for a string orchestra, some of which is electronically modulated with effects. An excerpt from what would become his composition *The Dorian Horizon* (1964) for string orchestra is included in the score. The mélange of the visuals of the moving sands and Takemitsu's music creates a stunning experience for the audience.

Jose Torres (1959), a documentary film of the Puerto Rican boxer by Teshigahara, has a score of Jazz music performed by a string orchestra. There is a famous story that when Takemitsu was asked what composer he would like to study in the United States, he replied with Duke Ellington. The jazz music he composed here is one of my favorites and fits the film perfectly. I have since learned that he originally composed and recorded this music for a jazz band but later rearranged it for a string orchestra because he was not satisfied with the way it looked in the film.

The music score for Masahiro Shinoda's *Pale Flower* was composed in collaboration with my father, Yuji Takahashi. They hired a large orchestra, but the orchestra had to play many unorthodox sounds, such as making click-clack sounds using the buttons of brass instruments, hitting the body of string instruments to make percussive sounds, and making the wind players exhale air without producing a note. Yuji Takahashi was studying with the Greek composer, Iannis Xenakis, at the time, and the orchestral score has a lot of string glissandi and sound mass clusters reminiscent of Xenakis' compositions, such as *Metastaseis* and *Pithoprakta*. During the gambling scene using Japanese *Hanafuda* cards (Flower cards), tap dancing was synchronized with the scenes of cutting the cards.

The music score for *Kwaidan* (1965) was created mostly using musique concrète. I write 'mostly' here, because in the episode of "Hoichi the Earless," the biwa and song are performed by Kinshi Tsuruta, and in the episode of "The Woman of the Snow," Katsuya Yokoyama's *shakuhachi* (a flute-like wind instrument) is the main instrument. The film consists of four episodes based on Japanese ghost stories collected by Lafcadio Hearn; the first episode, "The Black Hair," consists mainly of cracked sounds of bamboo and ice, hitting rocks from the island of Shikoku with a unique sound. Prepared piano and the bowed Japanese string instrument *kokyu* are also used. All the sounds of the snowstorm in the second episode "The Woman of the Snow" are created from shakuhachi of various sizes. Tape speed changes and modulation effects are used to further enhance the sound. In the third episode, "Hoichi the Earless," the biwa song composed by Kinshi Tsuruta is the central music that begins the episode. The sounds of the spirits of warriors who drowned at sea were created by slowing down a tape recording of chanting in traditional Noh plays. In the fourth episode, "In a Cup of Tea," the score is made from cut-up sounds of performances of *Futozao-shamisen* and *Gidayu* singing from Bunraku, a traditional puppet play from Edo-period Japan.

Toru Takemitsu was very much interested in its music, and he acted as music supervisor for the Bunraku film *The Lovers' Exile* by Martin Gross. Takemitsu also used cut-up sounds of the Bunraku Gidayu in *Double Suicide*.

The music for *Kwaidan* took six months to complete. My uncle, Kuniharu Akiyama, who specialized in musique concrète compositions, collaborated on the score along with the recording engineer, Junosuke Okuyama, and the sound man, Akira Suzuki. The idea was to replace the real sounds of the wind, the sea, and the breaking of wood with musique concrète. The music for this film has been released on record albums a number of times throughout the years.

When Takemitsu was commissioned to compose an orchestral work for the New York Philharmonic Orchestra, he composed *November Steps* for biwa (performed by Kinshi Tsuruta), shakuhachi (performed by Katsuya Yokoyama), and orchestra. This was his international breakthrough as a composer of contemporary music. I was at the world premiere, along with my parents and Takemitsu's daughter, Maki Takemitsu.

The most experimental of Takemitsu's film music was in the 1960s up to 1974 with Masahiro Shinoda's *Himiko* (1974). The music for *Himiko* has a lot of improvisational music performed by Takehisa Kosugi, Taj Mahal Travellers, Keiji Haino, and Magical Power Mako.

During the time I was with Keiji Haino's group, Fushitsusha, I asked Haino how he and the members of Magical Power Mako were able to perform on music credited to Takemitsu since Haino and Mako were rock musicians and not classically trained musicians who could read music. Haino said to me that Takemitsu would say "Give me a moan" and "more deeper" and so on until he got all the raw material he needed for the film. Many people were impressed with Keiji Haino's vocals on Magical Power Mako's first album. Haino could growl, moan, shout, and sing hard rock as well as in a high sweet tone. This must have impressed Takemitsu. Takemitsu gathered improvisational musicians including Takehisa Kosugi and members of his group, Taj Mahal Travellers, who provided the raw sounds that Takemitsu used for the soundtrack of the film.

From 1975 onward, with *Under the Blossoming Cherry Trees* (also directed by Masahiro Shinoda), Takemitsu started to compose more lyrical music for films using the orchestra, reminiscent of latter-day Debussy. In *The Ballad of Orin* (1977), Takemitsu confined himself to composing gorgeous melancholic orchestral music for the landscape scenes, because Orin in the film is a blind minstrel singer who accompanies herself on the shamisen, so there was already traditional music in the film.

I also like many of Takemitsu's later work for the movies, such as the soundtrack he composed for Hiroshi Teshigahara's *Rikyu* (1989) and *Princess Go-hime* (1992), and for *Night on Earth* (1991), directed by Jim Jarmusch. They were not as experimental as many of his earlier film works, but he described it as "an increased use of diatonic material... [with] references to tertian harmony and jazz voicing."[1] Unfortunately, Jim Jarmusch did not use the music that Takemitsu composed, as he was looking for something more experimental.

His daughter, Maki Takemitsu wrote to me about what happened:

Maki Takemitsu: Toru was so proud and completely satisfied with his work at the recording studio, which is quite rare of course. But on the contrary, I could tell what Jim felt right away: "This is not something I expected from the composer who wrote music for *Woman in the Dunes*." Toru was of course quite disappointed with Jim's decision, yet he respected that as he always felt that the film belonged to the director.

Ayuo Takahashi: Thank you for your very informative comment. This is something that few people would know. *Woman of the Dunes* is really a classic in world cinema, and the music set to the movements of the sands was perfect to convey the philosophical meaning in Kobe Abe's novel. The 1960s in Japan must have had a really interesting art scene. The 80s and the 90s were a completely different era. Perhaps Jim Jarmusch was looking for something more experimental and avant-garde like the noise guitar provided by Neil Young for his film *Dead Man*. I think the music Toru Takemitsu composed for this film is great on its own because it lets you visualize scenes in your mind. The different textures of sounds help the listener to do this.

This soundtrack of *Night on Earth* was included in volume 5 of the 5-volume box set entitled *Complete Takemitsu Edition*, released by Shogakukan in the mid-2000s. These box sets include the entire body of works composed by Toru Takemitsu in every genre of music.

---

[1]https://interlude.hk/toru-takemitsu/ from an article penned by Georg Predota.

I am proud to have been included as an arranger and performer in volume 5 of this box set; I also obtained permission to release the recordings I made for this release on my own on the site ayuo. bandcamp.com.

Figure 31   One-year-old Ayuo with Toru Takemitsu.

What is psychedelic?

I began studying music during the height of the psychedelic era in the United States, listening to Jefferson Airplane, The Doors, Grateful Dead, and Country Joe, and the Fish as I grew up.

A lot of psychedelic music at that time was aimed at inducing a state of ecstasy, removing listeners from their everyday world. Eastern Sufi music of the Middle Ages was known to have similar traits. There was a lot of influence from Eastern philosophy as well as drugs, but there was also a lot of music that was filled with strange mystic powers.

At the time, the psychedelic rock of San Francisco best portrayed that feeling. The Grateful Dead, Jefferson Airplane, Quicksilver Messenger Service, and Country Joe, and the Fish were the most iconic bands, and the Grateful Dead became known as the most representative of these bands.

There are many ways to listen to music. Grateful Dead guitarist Jerry Garcia once said that their music has become a drug to many fans. Just as there are numerous varieties of substances, there are also numerous varieties of music that have the potential to induce a variety of effects in individuals. For instance, there was a significant association between the drug ecstasy and British dance music, house, and rave culture in the 1990s. Crack was associated with the club music, Jungle. Many individuals frequented United Kingdom venues that specialized in such music while under the influence of drugs; the music itself was intentionally engineered to induce a state of consciousness comparable to that of those substances. In the 1990s, these types of chemical substances dominated the trip music scene.

When psychedelic music was at its peak in the 1960s, however, marijuana, hashish, other natural drugs, and acid were the norm. Cannabis can now be legally bought by people with cancer, AIDS, glaucoma, and other illnesses in California, Washington State, Colorado, and many regions of the United States as a source of pain relief simply by prescription. Unlike cigarettes, alcohol, and other narcotics, cannabis is deemed non-addictive, lowers blood pressure, and reduces stress. Some musicians who prohibit alcohol but permit marijuana in their bands have reported similar effects.

The influence of marijuana and hashish in music can be traced back about 3,000 years in the Middle East.

Creative individuals frequently discussed the potential musical benefits of hashish and marijuana use during the 1960s. In an interview with the magazine *Guitar Player*, Pete Townsend of The Who claimed that marijuana had fundamentally altered the way he produced and listened to music. I think a lot of other authors, musicians, and visual artists of the '60s felt similar. Outside of psychedelic rock, many people who came to hear contemporary composers, such as Terry Riley and La Monte Young, also used these substances.

Marijuana and hashish change your perceptions of both time and sound. I've had individuals remark that they felt as if a band was performing live right in front of them, even though they were only listening to their CD. Sounds become more readily connected with visual representations. Additionally, one's perception of time is constantly in the present moment, as opposed to advancing in a narrative fashion. Consequently, a considerable amount of trance music is based upon repetitive rhythms or movements within pre-established sequences of sounds, akin to the patterns observed in Iranian *radifs*, European modes, or Indian *ragas*, as opposed to conventional contemporary music and classical structures like the *ABCABC* pattern.

Music designed to change the brain and mind, such as psychedelic music, has existed since ancient times. They were frequently utilized in rites and rituals; such music was needed to communicate with the heavenly realm and to other worlds.

In religious ceremonies performed by African descendants of Latin America, such as *santeria* and *candomblé* (which became the basis for the rhythms in samba and salsa), the body is intoxicated by the repetition of the beat, and one enters a trance state in which the spirit of a god enters the body and reveals his messages. People smoke cigarettes and cigars at samba rituals because it is thought that the gods enjoy the smoke.

I once saw an excellent documentary film that depicted these situations in actual life today. It traced the history of samba in Brazil, as well as salsa in Puerto Rico and New York, back to African religious festivals. It demonstrated how current artists such as Milton Nascimento, Eddie Palmieri, and others continue an African legacy that began many, many years ago.

The repetitive rhythm intensifies and elevates your mental state while you dance. This music experience was prevalent not just in African music and dances but also in other parts of the world.

In the Appalachian Mountains of the United States, many traditional Christian ceremonies involved church attendees shouting and dancing in a trance-like manner reminiscent of rock music. Robert Graves, an English poet, stated in his book *The Greek Myths* that ancient Greek ceremonies of Bacchus involved the use of magic mushrooms, which induced an effect akin to LSD—causing individuals to dance and sing in a trance-like condition.

Repeating a mantra for an extended period yields similar results. You can transform a word into a power word. Suppose you determine that the word "Abracadabra" possesses magical qualities. Repeatedly practicing and genuinely believing in the magical properties of anything will eventually lead to a certain magical outcome; eventually, repeating it will induce a trance effect. Some argue that it might be considered a placebo or a form of brainwashing; however, similar teachings can be found in mysticism and many religions worldwide.

Psychedelic and trance-oriented music can have two contrasting effects. One benefit is that altering human consciousness can enhance awareness of previously unseen items and expose the mind to creative endeavors such as writing poetry, telling stories, or making artwork. Conversely, it can also make it easier for those in power to control people.

It is believed that the CIA distributed LSD to universities in the United States. The government prohibited the substance while promoting it, anticipating that students would believe that they were rebelling against the government by listening to rock music and using illegal narcotics. During the Cold War, the CIA undertook mind control experiments to rival similar operations being carried out by the Soviet Union.

Despite the legalization of marijuana in some US states in recent years, a former FBI narcotics agent was tasked with directly supervising the sales process of cannabis in Colorado.

Pete Townsend said that marijuana and hashish facilitate interaction between the right and left hemispheres of the brain. This condition was commonly pursued by saints and hermits in both ancient and medieval times via meditation and extensive training. In the Middle East, hashish, opium, and other drugs were occasionally used to momentarily experience sensations before achieving them via meditation alone.

According to psychologist Julian Jaynes, the prophets of the Old Testament must have been able to articulate intuitive sensations in their right brains via their left brains. He stated in his book *The Origin of Consciousness in the Breakdown of the Bicameral Mind* that the way we utilize our brains has evolved over the last 3000 years. David Bowie and many other musicians have said that this book was very influential, with Bowie even including a reference to the book etched in the run-out groove of the 1979 single, "Boys Keep Swinging," MIND YOUR BICAMERAL/YOUR BICAMERAL MIND.

It is now scientifically understood that the right brain is the sensory brain, and music and art are mainly enjoyed and created using this brain; while the left brain is the language brain, and theoretical thinking and analysis are done using this brain. Therefore, people whose left brain is damaged cannot speak well, but they can sing. It is also said that if a little electricity is applied to the right brain, the patient can hear the auditory hallucinations of songs and music.

Jaynes believed that the goddess of inspiration was referred to as the *muse* (from Proto-Indo-European root *men-*, the basic meaning of which is 'put in mind') because he theorized that in ancient times, the connection between the right and left hemispheres of the brain was stronger than it is today. He suggested that this connection was evident in the works of ancient Mesopotamian *Gilgamesh*, Greek Homer's *Ilias*, and various prophets in the Old Testament. He thought that the prophets must have really heard these words in their head. Their behavior could have resembled those with schizophrenia in modern times. He cited experiments with individuals with schizophrenia as evidence to support his point.

According to Jaynes' research, in the Delphic oracles of ancient Greece, words had to be chanted in Dactyl rhythms of classical poetry, where the rhythms are *long, short, short*. If the contents were not in Dactyl, the priests of the temple would translate them to fit the Dactyl rhythm pattern.

In ancient times, poetry was often sung. The same is true of poems that have survived since the Tang Dynasty in China, as well as of the Old Testament and ancient Greek poetry. According to W. B. Stanford, a scholar of Homer's Iliad, the ancient Greek Dactyl was sung on the root note and the fifth degree above it (*GCC, GCC*, if the root note is C).

The influence of hashish can be heard in the music of *rembetika* and *bouzouki* music recorded in Greece throughout the 1920s and 30s. The *bouzouki* is a three-course stringed instrument with a long heritage in the Middle East and is related to the Japanese *sangen*. Following World War II, the *bouzouki* was transformed into a four-course instrument closer to a mandolin, with its tuning adjusted to better accommodate Western music rather than its original Oriental roots. *Rembetika*, the Greek music genre, is influenced by musical traditions from the Orient including ancient Greece, Byzantine, Turkey, and ancient Persia. It originated from musical techniques that were disseminated from Persia and Arabia to Central Asia. Some tunes date back to the 19th century or before.

Following the collapse of the Ottoman Empire post World War I, all Greek Orthodox individuals residing in present-day Turkey were forcibly relocated to Greece. Former musicians from the Turkish sultan's court lost their livelihood and resorted to playing *bouzouki* and peddling hashish in Piraeus, the port city of Athens.

Four men from Piraeus returned home while puffing on hashish.
Two friends were there too,
One playing a bouzouki and the other smoking hashish from a pipe.

They invited me to play the bouzouki and smoke with them.
(lyrics translated from "Camel Rider's Dance")

These songs are played with a slow, hypotonic rhythm that reflects the traditional melodies from the Orient and its influence from cannabis. It was often believed that the *bouzouki* instrument was so closely associated with hashish-smoking communities that several record companies hesitated to record and distribute music played on it. During World War II, *Rembetika* and *bouzouki* music were used to accompany protest songs against the invading Nazis. Following the war, *rembetika* gained acceptance among the general public, yet it lost its bewitching atmosphere in the music, despite its technical improvement from its pre-war state. It grew more influenced by Western music. The music transitioned to a more commercial and pop sound, similar to how rock music evolved into a more commercial and pop style following the psychedelic and progressive era.

When I went to Athens in 1994, I bought the pre-war 3-course *Bouzouki*. This instrument was tuned *DAD* or *DGD* and was perfect for playing ancient modal music. I also used this instrument to play Persian songs. Unlike the Turkish *Saz*, which can play quarter notes between 'A' and 'Ab', the *Bouzouki* can only play notes in the standard Western scale.

The perception of time in Middle Eastern and Asian classical music often differs from that of Western music. This may be a contributing factor to the rise in popularity of Indian raga music in the United States during the late 1960s. It also significantly inspired psychedelic rock.

If you wish to experience the psychedelic sensations of the Grateful Dead, I would first recommend any album that contains a long-lived version of their song "Dark Star." The version on *Live/Dead* (1969) is classic, but I would especially recommend *Grayfolded*, a two-CD album produced by John Oswald featuring just new edits and re-mixes of the live versions of "Dark Star." Using a process Oswald calls *plunderphonic*, he edited fragments of over a hundred different performances of the song, recorded between 1968 and 1993, producing two new versions of the song each lasting over an hour. The first entitled "Transitive Axis" is the closest thing to a psychedelic trip I have experienced with just music.

The improvisation of this song gives you the thrill of traveling through a journey where you never know how it's going to turn out each time. You can sense the band performing without planning their next move. They allow things to happen because they want to surprise themselves as well. The band members' distinct individual characteristics weave together like threads of different hues, resulting in a rainbow-colored kaleidoscope of experiences.

Sometimes Jerry Garcia's guitar melodies and sounds alone have the power to transport you to another world, especially if you listen to it deeply and breathe in and out with the flow of music. At times it is atonal; at times it is funky. It emphasizes the significance of each moment, creating a sense of timelessness. The song lacks a predetermined form and takes shape as it is performed. This is the most similar sensation to the vastness of the cosmos. Listening to music of this nature helps one comprehend how music may have drug-like effects. The song is filled with thrills.

Sometimes music here is so powerful that it may induce a psychedelic experience without the need for substances. Falling asleep to this music in complete darkness may provide an immersive concert-like experience, enhancing your imaginative journey as you go off to sleep.

Yokoo Tadanori, Toshi Ichiyanagi, and the psychedelic music scene

It was in the late 1960s that I first met Yokoo Tadanori.[1] At the time, Yokoo felt pressured by the Japanese media, so he chose to leave Japan and spend some time in New York City. When Yokoo saw what was going on in Greenwich Village, he wondered why this kind of psychedelic culture was not getting into Japan, and he thought this was a chance to change the situation himself.

At the time, there were very few Japanese people coming to New York; Yokoo Tadanori, Shuji Terayama, Kishin Shinoyama, Toshi Ichiyanagi, Hiroshi Teshigahara, Toru Takemitsu, and Joji Yuasa, among others, were some of those people that I met during my childhood in New York.

This was the time when The Doors were on the cover of *13*, a pop idol music magazine popular among elementary school children. It was a period when the TV show *The Monkees* was popular among kids in primary schools, and the majority of children listened to rock music.

Yokoo and I talked about American psychedelic bands all the time when we met, since I was listening to many of them—including Jefferson Airplane, The Doors, and the Grateful Dead. We went to several rock concerts together, including a performance by Emerson Lake and Palmer at Carnegie Hall—just the two of us. Keith Emerson was a flamboyant performer who played the organ while leaping on top of it, resembling someone riding a wild horse at a rodeo. Yokoo informed my mother about the performance after observing them, imitating their gestures. We would often visit the Electric Circus and

---

[1]Yokoo Tadanori's name is written as family name/given name because this is how he requested it to be written. Toshi Ichiyanagi is written as given name/family name because it is already established that way.

the Fillmore East together. Yokoo, being from Japan likely perceived the city as being abundant with remarkable things.

For me, the society I was most comfortable with was the one I grew up in.

Yokoo believes that a person's personality develops from childhood to adolescence. He went on to write, "All of my work may be nostalgia for my own childhood." What he treasured throughout his life were the adventure stories he read in his youth. It was a special place for him that he could always return to.

Yokoo told me, years after we first met when I was eight years old, that he wondered what would happen to a child like me as I grew older. This was given that I had already been immersed in psychedelic culture as a child.

"I feared you'd go crazy. And with your parents, I had no idea what you'd become. But you appear to be doing all right," he told me.

When I said that my CDs issued on the Tzadik label in the United States were commonly referred to as 'Japanese psychedelic,' Yokoo answered that his own works were frequently referred to as 'Japanese psychedelic' overseas. However, categorizing Yokoo's work as 'psychedelic' would be a limited view of the range of works he has created.

Yokoo told me, "There was no psychedelic movement in Japan.... We labeled the music and fashion that had already been produced in America 'psychedelic,' but it was superficial. The conditions necessary for its emergence as a culture were not there in Japan at the time."

That may be the reason why my childhood stories cannot be effectively communicated in Japan. Despite many apparent similarities, the content and meaning in different cultures are distinct. I also believe the term 'psychedelic' is frequently misunderstood in contemporary times.

In 1969, Yokoo collaborated on a psychedelic record with contemporary music composer Toshi Ichiyanagi. At the time, Mr. Ichiyanagi was one of the few in Japan who created music that was closest in spirit to the original underground psychedelic music that I knew in NYC. The record album with Yokoo Tadanori, *OPERA "FROM*

THE WORKS OF TADANORI YOKOO" was one of these, but there are two others that I wish to mention here.

I especially like the music he created for the experimental short film, *Expansions* by Toshio Matsumoto. I first heard this on a DVD box set of films by Toshio Matsumoto, years after it was first released. I was astonished when I heard this. This, as well as his tape composition *Tokyo 1969* reminded me of the Velvet Underground. Then, I remembered that my parents gave him a copy of *The Velvet Underground and Nico,* with the banana jacket designed by Andy Warhol. This was our personal copy from 1967 when we were in NYC.

In 1969, Toshi Ichiyanagi would create music that people would say sounded like the Velvet Underground.

I also remembered that when my mother, my stepfather, and I came to visit Japan in 1970, Ichiyanagi took us to a club where records of psychedelic music were being played.

The two I mentioned above are listed in his list of compositions as follows:

Expansions (1969), for rock band and modulators, composed for Toshio Matsumoto's film of the same name.

Tokyo 1969 (1969), for various modulators, street sounds, and rock band.

He also made many electronic music for other films by Toshio Matsumoto.

I ran into Toshi Ichiyanagi near Shibuya station, shortly after I heard his music on the Toshio Matsumoto DVD box set, so I asked him about his work. He told me that some people want him to make music like that again, but he said *"ima sara"*—"That was such a long time ago, I think it's too late for that."

Ayuo: They sound so psychedelic. How did you compose them?

Ichiyanagi: I gave [the musicians] instructions on how to perform them.

Ayuo: Who were the musicians? How did you find them?

Ichiyanagi: They were musicians from Uchida Yuya and the Flowers.

(These musicians later became independent of their leader, Uchida Yuya, and renamed themselves The Flower Traveling Band.)

In the late 1960s to the mid-70s, Ichiyanagi often used electronics in his recordings and live improvisations. I would see him many times performing on an EMS Synth-A synthesizer, improvising with Takehisa Kosugi and Michael Ranta.

He also composed and performed minimal music. I saw him perform Steve Reich's *Four Organs* on electric organ and lead the ensemble. His composition for solo piano, *Piano Media*, is probably the best-known of his minimal works, and my favorite.

He also has a series of solo piano works named *Cloud Atlas*. The title of the 2004 novel by David Mitchell, as well as the subsequent film adaptation by the Wachowskis and Tom Tykwer in 2012, takes its title from this work.

In 1977, when Ichiyanagi performed at "The Media 3," an all-night festival featuring Terry Riley, he performed his own minimalist composition *Recurrence* on the electric piano—but there were drunks in the audience who would shout at him, "Hey, what's next?" as his minimalist music consisted of many repeating phrases. Someone who was near the stage told me later that he was trembling as he played.

Ichiyanagi's composition style began to change in the 1980s. Since he was very well trained in classical music, he returned to more conventional forms, composing symphonies, operas, and concertos. He was very successful in the classical music world, winning many awards. I like many of his later works, such as *Paganini Personal* for violin and piano, and *Transfiguration of the Moon* for *shō* (Japanese mouth organ) and violin. Some of his later orchestral works remind me of Arvo Pärt's compositions.

As I noted elsewhere, the underground experimental scene in Japan was falling apart in the late 70s. People like Takehisa Kosugi left Japan for the US. Kosugi joined John Cage, performing with the Merce Cunningham Dance Company for many years and succeeding him as music director after Cage passed away.

In June 2010, Yokoo said to me that creating a work of art should be a revolution in itself. He was talking about musicians who incorporate political messages into their art and music, thinking that that wasn't necessary.

I too believe that genuine art should have the power to inspire personal transformation through the power of art alone. Most popular Japanese music and dramas tend to concentrate solely on appealing to emotions, but I prefer works that can change the way people think about life itself.

Taj Mahal Travellers and Takehisa Kosugi

Until the mid-1970s, there was an interesting underground scene in Japan, but in the latter half of the 70s, things started to gradually change to a more conservative atmosphere.

Composer/violinist/voice performer Takehisa Kosugi and his Taj Mahal Travellers fit the vibe of the 60s and 70s. Each player was doing long cosmic improvisations using echo machines (now called delays). It was similar in some ways to the feedback-driven improvisations of early Pink Floyd and early Grateful Dead. There were elements of Indian music and elements of rock in that experimental music. Sometimes they would play all night long on the beach; the audience and performers were free to do what they wanted. They could play whenever they wanted, stop halfway through, and go out to eat. The music echoed with life of that era. No one was in a hurry. Music was made with the free and relaxed sense of time of that period.

A few people joined the improvisation singing the word, "AUM" (a word used in Indian meditation) during their performance. Each sound echoed inside throughout our body. The double bass player did not hold down the strings but moved his fingers over them playing with the harmonics (natural overtones) which went through an echo machine. They knew a number of simple but effective ways to improvise.

One night when I was in high school, I stayed at Takehisa Kosugi's apartment in Nakameguro. He filled five cups of tea and brought it in front of me, even though there were only the two of us.

"Which one should I take?" I asked.

"Well, now. Which one shall we start drinking with?" he said.

When I woke up in the morning, I was late for international school. He was blowing a hose in the kitchen, sounding like a whistle.

"Oh, shit, I'm late!" I said.

"Don't worry, I was late for school every day."

At the time, he was teaching a group of students, forming a group called East Bionic Symphonia. Chie Mukai was also a member of this group.

Times were changing, however, and the utopian dreams of the 1960s were gradually crumbling. People were no longer so relaxed that they could sit on the beach all day listening to improvised music. They were busy with real day-to-day life. Some people can live more freely than others, but there are many people for whom this kind of life doesn't suit them. In villages where people have known each other for a long time, people can live according to long-established traditions—but this isn't possible with groups of people who do not know each other.

The result will be a tendency for people to distrust each other and drift apart.

In 1976, Takehisa Kosugi decided to move to New York City. He left his Roland Space Echo machine and other effectors in my room. I started to record a lot of songs with those machines.

Takehisa Kosugi would later play some great violin solos on the song, "Birds of Paradise" for my album *Silent Film* in 1984.

John Cale Interview (from 2001): A musical journey from Xenakis, La Monte Young, Velvet Underground, and back to his roots in Wales

I had listened to John Cale's music since I was in first grade at primary school. I owned the Velvet Underground's self-titled first album, which had Andy Warhol's now-famous banana record jacket. It was one of the first records my parents bought in New York City; one day, however, it disappeared, and I asked what happened to it. My mother told me that she had given it to the composer Toshi Ichiyanagi. Ichiyanagi was one of the few 'serious' composers, who incorporated psychedelic music in his compositions.

While my father was studying composition with Xenakis, my father learned of a student in Massachusetts who caused a stir at a concert when he performed his own composition, during which he suddenly smashed a table in half with an axe. This was John Cale. He had traveled from Wales, UK, on a Leonard Bernstein scholarship, after being interviewed and approved by Aaron Copeland. In London, he was influenced by what he learned about the Fluxus art movement and began performing with the composer Cornelius Cardew, who was 24 at the time. Xenakis took a liking to him and invited him to come with him to New York City, where his piano composition was to be performed. This was to be his introduction to New York City.

Xenakis introduced him to other composers and people in the music scene there. He would later write that he didn't know why Xenakis chose John Cale to go with him instead of his other students. I think he must have sensed that John Cale was very talented and would come to play a major role in music.

Figure 32   Ayuo interviewing John Cale.

The Lower Eastside scene in New York City in the early '60s was a place where there were hundreds of people who called themselves poets, and everyone was connected through their work and their lovers. On any given night, any combination of musicians, poets, and dancers would show up to play on sidewalks, rooftops, or piers. Films doubled as sets for dancing to music, which would likely be interrupted by poetry reading. John Cale visited La Monte Young, who lived in a large loft; he kept a lot of turtles there, made yogurt, and feasted on organic food. His place looked like a hashish den. Everything was on the floor. He made a living by selling drugs, and John Cale became his assistant delivering his drugs. He joined his group, The Theatre of Eternal Music, which consisted of La Monte Young, Tony Conrad, Terry Riley, Angus Maclise, and himself. They spent hours experimenting with sounds. At first, they were playing a raga-blues style of music, but when John started to improvise with the natural harmonics on his amplified viola, La Monte started to calculate a just-intonation system. It took a year and a half of collaborating to create the music of The Eternal Theater of Music.

During this time, fellow experimental music composer, Tony Conrad taped hours of experimental music and improvisation in his apartment with John Cale; these are now available in a series of 3 CDs released by Conrad on his own label.

I often passed by when the Velvet Underground was performing in the Dom, beneath New York's legendary dance club Electric Circus. I was also at Max's Kansas City with my stepfather and mother when the Velvet Underground performed their final gigs with Lou Reed. When I was in junior high school, I bought and listened to all of Cale's solo albums, from *Vintage Violence* to *Helen of Troy*. They, along with the Velvet Underground and Lou Reed's solo records, became major inspirations for me as a lyricist and composer.

Ayuo: Are you living in New York now?

John Cale (JC): Yeah.

Ayuo: And you often go back to Wales?

JC: Well, I have family there, so whenever I can. I just found that I have a whole side of family that I didn't know about when I wrote my autobiography. On my father's side. I found a lot of information.... I was wrong in certain things and right in other things. Things that bothered me, when I was a teenager, which I am now clear about. There's an extended family on my father's side that I'd really ignored.

I didn't like my grandmother very much at all. Because my grandmother... she blamed me for my mother's illness in front of me. At the time, I didn't understand [it]. My mother had a mastectomy. And in that kind of society, it's so conservative. Nobody talked about what that was. Nobody talked about breast cancer. It was forbidden. So, nobody knew. Nobody understood. Nobody explained anything. And here is a 13-year-old boy who is trying to grow up and is very close to his mother. His mother disappears. And he is at a loss as to what's going on. So then, on my father's side, my aunt told me the other day that at my father's funeral, my mother told her something very revealing. My father who worked in the coal mines came from Cardiff, which was English-speaking, but when he married my mother and came to live with her in Garmont in South Wales, which is Welsh-speaking, my grandmother banned the use of English in the house, so that effectively shut him up.

I was so disgusted when I heard that.

Ayuo: So you weren't communicating with your father much.

JC: Not in Welsh. I couldn't speak Welsh to him because he couldn't speak any Welsh. And I didn't learn English until I was seven at school. There's that period there when communication was a problem. That sort of cleared up that whole period where it was murky.

There's a parallel here between language and music. Music itself is a language that can transcend English or Welsh, and the ease with which I could use it to communicate was a comfort I found nowhere else.

Ayuo: So when you grew up, what sort of music did you listen to?

JC: The radio. A lot of information came across from the radio.

I come from a very strict part of Wales, where it was very religious. "Don't play the radio on a Sunday." "But it's Bach." "No." In Wales, when I was 15, 16, 17... I used to lie in my bed with the covers piled up to bury the sound to listen to the Voice of America and Radio Luxembourg, just in awe of what is elsewhere.

That song in my CD, *Music for a New Society*—"Rise, Sam and Rimsky-Korsakov." That's Sam Shepard's poem, but it really captures that frame of mind, when your entire information about the world comes from the radio. Just in awe of what was elsewhere. And I've always enjoyed going to different places. Wherever I am, just listening to conversations and watching people, you get so much information about people and they're basically the same all the world around, only expressed differently. But it fascinated me. Eavesdropping in restaurants, and so on.

Ayuo: Was there not much traditional Welsh music?

JC: Plenty. I was part of some of it. I was just hired as a viola player playing in religious services, for oratorios, Handel's *Messiah*, and all those things in local orchestras.

Ayuo: I meant jigs.

JC: Those were the gigs. There were no clubs.

Ayuo (clarifying): I meant *Celtic Jigs*.

JC: No. That was an Irish thing. I think Welsh things were more singing.

What was some of your early music like?

Ayuo: What was some of your early music like, before you went to New York City? Were your early compositions more melodic, like the orchestral songs you would later set to Dylan Thomas' poems in the '90s in your album, *Words for The Dying*?

JC: Dylan Thomas is like what knowing Goethe is in Germany. Because it played such a major role [in my youth], I wanted to tackle it. I came at it… not from a composer's point of view when I learned it. When I was a kid at school, I was just overwhelmed by the noise of the language. What is in the language? So, trying to put more music into something that has so much music already in it is a tough challenge.

When I started working on those, Allen Lanier, from Blue Oyster Cult, and I went messing around in his studio and got the book *The Collected Poems of Dylan Thomas*. And the only way to deal with it was the way we did it. Which was to do all of it. We took the collected poems, and we did all the poems. We're going to set all of them to music. We're going to start on Monday, and we're going to finish it on Friday. We're going to go through the book and do all of it. And, that way, you just force your way into a pattern of having to solve a puzzle.

And yes. Most of the music I did before coming to New York was very melodic. And then it became very abstract. It was abstract because I was learning. You just hit out and you go through as much as possible.

About Xenakis

JC: Because I had studied a bit of the principles of mathematical philosophy, including the Fourier series and probability theory, before I met Xenakis, I kind of understood what he was getting at—but I felt that all this mathematics didn't have much to do with the actual experience of listening to the music because the music's great. It has this great noise. He knows how to orchestrate, and it's his orchestration that's really thrilling. It's also really strong, contemporary Greek music. It's national music. But in Europe, there's a kind of mindset that you have to explain what you're doing. What was great for me about John Cage was that he also had a methodology, but it was based on Zen. And it was a world view, not just justifying your activity.

The 3 CDs on Tony Conrad's label

JC: There are 3 CDs. They exist because Tony Conrad was patient enough to sit down and go through them. There's a lot of stuff.

There's a lot of stuff that you come up with when you're sitting around the room with some friends, trying to make a noise. Some are pretty funny.

One of them ("Sun Blindness Music") is on an organ. It's the Thomas organ that we used in the Velvet Underground. And I tuned it to La Monte's Just Intonation. And I stuck the keys down and improvised.[1]

The 3rd disc will have some pieces I recorded on a piano in the loft I lived in with Lou Reed, and the piano frame left after we took it apart. The very last piece is when we amplify the piano frame and make a very large noise with what's called a thunder machine. We lived above a fire station, and at the very end, a fireman comes up and the last thing you hear is him saying, "That's it. No more. You wanna do that kind of shit, go out to the countryside." And so, it's a great way to end the CD.

Velvet Underground

Ayuo: Velvet Underground is one of the most influential bands of the 60s. A lot of bands in the 70s and mid-70s were influenced by the Velvet Underground.

JC: They still haven't sold a million. Crawling along. Lou says they're just lying to us, but I don't believe it. They haven't sold a million records. It's something like 600,000, I think.

But they have a lot of influence. Nothing else.

Ayuo: The relationship between the avant-garde and rock [music] was talked about in the media.

JC: Now it seems the avant-garde is in rock. What we used to do was to push down the boundaries of what you can do on stage. Radiohead is pushing down the boundaries of what you can do on record, which is the structure of the song. Which is really surprising. They have altered the way the song structures normally are. It's very interesting what they do. Very expressive.

---

[1]These are excellent examples of what early minimalism was, and what the mid-60s experimental music scene was about. If you compare Cale's "Sun Blindness Music" with electronic music by Xenakis, you can feel the influence he received from Xenakis. Xenakis' music is calculated, but Cale presents a similar violent energy of sounds through improvisations with clusters.

Ayuo: I haven't gotten down to listening to Radiohead that much yet.

Are there any other groups you like listening to these days?

JC: I don't know. Yes. There's this one song on the new Leonard Cohen album. "Alexandra Leaving." I love that song. It's just a classic Cohen song.

About Nico's albums, an album with Terry Riley and others he produced

(From 1968, he produced and arranged a series of albums by Nico, which are in a genre of its own. The Indian harmonium (a hand-pumped organ), forms the center of her songs and he made gothic ethereal arrangements with viola, piano, harpsichord, bass, and percussion floating around her vocals, making the kind of music that sounds almost ancient or medieval, but was also totally new.)

JC: The concept with Nico was that she would put down the centerpiece, the anchor, and then I would do a lot of independent parts around it. Then we would take out the centerpiece, which is the harmonium, and just let all these suspended parts work like a mobile in the air.

That was kind of what I tried to do in *Music for a New Society*. We still ended up with rock 'n' roll songs, which is strange. That was a lot more experimental. That was one with no second takes. You have one chance. That's it.

Ayuo: The vocals are more emotional.

JC: Because you have to concentrate right there and then. And really, solving problems is when things come out of you that otherwise wouldn't. Because you're under stress.

Ayuo: Your first independent album was a duo album with Terry Riley.

JC: The way I got to do [my first solo album] *Vintage Violence* was to do Terry Riley first. Their idea was to put in into the studio with some of the contemporary composers to make them more popular. Give them a little more pop touch. So they wanted to do the same with La Monte. But they never got to La Monte that way. La Monte was too abstract. I remember the people at CBS were saying that we've been trying to get to La Monte, but that La Monte's concept was like a circle becoming smaller and smaller and smaller and nothing they could do could persuade him. But Terry was fine. I think what happened with Terry was that there were only 16 tracks in the studio, and we ended up putting two organ parts on one track, and he wanted to hear one of those organ tracks louder than the others, and he couldn't hear it. And he was very disappointed because when you made one of the organ parts louder, you couldn't isolate it. But, otherwise, it was fine.

Ayuo: Do you have good memories of the process?

JC: Yeah. It was fun. It was so fast.

Ayuo: One of the most well-known bands you produced in the 90s was Siouxie and The Banshees.

JC: That was a strange experience. It always seemed that everyone wanted to work on new materials, but nothing ever got done. It's like everybody said, 'Yes, we want to do that,' but it never actually got done and I could never actually figure it out. Because it seemed these were people who really enjoyed living on the edge and enjoyed experimenting and trying different things. Everybody was afraid of taking control. Or everyone felt that it couldn't happen unless somebody was in charge. And nobody wanted to be in charge. And I was waiting. They're a band and they'd been together for 15 years when I met them. That's a record for a band. So, we just got together and made an album, and that was it.

I learned from Patti [Smith] that you really have to be careful with bands. They're an organic whole. It's a family.

Ayuo: And you learned this from Patti?

JC: Well, when I first went into the studio with Patti, the first thing I said was "These instruments, they're old, they're warped." The first day in the studio, I replaced all their guitars. And to them, it was horrible, and I didn't realize that. I thought I was doing something good here. You won't have to worry about the instrument being out of tune because this is a good guitar. "Yeah, but I love my old guitar." You know what I mean. It caused all sorts of misunderstandings. So, when I got into Siouxie, there's a certain amount of respect for what they are into.

Ayuo: Nam Jun Paik had recently said that because we did so much in the 60s, "I feel sorry for the younger generation."

JC: That's a tough way of saying to the younger generation: get your shit together. You're in no different [of a] position than when we were young. You just overthrow generations of thinking. Between La Monte and Nam Jun Paik, there were performances, especially in Fluxus. Fluxus was the premier location for performance art. That's where it started, La Monte's piece, like *Composition 1960 #3*. I think what Nam Jun Paik was saying, is that because of what we did, we made life tougher for you. Bullshit. There are plenty of kids around who can dismiss Nam Jun Paik and say, "That is not the academy."

Ayuo: But the '60s were a period when people wanted to change things. People wanted to experiment to see what would happen.

JC: Yeah. And it was a lot of people. It wasn't just one person. It was everybody. Because there was no progress being made. Progress was left to people like Lenny Bruce, the poor guy. He was fighting a lot of demons. But he was fighting them all at once. He didn't necessarily know what the demons were. And it ended up being the Supreme Court. This forces you into a Marxist frame of mind. The only way to fight the system is to form another one. You'd have no success unless you had a system within which you work, you'd need a support group... No. You don't need a support group. I mean, I guess that the Viet Cong and everyone else proved that you do need a support group, but that's a different matter. That's really formulating a government. What we're talking about is overthrowing ideas. Like in the concert hall. And thinking about what is allowed in the concert hall. Taking an axe and smashing a table on stage was not allowed in those days, but they let me do it at Tanglewood. They didn't want to do it. They refused for about three weeks. Until, finally, they said okay. But the main thing about it was the shock of it. So, you really had to keep quiet about what you were going to do.

Yukio Mishima

In 1970, I spent about a month in Japan with my mother (Utako), and my stepfather (Mansour). Hiroshi Teshigahara had organized an exhibition of my mother's paintings in a gallery in Ginza, and we were all invited. My mother had been coordinating meetings in NYC for Hiroshi to promote his film *Summer Soldiers*, so he organized this exhibition in return. For me, this was the only time I was in Japan between kindergarten and the end of elementary school.

On the last night during my stay in Japan, I went to a party with my family, and the novelist Yukio Mishima was there. He was looking through photos of himself, taken by Kishin Shinoyama, and deciding which to use, asking my mother for advice.

Before he died, Yukio Mishima talked to a number of people we knew. He asked Mutsuro Takahashi, "Would you die for me?" Mutsuro responded, "I won't die for you." Three days before Mishima committed *seppuku* (ritual suicide) with a samurai sword, Tadanori Yokoo called Mishima to tell him that he wanted to travel to India. Mishima said, "There are those who can go to India and those who can't. You can go to India any time you want." He also said goodbye to three writers he respected the most: Jun Ishikawa, Yasuhiro Takeda, and Kobo Abe.

In this way, he was carefully getting ready to die.

He had longed to die for many years, and he wanted to show that he was not afraid. But I don't think his way was a good way to die.

The manuscript he handed to the publisher on the morning of his death contained the final chapters of a series of novels, with reincarnation as the theme, but the novel's finale revealed that there was nothing.

Reincarnation might just be a fantasy.

The ending reminded me of a poem in Cao Xuequin's novel *Dream of the Red Chamber*.

Translated into English, the meaning was as follows:
In the beginning, Creation had no abode;
Where, then, should we abide?
Since we came from the void,
then, we should return to the void.[1]

John Nathan's translations of Yukio Mishima's books, as well as Mishima's biography, were my first introduction to Japanese literature. Nathan and his Japanese wife, painter Mayumi Oda, were close friends with Mishima at the time, and his translations of Mishima's works were well-known in America and Europe.

Because of Mishima's influences, from Edgar Allan Poe to Oscar Wilde, I found his work very easy to read. I could read it in the same way I would read Western literature; I do not believe there were many Japanese books like that. Yukio Mishima and poet Shuji Terayama's works were inspired by Western literature, yet they sounded beautiful in Japanese to me. I have read that Terayama was greatly influenced by Mishima's choice of words.

Yukio Mishima first asserted that he was apolitical.

In the early sixties, when a magazine published a novel about the murder of the Emperor of Japan, right-wing activists mistakenly suspected that Yukio Mishima must have recommended the novel to the magazine, and even tried to have him killed.

However, when student demonstrations grew in the late 1960s, Mishima began to perform the same behavior as the "patriotic" characters he created in his writings. John Nathan, Ian Buruma, and Colin Wilson all regarded Mishima as an actor playing a part, not a real rightist.

Yukio Mishima often wrote about how he felt about student activists and political thinkers in his essays.

I believe he was right in one respect: many left-wing social activists in Japan were stating things that were comparable to those of the right.

---

[1] "A Dream of Red Mansions" by Tsao Hsueh-Chin and Kao Ngo translated by Yang Hsien-Yi and Gladys Yang. Foreign Language Press 1980. Chapter 87.

They were very much different from the left-wing activists I encountered in the United States in the 1960s. In the US, movies like *Woodstock* and *Easy Rider*, as well as the music of numerous hippie rock bands, demonstrate that the left wing wanted true democracy. Many students felt that unlike what the government claims, real democracy has not been achieved in America, and vowed that their generation will change that. This is what my teachers told us in NYC.

Japanese student activists were basically anti-American. They saw the United States as an imperialist enemy, favored Stalinism rather than democracy, and subsequently Mao Zedong's doctrine during the Cultural Revolution. They appeared to be aiming for a military, totalitarian government. Many people wanted solidarity with Asian activists. Yukio Mishima stated that those who think this way are actually patriotic and right-wing in their souls, but they are just hiding it.

They are ashamed of what Japan did in the Pacific War.

The experience of death

The following are from lyrics by Paul Kantner (of Jefferson Airplane), for the song "Starship." I've always felt that these words express what death is all about:

"At first/I was iridescent/Then/I became transparent/Finally/I was absent."

I will explain why.

In the late 1990s, I once traveled with the dancer, Maha, and an American percussionist named Robin who played Middle Eastern rhythms. During the trip, Robin told me that he's not afraid of death because he had already died once in a car accident—a near-death experience (NDE). He said that after being brought to a hospital, surgeons started operating on him. He saw the physicians operating on him as he hovered over his own body. He witnessed a world full of white light as he flew above the Earth in a state of peace. He was told by a voice that it wasn't yet his time, so he went back to inhabiting his earthly body.

I asked him, "What do you think might take place if you entered the light?"

He expressed his belief that he would have merged with the light and disappeared. To become part of the light (i.e., the universe).

I am not a believer in reincarnation, heaven, or hell. The following is what I believe in: We have one chance to make the best of what we have, therefore we shouldn't squander our potential. The universe is the creator. Every individual is an integral component of the cosmos and is formed from various permutations of energy within it. The different energies we sense from our surroundings often appear to us as gods and goddesses. We are connected with one another, so we should refrain from causing harm to one another.

We are created from the void, and so we return to the void. The void is not empty but is filled with the source of all creation.

In physics, the first law of thermodynamics asserts that total energy can be transformed from one form to another but cannot be created or destroyed. A fire transforms paper into smoke and ashes. Nothing completely new can be created, and nothing can be completely destroyed. It changes form into something different.

When someone we care about dies, their memories live on in our active imaginations. If they made music, we can listen to it. If they wrote words, we can keep reading what they wrote.

People who believed in reincarnation in ancient days often wasted human lives through sacrifices and wars. I get the impression that the rulers must have taught the people about reincarnation in order to exploit them. When I read about it, it appeared to me like a scam to trick people into working for a tiny elite group of rulers by telling them that they would have a better life in a future reincarnation if they worked hard for the rulers in this life. It is possible to make it appear to be true if one believes passionately in it, yet this can have the same effect as a placebo.

If we are taught to believe how precious one life is, we will not waste its potential. Life is full of so many possibilities. It's like a gift from the universe. We should all have the chance to make something of it.

Our body is all we have. Our consciousness comes from our minds. Part of us may become a part of a new life, but it does not happen in the way that many mystics claim. I don't believe in astrology or folk superstitions. They are frequently pursued by those who harbor a deep fear of the process of both living and dying. Life is filled with magic, provided one is able to discover it.

Carl Jung frequently cautioned his followers against writing anything that lacks scientific evidence. It might lead to accusations of the psychologist promoting religion and mysticism. Both Freud and Jung saw psychology as a science; embracing mysticism would undermine their objective and scientific approach to analysis. Carl Jung liked to study ancient and medieval texts because he was interested in how the ancient mind worked. After all, we still have the same brain as the ancients.

His work led to people discovering I Ching, ancient Taoist texts, alchemy, and its connection with European Renaissance music, and much study about ancient myths and folk tales. Jung's work is not about reviving mysticism. It is too bad that his name and some of his discoveries were hijacked by those who promote spiritualism, pseudo-science, and new-age beliefs.

As for burials, I would prefer to be buried in the soil. It's like a return to the earth. In time, what was once 'you' dissolves and joins the plants and trees. And the cycle of life begins again from the micro to the macro.

"We Are a Part of the Ocean"
(Lyrics by Ayuo, set to a melody by Jadranka)

Feeling the earth, we merge with soil
I feel the light within us
Sunrise in your eyes

And the force of life within
Looks for ways to be released
It's a part of you, a part of me
Like the plants, the fish, the birds
All things in life

We are a part of the ocean
Ocean is part of you and me

Every moment, we're born again
Flowing free in the sea
The force of life within

Every moment, we're born again
Flowing freely
Flowing freely
Flowing to the sea

Copyright owned by Ayuo Takahashi.
Registered @JASRAC.

Persian classical music and my stepfather, Mansour

Here I will discuss Mansour Malekpour, my stepfather, as well as the traditional Persian music that I was exposed to during my childhood. My childhood exposure to Persian music had a big influence on my music and poetry, introducing me to Rumi and Omar Khayyam's poetry and philosophy, as well as an improvisatory approach to music based on classical Persian modes. I later started playing this style of Persian classical music with Mansour.

Many conservative Muslims consider Sufi philosophy to be heretical. Music that incorporates words that reflect Sufi doctrine is sometimes prohibited from public performance in a culture that prohibits music. In such times of repression, they were preserved through home parties. Mansour was singing classical music at house parties attended by a large number of friends. Traditional Sufi music was often performed at home parties.

His grandfather, Ali Khan, was regarded as one of the greatest vocalists of Persian traditional music in the early 20th century, with an extremely unique voice. He used to sing for the Crown Prince of the Qajar dynasty. The Crown Prince constructed a Golden Cage to hang from a tree, and he sang from within it, accompanied by Persian instrumentalists on the ground around the tree. He was such an amazing vocalist that some claimed he cracked windows with his singing. Mansour's grandfather's songs are preserved on SP recordings from the early twentieth century. He also had a family member who performed Persian classical music on a piano that was carefully tuned to include a few quarter-tone intervals not found in Western tuning. It made the piano sound like the *santur*, a Persian hammered dulcimer. She recorded various records and CDs, which were released in Iran.

A year before I had to leave New York City, Mansour returned from Iran with a *setar*. I had already been playing the guitar at the time, and I attempted to play the *setar* several times, but it was quite difficult. When I moved to Japan and had to live away from my stepfather's house, I was reminded of the Iranian music I had heard as a child. I began improvising by combining Iranian modes with medieval European, Greek, North Indian, and Chinese classical modes.

Mansour handed me a book with the theory of improvisation in Iranian classical music, printed in five-line notation and in English, when we were able to meet more frequently again. We then started playing Omar Khayyam and Rumi verses together, accompanied by my Greek *bouzouki*. Mansour is capable of singing with the Tahrir nightingale vibrato, which is a characteristic feature of traditional Iranian singing. A related instrument to the Persian *setar* is the *bouzouki*; with a little tuning adjustment, you can play something akin to it without using quarter tones.

Mansour also sent me a volume of English translations of Rumi and other Sufi poems, which greatly influenced my songwriting.

Mansour and I have performed at cafes, temples, and other live venues. Some say it was the most amazing gig I had at the time. John Zorn intended to release my arrangement of Persian classical music, "Dastgah Chahargah," on his label, Tzadik, but as of the time of publication this was never released, so I self-published it on ayuo. bandcamp.com. There is also an arrangement of this piece as a solo piano piece in my collection of piano compositions.

My album *Songs from a Eurasian Journey* features several songs based on traditional Persian and Kurdish melodies. Some of the releases on ayuo.bandcamp.com also include them. I played these melodies with Peter Hammill, Dave Mattacks (of Fairport Convention), and Danny Thompson (of Pentangle).

Many classical Persian melodies are set to words from Sufi poets such as Rumi and Hafiz. Music is vital for Sufi followers in their quest for enlightenment. A great deal of Rumi's work exudes warmth, love, and comedy. Its meaning remains valid today.

Dastgah, in English, translates to "system," but it specifically denotes the twelve modes employed in traditional Iranian music. These modes can be equated to the twelve distinct colors observed in a prism of light. Both Persian and Indian classical music assign specific timeframes for the execution of each melody (scale), as well as distinct emotional and tonal characteristics. As an example, the "Nava" tune is performed during the evening, whilst the "Shur"— the fundamental basis for all twelve *Dastgahs*—is performed in the afternoon. The musical composition "Chahargah" is typically performed during the morning hours. "Homayoun" is performed during the twilight hours and symbolizes elements such as fire, intense joy, and the color green.

It is said that a master musician can read a poem written by a traditional poet and instantly know which *Dastgah* it is to be sung in.

Before the Meiji Era in Japan, musicians participating in folk festivals and rituals would often use the *I Ching* or the Yin-Yang Five Elements Theory in order to determine the appropriate musical choices for each specific time of day. During his trip to India to study traditional music, a friend of mine told me he discovered the rationale behind the association of specific *ragas* with particular times of the day. According to him, specific sounds resonate more effectively at specific time periods; the position of the sun and the humidity of the air both affect the vibration of sounds in the air. I experienced a similar sensation upon listening to Henry Purcell's music in England. I perceived that it was more suitable for the atmosphere in that particular area compared to other locations; however, I lack scientific proof to support this perception. It is a tradition that is almost forgotten by those who were raised with radio and television.

Hossein Alizadeh, a remarkable virtuoso of Iranian traditional music, was born in Tehran in 1951 and has been active since the 1990s. Alizadeh possesses exceptional expertise in playing the plucked string instruments *tar* and *setar*. Additionally, he composed several works for a Western orchestra. The harmony and melody of his compositions derive from the technique of Persian traditional music, rather than from the application of Western theory to Persian melodies. However, in my view, they possess distinctive qualities and exhibit a contemporary style. In addition, he has composed contemporary Iranian works that draw inspiration from the principles he has acquired in traditional music.

When I first heard his improvisations on CDs like *Homnavai*, I was surprised to discover that they reminded me of the Grateful Dead and Cream's improvised rock music from the 1960s. However, this was because those rock musicians were actually influenced by the sound of Indian *raga* music. According to Alizadeh, motifs in Persian classical music are similar to those in North Indian *raga* because they evolved from the same music and are based on the same improvisation approach. He has performed with well-known Indian musicians who share his approach to improvisation.

When you let yourself get swept away by the exceptionally organic music that these musicians have crafted, a tremendous sense of freedom envelopes you. Alizadeh has meticulously recorded all the motifs used in traditional Persian music; however, he maintains that he will always perform according to his emotions. He believes that a musician cannot authentically convey his emotions until he has achieved mastery over the techniques of traditional music.

Only when the musician is able to genuinely convey his own emotions in traditional music, in a manner that is suitable for his own life and era, will he be able to establish a means of connection with his audience.

The following part of this essay was written after the passing of my stepfather, Mansour Malekpour, as a tribute to him:

My stepfather, Mansour Malekpour, passed away last week after a few months of illness in March 2023. I lived with Mansour from the time I was in the second grade until the end of middle school. Those are the formative years of a person's life. My early years are the inspiration for nearly all of my music and writing, although I acknowledge that I was considerably more naive at the time. Mansour was very warm-hearted and looked after me and my mother very well. I am now preparing for a concert of classical music on Thursday, but I keep having flashbacks to the life I spent with Mansour.

Figure 33 1970. Mansour in San Francisco.

I was originally supposed to live in NYC as an Asian-American. While I was on a summer vacation in Japan, my mother unexpectedly ran off with another man, leaving me stranded in Japan. Many people still assume that I am Japanese, but Japanese is not my language and is not my culture. I spoke English at home and was in an English-speaking environment until I was 17 years old. Many people in Japan and elsewhere don't seem to understand that any culture you learn about from the time you are 18 years old will never become your own culture even if your ancestors come from that land. You are forever a foreigner, an 'outsider' in that land.

Mansour was from Iran and knew the traditional music and literature of Iran very well. We played music together live in 2000 and 2001 in Tokyo and Yokohama. Two years ago, my group, Yumemakura (Dream Pillow) performed a concert featuring Persian and Kurdish traditional music with Amin, an incredible singer of traditional Persian music who lives in Japan.

Many of the songs were based on poetry written by Rumi, the 13th-century Persian poet. I was first introduced to Rumi by Mansour, and we performed a song in 2001 that had verses written by Rumi. I sent Mansour a recording from the concert two years ago, which he seemed to enjoy very much.

Everything I do is a development from my early years in NYC, which was supported by Mansour. We went to see concerts of psychedelic and progressive rock and spent summers at two homes: that of conductor Seiji Ozawa and his wife Vera in Massachusetts, and that of composer Elliot Carter and his wife Helen Carter. During this time, I was very much influenced by Peter Gabriel's music theater performances and storytelling with Genesis.

Writing poetry, lyrics, and stories is what led me to do what I am doing now.

Figure 34   1974. Ayuo and Mansour playing with a cat in NYC.

Figure 35   2001. Ayuo and Mansour performing together in Tokyo.

Part V

Carl Jung, Joseph Campbell, and John Cage

Nothing happens in which you are not secretly entangled.
Nothing in you is hidden.
The stars are whispering to you all the deepest mysteries.
And the soft valley of the earth is the mother womb that is saving
you.

(Carl Jung, *The Red Book*, translated and interpreted by Ayuo.)[1]

Carl Jung is a psychiatrist/psychologist, known for his research on depth psychology and as the founder of analytical psychology. Jung wrote stories, poems, and paintings using active imagination, a technique in which he attempted to make direct contact with various images that emerged from the unconscious. In *The Red Book*, the illustrations are richly colored, and the text is written in decorative calligraphy reminiscent of medieval manuscripts. Jung considered himself a scientist and did not like to be seen as an artist, mystic, or occultist.

At first, like Freud, he began his research by analyzing dreams. However, even when we are awake, we can still experience the act of dreaming in other capacities, such as daydreaming. He began to treat the images that came to his waking consciousness as characters speaking outside of himself. Thus, he discovered that there was a woman inside him, and named her his *anima* (Latin for soul). His ideas about psychology were thus developed through such a series of experiments.

---

[1]These are from my own translations that I included in the Japanese version of *Outside Society*. In my performance of Carl Jung's "Dream Journals," all my fellow musicians preferred my translation over the official translation published in Japan because the official one tended to sound too academic to be recited in our live shows.

Jung came to feel that Freud was trying to turn psychology into a dogma of just Freud's own ideas. For Jung, the process of discovery was more important to him, so he allowed people serious about using Jung's method to use the same tools as he did, but with different conclusions. Jung did not want to make his ideas into a dogma. This is the interesting thing about Jung's method.

Jon Anderson, the vocalist and lyricist of Yes, often said that he would first capture the words from sounds, and then later try to figure out the meaning of the words. This is another type of songwriting that uses active imagination. Instead of writing out words to convey meaning, he searches for the meaning later from the verbal sounds he already made. In this way, he can find personal meanings to these words.

Many writers, painters, dancers, and musicians have been influenced by this kind of method. Hermann Hesse, an actual patient of Jung's counseling, was influenced by it in his novel *Steppenwolf.*

A lot of my works are also written in this way. These are the words from dreams in the waking state, like the words Jung heard and wrote down. I hear a word—often a word in English—and I write it down. I have never started from Japanese, as it is not a language that I feel deep within me. I do not believe that these words come from spirits or "the other world;" they emerge from the depths of my unconsciousness and originate from my personal experiences. The sound and rhythm of the words are often the starting point of a music composition.

One of the people who introduced Jung to the American mainstream was Joseph Campbell, a well-known mythologist. He discovered Jung's psychological books and the literature of James Joyce when he traveled to Europe in the late 1920s.

In the early 1940s, Campbell's friend, Xenia, a surrealist female sculptor, with whom he had often discussed philosophy and literature, married the composer John Cage. Campbell himself married Jean Erdmann, a contemporary dancer, and a student of his. Jean was a member of Martha Graham's contemporary dance company, but she and her friend Merce Cunningham decided to start a new independent company. For a while, Campbell, Erdman, John Cage, and Xenia lived together in New York City.

It is said that frequent and lengthy discussions of various philosophical ideas took place among them during this period. The poet Alan Watts later wrote a book reporting on these discussions of Buddhism and Eastern thought at the time. Cage tells us that it was through Campbell that he was first introduced to Eastern mystical thought as well as Buddhism and Zen.[2]

Around that time, Campbell introduced Cage to the ancient Chinese book of *I Ching* with a preface by Jung, who found that *I Ching* had a lot in common with his ideas of synchronicity. John Cage's compositional method of incorporating *I Ching* is called Chance Operations, which explored his concept of indeterminacy.

Jean Erdman choreographed some of Cage's music. This was the first concert of John Cage's music at MOMA. All four of them—Campbell, Erdman, Cage, and Xenia—appeared as music performers. "In those days, there was always a party, a performance, a discussion," Erdman said. However, this life ended when Cage became more involved with Cunningham and divorced Xenia.

Campbell's first important book with Henry Morton Robinson, *A Skeleton Key to Finnegans Wake*, is a critical analysis of Joyce's final text *Finnegans Wake*. This work by Joyce was to be a huge influence on John Cage.

When I was in junior high school, I went with my father to visit Cage and Cunningham at their home. I learned how to use the *I Ching* from Cage.

In the commentary to my album *Songs from a Eurasian Journey*, I wrote about the influence of Campbell's ideas on my music. The following is a summary:

What is civilization? What role did it play in the history of mankind? Even if we start from ancient China, Egypt, or Mesopotamia, it is only about 5000 years in the 4.6 billion years history of the earth. What happened 5000 years ago to create this life-organizing system known as civilization? When we look at those ancient cities, we realize that they were all planned and created with particular philosophical ideals in mind.

---

[2]There are many articles written about John Cage's friendship with Joseph Campbell such as the following: https://www.blackmountaincollege.org/edward-crooks-perilous-nights-and-shaggy-nags/

When the earth's climate was different from what it is now, people gathered near big rivers, built communities, and started to create civilizations there. Whether it be in ancient Mesopotamia or ancient China, the whole city was conceived as an imitation on earth of the cosmic order with the most important buildings—the temples and the priest-king's palace—as the highest and in the center. From what we know, the inspiration behind civilization seems to be based first on the discovery that there were five visible planets (Mercury, Venus, Mars, Jupiter, and Saturn) besides the sun and moon, which moved according to established laws and the notion that these laws should be the same as those governing the life and thoughts of mankind on earth.

Cities were organized architecturally in the design of a quartered circle centered around the priest-king's palace and there was a mathematically structured calendar to regulate the seasons of the city's life.

In ancient Mesopotamia, they measured three hundred and sixty degrees to represent the circumference of a circle and three hundred and sixty days plus five sacred festive days to mark the circle of the year. Five was a sacred number representing the spiritual energy from eternity.

In Ancient China, Korea, Vietnam, and Japan, the belief that all nature is made from the combinations of the five elements (water, fire, earth, wood, and metal) became an everyday concept. Symbolic relationships are worked out between the five elements with five directions (*north, south, center, east, west*), five planets, five colors (*black, red, yellow, blue, white*), the five notes in the pentatonic scale, as well as everything else conceivable was categorized into divisions of five.

Cities were built by placing all the houses and people in what would be its proper site, according to their relationship with the five directions. This was the foundation of *Feng Shui*. For example, because the north was considered to be the gate to the other world, graveyards, outcastes, and Buddhist temples were placed there; while the south was considered the human world, and the center where the palace was located was where the major festivities took place. The relationship between all the phenomena surrounding the human world was examined through the relationship between the symbolized elements.

In ancient China and much of East Asia, the philosophy of the *I Ching* and the doctrine of the *Yin Yang* and *Five Elements*, which is also the foundation of *Feng Shui* were the basis of these ideas. They were used in everything from how music and architecture were created to the scheduling of various events.

Musicians were often like shamans, serving as advisors and soothsayers to kings in many countries. The Irish harpists also played such a role in court, and many of them were actually executed when the English invaded the country. Until about 150 years ago, the Five Elements philosophy had been widely practiced in the East, including Japan and China. The Five Elements is a philosophy that reduces all the elements of the universe to the five elements of wood, fire, earth, metal, and water and examines the relationship between all the phenomena surrounding the human world through the relationship between the symbolized elements. In the ancient days, when the climate of the earth was different from that of today, people gathered around large rivers, built settlements, and began to build civilizations by creating cities around them.

In those days, music and mythology were not mere entertainment but were a functionally necessary part of civilization. The Five Elements in the East and Alchemy in the West were based on ideas that spread from Mesopotamia to the East and West at that time.[3]

The musicologist, Kurosawa Takao, wrote that the Chinese learned the theory of the pentatonic scale from the Mesopotamians and the Persians in the west some 5,000 years ago and further developed them. The underlying idea of this pentatonic scale is connected to the idea of the five elements. Mythology at that time had the role of explaining the universe and played a role similar to that of physics today.

The world that we now explain in terms of electrons and atoms was spoken of in terms of the names of gods and the existence of other dimensions. Mythologist Joseph Campbell is a strong advocate of the idea that 'all the myths of the world originate from a single source.' He also writes that myths must have spread from East to West with the development of civilization. I believe that in music,

[3]In the essay "Music and mythology," I have written in more detail, what these ideas were and the difference between the Eastern five-element concept and the Western four-element concept.

too, the development of musical instruments and musical theory spread in the same way as myths. Some people often call instruments such as *koto*, *bouzouki*, and *psaltery* 'ethnic instruments' or say that the music of such instruments 'feels ethnic,' but these instruments, like the piano and the guitar, were spread by trade and cultural exchanges between the West and the East.

Today, in many countries, classical music from the European Baroque onward is taught as if it is the foundation of music, but there was music that was born more than a thousand years before that through exchanges with Asia and the Middle East and beyond. This album, *Songs from a Eurasian Journey* began with the exploration of that music.

The Shosoin Repository in Todaiji Temple in Nara houses a collection of instruments with some musical scores featuring court music from many regions in Asia, such as Persia and Central Asia. These scores were brought from China during the Sui and Tang periods.

Gagaku is a music genre that developed in the Japanese royal court from the Tang Dynasty and ancient Korean court music and serves as the basis for much subsequent Japanese musical theory. They show how court music throughout the world had been connected in ancient times.

Jung's *The Red Book* is amazing. It was published in its entirety for the first time in the 21st century, and I think this should be regarded as a historical event.

When people are dreaming at night or imagining things during the day, they are on an inner journey. This is where we can find answers to what we really are. Your mind stops analyzing itself and you can look objectively at what the characters do as they appear, just as if you were watching a movie.

In his dreams, Jung saw himself as simply another character. He does not consider this to be "himself," but as part of a composite of multiple characters inhabiting the same mind. When exploring the depths of human consciousness, one encounters personalities that surpass individual identity. This encompasses more than just the collective unconscious. We delve into the ideas and historical accounts of deceased individuals.

Even if we encounter the grotesque, Jung advises us not to be afraid of it. Even if we meet the gods in a dream, Jung says, it is meaningless unless we can gain something from it. We are always surrounded by death. We leave death for a short time and then return to the world of death. There are words spoken from the world of the dead, but we don't see them anymore in modern society. *The Red Book*, Jung says, is the book of the dead for him. But he also says that it is not about what happens to us after death, but that it shows a way to be able to live side by side with death.

In the past, people tried to understand these things through metaphysics, Gods, myths, and Jesus Christ. What happens when we remove these religions and mythology, and explore what is inside of us through scientific psychology?

I believe that music and art have the same role as Jung's psychology.

Jung has written many words that are useful in daily life.

The following words are some examples:

"If you can understand your own darkness, you can understand the darkness of others. There is nothing more frightening to us than to accept ourselves completely for who we really are."

"People will do anything to avoid facing their own souls."

"If you don't become aware of what is in the unconscious, it will dominate your life. Becoming aware of the unconscious world is not possible without pain."

(Carl Jung, translated and interpreted by Ayuo.)

Music and mythology

Music, along with mythology, was passed from one country to another from the time humans created urban civilizations from village cultures over 5,000 years ago. The role of music and the arts in those early civilizations was not merely entertainment, but the cog and wheels of its civilization.

Mythology had the role of explaining the universe, a role similar to that of physics today. The physical world we now explain in terms of electrons and atoms was once explained by invoking the names of gods and goddesses and the existence of other dimensions. The 13th century Sufi poet, Rumi, can be read as though he were speaking of modern scientific knowledge in a good translation.

There always seemed to be several ways to explain things, as well. When we read the Old Testament today, we learn that several religions existed in ancient Israel. When we read Greek mythology, we notice that there are several overlapping myths, not just one. In that sense, differences of opinion must have existed back then, just as different scientists have different opinions about whether the universe is still being created and expanded today, even though the Big Bang theory is now widely believed. These differences are like the difference between Yahweh's creation of the universe and the Babylonian cosmology of perpetual seasonal rotation.

Lifestyle also changes the way people view the universe. In a male-centered patriarchal culture, like the ancient Hebrew culture, where hunting was the main way to get food, people often saw God as lightning. Thus, lightning became a symbol when Moses talked to God. Zeus in Greek mythology is also symbolized by lightning.

In contrast, in a female-centered matriarchal culture, the moon is often the central symbol, and the Moon goddess is the central figure.

The moon has a 28-day cycle of new moon, crescent moon, full moon, and lingering moon, which influences the monthly menstrual cycles of women in the cycle of menstruation, the follicular phase, ovulation, and the luteal phase. It is also analogous to the annual cycle of sowing seeds in the earth, growing crops, and harvesting them. In agrarian societies that continue to see plants reborn each year, many cultures have a strong belief that humans are also reborn. The moon was a central symbol of the goddess, as it controlled the tides and the female cycle. Burying the deceased also has the meaning of returning them to Mother Earth, and this belief remains from primitive times.

The labyrinth, or spiral, was considered the womb of the earth. Paintings and sculptures of these labyrinths and moon goddesses have survived in various places in Europe, Africa, and Asia—and they often have very similar features.

Cave paintings from primitive times are said to have been painted by shamans to show the mysteries of life and the universe. It is believed that rituals were performed there, and paintings were drawn deep in the dark so they would appear faintly, creating a magic effect in these rituals.

Contemporary concerts, dances, plays, and films can be thought of as extensions of those rituals. Rock concerts, especially from the late 1960s onwards, have always attempted to alter the human senses with light shows, high volumes, and energy—and in some cases with drugs. Ancient shamanistic rituals often created high energy around repeated drum beats and incantations, hoping to create a trance-like state of altered consciousness. I believe traces of this can still be found in the Japanese festival of drumming.

One thing that mythology and music have in common is that they stimulate and change the consciousness of their listeners by interacting with something beyond our everyday awareness. This interaction between the place where time flows as in everyday life and the space where time stands still as in a different dimension exists in various myths around the world. The cultural anthropologist, Levi-Straus, made a chart of Dream Time (infinite time) against Normal Time in myths. This is where the world of man meets the world of darkness, or where man meets fairies from another dimension. The same story of fairies from the other world in the Japanese tale of "Hagoromo" can be found in China, in the Middle Eastern collection of stories, *A Thousand and One Nights*, and in Irish mythology.

In the story known as "Urashima Taro" in Japan, there is a palace under the sea where everyday life and time move much slower so that a few hours become a few hundred years in earthly time. This same story is told in Ireland as the story of "Ossian." In this story, a beautiful woman named Niamh rides out of the sea on a horse and takes Ossian to the "land of the eternally young" in the sea. After spending some time there, Ossian misses his home and wants to return. Niamh gives him the horse and tells him never to touch the ground. But when he returns to the ground, he finds that all his friends have been dead for years—300 years have passed. The people living in what was once his homeland are a race of short people. To them, he looked like a giant. At one point, he saw a large group of people trying to move heavy marbles to build a building. When he tried to help them, he fell off his horse; the moment he touched the ground, he became a gray-haired, blind old man.

In music, as in these myths, the same instruments and theories have spread east and west. There are two ways of explaining this. One is by synchronicity, and the other is that civilizations have always been connected to the East and West through trade routes such as the Silk Road. Contacts between different kinds of people, through trade and invasions have always existed, except in very secluded places such as Papa New Guinea and places like the Amazon. Joseph Campbell, the scholar of mythology, has written books on the latter. He also points out a theory that civilizations in Central and South America must have had some trade through the Pacific Ocean because they have similar musical instruments. My album *Songs from a Eurasian Journey* was inspired by Campbell's ideas on how world mythology is connected.

In both the East and the West, there existed philosophical theories that connected music with mythological theories of the universe. In the West, the theory of harmony in Renaissance music was connected with alchemy. The harmonic music that emerged during this period became the foundation of subsequent Western music and is the most fundamental theory of both classical music and rock. When I interviewed Anthony Rooley, the leader of The Consort of Music in London, he explained to me that in the Renaissance, the universe was seen to be made up of four elements: earth, water, fire, and air. In music, this corresponds to bass, tenor, alto, and soprano, and in turn to the order corresponds to Saturn, Moon, Mars, and Jupiter.

The mathematician and researcher of ancient mysticism, P. D. Ouspensky wrote in his book *A New Model of the Universe* that Jehovah was spelled in ancient Hebrew with four letters: Yod, He, Vau, and He—which correspond to fire, water, air and earth. They also correspond to four directions: east, south, west, and north.

This tradition was kept in medieval alchemy.

In English Renaissance music, such as John Dowland's songs, the bass sings the harmonic root, like the earth; the soprano sings the central melody, like the air; and the alto and the tenor have the role of predicting the melody and breathing life into the song through rhythmic interplay. This influence of Kabbalistic alchemy is not only in music but also in painting and literature such as in the works by Shakespeare and Spenser. Frances Yates, a Renaissance scholar, has written a book entitled *The Magical Renaissance: Occult Philosophy in the Elizabethan Age*, which explains these influences in detail.

In East Asia, *I Ching* and the theory of *Yin-Yang* and the Five Elements of Nature have been used in many things in life, from music to the customs of daily life. In ancient Chinese texts, it was written that the theory of the Five Elements came from the Persians or the Mesopotamians living in the west of China. The form we know today, however, was formulated in China and introduced to all the surrounding countries influenced by Chinese culture including Korea, Vietnam, and Japan.

It is a way of thinking that divides the basic substances that make up the natural world into the five elements—wood, fire, metal, earth, and water. A trained Taoist or a religious priest tries to grasp their properties in all things. This includes music as well as architecture. *Feng shui*, or Chinese geomancy, still influences architecture and the rules in religious festivals today in these countries. The human body is also considered to be a microcosm of the universe, and all the parts of the body are also divided into the five elements.

There is also music of the five-tone scale based on the five elements. These scales are at the root of all kinds of traditional Chinese, Korean, and Japanese music, including *Gagaku* (ancient Japanese court music) and the *Shomyo* (Buddhist chanting). However, the way they sound, and how they are performed depends on what kind of meaning is intended.

Although it is generally believed that the performance style of court music has not changed since it was brought to Japan from Tang

Dynasty China, it is hard to imagine that all these compositions and songs were performed at such a slow tempo. In literature from Tang Dynasty China, it is said that "Etenraku," a very popular composition today in Japan, was originally a round dance from a Turkic tribe living in the western parts of China, where the people danced in a circle. Today, it is often performed at New Year's celebrations at a very, very slow tempo.

It's hard to imagine a round dance performed so slowly!

When these Turkic compositions are revived and performed in China, Chinese scholars use the present music of the Kazakhs and the Uyghurs as a reference. No one can be sure because no recordings exist from 1500 years ago. As a result, one common problem when recreating Tang Dynasty songs is the interpretation of their tempo.

Atoms are made up of vibrations or waves. Sound waves are vibrations that travel through the air. Light waves are electromagnetic vibrations. The sounds of plucked strings and the air vibrating with music move our bodies and spirits by sending us certain types of energy.

Because we believe the universe, including humans, is made of atoms, the frequency of the waves in the pitch of music, as well as in the colors of a picture, can influence our being.

Traditionally, the five-element system in the East and four-element systems in the West have been used to explain the connection between the universe and the arts, including music and ritual in ancient and medieval times.

Figure 36   Five elements in Chinese.

Folk society

There is a certain shared theme in all my songs based on *A Dream of a Red Mansion*: "What We Look Like in the Picture," "Izutsu," "Lament," and "Annabel Lee." It tells of an old village that has existed for years, a place where everyone has known each other since childhood, from birth to death. There is a boy and a girl. Since childhood, they have known each other, and when they grow up, they get married. When one dies, the other talks about the old days and reminisces about them. These works are centered around these themes. A world like this is the opposite of the one I grew up in.

"What We Look Like in the Picture" is inspired by *Six Records of a Floating Life*, an autobiographical work by the Chinese scholar and artist, Shen Fu. "Izutsu" is based on a *Noh* play written by Zeami Motokiy. "Annabel Lee" is a poem written by Edgar Allan Poe, a 19th-century American writer. "Lament" is a melody set to my own translation of the beginning of Li Bai's poem, from English to Japanese.

Each of them originates from a different place and time, but they share a common theme.

One of Yukio Mishima's early works is called *Diary of Prayers* (*Inori no Niki*). It seems to me that he may have modeled this on Poe's "Annabel Lee." After finishing this work, Mishima added a quotation from the text of Ise Monogatari, on which "Izutsu" is based, as an epigraph. He writes that he did this because he found a common theme in the story of "Izutsu" after he finished writing it.

I think people who are interested in these stories are also people who are thinking about issues of questioning identity. In his analysis of American literature, the British writer D. H. Lawrence wrote that Edgar Allan Poe played an important role in America's search for a new identity. Poe lived in the early days of American independence—a time of change and search for a new identity. Poe depicted ghosts wandering through a dying old European-style town. The world that Poe depicted was far more like medieval Europe than what was written in Europe itself. Lawrence wrote that those who came to America from Europe could not move on to the next stage until they had first reaffirmed where they came from and saw the old world crumble, to become like ghosts in their midst. The next step was to create a new identity in the new land.

Poe was the first poet I read while I was growing up in New York City. Poe envisioned many of his masterpieces in Riverside Drive Park, near where I lived when I was eight years old. An old bench with his name still stands there.

My parents have divorced and remarried so many times that I don't have a single culture or home to call my roots. When I was a child, I had been relocated from one country to another, from the time I can remember. With every passing year, my society, my friends, and even those in the roles of my parents changed.

New York, Berlin, and Paris were hubs for artists and would-be artists seeking out new cultures in the 1960s. Many of them returned to where they came from around 1975 after realizing they would never be able to form an international community due to their lack of understanding of each other.

Kurt Vonnegut was the American author I read most when I was in junior high school. In one of his essays, he wrote that his cultural anthropology teacher at university, Robert Renfield, was a huge influence on him. Renfield, largely unknown today, was a scholar who wrote and spoke about "folk societies" and "dream communities." Renfield contends that despite many differences among primitive societies around the world, all of them shared one common characteristic: they were small, and everyone within them knew each other from birth to death. In addition, oral transmission of knowledge was the only method of passing on knowledge. As a result, old people were valued because of their memories and experiences. There was little change.

In those days, there was not much division of labor. Work done by one person was similar to work done by another. If everyone knew each other's feelings and pasts, they would treat each other as they would treat themselves. The reason humans came to treat other humans as objects, Renfield wrote, was due to the structures of society, which had lost sight of each other's feelings, so that the people could only see each other in their own interests. During the sixties, Vonnegut writes that hippies were trying to realize these dreams by founding communes. However, it was not successful.

Modern societies have always had such dreams of community. A yearning for the primitive life of Africa, Asia, and South America was evident in the world music boom of the 1990s. The manga artist Mizuki Shigeru saw an idealistic aspect to the communities of people he met in Papua New Guinea during World War II. However, many people who try to create a modern version of this longing often wind up creating strange religious and political cults.

These primitive societies, however, are filled with all kinds of discrimination if we take a closer look at them. Many African societies discriminate against white-skinned albinos. It is believed by some black Americans that the whites in Europe are the descendants of those who were discriminated against and thrown out of black society.

My composition, "The Drummer of the Forest," was inspired by an autobiography of a man who played talking drums in an African village. I felt his position as an 'outsider' of society was similar to that of the *Kawaranomono* in Japan. The *Kawaramono* were river-dwelling outsiders who became musicians, actors, and storytellers; *Kawa* is Japanese for river. It was said that they lived near a river so that they could easily travel. Most people in old Japan were prohibited from traveling, and so they lived all their lives in one village. Those who traveled abroad and tried to return were executed.

The *Kawaranomono* often had no stable home. In many countries, musicians and artists were outsiders kicked out of society.

Anarchists often claim that people do not need laws to control people. However, when we observe all of the discrimination and crime that exists in primitive societies, we realize we need to find ways to deal with these darker aspects of human nature. There are many people involved in progressive social and political movements who did not pursue that part of humanity in depth. People, such as Pol Pot or Che Guevara—who dreamed of revolution—wound up killing many people as a consequence of their actions.

Music, poetry, and dance were used by ancient societies to explain the origins of the world. Masses and passion plays were composed by medieval European musicians. The Brazilian samba tradition includes rituals like *candomblé*, which honors African deities. Originally, Hawaiian hula dances were also dedicated to gods and goddesses.

The mythologist, Joseph Campbell, once said that Grateful Dead concerts were the closest thing to ancient religious rituals in the 20th century.

As a child, I dreamed of creating a new "traditional music" for the future that incorporates all the new scientific advances and experiences of the 20th century.

"The Drummer of the Forest"
(composed and written by Ayuo)

I WAS A DRUMMER IN A SMALL VILLAGE,
DEEP INSIDE A WIDE GREEN FOREST.
THE PEOPLE THERE, LIVED IN THEIR PRIDE,
OF THE LIFE THEY'VE HAD FOR CENTURIES.
BUT THE PEOPLE THERE, THEY DIDN'T LIKE ME.
I WAS TOO DIFFERENT.
THERE WAS SOMETHING WRONG.
I WASN'T LIKE THEM.
SO THEY SENT ME AWAY TO THE EDGE OF THE FOREST,
TO LEARN THE DRUMS.
NOW DRUMMING WAS A PART OF THEIR LIFE;
EVERY RITUAL HAD TO HAVE DRUMS.
BUT THE DRUMMERS WERE ALWAYS
THOSE WHO WERE OUTSIDE THEIR SOCIETY.
THOSE THAT THEY KICKED OUT OF THEIR LIVES.

SO LEAVE THAT PLACE.
FIND ANOTHER LIFE.
LEAVE THAT MUD.
FIND WHERE I CAN FIT.

BUT THE DRUMS KEPT POUNDING IN MY HEART.
NOW I ALWAYS WANTED TO LEAVE THAT PLACE,
TO FIND MYSELF IN A BETTER SOCIETY.
SO WHEN THE GOVERNMENT MADE A PROGRAM,
TO SEND SOME OF THEIR KIDS TO THE BEST SCHOOLS ABROAD,
THEY CHOSE ME 'CAUSE THEY WANTED ME TO LEAVE.
I DIDN'T KNOW WHAT TO EXPECT,
BUT I WAS GLAD TO FIND A NEW LIFE.
SMALL TOWNS ARE SO FILLED WITH HATE,
AND PETTY ENVY,
'CAUSE THEY SPEND THEIR DAYS,
WATCHING EACH OTHER,
COMPLAINING SOMEONE ELSE GOT MORE THAN HE,
AND ALL THAT MUD,
THAT LIVES IN HUMANS,
ARE MORE IN THE AIR,
'CAUSE THERE'S NOTHING ELSE TO DO.

SO LEAVE THAT PLACE.
FIND ANOTHER LIFE.
LEAVE THAT MUD.
FIND WHERE I CAN FIT.

BUT THE DRUMS KEPT POUNDING IN MY HEART.

NOW I WENT TO A GOOD SCHOOL.
PROVED MYSELF.
GOT A JOB IN THE LAW.
'CAUSE I WANTED TO KNOW WHY I WAS TREATED LIKE THAT.
SO I COULD ALWAYS FIGHT,
WITH THE LAW ON MY SIDE.
BUT I TOLD MYSELF,
I AIN'T GOING BACK.
GONNA LIVE THIS LIFE,
WITH THE BEST SUITS,
WITH THE BEST HAIR,

WITH THE BEST LOTIONS.
SPENT HOURS DRESSING MYSELF,
LIKE A GOOD, CULTURED MAN.
THOUGH I KNEW THEY WERE THINKING,
'HE'S FROM THE JUNGLE,
PROBABLY LIVED UP A TREE,
PLAYED THE BONGOS FOR A LIVING,
LIKE THEY SHOW ON TV.'

BUT I SAID TO MYSELF:

'I'VE LEFT THAT PLACE.
FOUND A BETTER LIFE.
LEFT THAT MUD.
FOUND WHERE I CAN FIT.'

BUT THE DRUMS KEPT POUNDING IN MY HEART.

I WAS PROUD TO BE SO MODERN,
LIVING LIFE WITH THE MOST SOPHISTICATED.
BUT THERE WAS SOMETHING I FELT IN THE AIR,
I KNEW THEY WERE THINKING,
'HE'S NOT CIVILIZED,
HE'S NOT ONE OF US.'
AND ONE DAY IN FRONT OF THE MIRROR,
AS I SAT DOWN TO DRESS,
TO PUT ON MY LOTIONS,
AND TO DO MY HAIR.
I SUDDENLY SAID,
'I AIN'T DOING THIS NO MORE.'
I RAN OUT OF THE HOUSE,
HALF-NAKED WITH MY BONGOS.
PLAYED IN THE STREETS,
WHILE SOME OF MY FORMER FRIENDS
STOOD IN SHOCK.
WHILE THE OTHERS GRINNED,
SAYING THEY ALWAYS KNEW,

THAT HE WAS ACTING IT OUT.
NOW HE'S REVEALED HIMSELF,
SHOWING WHAT HE REALLY IS.

BUT I SAID TO MYSELF:

'LEAVE THAT PLACE,
FIND ANOTHER LIFE.
LEAVE THAT MUD.
FIND WHERE I CAN FIT.'

BUT THE DRUMS KEPT POUNDING IN MY HEART.

NOW I'M IN A BAND,
MADE RECORDS FOR A LIVING.
AND I TEACH THE DRUM.
AND SOMETIMES I'VE GONE
BACK TO MY OLD VILLAGE,
WHERE NOW THEY TREAT ME
LIKE A GUEST FROM ABROAD.
IT'S A STRANGE LIFE,
BUT HUMANS MAKE IT SO,
AND IN MY HEART, I ALWAYS REMEMBER
ALL THOSE TIMES I'VE SAID TO MYSELF:

'GONNA LEAVE THIS PLACE.
FIND A BETTER LIFE.
LEAVE THAT MUD.
FIND WHERE I CAN FIT.'

BUT THE DRUMS KEPT POUNDING IN MY HEART.

About rhythm

The beat is the first element of music that comes naturally to a child. All of us are familiar with our mother's heartbeat, even before we are born. I remember my child making beats on the drum machine and then playing keyboards over them when she was just a baby. She enjoyed it, and I enjoyed watching it.

To teach your child classical music, you need to force children to study it even before they are interested in doing it on their own. In the absence of this kind of musical education, a child will learn music by listening to the beat first. I was not encouraged to study classical music, nor was I exposed to classical music by my parents when I was a child. Thus, the beats were the first thing I learned about music.

Music learned from beats and rhythms is absorbed differently than music learned from scales, such as in classical music. You learn to connect sounds in a way different from harmony theory laws.

Rhythm is the foundation of most traditional music around the world. It is common for classical musicians to view ancient music through the lens of classical music when commenting on it. Just intonation might be discussed, for example, but not so much the use of ancient rhythms.

Rhythm is the most ancient and important aspect of Balkan Peninsula music, such as that of Greece. Their music from ancient times is characterized by its rhythm. They have many songs and music in rhythm meters, such as 9/8 and 11/8, which would be considered odd time signatures in other countries. These rhythms have a long tradition in the Balkan countries. From the earliest recorded times, poets wrote their poems to the number of beats to be used, then they clapped their hands to the rhythm, and dancers would dance to it.

It is believed by scholars that most Ancient Greek poetry, including the poems of Homer, was composed to be sung to music, and it is generally assumed that a short syllable was sung to a short note, while the long syllables were sung to longer notes or a group of two or three short notes. The earliest Greek poetry, the poems ascribed to Homer and Hesiod, is written in dactylic hexameters, of which the basic meter is as follows:

|- u u |- u u |- u u |- u u |- u u |- - |

For example, the most common rhythm used in Greek comedy was 5/8 with |♩ ♪♩| and |♩ ♫♪|.[1] This is derived from *rhythmic paeonic* (quintuple time), a genus recognized by Aristotle and Aristoxenus in which the thesis and arsis are in durational ratio 2 : 3 and is represented as — ‿ —. This is not common in Western music but is well-known in the folk music of Eastern Europe.

Dochmiac is a poetic meter that is characteristically used in Greek tragedy, expressing extreme agitation or distress."[2] This rather complex rhythm is as characteristic of tragedy as *paeonic* is of comedy. The base metrical scheme is: ‿ — — ‿ —, where the — represents the long syllable and ‿ the short.

However, any of the long syllables may be replaced by two shorts (‿‿), and either of the two shorts may be replaced by a long (—). In theory, 32 variants are possible, ranging from five longs — — — — — to eight shorts, ‿ ‿‿ ‿‿ ‿ ‿‿.

The ancient Greek *dochmiac* behavior presents an interesting analogy with the meter 3 + 3 + 2, in which the members can be exchanged as 3 + 2 + 3 or 2 + 3 + 3. "The asymmetrical groupings which are the essence of *dochmiac* rhythm are paralleled in the folk music of various countries, but particularly in that of the Balkans. Bartók's specimens of Hungarian folk music include a song from Transylvania which is in perfect *dochmiac* rhythm."[2]

In an interview with Tower Records' magazine, drummer Norbert Pfammatter of the Elina Duni Quartet told me the following: "Unlike syncopation in Africa, dancing with long and short steps creates the

---

[1]West, Martin, *Greek Metre*. Oxford University Press, pp. 108–115, 1982.
[2]West, M. L. *Ancient Greek Music*. Oxford University Press, pp. 140–145, 1994.

rhythms in Europe." Such a rhythmic approach to traditional poetry can indeed be found in many countries throughout Europe. In fact, Roman culture was no different.

Pythagoras and Aristoxenes were among the mathematicians and musicologists who wrote about how to analyze the musical scale. In Byzantine sacred music, which is Greek church music, the octave is divided into 68 points, of which the *minor* second degree is 7 points and the *major* second degree is 9 points and 12 points, depending on their surrounding notes. The sound might seem strange to those accustomed to Western music because it sounds quite different from music in equal temperament.

In exploring various types of music, we realize that we are not limited to 4/4, 3/4, and 2/4 as our average rhythms. Natural walking steps do not necessarily follow a 4/4, 3/4, or 2/4 rhythm. Modern music was responsible for averaging them out from long and short steps into a regulated meter.

It was also possible to achieve a common understanding of time by averaging it. Hours, minutes, and seconds became the same, regardless of day or night, winter or summer. This happened at the same time as when equal temperament music scales became the norm in the West during the 18th century. They are all relatively new.

From the old clocks, it can be observed that the hours in winter and summer in Japan were not the same. Before the 19th century, people used sundials to determine time: days in winter were shorter and nights longer, while days in summer were longer and nights shorter. An hour of daylight was longer in summer than in winter; hours were not averaged. Sundials and lunar calendars were used to determine when festival music would begin.

This may have been the most natural way of counting time and rhythm, but it's not suited to modern life. Modern life would collapse if an hour became longer or shorter according to the sun. It was common practice in Europe to place clocks in the middle of towns to announce the general time, and life became impossible if people failed to observe it.

In Greek or West Asian music, you'll hear more subtle microtones than in the Western scale *solfège* (do-re-mi-fa-so-la-ti-do). However, there used to be similarities centuries ago, even in European music—flat notes used to be lower and sharp notes higher, represented in microtonality. In other words, a D-flat note used to be higher than a C#, but now they are the same note.

As a result, complex harmony became possible instead of these fine nuances. The need for a mean time in daily life led to the development of a mean time and equal temperament in music, which led to Romantic music, Impressionist music, twelve-tone music, and atonal music.

As life changes, so does music.

The rhythm of the words we speak affects the rhythmic sense of the person who speaks them

In the 1960s, American jazz drummer Art Blakey experimented with a Pan-Afro-drum ensemble. He invited West African percussionists to perform alongside black American musicians who are descended from West Africans. He intended to demonstrate the commonalities between African-American rhythms and West African rhythms.

However, this endeavor was said to be unsuccessful. African-Americans and West African musicians did not have the same sense of rhythm. They didn't realize how much the language they spoke influences the rhythmic sense of an entire group of people. Those who grew up speaking English would develop rhythms that matched the way they spoke the language, whereas those who spoke a West African language developed rhythms that fit *their* way of speaking. Hip-hop/rap music recognizes this and makes use of the rhythmic sense of the distinctive African-American way of speaking. The same may be said for jazz, soul, and gospel music.

People absorb language and culture as they grow up in a specific society. Nationalists and racists would like to believe that language and culture are passed down genetically; however, all people absorb language and culture as they grow up through interaction with others in society. This is how language works.

In the 1990s, I read a book called *Dance of Life* by cultural anthropologist Edward T. Hall. This book addressed issues that I had always suspected instinctively regarding how one's sense of culture develops. It helped me understand how culture operates.

Hall wrote about it in a way that made it clear and helped people like me understand what culture is and how humans understand it.

I grew up in a mixed-race home in New York City in the 1960s, and I was unfamiliar with how Japanese people communicated with one another. I was never taught the language or about the culture by my mother.

If rhythms are viewed as a manner of using and dividing time, then my perception of rhythm differed from that of Japanese, European, and African-Americans. *Dance of Life* demonstrates this by examining the various ways in which Hispanics, Caucasians, and Native American Hopi people in New Mexico handle time. Time can be used in a variety of ways, and it can also be divided in a variety of ways. Different senses of time can coexist even within the same country.

Hall discovered that the way a certain group of people makes divisions in time greatly influences their sense of rhythm(s) in daily life. For example, there are no words for past or future tenses in the Hopi language—only the present tense. As a result, their sense of time was vastly different from Western countries. Many Westerners saw them as unable to keep time appointments. Hall analyzes these differences in time and rhythm.

What appears to be exotic superficially is not the real difference between cultures. The true difference between cultures is buried and preserved, much like a turtle's shell.

Hidden Differences: Doing Business with the Japanese is another book by Edward T. Hall. This book greatly aided my understanding of how people meet and communicate in Japan.

According to Edward T. Hall, before the Renaissance, God was conceived of as sound or vibration. Since the dawn of civilization, each geographical place has experienced time in its own distinctive manner. The blending and crossing of multiple ways of experiencing time resulted in a unique science of time for humanity.

Rhythm is the most binding force that holds people together, and rhythmic patterns are an important quality that distinguishes one person from another. Any rhythm that humans use is a cultural feature that exists in the environment from where the patterns are learned. Time has a bearing on the formation of the worldview of all people in a culture. The time frame patterns established are unique to each culture. As a result, according to Edward T. Hall, we need to learn the language of time in a specific culture as much as we would need to learn to talk and write the language of that culture.

"Dance of Life"

(written and composed by Ayuo)

It's about how you feel time,
Synchronizing rhythms in the dance of life.

When we talk,
Our nerves mesh,
Like gears in transmission,
Tuning our waves in phase.
And locking us in feeling,
In the dance of life.

We sync and dance,
How our rhythms relate,
On earth's energy fields,
Transcending space and time.
And locking us in feeling,
In the dance of life.

Time plays a role in life.
Individuals tied together.
Invisible threads of rhythms.
Isolated by hidden walls.

It's about how you feel time,
Synchronizing rhythms in the dance of life.

It's about how you feel time,
Synchronizing rhythms in the dance of life.
Dance the dance of life.

Copyright owned by Ayuo Takahashi.
Registered @JASRAC.

"Different Languages"

(written and composed by Ayuo)

Sometimes when you are all alone,
You think back to that time you once knew,
When every thought,
Was in a different tongue,
A language you could no longer speak.

And you'd realize as your mind goes back
You'd felt things, you could no longer say,
When every color
Was in a different shade,
A language you could no longer speak.

It feels strange,
The world didn't change,
But environments are a part of thoughts,
When every thought was in a different tongue,
In a language, you could no longer speak.

The difference between English and Japanese lyrics

During my time as a recording artist for MIDI Records in the 1980s, I had an interesting discussion with Minako Yoshida, the singer, lyricist, and composer, regarding the difference between English and Japanese lyrics.

As Ms. Yoshida explained, English lyrics can include double meanings, metaphors, and multiple instances of irony. Even when you sound like you're saying something definite and clear, you can add two or three layers of meaning. However, in Japanese lyrics, there is only one definite meaning, even in situations where it sounds like you seem to be saying something vague.

I have often been told in Japan that I speak too directly, and this makes people unable to understand what I am saying. In Japan, it is common to speak in a roundabout manner, even when one's intention is to say something directly, so the way words are used in Japanese is the opposite of how words are used in English. After hearing that, I felt like a mystery had been solved for me.

English lyrics, translated directly into Japanese, often feel forced and alter the image of the original song. It is not just the meaning that is important in English lyrics, but the sound. Many of them are designed to be listened to. The words in Shakespeare's plays sound like music when orated in English because they were written with sound and rhythm in mind. The same is true for rock and rap music.

As we grow up, we think with words. As we watch children learn a language, it appears they already have the basis for learning a language and the ability to communicate; the languages they learn depend on where they grow up. It is not uncommon for many of us who lived in the US until around the age of 15 and spoke English both at home and at school until the age of 17, to think in English, the language of our upbringing, although some people in Chinatown and Puerto Rican communities speak the language of their ancestors.

As far as I was concerned, I realized that I could only think in English because I was never taught Japanese as a child. Whenever I make music, I usually begin by writing words in English, and then add sounds to them. This applies not only to songs, but to piano pieces, string quartets, and instrumental pieces for commercials and movies as well. To create images, I use English words. Music or melody don't appear in my head directly. No sounds come to mind if I don't think of the words.

This isn't just about thinking about lyrics. This process is different from thinking about meaning. There might be something to do with rhythm. An image might be involved. Several of those elements may be present at once in the words.

Even if I write down the music and hand it over to the performer, it may not be expressed properly if the performer doesn't understand what I'm trying to convey. If I play it myself, I can change the tempo or dynamics as I see fit, based on my feelings; however, even if I write all the specifications down in the score for a different performer, it may end up sounding somewhat different. This can happen if the performer cannot understand what I am trying to express.

When I was asked to write a pop song with Japanese lyrics around 1990, I wrote the words in English first, and then the music followed. In Japanese pop music, the melody is often written first, and then the lyricist adds lyrics to match the melody, so the lyrics I wrote weren't used in the final song—but if I hadn't written the words in English first, I would not have been able to write the song at all.

During the early 1980s, a musician once told me, "The Japanese can understand English and American rock music better than those raised in the West. Because we don't understand the lyrics, we can hear the sounds better." This sounded ridiculous to me. Music is created to express something. If someone doesn't understand the words, how can they understand what the musician is trying to express? I know that what he was trying to say was the lyrics can get in the way of being able to appreciate the music purely on its own.

Many people believe that the Japanese communicate in ways other than speech. You can often encounter a man grunting "um" to signify a variety of different things, depending on the situation. There are countless instances when someone says something so vague that you are unsure whether he is agreeing or disagreeing with you. However, if you don't recognize what they're trying to convey without using words, you'll be accused of *kuuki wo yondeinai*— or 'not reading the air.' I believe this resulted from centuries of isolation. Those who left Japan and attempted to return would be executed. Without a permit, people were not permitted to leave their hometowns. This '*Sakoku*' isolation policy caused individuals to communicate more like animals, using body language instead of using words too directly.

Animals don't do things that are meaningless. That's why linguists, like Steven Pinker, study the way animals use sounds. Animals don't communicate with spoken languages like humans, since they mostly communicate with body language; when they make sounds, it is an extension of their body language. Each meow of a cat isn't a word that can be directly translated, and yet the cat is meowing to express a certain meaning. Sounds are expressions of meanings.

If, as Minako Yoshida said, there is only one clear meaning in what seems vague in the Japanese language, then this makes it hard to create metaphors that can contain different meanings in a single poem. Writing things directly would make the words feel as though they were imposing a single meaning on the reader.

When China and Japan normalized diplomatic ties, Zhou Enlai (the Chinese prime minister), said to Kakuei Tanaka (the Japanese prime minister), "We are sorry for having passed on the *Kanji* (Chinese characters) to Japan."

Because *Kanji* was derived from pictures, it is difficult for words to have several different meanings. This, I believe, causes the Japanese to focus more on the meaning of words than Westerners. In Japanese, the meaning of the words holds more weight. It seems to me that this is the misfortune of the Japanese language. I don't know if it is the same in China, since the Japanese language itself is a very different language from Chinese and the *Kanji* was an adopted form of writing.

Couldn't they have done something with *hiragana* and *katakana*, like Korea did with the *Hangul* alphabet?

Is it too late now?

Classical music's influence in Rock music[1]

Some time ago, my composition teacher, Minao Shibata, said something like this:

> The era of Mozart and Beethoven marked the period of European civilization's expansion towards global dominance. When we study Western music nowadays, we focus on this historical period because it is when society's framework and the scientific way of thinking were developed that influence our current culture. Wagner and Verdi's music have a sense of grandeur and power as if one has reached the pinnacle. The same may be said about the literature and other arts of the period.

With the end of World War II, American civilization became the center of the world, and its consumerist culture spread around the world. Rock and Roll, comics, Hollywood movies, television, and pop art became the central culture in many people's lives.

But this culture from America is still young. We don't know what will be left as a tradition after 100 or 200 years. Will the Beatles or Joni Mitchell's songs remain classics?

Let's trace the history of European music, which is the tool for the current way we create music. What does rock music today take from the traditions of Western classical music?

Thoreau and other 19th-century philosophers often wrote that civilization begins in the east with the sun and moves westward. Europeans in the Middle Ages learned mathematics, science, and music from the Arabs who ruled Spain at the time, passing on the traditions from ancient Greece. The Arabs are said to have learned

---

[1]An article written for a rock magazine *Keyboard Special* in 1985 and revised before its publication in the book.

about music methods and techniques from Greek slaves who were taken to the Middle East. Therefore, the modes used in medieval music are called Greek modes (church mode, church melody).

However, we know today that they were different from the actual modes that the ancient Greeks used. The Europeans adapted names such as Dorian, Lydian, and Phrygian, but the sounds and music theories were completely different.

Examples of medieval modes (on the scale of C):

Ionian: C,D,E,F,G,A,B,C

Dorian: D,E,F,G,A,B,C,D

Phrygian: E,F,G,A,B,C,D,E

Lydian: F,G,A,B,C,D,E,F,

Mixolydian: G,A,B,C,D,E,F,G

Aeolian: A,B,C,D,E,F,G,A

Locrian: B,C,D,E,F,G,A,B

The Spanish Arabs of the time introduced numerous instruments that would later be used in Western music. The *oud* became the lute and later the mandolin of today, and the Persian *setar* became the guitar. (*Tar* means strings in ancient Persian, so *setar* means three strings.) Rhythm patterns introduced by the Arabs were also used in compositions. In medieval Spain, there are written records and illustrations of Arabs and blacks singing and playing the hymns of the Virgin Mary together with the Christians. The Clemencic Consort reproduced these songs in masterful performances on their recordings of *Cantigas de Santa Maria*.

There used to be a country called Provence in the south of France, next to Spain. The culture there became more highly developed than in other European countries during the Middle Ages. However, the Pope and the King of Northern France destroyed the culture in Provence in a political power struggle, using religious intolerance to incite the soldiers and the masses against those living in Provence. However, before this happened, in the 12th century, many troubadours were living there who composed new minstrel songs that influenced all of Europe. These songs were strongly influenced by the Spanish and the Arabs. Many of them were love songs, and they left many masterpieces of poetry and music, deeply influencing the *Trouvères* of Northern France and the Minnesingers of Germany. These held simple melodies, but they still sound very fresh and original when they are played in a good arrangement.

Many of the songs are very similar to rock, either played in the *ABABAB* verse format with harp or guitar accompaniment or when played by an acoustic band. Jim Morrison of The Doors often said in interviews that the rock music of the 1960s will most likely be remembered the way medieval troubadour music is now remembered. There was a renewed fascination with the medieval period in the 1960s. A folk club venue named The Troubadour was founded. The troubadours became romanticized, just as 1960s rock music has since been romanticized. Singer-songwriters were often seen as the modern version of what the medieval troubadour was doing during their time.

Rock music in the 1960s became very much influenced by Indian music and other music from Asia and Africa. Modal songs began to appear in pop songs. "Scarborough Fair," a folk song from England, became a huge hit. "The End" by The Doors is heavily influenced by Indian sitar music. "China Cat Sunflower" by Grateful Dead was influenced by Japanese haiku in the lyrics.

During the 60s, many bands played improvisations and jam sessions centered on drones (sustained bass) like in medieval European music and many Indian and Asian music. You can hear them on records that are now considered psychedelic masterpieces by bands such as The Byrds, Country Joe and the Fish, Tyrannosaurus Rex (early T Rex), Jefferson Airplane, Daevid Allen and Gong, Third Ear Band, Hawkwind, Neu, and many, many others.

Around the same time, there was a folk revival movement in America. Bob Dylan, Joan Baez, Judy Collins, Joni Mitchell, and others were leading artists of the revival of folk songs, the traditional folk music that had been passed down through generations. Many of these songs were similar to those of the medieval troubadours since they became part of common culture during the Middle Ages and remained with the people. However many scholars have traced the source of some of the songs to those that originated in the Middle East.

In the seventies, Steeleye Span and Fairport Convention created a genre that later became known in Japan as British Trad.[2] They played many traditional songs from England, Scotland, and Ireland, along with original songs. Martin Carthy, who played with Steeleye Span also developed a unique guitar style of his own and a guitar tuning that is of his creation. He often makes the guitar sound like a medieval instrument.

Just as Gregorian chants are still sung to this day, the music of medieval minstrels still serves as a foundation for Western music.

From the end of the Middle Ages, the *Ars Nova* (Latin for "new art") movement spread to architecture, music, and art. In music, a French composer named Philippe de Vitry wrote a manifesto for *Ars Nova* music in 1325. In this new polyphony, the 5th, 3rd, and 6th degrees were positioned as *consonance*; the minor 2nd, major 2nd, minor 7th, and major 7th degrees were positioned as *dissonance*. The augmented 4th and diminished 5th degrees were called the devil's notes and absolutely avoided, although using them now is fashionable and became so from the late 19th century. Many compositions of polyphonic music with complex intertwining rhythms were composed during this period.

One notable composer during this period was Guillaume de Machaut; his "Hockett" and his *Messe de Notre Dame* influenced many classical composers in the 20th century.

Guillaume de Machaut also composed many isorhythmic motets. These are compositions in which melodic and rhythmic patterns of different lengths are repeated in succession. In this way, while treating pitch separately from rhythm, it is possible to compose works that systematically integrate interesting counterpoint and complex rhythms, including polyrhythms.

However, Machaut not only composed these rhythmically intricate pieces but also composed monophonic French songs in the *Trouvère* tradition of poetic forms. These days, this would be the same as composers, who would compose both in the classical contemporary style and the more popular style of the day.

One example of the relationship between melody and rhythm in an isorhythmic motet:

---

[2]In the UK it is called folk rock, but to distinguish it from bands like The Byrds, Japan used the word *trad*—abbreviated from the word traditional.

Melody 1 I Melody 1 I Melody 1
Rhythm 1 I Rhythm 1

The *Ars Nova* techniques resurfaced in the twentieth century, influencing many composers including Igor Stravinsky, Olivier Messiaen, Alban Berg, and Pierre Boulez. In Japan, this kind of method is also used in the works of Jo Kondo, among other composers. In the *Requiem* by Johannes Ockeghem (1410–1497), the tenor voice sings in 2/1 time, while the counter-tenor sings in multiple meters: first in 3/1, then in 6/2, then in 6/4, then in 3/2, and finally returning to 3/1 time. Such complex rhythmic counterpoint creates the impression of the interplay of a multi-layered grand procession of sounds. There is an absence of symmetrical clarity, with lines soaring into the infinite. The melodic lines are of heavenly length.

Ockeghem's counterpoint is said to have later influenced Bach.

The late Renaissance and Baroque periods saw the development of our present harmonic theory. In those days, the score showed chords by numerical figures written below the *Basso Continuo*—the bass line often performed by the cello and the harpsichord on the left hand. The composer normally just wrote the bass line and indicated what the harmony should be (which chords should be played) by writing numerical figures underneath the music. The numerical figures give the intervals from the bass note up. The player made his own interpretations of what the actual notes would be. More improvisation was allowed in those days.

In the classic age, many people tried to adhere to the way of music as described by the ancient Greek philosophers and mathematicians. Rhythm begins with human breathing and defines the rhythm of life, while harmony represents the harmony of nature and the cosmos, including for humans, and music is meant to uplift humanity and instill a sense of beauty in us. This is also the time when the instruments used in orchestras today were created.

A revival of medieval legends and tales began during the age of Romanticism in the 19th century. The fairy tales we read as children, such as "Snow White," were compiled by the Brothers Grimm and Hans Christen Andersen during this period. Scholars turned their attention to folk tales and songs that had been handed down from generation to generation among the people. This was the age when nation-states were being created. Art and culture that belonged to the "people," instead of the aristocracy, were needed. Composers such as Richard Wagner composed works based on European literature, legends, and myths.

Another notable figure, Novalis re-read the works of the medieval bards and was enchanted by the magical beauty of their poetry. Novalis emphasized the concept of *Innerlichkeit* (inner light). Wagner was influenced by Novalis and the philosopher Arthur Schopenhauer when he composed *Tristan und Isolde*.

Interest in Eastern literature and culture grew among the intellectuals of the 19th century. Schopenhauer was influenced by Indian Hinduism and Buddhism. Wagner researched Arabic music when he discovered its influence on medieval European music. In his opera *Parsifal*, he attempted to compose a traditional medieval tale with an Arabic melody. The work is also said to be the first Impressionist work and would serve as a major influence on Claude Debussy.

Mahler's song cycles continued in this tradition. Mahler's *Des Knaben Wunderhorn* (The Child's Wonderful Horn) is a work based on a folk song, composed to sound like a popular folk song with orchestra and piano accompaniment.

From the turn of the century, many classical composers, such as Ralph Vaughan Williams in England and Béla Bartók and Zoltán Kodály in Hungary, began notating and collecting folksongs that they would incorporate in their compositions. It was vital to accomplish this at this time because live performances of folk songs began to wane in popularity—especially after World War I—as radio broadcasts became the primary means of listening to popular music. In the 1960s, during the folk revival scene, songs from these British collections would be arranged by Joan Baez, Judy Collins, Martin Carthy, Fairport Convention, and Steeleye Span. In Hungary, Márta Sebestyén and the ensemble Muzsikás would arrange many of the songs collected by Kodály and Bartók to popularize them for world music and folk audiences.

The influence of popular music in classical music became even more significant. Erik Satie, who earned his living as a cabaret pianist in his early days, adapted many popular songs and composed his own songs in the popular style of the day. The best known are his own "Je te veux" and "La Diva de l'Empire."

Ragtime music, which originated within African-American communities in the late 19th century and became a distinctly American form of popular music, not only influenced early jazz but many European classical composers, such as Claude Debussy, Erik Satie, and Igor Stravinsky.

George Gershwin started as a composer of popular songs for Tin Pan Alley, but at this time began to incorporate influences from the new harmonic chordal progressions developed by impressionist composers in Europe. In the 1920s, he even tried to study with Maurice Ravel, who rejected him, telling him: "Why become a second-rate Ravel when you're already a first-rate Gershwin?" By that time, Gershwin had already composed works such as *Rhapsody in Blue*, *Blue Monday*, and *Lady Be Good* and was composing *An American in Paris*—all works which have since become a part of standard and classical repertoire.

There were many other composers of jazz music and Broadway musicals that were influenced by impressionist harmonies. Even Debussy's composition, *Rêverie*, was made into a hit song, "My Reverie," in 1938, as performed by Bing Crosby, Mildred Bailey, Glenn Miller, Ella Fitzgerald, Dizzy Gillespie, Sonny Rollins, and many others.

Kurt Weil had been thinking and writing about incorporating jazz in his music before he met the playwright, Bertolt Brecht, with whom he would collaborate heavily with. Weil's songs had advanced harmonies since he was influenced by 20th-century composers such as Ferruccio Busoni, Gustav Mahler, Arnold Schoenberg, and Igor Stravinsky. Weill's music was admired by composers such as Alban Berg, Alexander von Zemlinsky, and Darius Milhaud.

Alban Berg, in his opera *Lulu*, composed the most interesting blend of atonal music and jazz, way before modern jazz; many later jazz critics would say that Berg composed what would become modern jazz within his opera, foreshadowing the developments in post-war jazz.

Berg spent two years writing *Lulu*'s script. He made it into one opera from two plays by playwright Frank Wedekind and wrote the lyrics for the arias. While writing the script, he must have been thinking about how to structure the music. He often wrote the words before he wrote the music. Schoenberg said that even Berg's instrumental music was also like songs. Theodor W. Adorno, a prominent philosopher, wrote that the musical appeal of *Lulu* lies in the fact that the melody is central. Berg took the time to create a way of twelve-tone music that differs from Schoenberg's.

Perhaps the melodies came to mind first, along with the words, and the methodology for using the melodies was thought up later. Some parts of his music are composed more like *Ars Nova* or Renaissance contrapuntal music; others have very advanced harmonic movement, composed years ahead of the postwar modern jazz sound. Berg's use of jazz was more all-encompassing than Kurt Weill's. Broadway musical composer Stephen Sondheim has also said that Berg's operas were a major influence on his music. It is so melodious that it is hard to imagine that the 12-tonal systems that were used were created first before the melodies.

Barbara Hannigan's performance of *Lulu* in 2012 seems to understand the heart of this work. Says Hannigan: "When I sing Lulu, I feel like I'm expressing the inner life of the composer." There is a bit of a similarity between the life of the composer and the woman Lulu, the protagonist of the opera. Director Krzysztof Warlikowski studied Berg's biography and incorporated it, introducing Berg's daughter Albine as a phantom, as well as the phantom of Lilith, who is said to have existed before the Old Testament Eva. The aim was to create a 21st-century setting that transcended Berg's detailed stage designations.

The story begins when Lulu is 15 years old and ends when she is killed by Jack the Ripper at age 18. Lulu has no parents. She was made the mistress of middle-aged Dr. Schön when she was 12 years old, after trying to pick up his wallet on a street corner. He marries Lulu off to another man several times while continuing to date Lulu in the shadows. When Dr. Schön gets engaged, Lulu blackmails him into marrying her. But the marriage doesn't work out, and Dr. Schön threatens Lulu with a pistol. Lulu takes the pistol and shoots him dead. Later, Lulu escapes from prison and escapes with Dr. Schön's son Alva. There is no other way left for Lulu except prostitution to survive. Alva is killed; finally, Lulu is also killed by Jack the Ripper.

At the age of 15, Berg became involved with a 30-year-old woman, and when he was 17, she gave birth to a daughter, Albine. Berg was still a boy, and he was unsure of what to do. After attempting suicide, he tried to relieve his problems by making music. His older sister saw him attempting to do so and took him to a teacher in town who taught composition; that teacher was Schoenberg. Berg had no money to pay for lessons, but Schoenberg, seeing Berg's talent, agreed to teach him for free. For Berg, this was a lifesaver. At Schoenberg's place, he also met the composer Anton Webern, who would become his lifelong best friend.

In this day and age, many people are growing up in broken families, and incidents of abuse are often written about. I think the reason this work is now in the 21st century and is considered the greatest operatic work of the 20th century is because it conveys such content so strongly.

The philosopher, Slavoj Žižek, who has become very popular in recent years, often quotes the Hegelian thinker Theodor W. Adorno, who was a student of Alban Berg. Adorno saw Berg's works *Lulu* and *Wozzeck* as important works that depict people being exploited in modern society. He believed that by seeing the darkness in society, people might reflect on its problems and change their behavior. Adorno was dismissive of the ideas of Bertolt Brecht and Hans Eisler, another disciple of Schoenberg, who even embraced the great purges that Stalin waged in the Soviet Union.

I first heard *Lulu* when I was 20 years old. I was greatly moved by the melody and the words sung in the opera.

Alban Berg is one of my favorite composers. I arranged his "Lullaby" from the opera *Wozzeck* for my album *Memory Theatre*. This song is in ABAB form, and the harmony is made from the superimposition of the fourth degree. Using synthesizers and samplers, I made the song sound closer to popular music and had the Japanese singer Epo sing the melody.

Atonal music and serial music made counterpoint as important as it was in the Middle Ages. Isorhythm techniques in composition can be found in many of Berg's compositions, including the opera *Wozzeck* and the string quartet *Lyric Suite*. Isorhythmic techniques can also be found in the works of Oliver Messian, John Cage, Igor Stravinsky, and many others.

In 1967, *Sgt. Pepper's Lonely Hearts Club Band* by The Beatles is known for incorporating a wide range of stylistic influences including vaudeville, circus, music hall, avant-garde, and Western and Indian classical music.

Both John Lennon and Paul McCartney became interested in avant-garde and electronic-music composers such as Karlheinz Stockhausen, John Cage, and Luciano Berio. In the song "A Day in Life," there are passages of orchestral glissandos that were partly improvised in the avant-garde style. *Musique concrète* techniques are used in the recording, showing the influence of electronic and experimental composer Pierre Schaeffer.

There is also music in the Indian classical style. George Harrison wrote "Within You Without You," inspired by his sitar teacher Ravi Shankar.

The *sitar, tambura, dilruba,* and *tabla* were performed by Harrison and members of the Asian Music Circle.

"She's Leaving Home" is a song written by Paul McCartney and John Lennon, accompanied by just a small string orchestra arranged by Mike Leander. I later arranged this song for solo piano, as commissioned by Aki Takahashi, and recorded it for Toshiba EMI.

Recognized classical composers such as Luciano Berio, Aaron Copland, John Cage, Ned Rorem, and Leonard Bernstein helped legitimize the Beatles as serious musicians.

Pink Floyd (with Syd Barrett) were recording their album, *The Piper at the Gates of Dawn*, in the studio next door at Abbey Road studios at the same time as *Sgt. Pepper's Lonely Hearts Club Band*. The members of The Beatles would drop in to check what they were doing and invited the members of Pink Floyd to sit in on The Beatles' session for the song "Lovely Rita."

This debut album by Pink Floyd is a pivotal psychedelic rock recording. The album had both long-form improvisational pieces as well as short pop songs written and composed by Syd Barrett. Even in his short 3-minute songs, there were influences from electronic music and musique concrète. Syd Barrett also set James Joyce's poem "Golden Hair" to a song with guitar accompaniment.

Pink Floyd was sometimes booked with AMM, a free improvisation group, at the UFO club in London. Pink Floyd was very much interested in avant-garde music, and their incorporations from the avant-garde would take things one step further in rock music. AMM at this time consisted of Keith Rowe on guitar, Lou Gare on saxophone, Eddie Prévost on drums, Lawrence Sheaff on bass, and the composer/pianist Cornelius Cardew in 1966, performing on piano and cello. Keith Rowe showed me, some of the unusual guitar techniques that he showed Syd Barrett when I met him in 1986.

Meeting them led me to record in Bath, England with David Lord.

Among the many LPs influenced by *Sgt. Pepper* was Jefferson Airplane's *After Bathing at Baxter's* and the Rolling Stones' *Their Satanic Majesties Request*.

Both Jefferson Airplane and Grateful Dead were bands that grew out of the psychedelic scene in San Francisco, which incorporated many avant-garde experimental music techniques in their recordings. This was especially so in *After Bathing at Baxter's* and *Crown of Creation* by Jefferson Airplane, and *Anthem of the Sun* and *Aoxomoxoa* by Grateful Dead.

"Rejoyce" by Grace Slick of Jefferson Airplane is based on James Joyce's novel *Ulysses*. It refers to the book's characters, borrows a few lines of the text, and sets it to a Gil Evans–inspired jazz with Arabic tones and hypnotic *flamenco* rhythms. I am certain that Spencer Dryden's "Chushingura" on Jefferson Airplane's *Crown of Creation* was inspired by Toru Takemitsu's film score to *Kwaidan*, although I have not read about this anywhere.

Phil Lesh and Tom Constanten of Grateful Dead both studied avant-garde music and extensively brought its influences to the band. *Anthem of the Sun* was assembled like a collage from both studio and live recordings, interspersed with segments of prepared piano that sounded like a gamelan orchestra. Grateful Dead would continue to perform avant-garde improvisations in their live set, sometimes atonal with a lot of the most contemporary electronic effects.

The Velvet Underground were a New York group, whose integration of rock with the experimental avant-garde made them one of the most influential bands in alternative music. The group was formed by Lou Reed, who studied poetry at Syracuse University under Delmore Schwartz, before working as a pop songwriter for Pickwick Records; and John Cale, who studied composition with Iannis Xenakis before joining La Monte Young's ensemble The Theatre of Eternal Music. The group completed the initial line-up with percussionist Angus MacLise, who was also a member of La Monte Young's Theatre of Eternal Music, alongside John Cale, Tony Conrad, Marian Zazeela, and Terry Riley; and Reed's college friend Sterling Morrison, who majored in English literature. The interview

I conducted with John Cale in this book goes in-depth into his background.

Emerson, Lake, and Palmer performed several rock arrangements of classical compositions, from J. S. Bach and Modest Mussorgsky to 20th-century composers such as Béla Bartók, Aaron Copland, Sergei Prokofiev, and Leoš Janáček. Emerson was the first artist to tour with a Moog synthesizer; ELP's record deal provided funds for Emerson to buy his own Moog modular synthesizer, and his performances were vital to the development of newer Moog models.

The influence of the music from the romantic age can be heard in Yes. Jon Anderson, the singer, often says that Sibelius, Delius, and Stravinsky were an influence, but the folk-song influence in Yes reminds one of Mahler.

Today, in the 1980s, we see Brian Eno's conceptual influence from John Cage and Ryuichi Sakamoto's works, using impressionist techniques influenced by Debussy. The Art of Noise was named after Luigi Russolo's *L'arte dei Rumori* (The Art of Noises) based on the idea of avant-garde art futurism, which states that "I will make music with noise"—including mechanical sounds as well as natural sounds. Wim Melton, who formed the ensemble, Soft Verdict, recorded many works of post-minimalism for the label Les Disques du Crépuscule; he also published a book titled *American Minimal Music*, a study of works by La Monte Young, Terry Riley, Steve Reich, and Philip Glass.

Virginia Astley is influenced by Mahler and composes music that could be performed in a classical concert.

Popol Vuh was a German musical collective founded by the composer, Florian Fricke, incorporating influences from the music of India, Tibet, Africa, and pre-Columbian America. They created a unique soundscape that could be described as both minimal or psychedelic and could be listened to as contemporary world music or as new age/ambient. His music often featured religious motifs and mantras that were repeated over and over. Other members included singer, Djong Yun (the daughter of composer Isang Yun), and drummer-guitarist Daniel Fichelscher (son of the legendary jazz pianist Toby Fichelscher). They contributed soundtracks to films of Werner Herzog, including *Aguirre, der Zorn Gottes* (Aguirre, the Wrath of God), as well as *Nosferatu, Fitzcarraldo, Cobra Verde, Herz aus Glas* (Heart of Glass), and *Jeder für sich und Gott gegen alle* (The

Enigma of Kaspar Hauser), in which Fricke appeared. *Das Hohelied Salomos* ("The Song of Solomon") is my favorite album by them.

On many of my albums, I've used the modes used in medieval music.

I aimed to create music that could be placed in any genre just by changing the instrumentation. My composition *A Turquoise Mirror* can be played as a classical piece for violin and piano, or as a song for a psychedelic rock band without changing the basic arrangement. Only the instrumentation is changed, and the drums are left out. This composition can be heard as a classic composition for violin and piano in my album *Memory Theatre*, or as a rock song in my rock compilation on ayuo.bandcamp.com.

Here, I have briefly explored how rock music has been influenced by classical music from the Middle Ages to the 20th century.

New art and music are often created from absorbing classical literature, art, and philosophy, as well as from popular culture. Inspiration may come from other cultures or other periods in history.

What will future generations take away from what we do today?

Influences from Joni Mitchell and my mono opera *Izutsu*

Joni Mitchell has had a significant influence on much of my music. This may be broken down into three elements:

(1) Guitar Tuning:

She herself said that if all transpositions are counted, there are around 50 different tunings that she created for the guitar. Her 2014 songbook, *Joni Mitchell Complete So Far*, lists 35 tunings. She rarely plays her pieces in the usual tuning of *EADGBE*, but uses tunings such as *CGBbEbFBb* and *CCEGCE*. In this way, the strings sound as colorful as the colors in Van Gogh's paintings.

One of the reasons that she had to come up with so many different tunings is that her use of harmony is unique. She uses chords such as Em7sus4 and sus2, which are often interpreted as dissonant chords with a lot of tension or impressionistic sounds from a traditional Western music point of view. Jazz also uses such chords, but Joni's harmonic progressions are quite different. Although it has a similar sound sometimes with the guitar chords used by João Gilberto, Gilberto is also influenced by cool jazz. Joni Mitchell began her music career playing folk, which often has modal melodies based on medieval European music.

One of the reasons she had to create different tunings is because she had a severe case of polio when she was a child. Her hands could not hold down the chords she heard in her head, so she had to change the tuning of the guitar to play them.

From the time I bought her songbook, *For the Roses*, I've tried out all her guitar tunings and started writing songs with them.

Joni once said, "I make the guitar sound like an orchestra. The thicker lower three strings are the double bass, cello, and viola, and the thinner top three strings are the winds." On the album *Shine*, I got the feeling that she is playing the midi guitar as an extension of this.

(2) Lyrics:

Songs like "Woodstock," "Both Sides Now," and "The Circle Game" are well-known and have become standard songs that represent my generation. But I was influenced by how cinematic the lyrics of her song, "Chinese Café" are. Listening to it was almost like watching a movie inside your head.

"Chinese Café" is the name of a cafe where she and her friends used to go as teenagers to listen to rock and roll music on the jukebox. The song begins with a conversation with Carol, whom Joni used to hang out with back then:

"Carol, we've reached middle age. We were both wild back then, when rock 'n' roll was still in its infancy. But your kids have grown up 'serious' and I couldn't raise mine. Nothing lasted very long."

In the middle of these reminiscences, the song suddenly changes to the '55 hit "Unchained Melody," a song that was often played on the jukebox in the early 60's. In "Unchained Melody," the lyrics note that *"time goes by so slowly,"* which is the opposite of "nothing lasts for long." When I heard it, I was so moved that I felt goosebumps, as if an old photograph suddenly fell from an unexpected place. It was like in a movie, when old scenes are suddenly shown in black & white. It makes you think about the different perceptions of time that we have in our life. "Chinese Cafe" ends with "where does the time go?"

When I composed *Izutsu*, a mono opera based on a *Noh* play by Zeami, I was thinking about this kind of use in presenting time in the lyrics, and of how masterfully these lyrics were performed.

Izutsu is classified as a "madwoman's play." The main character, a woman, appears as a ghost at an old well where she remembers playing with her husband as a child, and dances while singing. When they were in their teen years, they were shy towards one another, but after dedicating songs to each other, they marry; despite one affair in their adult years, they live out their lives together. The man, Narihira, dies first. The woman cannot let go of all the memories she had of their years together; she dresses in her husband's robes and tries to transform herself into him. She looks at the mirror and says: "It is as if Narihira, the man of long ago with whom I was engaged, is exactly as he was in his former days."

Reading the work, it reminded me of stories by Edgar Allen Poe that I read in my childhood. It is beautiful and spine tingling.

Izutsu was released on Tzadik Records in 2000. A duo version with just the singer Makiko Sakurai and Ayuo is released on ayuo. bandcamp.com.

Here are some of the lyrics translated into English:

Once, long ago, in this land,
Lived two families, house by house.
In front of their gates was a well,
Where the children came to talk,
And watch themselves in the mirroring water.
Side by side, sleeve to sleeve,
And pure the water in their hearts,
That it knew there was no sound to disrupt them.

But as the moons and suns passed by,
They grew up to know modesty,
And one day, he wrote to her,
Words colored by a flower in his heart.

Well, the old well,
Where we stood by,
And measured our heights.
I've grown taller,
Since I saw you last.

And she also sent him a poem:

My tresses flow past my shoulders,
If not for you,
For whom shall I put up my hair.

Exchanging poems,
She became known

As the 'lady of the well',
The old name for Aritsune's daughter.

The Lady of the Well:
From the old days by the well,
Moons and years have passed by,
And now Narihira is no longer with us.
Wearing the old robe he left me,
I dance as a man,
The flowery sleeves were tossing like swirling snow.

He once sang:
"Is this not the same moon,
As in the past?
Is this not the same spring,
As in the past?,"
But, when did he sing it, I wonder?

The Lady of the Well and a Phantom Chorus:
With his headdress and his robe,
She no longer looks a woman,
But becomes a man.
Narihira, as he is remembered.

(She looks in the mirror and weeps.)
There I see you before me,
My love, and it brings me back so much.

The Lady of the Well:
I see myself and yet it brings me back.
My loving husband as a phantom,
A withered flower, all color gone,
But his scent remains.
The temple bells of Ariwara,
Toll in the growing redness of dawn.
An ancient temple,
The wind sighs through the pines.

And the leaves break the dream into awakening.
The dream breaks,
And the day begins.

(from *Izutsu* by Ayuo)

(3) Melody:

Another important element is the melody. When I first heard Prince sing "A Case of You" on the Joni tribute CD released in June 2007, I was surprised—he sang the same melody and lyrics as Joni, but the words resonated with completely different nuances.

In Joni's works, there are songs with catchy folk-like melodies like "Circle Game," standard jazz melodies like "Both Sides Now" and a narrative, story-telling approach like "Hejira." Some use dissonant harmonies, and some are modal.

Every single Joni album is different. She has an album of her songs arranged with a full orchestra, an album of jazz songs with advanced harmonies that Charles Mingus wanted her to complete, albums of songs backed with synthesizer programming, as well as many albums of songs which were recorded by her alone on guitar, piano, electric guitar, or midi guitar.

Her most recent studio album, *Shine*, was released in 2007. Joni's vocal range was narrower than before, but her expressive power became deeper. Many of the songs on this album focus on various issues facing our crumbling society today, such as environmental issues. At the time it was released, she said in interviews that her generation might have been the last generation to hope to change society for the better. "Nowadays, I think it seems very unrealistic to have hopes for the future. But I still want to hold on to hope, even though I know it is unrealistic," she said.

Shine ends with "If," a re-writing of a poem by Rudyard Kipling, author of *The Jungle Book*; it reminds one of Buddhist sayings. "If you can fill the journey of a minute with sixty seconds worth of wonder and delight, then the earth is yours and everything in it. But more than that I know you'll be alright." (The original that Rudyard wrote was: "If you can fill the unforgiving minute with sixty seconds' worth of distance run... you'll be a Man, my son!")

The song "Night of the Iguana" was written based on the novel of the same name by Tennessee Williams. In this novel, there is a character named Father Shannon who has internal sexual problems, which manifest themselves as hysteria, and he is thrown out of the church. He then takes a job as a tour bus driver, but he is not free from his problems.

In this day and age, "experimental" works do not consist of avant-garde sounds. What "experimental" means is to continue to create the expressions that are true to what the artist believes is necessary in his or her own time.

When Joni toured the US with Bob Dylan and Van Morrison, a few years before *Shine*'s release, the two male artists sang mainly their well-known songs, but Joni Mitchell always played her new songs.

In America, Joni Mitchell's old songs—along with those of Dylan—have had such an impact that they have become like folk songs: a part of the culture; a part of many Americans' lives. That's why it was very important for her to make an album with this kind of completely new content at the beginning of the twenty-first century.

Yokoo Tadanori: The hometown is the source of creation[1]

I seem to like the image of death. For some reason, adorning myself with images of death while fearing death at the same time, gives me a sense of security. This is accompanied by an irresistible sense of pleasure. I intuitively felt that if life is fictionalized by making death a routine part of everyday life, the distinction between life and death disappears and we are freed from the fear of death.

—Yokoo Tadanori

From February to May 2018, an exhibition titled "Yokoo Tadanori's Journey to the Next World" was held at the Yokoo Tadanori Museum of Contemporary Art in Kobe. This exhibition was divided into four chapters: a 1970 collection of nude photographs of women, themed on Dante's *Divine Comedy*; a 1974 poster themed on a scene from Dante's *Divine Comedy*; the Red Series; and drawings from the 1980s depicting women's backs and women with their faces hidden.

As a schoolboy, Yokoo watched the cities of Kobe and Akashi burn in the bombing from dozens of kilometers away in his hometown of Nishiwaki. "It was beyond the mountains," he said, "but it was an unimaginable hellscape. When I paint a red picture, what comes back to me is that red, burnt sky, but at the same time it turns into music played by the countless stars in the galaxies that flow through that red sky like a great river." Yokoo was able to conquer his fear of death by drawing his works of the Red Series.

Yokoo's paintings of his hometown of Nishiwaki distinctly show his formative experiences. The hometown is the source of his artistic creations.

---

[1]This article was commissioned by Yokoo Tadanori Museum of Contemporary Art and published by *Intoxicate* magazine in 2018.

Tadanori Yokoo: Posthumous Works (1968) was the title of his first collection of works. In 1968, in an attempt to change his overly busy life, Yokoo brought out a "declaration of death" and spent four months in New York absorbing its culture. I often saw him during this time.

Yokoo later said, "If it hadn't been for that encounter at the peak of psychedelic culture, I wouldn't be doing what I am today." I think it must have been the same for Shuji Terayama. There was a potential for a new world to begin. It was a culture that could only be experienced at that time, and only if you were there.

Yokoo Tadanori used to talk to me often, although I was still a child—just eight years old at the time. I would go with my mother, Yokoo, and Shuji Terayama to Electric Circus, a hippie hangout disco. A lot of people were doing drugs and dancing around. Yokoo and I would also go to rock shows together. I grew up seeing the same things that adults saw. Yokoo later told me that he thought I might grow up crazy.

Whereas Yokoo grew up in Nishiwaki, I grew up in New York City amid the psychedelic culture. As I grew older, I experienced a stronger connection to the years I spent living in Greenwich Village as a child. Along with my fellow students, the artists and musicians I encountered during that time are an important part of this. Yokoo Tadanori has always been a part of my formative experiences.

Yokoo's recent series of paintings of a woman whose face cannot be seen is connected to the image of death. The woman is an existence that never dies, and she is also the source of life to which people return in death.

Although I have never discussed Carl Jung with Yokoo, the Jungian psychologist James Hillman describes Jung's *Red Book* as a book of the dead. Speaking on the *Red Book*, Hillman observed that "we are surrounded by the dead in everyday life."

But the 'dead' in our active imagination, not the historical ones, is what Hillman refers to. Not ghosts, but parts from our inner psyche—perhaps archetypes from our unconscious. This psychological process emerging from Jung's *Red Book* can be applied to creative art and literature.

Here are some quotes from Yokoo from around the time of this exhibition:

The hometown is like the womb. Without a place like this, a person would never be born or raised. But I believe that the world of death is also located deep inside the womb. Assuming that the human soul dies before later being reborn. One might also say that our hometown is also connected to the world after death.[2]

As long as we live, we all think about death somewhere in our minds. Artists and philosophers are constantly expressing the questions of where they come from, where they are going, and who they are in their works.

Human beings seek freedom in life. But true freedom is impossible as long as it is in the physical senses. If you want true freedom, you will have to live death in the body. Isn't that what we call art?[3]

Life and death are not relative to each other. They are one thing.[4]

—Yokoo Tadanori,
Yokoo Tadanori's Journey to the Next World (2018)

---

[2]Tadanori, Yokoo. *I Don't Intend to Die*. Poplar Publishing, 2016, p. 43.
[3]Tadanori, Yokoo. Kaiga no mukogawa/Boku no uchigawa (The Other Side of the Painting/The Inside of Me). Iwanami Gendaizensho, 2014, pp. 64–65, Quotes translated by Ayuo.
[4]Ibid.

Part VI

Outside Society: People Without a Country—The poem

Everybody's home is where they grow up.

This is where our language and culture are formed.

Our bodies are passed down from our forefathers.

But our culture is molded by our surroundings.

Epigenetics, a scientific term, could be used as a metaphor for this.

It may sound simple, but the simplest things are the most misunderstood.

People who grew up in New York City spend their entire lives thinking from the viewpoint of the New York of their childhood.

An Arab who grows up in London considers his upbringing to be his home; as such, he understands his parents' beliefs through translations.

Which are not the same as the original.

His parent's generation assumes that he is rebelling against them.

Because he argues with them.

But he is just being himself.

They just come from different cultures.

And different languages.

But what will he do if the people of his homeland—where he was raised—don't even accept him as one of their own?

A fanatical cult may provide him with an identity that no one else could.

What happens when a person, who grew up in a distant land, travels to the home of his parents?

"You're NOT one of us," they will tell him.

"You're not like us—you are different!" they will say.

"You are not *Japanese*," is what they often told me.

But didn't all humans originate in Africa?

We've traveled far and wide before reaching the place where we call home.

Even now, the journey continues.

The United States of America was created only 250 years ago.

Many people travel each year.

More than ever before.

The future will have more immigrants.

The future depends upon what these people do.

Will they become:

A NEW People in a NEW land?

A NEW nation?

Or will they be a 'people' without a state?

The future depends on what they do.

Those who live on the outside of society know

that national 'identity'

Is an artificially made-up thing.

People who live *outside* of society

Do *NOT* need such an identity.

Discography

Albums released in Japan:

Carmina (1984)
Silent Film (1985)
Shizukani Okitegoran (1985)
Memory Theatre (1985)
Nova Carmina (1986)
Blue Eyes, Black Hair (1995)
Heavenly Garden Orchestra (1995)
Songs from a Eurasian Journey (1997)
Earth Guitar (2000)
Stoned (2002)
E no Naka no Sugata (What We Look Like in the Picture) (2006)
dna (2009)
Outside Society (2019)
ayuo.bandcamp.com (2024)

Albums released in the United States:

Izutsu (2000)
Red Moon (2004)
AOI (2005)

Albums released in South Korea:

Songs from a Eurasian Journey (1998)

Albums produced by Ayuo:

Kazue Sawai/*Me to Me* (*Eye to Eye*) (1988)

Albums released on ayuo.bandcamp.com:

Since 2020, there have been over 23 releases on the website ayuo.bandcamp.com. The list is growing each year. The following are available now:

Compilation Part 2 Rock Music
Compilation Part 1 Ambient and Classical Music
Ayuo and Makiko Sakurai Duo: Izutsu and Tang Dynasty Music
White Time: Music for Theater
Animation and Electronica
OEDIPUS REX: A Musical
Bouzouki Rock and Jazz
The Day the Second World War Ended
Open Tuning Guitar Songs
Classical Japanese Poetry Set to Original Songs
Rok Opera: Blue Eyes Black Hair
Japanese Folk Songs for a Rock Band
Beyond Progressive Rock
Early Spring – Kankyo Ongaku – Ambient Music
Borderline Rock Music
Music For Harp, Bouzouki, and String Instruments
Face of Another – Songs by Toru Takemitsu, Arranged by Ayuo
Piano Compositions by Ayuo, performed by Yuji Takahashi
Experimental Music/Graphic Notation
Ambient Guitar
Dark Beauty
At Heart I Am a Child with No Home
Outside Society

About the Author

Ayuo Takahashi was born (October 19, 1960) in Tokyo and spent his early childhood traveling with his parents in Germany, Sweden, and France. His father, Yuji Takahashi, is a composer of contemporary classical music and a pianist known for premiering works by Iannis Xenakis and John Cage. Ayuo and his parents settled in New York City in 1966. Ayuo grew up listening to both the new avant-garde experimental and contemporary music and the psychedelic rock music of the 1960s. He often went to museums, art galleries, and cinemas to see contemporary art exhibitions and the new cinema. At the same time, he also saw traditional Japanese Noh plays and heard ancient and medieval music from Japan and Europe. All these were to become important influences in Ayuo's music and music-theater pieces. Ayuo's parents divorced in 1969, and Ayuo's mother married an American of Iranian descent, Mansour Malekpour, who came from a family that performed Persian traditional music. This gave Ayuo the opportunity to hear Persian traditional music, which was also to have a lasting influence on his music. Mansour's grandfather, Ali Khan, was recognized as one of the greatest singers of Persian traditional music in the early 20th century, and his voice was regarded as exceptionally unique. He used to sing for the Crown Prince of the Qajar dynasty. With Persian instrumentalists on the ground surrounding the tree, the Crown Prince created a golden cage that hung from a tree, and Ali Khan was singing from inside because he was rumored to be able to sing like a nightingale. Ayuo also grew up listening to American psychedelic rock and British progressive rock while living with his stepfather, Mansoor Malekpour, in New York in the 1960s.

From the time he was in elementary school, he met artists Yokoo Tadanori and Andy Warhol, novelist Yukio Mishima, film director Hiroshi Teshigahara, and musician Yoko Ono. Beginning with 1960s psychedelic culture and influenced by Peter Gabriel, Joni Mitchell, Lou Reed, John Cale, and medieval minstrel music, he envisioned a synthesis of music, literature, and philosophy. In 1975, Ayuo's mother and step-father separated, while Ayuo was visiting his father in Japan, forcing him to live there.

He later wrote that the time spent with his stepfather was the happiest and influenced his music and musical theater work significantly.

Adjusting to life in Japan as a teenager was difficult, and Ayuo later made it the main theme of his CD *What We Look Like In The Picture*, released in 2006 from Zipangu in Japan. Ayuo spent his high school years writing poetry and appearing in poetry-reading competitions.

Ayuo joined Keiji Haino's group "Fushitsusha" in 1979 and performed improvisation with many musicians in what was the final period of the "free music scene" of Japan in the 1970s.

His first solo record, *Carmina*, was recorded in 1983 and released in 1984 by Epic-Sony. Since then, he has released over a dozen solo albums, collaborating with a diverse group of individuals, including Peter Hammill, Ryuichi Sakamoto, Danny Thompson, Maddy Prior, Takehisa Kosugi, Carlos Alomar, John Zorn, Bill Laswell, Dave Mattacks, Yohji Yamamoto, Jadranka Stojaković, Hiromi Ōta, Yoko Ueno, Clive Deamer, Mikigami Koichi, Wataru Ohkuma, Aki Takahashi, Mie Miki, Kazue Sawai, and many Japanese traditional musicians. Three CDs of his music have been released in the United States from the TZADIK label in the 21st century.

Ayuo has composed music for films, ballet, contemporary dance, and theater. *Border Line*, directed by the Japanese-Korean film director Lee Sang-il in 2002, features music mostly performed alone by Ayuo.

In 2020, the compilation album *Kankyo Ongaku: Japanese Ambient Music*, which includes Ayuo's composition "Nagareru," was nominated for a US Grammy Award.

In recent years, Ayuo's work has increasingly included music theater and chamber music mixed with dance and theatrical elements.

His recent works have been released at ayuo.bandcamp.com.